MINISTRY OF EDUCATION

Half Our Future

MINISTRY OF EDUCATION

Half Our Future

*A Report of the Central Advisory Council
for Education (England)*

LONDON
HER MAJESTY'S STATIONERY OFFICE
1963

Foreword

This report is the outcome of a reference given to the Central Advisory Council for Education (England) by my predecessor, Lord Eccles, in March 1961.

I am sure there is a need for wide public discussion of many of the Council's findings and recommendations. The teaching profession, the local education authorities and the Government will need to consider, both individually and jointly, the many recommendations that call for new initiatives, particularly in the fields of research and development. But I agree with the Council that there is above all a need for new modes of thought, and a change of heart, on the part of the community as a whole. We who are professionally and constitutionally concerned with the work of the schools cannot hope to discover the true needs of these pupils, and the best means of meeting them, without the backing of widely informed public opinion.

We therefore owe a great debt of gratitude to Mr. John Newsom and his colleagues on the Council for the skill and care with which they have defined the problem, and so admirably prepared the ground for what I hope will be a general raising of sights in our attitudes towards these pupils. Their potentialities are no less real, and of no less importance, because they do not readily lend themselves to measurement by the conventional criteria of academic achievement. The essential point is that all children should have an equal opportunity of acquiring intelligence, and of developing their talents and abilities to the full.

EDWARD BOYLE

August, 1963.

August 7, 1963

Dear Minister,

Your predecessor, Lord Eccles, asked the Central Advisory Council for Education (England) in March, 1961 to advise him on the education of pupils aged 13 to 16 of average and less than average ability.

I have much pleasure in submitting our report,

Yours sincerely,
JOHN NEWSOM
(*Chairman*)

The Rt. Hon. Sir Edward C. G. Boyle, Bart., M.P.

MEMBERSHIP OF THE
CENTRAL ADVISORY COUNCIL FOR EDUCATION (ENGLAND)

Mr. J. H. Newsom, C.B.E. (Chairman), Joint Managing Director, Longmans Green and Co. Ltd. (formerly County Education Officer, Herts.).

Mr. R. H. Adams, Principal, Kingswood Training and Classifying Schools, Bristol.

Miss C. Avent, Careers Advisory Officer, L.C.C. Youth Employment Service.

Mr. D. B. Bartlett, Chief Education Officer, Southend-on-Sea.

Mr. S. W. Buglass, Youth Training Officer, Imperial Chemical Industries.

Alderman S. M. Caffyn, C.B.E., Chairman, Education Committee, Eastbourne; Chairman of Council of the University of Sussex.

Mr. A. B. Clegg, Chief Education Officer, West Riding of Yorkshire.

Professor B. A. Fletcher, Director, The Institute of Education, Leeds University.

Mr. F. D. Flower, M.B.E., Principal, Kingsway Day College, London.

Dr. H. Frazer, Headmaster, Gateway School, Leicester.

Mr. A. J. N. Fuller, Headmaster, Oldborough Manor County Secondary School, Maidstone.

Miss M. G. Green, Headmistress, Kidbrooke School, London.

The Rev. H. W. Hinds, Rector of St. Peter, Walworth, London.

Mrs. A. J. Hirst, Staff Relations Manager, J. Lyons and Co. Ltd. (Joined the Council, March, 1962).

Mr. R. M. T. Kneebone, Headmaster, Beckfield Secondary Modern School, Acomb, York.

Dr. Kathleen Ollerenshaw, Member of Manchester City Council and Education Committee

Miss B. Paston Brown, Principal, Homerton College, Cambridge.

Miss E. M. Pepperell, Assistant Director, Industrial Welfare Society.

Alderman A. H. Quilley, M.B.E., Chairman, Hampshire Education Committee.

Mr. J. Scupham, O.B.E., Head of Educational Broadcasting, British Broadcasting Corporation.

Miss E. L. Sewell, General Secretary, The National Association of Youth Clubs.

Miss A. M. Simcock, M.B.E., Headmistress, Moss House Secondary School, Manchester.

Mr. W. J. Slater, Lecturer, Department of Physical Education, Birmingham University.

Mr. J. E. Smith, Headmaster, Sheldon Heath Comprehensive School, Birmingham.

Mr. C. A. Thompson, Principal, Brooklyn Technical College, Birmingham.

Mr. N. G. Treloar, Education Adviser, British Insulated Callender's Cables Ltd.

Mr. D. Winnard, Secretary, Education Department, Trades Union Congress (Joined the Council, March, 1962).

Miss K. A. Kennedy, Assessor.

Mr. D. G. O. Ayerst, H.M.I., Assessor.

Mr. R. J. W. Stubbings, H.M.I., Assessor.

Mr. J. W. Withrington, H.M.I., Assessor.

Miss M. J. Marshall, H.M.I., Secretary to the Council.

Miss M. L. Smith (Clerk).

The Council began work under its present terms of reference in March, 1961 under the chairmanship of Lord Amory, who resigned in June 1961, following his appointment as High Commissioner for the United Kingdom in Canada. Dame Anne Godwin (resigned November 1961) and Miss N. Newton Smith (resigned December 1961) were also members of the Council during this enquiry.

Note. The estimated gross cost of the preparation of the report is £12,814 of which £7,264 represents the estimated cost of printing and publication.

Table of Contents

PART ONE

FINDINGS

PART TWO

THE TEACHING SITUATION

List of Tables, Diagrams and Illustrations

Introduction

The most important of our recommendations is implicit in the whole of our report even though it will not be found specifically in the text. We are concerned that the young people whose education we have been considering should receive a greater share of the national resources devoted to education than they have done in the past, and by resources we do not mean solely finance, although this is important. Our pupils constitute, approximately, half the pupils of our secondary schools; they will eventually become half the citizens of this country, half the workers, half the mothers and fathers and half the consumers. Disraeli once said that on the education of the people of this country its future depended and it is in this sense that we have entitled our report "Half Our Future".

We are concerned that there should be a change of attitude towards these young people not only among many of those who control their education but among the public at large and this cannot be achieved solely, if at all, by administrative action. It involves a change of thinking and even more a change of heart. Our particular recommendations are, nevertheless, within the compass of the Ministry of Education, the local education authorities and the teaching profession. We cannot stress too strongly that the solution to these problems is not necessarily to be found by a reorganization of the present pattern of secondary education. However large or small the school, whether it is one-sex or co-educational, however wide its range of intellectual ability, the problems peculiar to the pupils we have been considering still remain to be solved.

We fully endorse and reaffirm the conclusion reached in the Council's last report that there is an urgent need to raise the school-leaving age to sixteen and that a specific date should be announced for the implementation of this decision. We maintain that during the whole secondary period the full-time education of pupils should be either in school or based on a school, despite the fact that we consider it important that the older pupils should have experience outside its confines. We consider that much fuller use should be made of the natural interests of older boys and girls in the work they will eventually undertake and that this fact should be reflected not only in the content of the curriculum but in the method of teaching and, above all, in the attitude of the teacher to the pupil when the pupil is, in effect, a young adult. We do not minimize the importance of maintaining the high educational standards required from the members of the teaching profession when we stress that, for the pupils we are considering, it is of quite exceptional importance that they should have an equally high capacity as teachers. By their very nature these young people require outstanding professional skill and inspiration from those who care for them and we consider that this fact should be recognized both in their training and in the position they hold in the school. It is for these reasons that we have concentrated on these matters which we consider to be the kernel of the problem and have not discussed, as some people would have expected us to do, the organization of the secondary school pattern throughout the country.

We have been impressed by what the schools have achieved since the concept of secondary education for all was initiated. We have been particularly struck by the steady growth in the standards of literacy (described in chapter 21) and there is no sign that the rate of improvement is slackening. But there is some evidence that young people of the same ability who attend recognized private schools and remain there in small classes until well beyond the statutory leaving age can achieve standards very different from those normally found. Moreover in many other countries the pupils remain at school till a later age than in the United Kingdom. From this we deduce that it is not possible to generalize about the capacity of the average and below average until we have had an opportunity of keeping them at school for a longer period and in smaller classes. It is possible that the potential of these children is very much greater than is generally assumed and that the standards they could achieve might surprise us all. The demonstrable improvements of the past decade have happened despite the fact that it is only in the last few years that the majority of the schools have been provided with the buildings, equipment and teaching strength to cope with the situation and even now, as our survey has shown, there are gross deficiencies still to be made up. We agree with the first chairman of the Central Advisory Council, Sir Fred Clark, who said that only after a diagnostic twenty years would it be possible to decide whether a particular structure of secondary education was likely to be beneficial. It is misleading to assess the success of secondary modern schools when they are still a long way from having had this period with adequate resources to achieve their purpose. It is, of course, even more premature to attempt a reasoned judgement on comprehensive and other types of secondary organization.

We make no apologies for recommendations which will involve an increase in public expenditure on the education of the average pupils. Their future rôle politically, socially and economically is vital to our national life but, even more important, each is an individual whose spirit needs education as much as his body needs nourishment. Without adequate education human life is impoverished.

And the bill which has to be presented is not limited merely to full-time education at school. It was not our remit to discuss the contribution which the youth service should make or the need for further education after leaving school; but we may insist that the boys and girls with whom we are concerned need these services as much as any section of the community.

Our report is not simply addressed to those who have the power to take administrative action. They need the support, perhaps sometimes the incitement, of an informed public opinion. It is there for the asking. Never before has the cause of education had so much popular support. Why, then, worry? Our anxiety is lest the relatively unspectacular needs of the boys and girls with whom we have been concerned should be overlooked. They have had far more than their fair share of thoroughly unsatisfactory buildings and desperately unsettling changes of staff. Given the opportunities, we have no doubt that they will rise to the challenge which a rapidly developing economy offers no less to them than to their abler brothers and sisters. But there is no time to waste. Half our future is in their hands. We must see that it is in good hands.

Terms of Reference

"To consider the education between the ages of 13 and 16 of pupils of average or less than average ability who are or will be following full-time courses either at schools or in establishments of further education. The term education shall be understood to include extra-curricular activities."

Principal Recommendations

(These follow the order of the chapters of the report)

In order that the children with whom we are concerned should have an effective secondary education, we recommend that:

1. An immediate announcement should be made that the school-leaving age will be raised to sixteen for all pupils entering the secondary schools from September 1965 onwards.

2. A programme of research in teaching techniques designed, particularly, to help pupils whose abilities are artificially depressed by environmental and linguistic handicaps should be instituted by the Ministry. The programme should include an experimental school run in co-operation with a teachers' training college whose staff is specially strengthened for the purpose.

3. An interdepartmental Working Party should be set up to deal with the general social problems, including education, in slum areas. Particular attention in education should be paid to the need for stability of staffing; the size of schools; and to the design and function of school buildings in these areas as part of the general community provision.

4. (*a*) All schools should provide a choice of programme, including a range of courses broadly related to occupational interests, for pupils in the fourth and fifth years of a five year course, and should be adequately equipped to do so.

(*b*) Equally, attention should be paid both to the imaginative experience through the arts, and to the personal and social development of the pupils.

(*c*) Excessively fine grading of ability groups should be avoided; more than three broad groupings is probably unnecessary, and groupings in the final years at school should be largely based on subject or course choices.

(*d*) Every effort should be made to emphasize the status of the older pupils both through school organization and in the design of school buildings.

5. (*a*) The hours spent in educational activities, including the "extra-curricular", should be extended for pupils aged fourteen to sixteen. Some experiments by local education authorities and schools in different types of extension of the school day should be encouraged by the Ministry.

(*b*) The implications for the staffing establishment of schools and the conditions of service, including the financial, should be examined; as also should be the demands which would be made by an extended use of school buildings.

6. The Ministry and the local education authorities should undertake a joint survey to establish accurately the scale on which provision for residential courses of all types is available, how far it is meeting demand, and the estimated cost of providing some residential experience for all pupils in the course of their school life, especially for a substantial number of pupils during their final two years at school.

7. The local education authorities should consider a revision of the Agreed Syllabuses for religious instruction to determine whether adequate provision is made for the needs of the older boys and girls with whom we are concerned, and whether they leave sufficient scope for teachers to develop methods which start with the actual problems which the pupils have to face.

8. Positive guidance to adolescent boys and girls on sexual behaviour is essential. This should include the biological, moral, social and personal aspects. Advice to parents on the physical and emotional problems of adolescents should be easily available. Schools of whatever type should contrive to provide opportunities for boys and girls to mix socially in a helpful and educative environment.

9. (a) The school programme in the final year ought to be deliberately out-going—an initiation into the adult world of work and of leisure.

(b) All links with, and knowledge about, the youth employment service, further education, the youth service and adult organizations need strengthening.

10.(a) The schools should provide all sixteen year-old leavers with some form of internal leaving certificate, combining an internal assessment with a general school record, irrespective of any external examinations they may take.

(b) They should resist external pressures to extend public examinations to pupils for whom they are inappropriate, or over an excessively large part of the programme for any pupils. They have a special responsibility to offer the non-examination pupils an educational experience which is worth while.

(c) No pupils should be entered for any external examination before the fifth year; schools should look ahead to a situation in which all pupils will be in full-time education to sixteen.

11. The Ministry in conjunction with local education authorities should arrange an experimental building programme, to try out different forms of school organization and teaching methods in buildings designed for the purpose; at least one such experiment might be run in conjunction with a teachers' training college.

12. Meanwhile action should be continued and, indeed, accelerated to remedy the existing functional deficiencies of schools, especially in relation to provision for practical subjects, science and libraries, by:

(a) relieving otherwise good modern buildings of the effects of over-crowding;

(b) replacing buildings which are totally inadequate to modern educational needs.

13. (a) Provision for all practical subjects should be reappraised, and extended workshop and technical facilities provided, whether wholly within the schools themselves or jointly with further education institutions.

(b) All secondary schools should be adequately provided with modern audio-visual aids, and with facilities for using them; in particular the planning of secondary schools should take account of the use of television, as a permanent teaching aid of great potential value, and of equipment for foreign language teaching by modern methods.

14. The policies on which the teacher training programme is based should be reconsidered to ensure that a substantial proportion of teachers in the secondary schools receive a training of the "concurrent" type.

15. The training colleges should be staffed and equipped to enable students to teach pupils of secondary age in one main subject and in at least one, and preferably two, other subjects, with the possibility of a choice of subjects which cuts across the conventional divisions of "practical" and "academic" subjects.

16. (a) The training of teachers should include preparation now for the new demands which will be made on them by the raising of the school-leaving age.

(b) A training requirement for graduates should be introduced at the earliest practicable moment, and the date announced in advance.

(c) As an interim measure there should be an emergency programme of in-service courses to help graduates and other teachers who have attained qualified status without training to deal with the problems they encounter in the schools. The content and conditions of the training course for graduates should be reviewed in order to make voluntary training more attractive.

Part One

Findings

"A boy who had just left school was asked by his former headmaster what he thought of the new buildings. 'It could all be marble, sir,' he replied, 'but it would still be a bloody school.'"

"I enjoyed my school life very much. I wanted to stay on, but there wasn't any room." Fifteen year-old leaver.

"*Incentives for Good Behaviour*. At school: House points; stars for work and service; public commendation after Assembly. At home: a drink of shandy; staying up late; staying out late; wearing make-up; having a hair-set; use of other people's clothes; money; cigarettes." Headmistress.

"We believe that the parents are solidly behind us in our work, and the co-operation they display is most encouraging." Headmaster.

"Outside the very narrow range of their immediate experience, their vocabulary was tragically poverty-stricken."

"The school's outstanding strength is its social achievement. The girls are fluent and confident and entertained the visitors with an easy grace which would have done credit to a grammar school sixth form."

"Our headmaster thought the school was marvellous and wouldn't face up to facts." Fifteen year-old school-leaver.

CHAPTER 1

Education for All

1. Boredom with everything school stands for, or enthusiasm? Conflict between school and home, or mutual support? Tongue-tied inadequacy, or social competence? What is the true picture of the educational situation of hundreds of thousands of young people today?

2. We believe the answer matters to many people besides the Minister to whom this report is formally addressed. Our terms of reference direct us to enquire into the education of pupils of "average" and "less-than-average" ability. If those words have any precise meaning at all, they must refer to at least half the children in the country—every other pupil in school, every other child at home. We have tried, therefore, in setting out our main ideas in Part One of this report, to keep in mind a wider public, especially parents. Part Two, which considers some aspects of school organization and class-room matters in more detail, is addressed more particularly to the teachers. Part Three describes in detail a survey of a representative sample of schools undertaken by the Council.

3. As the quotations from our evidence on the page opposite indicate, no simple generalizations will apply to all the pupils, and no one formula dispose of all the problems with which this report is concerned. But what we have seen and heard and read has seemed to lead inevitably to a number of beliefs. We shall argue them later at length, but they might be summarised as follows. Despite some splendid achievements in the schools, there is much unrealized talent especially among boys and girls whose potential is masked by inade-quate powers of speech and the limitations of home background. Unsuitable programmes and teaching methods may aggravate their difficulties, and frustration express itself in apathy or rebelliousness. The country cannot afford this wastage, humanly or economically speaking. If it is to be avoided, several things will be necessary. The pupils will need to have a longer period of full-time education than most of them now receive. The schools will need to present that education in terms more acceptable to the pupils and to their parents, by relating school more directly to adult life, and especially by taking a proper account of vocational interests. Possible lines of development can be found in many good schools now, but experiment is required, both in the content of the school programme and in teaching methods. Finally, the schools will need strong support in their task, not least from parents, and they will need the tools for the job, in the provision of adequate staff and buildings and equipment.

4. Such is our thesis. Who are the boys and girls with whom this report is concerned? "Our children", as we came to call them, cannot be defined as any exact percentage of the population; and a full description of what we have learnt about them from our survey must come later. But if we ask where they are to be found at the present time, they are the boys and girls who form the majority of pupils in the secondary modern schools, or who are in the middle and lower forms of comprehensive schools. Or to put it another way,

we can think of an area, typical of much of the country, in which up to about a quarter of all the pupils who leave the primary schools go on to secondary grammar or secondary technical schools. The remaining three-quarters, apart from a small number who may be provided for in "special" schools for the severely physically or mentally handicapped, will go to secondary modern schools. In the latter, there will be an "above average" group, including some pupils who show themselves capable of doing work similar to that done by many pupils in a grammar school. There will be a second group, generally much larger, who represent the "average" boys and girls of their age; and a third, usually smaller, group, of those who have considerably more difficulty in remembering and applying what they learn, and who certainly work more slowly. Finally, we can pick out a fourth group of really backward pupils who have a struggle to attain an elementary mastery of reading, writing and calculation. No description of the size of these various groups will be accurate for all schools, but however uncertain the frontiers, all these territories have to be included in the educational map.

5. It was not part of our brief to consider the structure of secondary education, and we have not made any assumptions about what that may be, or ought to be, in the future. The description above will not fit some areas where different schemes of secondary organization are in operation, but it reflects what most commonly happens now. Whatever the local pattern, the educational needs of the boys and girls are the same. For brevity's sake, we discuss those needs throughout this report largely in the context of the secondary modern school, but the observations apply to "our" pupils wherever they are found.

6. We had difficulty with our terms of reference. "Average" and "below average" are full of pitfalls. The words themselves are useful enough, as ways of trying to identify in broad terms two large groups of pupils; but unluckily they often carry emotional overtones: the idea of "below-average ability" easily suggests "below-average people", as though the boys and girls so described were being regarded as generally inferior and in some way less worth educating than their "above-average" brothers and sisters. There can be no question of regarding one human being as less valuable than another, but though distinctions are difficult, some have to be attempted. Anyone involved in the job of teaching knows that the range of capacities to be encountered among the pupils of even a single school is very wide, and that to fail to take account of this is neither realistic nor likely to be in the pupils' own interests. In order to help individual boys and girls, the teacher needs first to appreciate their difficulties. Whether the individual ceiling of attainment for some, perhaps many, pupils could be higher, is an important matter which needs separate consideration; but that differences exist within any group of boys and girls is a fact of experience.

7. Another fact, perhaps not often enough emphasized, is that the standard indicated by "average" is rising all the time, and perhaps never more rapidly than in the last twenty-five years. As the life of our society becomes more complex, new demands are continually made on all of us; and this is as true in relation to our personal lives as it is in relation to the changing economic life of the country as a whole. The amount which men and women need to understand, and the range of experiences with which they are required to deal in all the daily business of living, are continually extending. The mysteries

of one generation become the commonplaces of life to their grandchildren. In this sense standards do rise.

8. This is not often apparent, because we are seldom in a position to compare, directly, the achievements of pupils of one generation with those of another. In a later part of this report, in which the results are described of a series of tests designed to show the pupils' capacity to read with understanding, there is a clear record of improvement. A test score which even fourteen years ago would have been good enough to put boys or girls well into the above-average category would today put them firmly into the below-average group. Over the intervening years the general level of performance has risen. One of the reasons why there is a quite proper anxiety over the general standards of literacy today is not that fewer and fewer people can read and write, but that more and more people need to do so with greater competence.

9. The point is, could many people, with the right educational help, achieve still more? If they could, then in human justice and in economic self-interest we ought, as a country, to provide that help. Any substantial recommendations affecting provision for half the population are bound to cost money. Are we prepared to foot the bill? We are conscious that, although there is a strong body of public opinion urging expenditure on education as a vital investment, the emphasis at present is almost invariably on the higher education of the most gifted. And with the prospect of a steady, long-term increase in the child population, the cost even of maintaining the existing services is mounting so rapidly that the competition for educational priorities is acute. We therefore think it essential to state at the outset the economic argument for investment in our pupils.

10. Briefly, it is that the future pattern of employment in this country will require a much larger pool of talent than is at present available; and that at least a substantial proportion of the "average" and "below average" pupils are sufficiently educable to supply that additional talent. The need is not only for more skilled workers to fill existing jobs, but also for a generally better educated and intelligently adaptable labour force to meet new demands.

11. In spite of popular belief to the contrary, technological advance—especially the introduction of automatic processes—is not leading to widespread unemployment among skilled workers or to the destruction of the level of skill. Skills may be changing and some individual skills become less important while new ones emerge, but the forecast made in 1956 in a government report on "Automation"[1], that on the whole the level of skill will tend to rise rather than fall, is being fulfilled. If anything, the progress of automation and the application of other technological developments are likely to be delayed by lack of trained personnel.

12. This was recognized in the 1962 White Paper on Industrial Training, which stated that, although both 1961 and 1962 saw welcome increases in the number of apprentices recruited, "Even so, it remains doubtful whether the number of new entrants into skilled occupations will be sufficient to match future needs. Experience in the United States, for example, suggests that technological progress requires an increasing proportion of trained and technical manpower in the working population, with a correspondingly smaller demand

[1] Department of Scientific and Industrial Research: "Automation", 1956.

for unskilled and semi-skilled labour. The same is true here. The great majority of unfilled vacancies call for some degree of skill, while a high proportion of the adult unemployed are labourers."

13. This trend in industrial employment is matched by a second, the expansion in employment in service occupations at a level that makes new demands on their employees. The retail trade for example, is increasingly looking for a better educated recruit who will neither be an errand boy nor possess an encyclopaedic knowledge of the product he sells, but be more capable of understanding and reacting effectively to the human situation in which he finds himself.

14. These developments are still at a relatively early stage, but the trend is clear, and should be setting the vocational pattern to which our educational system is geared. Other advanced industrialized countries are also having to look critically at their educational systems, and attempts are being made to measure the national reserves of ability.

15. Can our pupils be regarded as one such reserve of ability? Will a substantial investment in their education produce people capable of fulfilling the industrial rôles indicated above? If we look at what has happened when popular education has been extended in the past, the answer is an optimistic "Yes". New provision has always elicited new responses. Intellectual talent is not a fixed quantity with which we have to work but a variable that can be modified by social policy and educational approaches. The crude and simple answer was given by Macaulay 139 years ago:—[1] "Genius is subject to the same laws which regulate the production of cotton and molasses. The supply adjusts itself to the demand. The quantity may be diminished by restrictions and multiplied by bounties."

16. A more subtle investigation into what constitutes the "restrictions" and the "bounties" in our society is of far more recent growth. The results of such investigation increasingly indicate that the kind of intelligence which is measured by the tests so far applied is largely an acquired characteristic. This is not to deny the existence of a basic genetic endowment; but whereas that endowment, so far, has proved impossible to isolate, other factors can be identified. Particularly significant among them are the influences of social and physical environment; and, since these are susceptible to modification, they may well prove educationally more important.

17. The problem is not solely a matter of social conditions. There are still large differences in the progress and attainments of children who appear to start with equal advantages, and even brothers and sisters in the same family differ from each other in talents. Factors of health and growth, character and temperament come into it, as well as native wit, which must be reckoned with, even if it cannot as yet be precisely measured. But when we refer to pupils in this report as "more able" or "less able" we are conscious that the terms are descriptive rather than diagnostic; they indicate the facts about the pupils' relative performance in school, but not whether that performance could be modified given different educational approaches.

18. There is very little doubt that among our children there are reserves of ability which can be tapped, if the country wills the means. One of the means is a longer school life. There is, surely, something of an anomaly in the fact

[1] T. B. Macaulay (1824) "On the Athenian Orators".

that whereas a five-year secondary course is regarded as an essential minimum both for our ablest children in the grammar schools and for those of very limited capacities indeed, in schools for the educationally sub-normal, less is demanded for the large majority of children who neither progress as quickly as the first group nor are as severely limited in their potential as the second.

19. Our terms of reference imply, and the whole argument of our report assumes, a school-leaving age of sixteen for everyone. We have again considered the position with great care, and we have unhesitatingly come to the same conclusion as the Council reached in 1959: "This is a duty which society owes all its young citizens". The evidence presented to us makes it clear that in the last few years there has been a marked strengthening of conviction in this matter, both among those professionally concerned with education and among the interested general public. The percentage of pupils who voluntarily remain at school beyond the minimum age of fifteen has doubled in the secondary modern schools since 1958,[1] and this in itself testifies to an increasing confidence in the schools and to a belief on the part of many parents in the value of a longer education for their children. Already in some modern schools, pupils are voluntarily remaining not only for a fifth but for a sixth year, and we have little doubt when the formal school-leaving age is raised to sixteen, there will be more pupils voluntarily choosing to stay to seventeen and even eighteen.

20. But the decision to raise the school-leaving age should not therefore continue to be deferred and progress left to follow its voluntary course. There are still too many boys and girls who, otherwise, will leave at the earliest permissible moment, whatever their potential abilities, because outside pressures are too much for them. Again and again teachers confirm that the pupils with whom we are especially concerned stand to gain a great deal in terms of personal development as well as in the consolidating of attainments from a longer period of full-time education—but it is just these boys and girls who most readily succumb to the attractions of the pay-packet and the bright lights it commands.

21. Besides, in the national economic interest we cannot afford to go on waiting. Others are already ahead of us. It is true that we start school a year earlier than most other countries, but there is no reason to assume that the majority of our children are ahead of other people's at the age of fifteen when they leave school. In the United States nearly two-thirds of the population are at High Schools until the age of eighteen, and there is currently much concern over "the drop-outs", many of whom have stayed at school till sixteen. France, with problems of shortages of teachers and of accommodation comparable with our own, has already raised the school-leaving age from fourteen to sixteen for all the pupils who started school in or after 1959.

[1] In 1962, rather more than one-sixth of the age group in secondary modern schools for the country as a whole, and a very much higher percentage for some individual schools and areas. The demand for a longer education is also reflected in the proportion of pupils staying on in the comprehensive schools, and account must be taken of the pupils in full-time courses in further education, particularly in areas where it has been a matter of local policy not to provide fifth year courses in the modern schools. It must be noted, however, that only 45 per cent of all fifteen year-olds in 1961–62 were in any kind of full-time education, at school or in colleges of further education, and quite certainly the great majority of these were not the pupils with whom this report is essentially concerned.

22. The French procedure of naming the date on which the higher leaving age will become operative well in advance strongly commends itself to us. In this country, we cannot now afford to wait another ten years until boys and girls who have not yet entered the primary schools become fifteen. But, if the decision were taken quickly, a leaving age of sixteen could be made operative for all pupils who enter the secondary schools in or after 1965: that is, the first year of full-time compulsory education up to the age of sixteen would be 1969—70. The Crowther report urged the claims of the years 1966–69, when the secondary schools will experience a relative easing in the pressure of numbers, as the most apt for introducing the higher leaving age. The chance of using that spell is virtually gone, but in 1970 at least the actual numbers of boys and girls who will reach the age of fifteen, and who would be the first to be affected by the new provision, are relatively low—655,000 compared with 663,000 in 1969 and with 738,000 in 1975. There would be advantage in making the change when the first age group to be affected is relatively small. There are, in any case, undoubted advantages in taking the decision and announcing the date five years in advance: in this way, the pupils and their parents know from the beginning of the secondary course where they stand, and both teachers and administrators can make their plans with a definite goal ahead.

23. There is one other point about our terms of reference which we must make straight away: they appear to leave open the possibility that when the school-leaving age is raised, some pupils below the age of sixteen may be following full-time courses in colleges of further education. We are ourselves convinced, and have found almost unanimous agreement among those who have contributed evidence, that the schools should be responsible for boys and girls up to this age. This does not rule out the transitional use of the colleges for the full-time education of fifteen to sixteen year-olds, in the period before all secondary schools have the buildings, staffing and equipment to provide a fifth year for all their pupils. Interim arrangements, however, ought not to involve the creation or enlargement of further education establishments so that the temporary expedient becomes a permanency. We say this not in any criticism of the work now being done with full-time fifteen and sixteen year-old students in colleges of further education: these students are in any case mostly among the abler boys and girls of their age group, rather than those with whom this report is especially concerned. But when the school leaving age is raised to sixteen for all, there will be a fundamental change in the whole educational situation, and the schools must be equipped, staffed and re-orientated in their working to meet it. If they do their job well, the colleges of further education will have to meet rapidly increasing demands for courses by older school leavers.

24. Active co-operation between the schools and colleges will, however, be essential, and in some areas it might well prove an admirable arrangement to allow pupils to attend a local college for some part of their final year's programme, in order to take advantage of special equipment and facilities. There is everything to be said for extending the pupils' experience beyond the school walls at this stage, and this is one promising way of doing it. But the ultimate responsibility for the pupils' welfare up to the age of sixteen should rest with the schools, and the educational programme, though increasingly outward looking, should be school based.

25. Clearly, the value of offering all pupils a longer experience of full-time education depends in considerable part on the resources of staffing and on the material conditions, in terms of buildings and equipment, which the schools may be expected to enjoy. From the findings of the National Advisory Council on the Training and Supply of Teachers it is clear that on current policies there will be a continuing shortage of teachers into the 1980's. This will be less acute for the secondary than for the primary schools, but we are well aware that the effect of conditions in the primary schools, particularly on pupils who do not learn easily, could have marked significance for success or failure at the secondary stage. On material needs, our own survey of schools gives some indication of the size of the task of bringing all school buildings up to the standards which have already long been established as desirable, quite apart from the need to improve further on those standards to take account of changing educational ideas and teaching methods, and of the growing number of older pupils staying on.

26. In attempting, therefore, to indicate what we believe to be educationally desirable, we realized that we might appear economically unrealistic; on the other hand, we see no reason to assume that the proportion of the national income spent on education is unalterable. We have tried, in the later sections of this report, to suggest both what educational developments can be undertaken here and now, especially by the more fortunately placed schools, and in what ways improved resources in staff and facilities will ultimately be needed for all schools if they are to develop as they should.

27. We realize that much of what we have to say, particularly about the content of the final year of a longer school course, is speculative. It is necessarily so, because one of the facts about "our" pupils is that they constitute so far only a small minority of those boys and girls who have voluntarily stayed on at school. There is as yet little store of experience within the national system of education in this country of teaching them right up to the age of sixteen or of testing different teaching approaches. We do not yet know what their achievements might be given a longer school life, a suitable programme, and work in reasonably sized groups with teachers of high quality. The analysis of the problem which both our witnesses and we ourselves have made convinces us that the solution can only be found in action; and that through experiment it can be found.

RECOMMENDATIONS

(a) An immediate announcement should be made that the school-leaving age will be raised to sixteen for all pupils entering the secondary schools from 1965 onwards. The year in which the new leaving age first becomes operative would then be 1969–70, when the number of fifteen year-olds involved is relatively low. (paras. 19–22)

(b) Full-time education to the age of sixteen should be school-based. This is not to preclude some part of the school course in the final year being followed off the school premises, e.g. in a college of further education. (paras. 23 and 24)

CHAPTER 2

The Pupils, The Schools, The Problems

"I can't help feeling wary when I hear anything said about the masses. First you take their faces from 'em by calling 'em the masses, and then you accuse 'em of not having any faces."—J. B. Priestley, "Saturn Over the Water".

28. We feel the same wariness in generalizing about "average and below average pupils." There were well over two and three quarter million boys and girls in maintained secondary schools in 1962, all of them individuals, all different. We must not lose sight of the differences in trying to discover what they have in common. It is however, useful to put together what is collectively known about "our pupils", even though the result may not be an exact likeness of any one of them.

29. We took a national sample of secondary modern schools and asked the heads not only to give us a great deal of information about their schools and the local background, but also to complete individual questionnaires on one in three of their fourth year pupils. As a result, we obtained pen-portraits of 6,202 fourteen year-old boys and girls, who between them represent a cross-sample of all the pupils in those schools, from the ablest to the weakest. The heads gave their own assessments of each pupil's general capacities, as compared with other pupils in that school; in addition, all the pupils in all the schools took an identical test (described in Chapter 21 of this report), so that it was possible to make some comparisons between them, even though they came from many different schools in different parts of the country.

30. A similar procedure was followed with a national sample of comprehensive schools, and with a group of schools specially selected for the known difficulties of their social and physical environment. Full details of both these sections of the survey are given in Part Three. To simplify the general discussion of the survey results, references in this chapter and subsequently are to the secondary modern schools sample only, unless otherwise stated.

31. It was also possible to extract further information which has a bearing on our subject from the National Service Survey results recorded in Vol. II of the Crowther Report. Based on these two sources, a brief description of the pupils in the sample might run something like this. A third of them live on housing estates, which may be bright and modern, like those of the new towns, or drab and ageing, as are some of those built in the early years between the wars. Just under a fifth live in the old and overcrowded centre of some big city or industrial area, where there are few amenities and often a concentration of social problems; for brevity we later refer to these as "problem" areas. Another fifth of the pupils is made up of boys and girls from rural and from mining districts; and the remainder come from areas which do not fit into any one of these categories and are generally mixed in character.

32. We did not obtain information on the occupations of the fathers of the pupils in our sample, but on the basis of the Crowther Survey, five out of six are likely to be children of manual workers skilled, or unskilled. Many attend

schools housed in attractive, post-war buildings, some of them built on the estates on which the pupils live; but many of these new schools are having to cater for many more pupils than they were designed to hold, and two-fifths of all the schools in our sample were in seriously inadequate premises. They are rather better off in respect of playing fields, but in the large towns playing fields have sometimes inevitably to be an awkward distance from the school, and the schools in the problem areas come off worst in every way, outdoors and indoors.

33. These boys and girls have seen a good many changes of teacher. Indeed, many of them must have been in their secondary schools longer than most of their teachers. Of the teachers who were on the staff when the pupils entered the schools in 1958, only half the women were still there in 1961, and about two-thirds of the men. Not only had many new teachers come, but there had been a great many comings and goings in between.

34. Most boys and girls in their teachers' opinion, are co-operative and behave well in school; only a small minority, under five per cent of the pupils in the fourth year at school, present serious problems of discipline. The pupils are liable to be absent from school, on average, for about ten days in the course of the year, but usually for acceptable reasons. They do their homework, if any is regularly required of them, but half of all the pupils in the modern schools are not given any homework. Nearly half the boys do some part-time paid job; only a small minority of the girls are so employed, perhaps because more claims are made on them to do domestic chores at home, as the heads of the schools often observe. About a quarter of all pupils belong to some school club or society, and nearly half, including many of the same enthusiasts, to some organization outside school.

35. Much of this description applies to all the pupils in the schools. It is, however, possible to draw some distinctions between our average and less than average pupils, and the rest. There is a slight, but definite, tendency for the less able pupils to be smaller and to weigh less than the brighter pupils— the puny-looking child, as it turns out, is not so likely to be the studious bookworm. It may well be that there is a comparable development in physical and in mental growth in the years of adolescence—a good deal of medical research suggests that there is; but it is also notable that the less successful children tend to come from the larger families (this is true irrespective of social class or background), and there is some evidence that children in small families tend to be taller and heavier. On the other hand, there are no generally significant physical differences between children from one environment and another apart from the exceptionally adverse areas discussed in the next chapter.

36. It seems that the less able the pupils, the more likely they are to be away from school, for longer periods, and more often without adequate excuse. They are also very much less likely than their abler fellows to be set homework. It is clearly worth asking how far frequent absence, and the lack of the extra practice which bright pupils get through homework, help to make the weak pupil weaker still. Contrary, perhaps, to what might be expected, there was no evidence, at least as far as the test score was concerned, that school work is adversely affected by pupils doing a part-time job.

37. What kind of places are the schools to which the pupils go? It is as difficult to do justice to them in a few generalizations as it is to describe the pupils.

Last year, there were 3,668 modern schools in England, making up rather more than two-thirds of the total of all secondary schools. The 1944 Act changed the name and status of the old Senior Elementary Schools to Secondary Modern Schools, but at first changed little else. When the school-leaving age was raised to fifteen in 1947, the country was faced with the enormous task of discovering how to provide an effective secondary education for a large part of the population which had never remained so long at school before. The teachers had to gain their experience on the job, often in old and unsuitable buildings and often without adequate books and equipment. These schools, and the even younger schools which have started up since, have had to plan their development ahead through a period which has seen in every field of education chronic shortages of teachers and overcrowding of classes. Much of the gathered wisdom of the old Senior Schools was lost in the shattering upheaval of the war, and the newly-designated Modern Schools had no collective tradition or reputation to support them; on the other hand, the very absence of a set pattern has attracted men and women with a zest for pioneering. As a result, the schools are growing up—for the process is still going on—very varied in character.

38. Over the last eight or ten years, they have been helped by a massive programme of new school building. In the period 1954–61, 1,808 new secondary schools in England and Wales were completed, the majority of them secondary modern schools; before the 1960s are out,[1] nearly two-thirds of all secondary pupils may be either in new schools or in enlarged older schools. The contrast however, between those schools now housed in new premises, and those still making do in pre-war, sometimes pre-twentieth century, elementary school buildings, grows sharper, and even the most splendid new buildings have not uncommonly been severely overcrowded since the day they opened. Nevertheless, imaginative design and construction, lightness, gay colour in decoration, and attractively laid out grounds, are among the most striking outward signs that the new schools have begun to come into their own.

39. Other changes, just as notable, have been happening inside the buildings, so many and so rapidly that it is doubtful if even the parents of the present pupils can realize just how different schools may be from the places they remember from their own school days. Most schools are making strenuous efforts to establish contacts with parents, sometimes with poor response: a school doing excellent work can have the dispiriting experience of only a handful of people turning up for a meeting called especially for the parents' benefit. But schools are large and busy places, and there is in any case so much more going on than can easily be absorbed in occasional visits. Communication is still difficult.

40. Probably the development which has caught most public attention is the growth of a variety of courses mainly, but not necessarily, leading to some external examination, for the older and abler pupils. These have undoubtedly been effective in inducing large numbers of boys and girls to stay longer at school, and in convincing their parents that to do so was worth while. Rather more than one pupil in six was staying beyond the minimum leaving-age in modern and all-age schools in 1962 over the country as a whole. In some individual schools and areas, the proportion was very much higher.

[1] i.e. when the building programmes for 1960–65 are completed.

41. Much else is changing. Visitors to one of the really fortunately placed schools are likely to be struck by the attractiveness of the newer text-books, the plentiful library books, the well-furnished library room. They may see a more generous provision of special rooms and equipment for science, cookery, needlework, woodwork, metalwork, art and crafts in general; and facilities for physical education on a scale which an older generation of pupils never knew. They may find there are subjects on the timetable which never figured in their own experience—a modern language, engineering, or commerce, for example; and certainly if they venture into the classrooms they may find " old " subjects covering a wider span of interest and being presented in unfamiliar ways. It is possible that the class will not be there at all, because the pupils have gone off to do field work in geography or biology, learning to search out more information for themselves, rather than receiving it all in notes from the teacher. Parents will certainly think the activities in physical education bear little resemblance to the more regimented drill procedures of not so many years ago. They may, if it is an exceptionally well provided school, even be a bit suspicious of the variety of equipment that seems to be supplementing chalk and talk these days—filmstrips, films, records, radio, tape-recorders, perhaps television; but they will concede that these pupils are lucky in having many more sources of illustration and interest. Most schools would feel that they have fewer of these aids than they could profitably use. Visitors may find the buildings lighter and brighter and a good deal less austere than their remembered picture of "school", and they may be aware of a generally easier atmosphere and less formal relation between teachers and pupils. The school notice boards, with their news of clubs and societies, choirs and instrumental music, local expeditions and trips abroad, may suggest the lively sharing of interests which goes on in out-of-school time.

42. These activities outside the limits of lesson times are a valuable and distinctive feature of school life, not least, perhaps, in the way they are literally widening the pupils' horizons. One outstanding, but by no means unique school, quoted in our evidence, has undertaken in six years sixteen holidays abroad and twenty-six in this country: the programme has included visits to Stratford, Edinburgh and York; geographical surveys in the Isle of Man, Yorkshire and the Lake District; historical studies in Lancashire; cycling and Youth Hostelling trips in many parts of this country; crossing the Norwegian ice cap above Hardanger, traversing mountain ranges in Austria, making a two-hundred mile high level walking tour in Switzerland, walking and climbing in the Dolomites in Northern Italy. Means of helping pupils who could not otherwise afford the journeys have been found, and pupils of every grade of ability have taken part, although the abler boys and girls have undoubtedly participated most.

43. We have dwelt on these aspects of the younger secondary schools first because they are not appreciated as widely as they ought to be. Educational journals week after week carry news of enterprising experiments in ways of making school life still more rewarding, but too little of this trickles through to the general public. Other patient work goes on which is scarcely recorded at all, except in inspection reports, because although immensely valuable, it is not necessarily novel or dramatic in character. Yet knowledge of both sorts of progress is needed, to put into perspective those disturbing accounts which do provide headlines in the national press, when some schools or teachers are

overwhelmed by problems of exceptional difficulty. Such situations certainly occur, and we are rightly perturbed when they do: but they are not typical, and they have often been luridly, even inventively presented. A well-informed public opinion could be of great support to the schools, not least to those in the gravest difficulties. Education needs a better communications service.

44. Secondly, we want to affirm quite clearly that the record of secondary education since 1944 is essentially one of progress in the face of formidable obstacles. We have criticisms and anxieties to express in the pages which follow, but they are to be read against this background of substantial success.

45. Why, then, not let well alone? Because very far from all the schools are as happily placed as the one in our generalized and somewhat rosy description; and because, although educationally we are scoring some gratifying hits, this increases concern about the misses. In respect of the physical conditions under which teachers and pupils are required to work, much of what was acknowledged in the Minister's statement in 1958 still has force.[2] "Some are secondary schools only in name or are accommodated in buildings long since out of date which it would not be sensible to improve where they stand . . . Others, though satisfactory for smaller numbers, are overcrowded . . . Others, again, though adequate in some ways, lack some of the facilities needed for proper secondary education, above all in scientific and technical subjects". Of the schools in our own sample, only a quarter in 1961 had an adequate library room which they were able to keep for its proper use, and more than another quarter had no library room at all. A third of the schools had no proper science laboratories. Half had no special room for teaching music, and these included many schools in which the single hall had to serve for assembly, gymnasium and dining.

46. The greater the number of people who prove to be educable beyond all previous expectations, the stronger the suspicion grows—and the teachers are among the first to voice it—that the rest may have been underestimated also and that we are somehow failing a substantial number of young people. At the same time, the stronger the contrast becomes between those who are successful and those who are not, especially judged by those criteria which the world outside school most readily applies. There are differences over the country in the extent to which courses extending beyond the age of fifteen are available, as well as in the proportion of pupils who actually stay on. There are differences within a single school in how well it provides, or is able to provide, for pupils of varying abilities: most of the distinctive courses which have proved so successful have, for understandable historical reasons, so far been designed for the abler pupils. It would be idle to pretend that all the rest of the pupils are satisfied or satisfactory customers.

47. Too many at present seem to sit through lessons with information and exhortation washing over them and leaving very little deposit. Too many appear to be bored and apathetic in school, as some will be in their jobs also. Others are openly impatient. They "don't see the point" of what they are asked to do, they are conscious of making little progress: "The reason why I left at fifteen is because I felt that by staying on I should be wasting two years learning nothing. I could have worked harder, but what's the use if you don

---

[2] "Secondary Education For All. A New Drive", H.M.S.O. 1958.

get any encouragement?" argues one girl. A headmaster acknowledges, "There are far too many of our slow and average children who long ago reached saturation point doing tedious and hateful work year after year". They are provoked not only by the tedium of the work but also by resentment at being treated as children: "We had the feeling that if they treated us like little children we'd behave like it". "The teachers were nice but they just didn't seem to go about teaching us as well as we'd have liked. They couldn't control us because they treated us like children, and even kept telling us we were only children."

48. These girls and boys must somehow be made much more active partners in their own education. Whatever their natural endowments, they all need to attain self-respect and a reason for wanting to work well. Unless they do, no one can honestly justify extending the educational process by another year for them. Yet these pupils badly need the extra time, to enable them to grow up a little more as persons, to add to their general knowledge and understanding, and to strengthen their attainments. They are going out into a world of extreme complexity, which will certainly make taxing demands on them in their personal lives, if not in their jobs; and even in their jobs, there is no knowing what may lie ten or even five years ahead for any one of them. They will need all the resources the school can give them.

49. Some of their discontent is related to the restiveness of adolescence which affects all young people in some degree. But others, as well as the pupils, are not happy about the situation. Employers complain not only of poor attainments but of the inadequate speech and inability of boys and girls to manage their dealings with other people. "It is not so much that they are ill-mannered, but that many of them have a complete lack of any social skill". Other contributors to evidence write to us: "We feel bound to record our impression that very many of these less gifted young people are socially maladroit, ill at ease in personal relationships, unduly self-regarding and insensitive; their contact even with their peers is often ineffectual; they understandably resent being organized by adults but show little gift for organizing themselves". These are serious criticisms, certainly not applicable to all our pupils, but not, either, easily to be dismissed. This matter of communication affects all aspects of social and intellectual growth. There is a gulf between those who have, and the many who have not, sufficient command of words to be able to listen and discuss rationally; to express ideas and feelings clearly; and even to have any ideas at all. We simply do not know how many people are frustrated in their lives by inability ever to express themselves adequately; or how many never develop intellectually because they lack the words with which to think and to reason. This is a matter as important to economic life as it is to personal living: industrial relations as well as marriages come to grief on failures in communication.

50. The evidence of research increasingly suggests that linguistic inadequacy, disadvantages in social and physical background, and poor attainments in school, are closely associated. Because the forms of speech which are all they ever require for daily use in their homes and the neighbourhoods in which they live are restricted, some boys and girls may never acquire the basic means of learning and their intellectual potential is therefore masked. Perhaps the boy who said "By the time I reached the secondary school it was

all Chinese to me" was nearer the mark than he realized. This cannot explain the difficulties of all our pupils, some of whom enjoy most helpful home conditions. But it may underlie the relative failure of large numbers of boys and girls, and partly account for the undue proportion of children from working-class backgrounds who appear as below-average.[3] If this is so, then here is a problem which can be tackled educationally although research and extensive experiment will be needed to discover the right teaching techniques.

51. There remain other handicaps of environment, besides the linguistic, which may be working against the schools or the individual pupils. The next chapter considers the problems of schools in exceptionally under-privileged areas.

RECOMMENDATIONS

(*a*) Attention should be given to the functional deficiencies of many schools. Some of these deficiencies are due to overcrowding rather than to the age of the buildings, but others are characteristic of buildings which are totally unsuitable and inadequate; the deficiencies from whatever cause affect adversely the secondary education which can be offered to older pupils. (para. 45)

(*b*) There is an urgent need for research into the problems of environmental and linguistic handicaps, and of experiment in teaching techniques for overcoming the learning difficulties they create. (paras. 49 and 50; cf. also Chap. 12 para. 291)

---

[3] The evidence is in Chapter 1 of Part Two, Vol. II of "15 to 18". A similar argument is developed in Chapter 21 of this report.

CHAPTER 3

Education in the Slums

52. There is no need to read the melodramatic novelists to realize that there are areas, often near the decaying centres of big cities, where schools have more to contend with than the schoolboy's traditional reluctance. These are the districts where, as Mr. J. B. Mays puts it,[1]

"We find many different kinds of social problems in close association: a high proportion of mental illness, high crime and delinquency rates; and above average figures for infant mortality, tuberculosis, child neglect and cruelty. Here, too the so-called problem families tend to congregate. Life in these localities appears to be confused and disorganized. In and about the squalid streets and narrow courts, along the landings and staircases of massive blocks of tenement flats which are slowly replacing the decayed terraces, outside garish pubs and trim betting shops, in the lights of coffee bars, cafés and chip saloons, the young people gather at night to follow with almost bored casualness the easy goals of group hedonism."

53. What does it feel like to be responsible for a school serving such an area? What is the interaction between neighbourhood and school? We asked the heads of schools included in our survey to write freely about their problems. This is some of what they had to tell us.

54. First, the physical surroundings.

From London: The neighbourhood presents a sorry picture of drab tumble-down dwellings in narrow mean little streets, relieved by open spaces made recently by the demolition experts, and the dreary bomb sites that have served as rubbish dumps since the last war. Overcrowding still persists in the remaining slum dwellings where people of all nationalities compete for shelter. The homes of our children are in a deplorable condition. Damp and badly maintained, many of them are over-crowded. Large families live in two or three rooms. Toilet requirements are inadequate, giving rise to difficulties through too much sharing. Slowly the Council building scheme is providing new dwellings in the blocks of flats that are now beginning to rise near the school.

From the Midlands: The school is situated alongside a large sauce and pickle factory, and there is also a large brewery just behind it. The odours of vinegar and beer are constantly present and the air is full of soot particles. Many congested streets converge on the school buildings, the houses in these streets being tightly packed in terraces and courts. They are mainly of the back-to-back variety and accommodation usually consists of one room down, in which the whole family lives, plus T.V., and two to four bedrooms upstairs.

From Yorkshire: The estate was built a generation ago to house the people of the first slum clearance areas of the city. It forms a pocket about one mile from the city centre. The area has no shopping centre, recreation

[1] "Education", 15th June, 1962.

centre or community centre of its own . . . Gardens are a good reflector of the attitude and outlook of householders. Here it is obvious that few take any interest whatever in the appearance of the garden. Fences (iron) were removed during the war and that may be a contributory factor in the dilapidated condition of most.

From Yorkshire again: The area has an exceptionally high deposit of industrial dirt. The school itself has for neighbours two works within twenty yards of the playground wall, and three more within a radius of 200 yards. A railway and a canal are also within 50 yards of the school. Houses are terraced in dirty and badly illuminated streets and most are due for demolition. This has, in fact, already started in some streets in which a number of uninhabited houses offer tempting opportunities for mischief. Only one to two per cent of the houses have indoor sanitation and 36 per cent a hot water supply . . . A large proportion of fathers spend their working life in an atmosphere of heat, dirt, noise and mechanical violence. Communication can only be carried out by shouting and the effects of this can be noticed in the home, in the street and in places of entertainment. There is, therefore, a great tendency for boys to shout at each other in ordinary conversation.

From the Midlands: The children live in back to back houses which are badly designed, badly lit, and have no indoor sanitation—four or five families share one public toilet in the middle of the yard. Few of the children living here have ever seen a bathroom, and in some homes there is not even a towel and soap. Canals and railway lines run alongside the houses giving bad smells, grime and smoke and noise. All these homes have overcrowded living and sleeping quarters, for example, ten or eleven people may sleep in two beds and one cot. The living room usually measures about 10 × 9 ft. and combines gas stove, cupboard, sink and small table. The children are restricted to playing in the small yard or the pavement of the main road.

From Lancashire: The homes are nearly all tenement flats, erected a generation back, or maisonettes or multi-storey flats built within the last four or five years. Almost all the dwellings are well-kept by their own standards, though some of the housecraft ideas are sketchy. A growing number have washing machines in the £80 to £100 class on H.P. All, of course, have T.V. Amongst the girls there is still an obvious need for personal hygiene, even at the level of clean necks and brushed hair for school. Some of the mothers make startling objections to school complaints of head lice, fleas, body odour etc. Nevertheless, there is a great improvement on pre-war standards.

55. Next, then, the population.

From London: In recent years there has been a comparatively large immigration into the area especially from the West Indies, Southern Ireland and Cyprus.

From the Midlands: In most cases the parents, grandparents, and even great grandparents of the present boys are old scholars. The area is a very tightly knit community, and, in some respects, there is a genuine pride in the old school. An increasing number of families are being rehoused on the outskirts of the city, but many of the houses are being repaired to accommodate coloured immigrants from India, Pakistan and the West Indies.

From Yorkshire: The estate was given a great deal of unfavourable publicity at the outset and the impression made on the rest of the city remains. A clannish attitude tended to develop; strangers were not readily accepted. People who come to live here and have initiative and drive find little cooperation from the remainder so, whenever the opportunity comes, they leave. Replacements are invariably poor both financially and intellectually.

From Lancashire: We have a mixed population of white and coloured people dependent on industries and services closely connected with the port. The coloured population is very mixed from pure coloureds from the West Indies, Africa, India and Malaya to various half-caste groups . . . Families frequently change their address. This is especially true of the coloured children, but on the whole they seem to come from better cared for homes than others.

From Lancashire again: The girls are all drawn from the immediate neighbourhood within an area of a half square mile, all of the same racial and religious stock, Irish and Catholic, and almost all are the children of unskilled labourers who are in full employment. The community is very stable despite recent slum clearance and most of the children are descended from former pupils.

56. This brings us on to family life and general social behaviour.

From London: The children are generally exceptionally friendly, very generous and sympathetic towards one another. On the other hand, some quarrel readily. Tempers flare up instantly on very little provocation and die down just as quickly. Others resort to blows and lose all self-control . . . There is no participation in hooliganism. Very rarely do we find pornographic drawings or remarks in books or on walls. Living in the middle of one of the worst vice areas in London, it is very remarkable indeed to note that the children are surprisingly clean in thought and word and deed . . . Discipline at home seems to come about not so much through any governing principle or convictions, as perhaps by expediency, and is attained largely through fear of punishment, loss of temper, bad language, threats and over-indulgence. The children are often confused and bewildered by these various means . . . Any sort of physical approach, even as slight as a touch on the shoulder, can be received with great resentment and quick defensive action—possibly due to severe and repeated corporal punishment from dad at home. If dad is too heavy-handed, mum often protects the child from such punishment by lying or making light of certain misdeeds. In either case the child soon accepts the fact that he is "getting away with it". Naturally he strongly resents it when he is found out at school.

From London again: The Victorian concept of father still persists. He is the supreme head of the household, his wants are the first attended to, then come those of the sons, then of the mother, and finally, those of daughters. The boys will have a spare-time job and guaranteed pocket-money, for the girls pocket-money can be a matter of chance or the result of domestic work in the home.

From Yorkshire: The girls accept drunkenness as part of the normal pattern. They are amused by it; regard it as the normal way in which to celebrate. Even in good homes the parents will provide cases of beer for a 15 year-old's birthday party. The first form will give detailed accounts in essays of the quite revolting scenes when father comes home drunk. One dainty and sensitive little girl wrote: "You'd have died with laughing at my Dad . . ." In the same way they regard bad language as the normal. When we say that many men do not swear in their homes etc., they accuse us of teasing, or lying. They *know* that we are wrong and say so. Any *real* man swears and drinks. I think many of the "fringe" group of girls are saved from sexual intercourse by the fact that the young men who approach them do so quite openly. They make their requests in the first moment after meeting the girls in the street; and, unless the girls give immediate consent, they leave them to find a more readily obliging partner. If there were "petting parties" first the situation could be very different. At home washing is a real difficulty. The girls have what may seem to the outsider a foolish modesty in these matters. I have learned to see that in some cases they are wise not to undress to wash properly in front of brothers and fathers.

From Lancashire: There are many broken homes. Twenty-two per cent have no father, 5 per cent no mother; these figures may be higher in reality. At home corporal punishment (belting, a crack, a good hiding) is a common punishment. Some of it is severe and I have known a boy run away and sleep out for several nights for fear of the beating which he expected . . . Gambling is common in phases among the boys, with cards, tossing coins etc. Betting on horses and pools is not infrequent, but then fathers send their sons to the local bookmakers to lay bets and collect winnings, even pursuing them into school to retrieve the money. Obtaining money by violence or threat is a fairly common form of bullying younger children.

From Lancashire again: The (Roman Catholic) parish clergy hold a unique position in dockside parishes, however relaxed some parishioners may be in religious observance. The parents are amenable to quite slight pressure from the school, perhaps because the school has been under the Sisters for nearly a century, though the general moral standpoint which we all share has a good deal to do with it. The people are decent and good-living; there are strikingly few broken homes and illegitimate children. Families are still fairly large, and there is a great family sense so that, even when mothers are out at work, there is always some relative, usually the grand-mother, to turn to . . . Although there is a great deal of talk of "murdering" and "battering", I have only come across two cases in six years of girls severely beaten by father or mother. The parents are foolishly generous and quite inconsistent in their treatment of the children who are adept at evading consequences. The bad language shrieked from the top balcony of the tenements sounds appalling but appears to be rather a maternal safety valve than a heart-felt threat. Indeed, the children are very much loved and secure in their family affection. Every new baby is welcomed to an extra-ordinary extent. The girls are very kind to little ones and to the old. I have never come across an instance of rudeness or unwillingness to oblige an old person, though this may be due to caution, since grandparents are still powerful. They are rude to neighbours, carrying on family quarrels with gusto, and fights are common. I have much work in keeping fights out of school, and it is horrifying how even "good" girls all flock to watch a fight anywhere. The girls will fight as fiercely as the boys if they get the chance. Most girls stay up very late but few stay out. Those who do, stay on the tenement landings in the semi-darkness with the boys. Their main amusements are gambling, singing or cat-calling, horse-play and some sex-play. Sexual laxity is rare in this district under school leaving age. I have had no schoolgirl mothers and only three girls who tried their hand at soliciting or got into the company of a prostitute by choice. Girls marry very young, so, whilst doing all we can to deter them from marriage before 18, we do our best in the Fourth Year course to give then some training for their career as wife and mother.

A final contribution from Yorkshire: What can we do about rehabilitation when girls have got into serious trouble of some kind? In school we have little difficulty. It is easy to pick them up and let them begin again, as regards those who have left we cannot do a great deal. Certainly the fact that Old Girls (especially the weaker brethren) are encouraged to come back to school *whatever* has happened seems to have been useful. We are often able to try to do that part of the task of rehabilitation for both young and old which would have been the business of the local priest or doctor at one time. In these days very few will go to the clergyman—they do not know him. And the doctor is now one of a team—and often they do not know him either. So they come to school, sure at least of a hearing and—"no gossip afterwards".

57. The picture which these heads have so movingly drawn for us make it clear that the social challenge they have to meet comes from the whole neighbourhood in which they work and not, as in most modern schools, from a handful of difficult families. The difference is so great as to constitute a difference in kind. Inevitably their pupils as a whole are not as good at school work as those from more fortunately placed homes. Inevitably, too, their general level of manners is lower and the risk of their falling into delinquency is greater than average. Considering the base line from which schools in slums start, their achievements in formal, personal and social education often equal the achievements of schools in better neighbourhoods. Sometimes indeed they are better. The strict objective test of reading which we applied shows that although the average reading age of their pupils is seventeen months below the average, a quarter of the schools in the worst areas scored an average mark which was at or above the mean for all modern schools in the country. This is a splendid achievement. In the slums, as everywhere else, there are good, bad and indifferent schools. No doubt the failure of a bad school in a slum is more total and more spectacular than in a middle class suburb because of the lack of parental and community support to bolster up the industry and moderate the behaviour of the pupils. But we have no reason to suppose that bad schools are more frequent in slums than elsewhere.

58. What about the schools themselves? We have been careful in this chapter to write of "schools in slums", not of "slum schools". This distinction, however, can hardly be maintained as far as buildings are concerned. Forty per cent of all the modern schools in our sample had buildings which must be condemned as seriously inadequate. The corresponding figure for the slums is 79 per cent. Two illustrations may be given of what 'seriously inadequate'

means. The first is a typical example; the second is worse than typical but
by no means unique. They have been chosen because these schools happen to
have the best attendance figures in this special slum group. The fact that their
attendance is up to or above the average for all modern schools, shows how
devotion can overcome difficulties.

A boys' school of 284 *pupils.* Average attendance 91·5 per cent. A very old
building with nine large classrooms. In addition there is an art and light
craft room. There is a library, but it is smaller than a normal small classroom, and a laboratory, but it can only take 20 boys at a time. There is a
very small hall without a stage but no gymnasium, dining room, medical
room, or, indeed, any other special room. Two outside centres provide
between them 9 sessions of woodwork per week, in addition to what is
done in one woodwork room at school. A playing field is being provided
for this and neighbouring schools, but was not in full use at the time of the
survey. All school matches have had to be played on opponents' grounds.
There is an old swimming bath (70 ft. by 30 ft.) ten minutes away without
facilities for diving. Three sessions of 40 minutes are available per week—
insufficient for all who wish to swim.

A girls' school of 209 *pupils.* Average attendance 93·0 per cent. A very old
building with 7 classrooms of 480 sq. ft. each, one of which is at present
used for art and music as there is no teacher for the seventh class. Four are
separated by moveable wood and glass partitions. There is no hall, gymnasium, dining room or special room of any kind. There is a small roof
playground, very exposed to wind and weather but no fixed P.E. equipment.
Netball is played in the courtyard of nearby tenements. Science has to be
based on one corridor cupboard. There is a sink, gas and electricity. There
are good cupboards, ironing boards, sewing machines and a fitting corner
in one classroom. There is no room for light crafts. Class libraries and
subject libraries are kept in portable infant type cupboards. There is
sufficient time allocation at a housecraft centre to give the 2nd, 3rd and
4th years one session per week. Four forms each week are able to visit an
L.E.A. playing field half an hour away by bus. There is a very old swimming
bath with poor accommodation near the school which is available for one
hour per week (2 classes).

59. Conditions such as these must inevitably have an adverse affect on staffing.
As far as the actual ratio of teachers to pupils is concerned these schools are
no worse off than the general run: indeed many of them have a marginal
advantage. But all our evidence stresses the need for continuity of teaching
and stability in staffing. The heads of schools in the slums have nearly all
pointed out in their evidence the value of teachers who are now meeting the
second and even the third generation of pupils from the same family. But
besides the need for such men and women who have won a place in the
tradition of the neighbourhood there is an equally great need for what may
be called short-term stability—that is to say stability over the period of a
pupil's school life. It is this stability which we have tried to measure in our
survey.

60. How many teachers who were in the schools in 1958, when the pupils
in the survey were admitted, were still there in 1961? How many had
come and gone in the interval? How much bigger was the staff in 1961?
The following table answers these questions taking the 1958 staff as 100.

	Men		Women	
	All Schools	Schools in Slums	All Schools	Schools in Slums
1958 staff still there in 1961	64	52	50	33
Teachers who came since and have stayed	50	42	61	68
Teachers who came and went	27	82	44	65

The true situation is probably even worse than these figures since a slight ambiguity in one question led some schools to underestimate the number of transients—small wonder, then, if boys and girls eyeing a new teacher are doubtful whether he will stay long enough to make it worth their while to settle down and really work for him. In these slum schools there was only an even chance that a woman who joined the staff later than the beginning of the Christmas term in 1958 would still be there in September 1961; for men the odds were two to one against. Only a third of the women and half the men had been on the staff for more than three years.

61. Four other ways in which schools in slums fall markedly below the general run follow as almost inevitable consequences from poor staffing and poor premises. First, very few boys and girls want to extend their compulsory school life by even one or two terms. Secondly, the less able pupils spend more of their time in ordinary classroom work than in other modern schools. In only ten per cent of the schools in slums compared with 21 per cent of all modern schools, do the less able pupils spend roughly half or more of their time on "practical subjects", including physical education. Thirdly, only one in eight fourth year pupils belong to school clubs or societies compared with one in four in modern schools generally. Lastly, homework is much less common in schools in slums. Sixty-nine per cent of the fourth-year boys and fifty-nine per cent of the girls get no regular homework compared with forty-nine per cent of the boys and forty-three per cent of the girls in modern schools as a whole.

62. What proportion of all modern schools are what we have called "schools in slums", and what proportion of boys and girls attend them? There is no satisfactory objective criterion of a slum. In the north of England especially there are still a very large number of highly respectable neighbourhoods in which the buildings are so far below modern standards that the houses may well be considered unfit. These are not slums in our definition. Only where there is an unusually high concentration of social problems as well have we classified a neighbourhood as a slum.

63. The particular schools in slums with which we have been concerned in this chapter are not included in our representative sample of four per cent of all modern schools. They are an additional group which was specially selected so as to make sure that we had adequate information about schools working in the most difficult of all neighbourhoods. This additional group was necessary because, although there was only a one in ten million chance that the worst ten per cent would be totally excluded, there was a one per cent chance that the worst three per cent might be unrepresented.

64. It would, of course, be quite wrong to think of a sharp frontier separating slum from non-slum. The transition is gradual and included in our representative sample there are, as it happens, some schools which appear to be as badly situated as any in the special slum group and others which face nearly,

but not quite as difficult a task. Inside the sample we have grouped together all the schools which serve neighbourhoods of bad housing with bad social problems. These we have called "problem areas" to distinguish them from the special group of schools in slums. We know, therefore, the size of the problem areas. Twenty per cent of the schools served "problem areas" and were attended by eighteen per cent of all pupils.

65. If the schools in problem areas are compared with modern schools generally, they suffer in much the same kind of ways as the schools in slums, though not to the same extent. Thus, to take one illustration only, the average reading age of the fourth-year pupils in the problem area schools was eight months lower than the average for modern schools generally. In the schools in slums it was nine months lower still—seventeen months in all. In paragraph 60 the fact that the schools in slums have less stability and more turnover in staffing emerges clearly. This is evidence that the same thing applies, to a lesser extent, in the problem areas, although if we had no data beyond the sample of 150 modern schools the difference would not stand clear of sampling fluctuation. The special group may be regarded as the tail end of a much larger sample.

66. Had it been practicable to have worked with a much larger sample a fairly close estimate of the total number of schools in slums might have been made. The actual procedure gives a rather loose estimate of between three and ten per cent, say, seven per cent with a further thirteen per cent sharing many of the same disadvantages.

67. Nothing that we have seen or heard leads us to believe that the strictly educational problems of the less able pupils are different in slum schools from other schools. The approach which is most likely to succeed in modern schools generally is the most suitable also in the slums. There is, therefore, no chapter in Part Two of our report dealing with their problems in isolation; all the chapters of that Part in our view apply as much to schools in slums as to schools elsewhere.

68. But schools in slums do require special consideration if they are to have a fair chance of making the best of their pupils. They seem to us, for instance, to need a specially favourable staffing ratio. Even more they need measures which will help them to secure at least as stable a staff as other schools. Perhaps this can be secured simply by making it clear that professionally it is an asset to have served successfully in a difficult area, that work there can be intellectually exciting and spiritually rewarding, that these are schools in which able teachers may want to serve and make their career as so many of their gifted predecessors have done. One headmistress wrote to us "the staffing of schools in difficult areas is made more difficult by those administratively responsible who take the line, 'It's no good asking folks to come down here—they wouldn't put up with it'. In fact this is not true. Four able teachers have *asked* to come to this school, and their request has been ignored." Perhaps then a change of wind will be sufficient.

69. But perhaps more tangible inducements may be needed. One suggestion is contained in an appendix to this report. Another might be the provision of good residential accommodation for teachers near the schools. This is something which ought to be examined, however, not only as a device for recruiting teachers, but also for its bearing on the whole life of the community

in which they would then be living as well as working. In helping to solve a purely school problem we might be slightly relieving that uniform residual nature of the population which helps to make a slum.

70. There is another aspect of the staffing problem which also overlaps strictly education boundaries. There is no doubt at all about the need for a good deal of social work in connection with the pupils. Problems of poverty, health and delinquency are involved. Nearly twice as many fourth-year pupils get free dinners as in modern schools as a whole. Twice as many boys are under five foot high, and twice as many under six and a half stone in weight.[1] Among third-year pupils, half as many again as in modern schools generally missed more than half a term's work—two-thirds of them because of ill-health. There is also a worse problem of truancy: half as many again could not satisfactorily explain their absences. One in six of the third-year girls were in this category. We have no hesitation in saying that these figures from our survey taken in conjunction with the general picture given by the heads make a good case for the employment of trained social workers. But should they be school-based? This is a different and more difficult problem. Behind each absence there is a story which may well involve several different social agencies.

71. The fact that 79 per cent of the secondary schools in the slums were seriously inadequate points to the need for a bold re-building policy which is indeed under way. Several of the schools in our survey have already been replaced. It might be thought that a re-building policy at least was something that could be decided on purely educational grounds. It is not so. The general tendency on educational grounds, rightly or wrongly, has been for small schools to give place to larger ones. But the heads of the schools in our special slum group are convinced believers in small schools to meet their special problems which are social, as we have seen, rather than educational. The question of size is also relevant to the problem of how to tackle the welfare of the new immigrants who are often of different ethnic and cultural groups from their neighbours. There are three possible educational solutions. They may attend the local county school in which they will form a distinctive and compact group. If the school is small and draws its pupils from a confined area they may soon provide a quarter to a third of the pupils. Or they may, like the Irish Roman Catholics in many places, attend a voluntary school that is virtually their own. Or they may lose their group identity either by being divided between many small schools, or by being sent to a very big school with a catchment area so large and carefully drawn that they cease to be a conspicuous group. Which is the right decision cannot be settled on purely educational grounds.

72. We are clear, too, that an adequate education cannot be given to boys and girls if it has to be confined to the slums in which they live. They, above all others, need access to the countryside, the experience of living together in civilized and beautiful surroundings, and a chance to respond to the challenge of adventure. They need priority in relation to school journeys,

---

[1] The average figures for boys, which are free of sampling fluctuation, are

in height—	All modern schools	64·5 in.
	Schools in slums	63·2 in.
in weight—	All modern schools	116·9 lbs.
	Schools in slums	112·5 lbs.

There is no such discrepancy in height or weight for girls. The reasons for this remain a matter for speculation.

overseas visits, and adventure courses. Clearly this is an educational matter, but it is not solely one. Children below school age, young workers, older people—the whole community—need to have a stake in something more than the streets in which they live.

73. In the last four paragraphs we have been concerned with the fact that certain problems which are primarily educational have wider social implications. Whatever is decided by the educational authorities in these matters will have repercussions on other social agencies. It is equally true that decisions made in other fields—in housing, for example, or in public health—will have reactions in the schools. There may well be a case, as has been suggested to us, for really short term residential provision in their own neighbourhood for boys and girls who are in especially difficult or distressing home circumstances, or who may be in danger of lapsing into serious delinquency. If this is so, the relation of such a plan to the schools is something which might be explored jointly by the services which would be involved. In the slums the need for reform is not confined to the schools. It is general. Because no social service is "an island to itself" there may be a case for an inter-departmental working party to plan the strategy of a grand assault, but not at the expense of postponing the opening of the campaign.

74. Here, then, are some of the things that seem to us need tackling if we are to give the schools in the slums a fair chance. The bill we have presented is large. It is larger than it might have been because the account has been allowed to go too long unpresented. But adequate education in slum areas will always be expensive, more expensive than average. It looks to us as if it has often been less expensive than average, and therefore pitifully inadequate. It is time for a change.

RECOMMENDATIONS

(a) An inter-departmental working party should be set up to deal with the general social problems, including education, in slum areas. (para. 73)
(b) Particular attention should be paid to devising incentives for teachers to serve and stay in these areas. (paras. 68, 69)

CHAPTER 4

Objectives

"If your machine was working well . . . you went off into pipe-dreams for the rest of the day . . . You lived in a compatible world of pictures which passed through your mind like a magic lantern, often in vivid and glorious loony-colour".
Alan Sillitoe, "Saturday Night and Sunday Morning".

75. Before they can tackle their problems the schools have to be clear about their ultimate objectives. What ought these to be for our pupils? In any immediately foreseeable future, large numbers of boys and girls who leave school will enter jobs which make as limited demands on them as Arthur Seaton's: can their time in school help them to find more nourishment for the rest of their personal lives than loony-coloured phantasies?

76. Most teachers and parents would agree with us about general objectives. Skills, qualities of character, knowledge, physical well-being, are all to be desired. Boys and girls need to be helped to develop certain skills of communication in speech and in writing, in reading with understanding, and in calculations involving numbers and measurement: these skills are basic, in that they are tools to other learning and without some mastery of them the pupils will be cut off from whole areas of human thought and experience. But they do not by themselves represent an adequate minimum education at which to aim. All boys and girls need to develop, as well as skills, capacities for thought, judgement, enjoyment, curiosity. They need to develop a sense of responsibility for their work and towards other people, and to begin to arrive at some code of moral and social behaviour which is self-imposed. It is important that they should have some understanding of the physical world and of the human society in which they are growing up.

77. Our pupils, because some of them acquire skills slowly, and others only with the utmost difficulty, may be in danger of spending their whole time at school in continual efforts to sharpen tools which they never have opportunity enough to use. They may be kept busy, and yet never have their minds and imaginations fully engaged; and leave school very ill-equipped in knowledge and personal resources. Again, because many of them do not acquire or retain factual knowledge easily, the range of information and ideas to which they are introduced may be seriously inadequate. Yet it does not follow that because they will not long remember everything they have thought and talked about in school—who does?—the experience will be of no value. How is it possible to devise for pupils of only moderate, and in some cases very limited, skills, a content of education which exercises their minds and emotions and feeds their imagination? What kinds of experiences will help them to develop their full capacities for thought and taste and feeling? Without some satisfactory answers, both the individual and society remain that much the more impoverished.

78. There are some aspects of our times which must affect anyone growing up to-day, and of which education ought to take account. This is a world in which science and technology are making spectacular extensions to human

experience; it is also a world in which the threat of nuclear war has been present ever since the boys and girls now in school were born. At homely levels, machines and tools enter increasingly into every-day living. The conditions under which our pupils will work and live out their lives may be very different, even from what their parents now know. All this requires at least a vocabulary for discussion, at many different levels of understanding.

79. This too is a time when economic inter-dependence is bringing the countries of the world much closer together, and sheer factual knowledge of how people of other nations and races and religions live is becoming urgently necessary. For the boy and girl at school, this need not be a matter of geographical and economic abstractions, but of achieving, for example, some compassionate insight into what it means to say that half the world is undernourished, or of learning how to get along with foreign neighbours.

80. This is a century which has seen, and is still seeing, marked changes in the status and economic role of women. Girls themselves need to be made aware of the new opportunities which may be open to them, and both boys and girls will be faced with evolving a new concept of partnership in their personal relations, at work and in marriage.

81. In western industrialized countries, the hours which must necessarily be spent in earning a living are likely to be markedly reduced during the working lifetime of children now in school. The responsibility for ensuring that this new leisure is the source of enjoyment and benefit it ought to be, and not of demoralizing boredom, is not the schools' alone, but clearly education can play a key part. A great deal has been written elsewhere about the impact of all the vastly extended means of mass communication and entertainment. Certainly everybody needs, as never before, some capacity to select, if only in the interests of fuller enjoyment, from the flood of experience continually presented. Our pupils, more than most, need training in discrimination.

82. These are issues especially relevant to the present day. Clearly, there are others, of great importance, particularly those concerned with conduct and with religion, which recur to some extent for every generation. But it is surely not necessary to labour further the point, that there are public events and fields of ideas and of knowledge which have significance for everyone. To ignore them is not only to do a disservice to all young people, but to throw away many obvious sources of interest and stimulus to learning. The experience of some of the most successful teachers confirms that boys and girls can enjoy intellectual effort and respond to aesthetic experiences, even though their own attainments, assessed in terms of "basic skills", may be very modest. Adolescents, at any level of ability, are not indifferent to important aspects of human life and behaviour. They may ask searching questions about the most profound problems. The fourteen-year-old boy, from the lowest fourth year class, who wrote the words quoted below, needed more than help with spelling and punctuation:

> "I have many times thought about religion I have gone to many Churches and gone to many meetings to find out the truth about God. I think there is a God but I do not think he his in heaven because men have studied science and found out the moon his far away it his cold and dead and the sun his burning and the stars are billions of years away and the sky is just space so where can God be."

83. How are the schools to set about meeting these deeper educational needs? When parents ask their children what they do at school, the answers tend to be about particular lessons and subjects—arithmetic, woodwork, geography. That is understandable, because that is how the experience of each day is made up. Sometimes, it may seem as if that is all school is about, especially to the more dissatisfied customers, who go on to ask "What's the use?" But it is not the whole of what school really is about. The separate lessons and subjects are single pieces of a mosaic; and what matters most is not the numbers and colours of the separate pieces, but what pattern they make when put together. Some of the most urgent questions which all secondary schools are having to ask themselves just now are about the total patterns of the curriculum, for all their pupils. They are finding that it is not enough to tinker with the separate pieces.

84. That is why it is not possible to offer a short and simple formula for the education of our pupils, in terms of additional lessons in English or more time in the workshop or extra bits of knowledge in this subject or that. The significant thing is the total impact. What will these young people be, and know, and be capable of doing, as a result of their time in school? No sixteen year-old, or even eighteen year-old, is a fully finished product as a human being; but each additional year in full-time education ought to be assisting the pupils in their progress towards maturity, and equipping them a little better to play their part in the world.

85. In trying to fulfil their larger aims, many schools are perplexed by their difficulties over the immediate means. There is potentially a large range of means available, not only in direct lessons of all kinds, but in many out-of-school activities and in the experiences of social and communal life which the school provides. But not all schools are equally well endowed. Some are lacking in particular kinds of accommodation—library or science laboratories or craft rooms or gymnasium; many others are short of teachers, or lacking in teachers with knowledge and interest in particular subjects. These inadequacies are seriously hampering, and we do not wish to minimise them. But they may be less serious in their consequences if a school can build from strength, giving particular emphasis to those educational experiences which it is best able to provide, but not necessarily assuming that there is a fixed range of subjects which must be included at all times for all pupils. There may be more than one way of attaining the same objective.

86. There are, in any case, some objectives which can and ought deliberately to be pursued through every part of the curriculum. Very high in this list we should place improvement in powers of speech: not simply improvement in the quality and clearness of enunciation, although that is needed, but a general extension of vocabulary, and, with it, a surer command over the structures of spoken English and the expression of ideas. That means seizing the opportunity of every lesson, in engineering or housecraft or science as well as in English, to provide material for discussion—genuine discussion, not mere testing by teacher's question and pupil's answer.

87. Discussion should be used to develop judgement and discrimination. This may apply to enjoyment in music or art or literature; to taste and craftsmanship in the workshop; to a sense of what is appropriate behaviour in a particular situation, which will generally involve some consideration of other

people's feelings and points of view; or to an appreciation of what is relevant to the immediate task in hand. It does not follow, because the actual tasks undertaken may be relatively simple, that the pupils cannot be guided into thinking about them critically. They badly need this general strengthening of critical powers. One of the ways in which they are specially vulnerable as young adults is in their inability to see when they are being got at, particularly through some modern sales methods and commercial entertainment. There is much scope for valuable work which schools can undertake with their older pupils, both in consumer studies and in examining the influences extended by newspapers, magazines, comics, advertisement hoardings, films, and television. But it would be wrong to leave pupils with the idea that everything they like is bad, or that all criticism is negative. A sound, positive judgement must start with valuing properly the good things they enjoy.

88. Parents and employers are naturally anxious to be assured in all this that sufficient attention is being paid to basic skills. It is sheer common sense to urge that every possible opportunity, throughout the whole of school work, be taken to provide the pupils with practice in reading, writing and elementary mathematics, and in searching out information for themselves. It may be that pupils will gain some of their most helpful practice in writing outside the English lesson, from trying to give in their own words an account of a science experiment or a geographical expedition. In this way, when they have something definite to say, the pupils may learn the difficult art of writing that simple, straightforward English which is always being commended to them as though it were an easy thing. Work in the craftshop or the housecraft room, or on the school farm, or for that matter in designing the scenery and selling the tickets for the school play, may involve practice in arithmetical calculation, and the point of getting the sums right may seem more obvious than if the same sums appeared in a text book exercise. There are other important aspects of English and mathematics to be covered in school besides these; but every advantage ought to be taken of such direct applications in other subjects.

89. In short, we are saying that whatever lessons appear on the timetable, it is essential that the pupils be helped and stimulated by them to enlarge their understanding and practise their skills; that some direct experience, which can mean, for example, listening to a broadcast or watching a film, as well as actively doing or making things, will often provide the most effective starting point for discussion; that from this they can advance to some critical evaluation, perhaps a search for further knowledge, and to making some written record, where this is appropriate, of what they have been doing. All of this bears a good deal of resemblance, we are aware, to the experience of learning offered in a lively junior school. The main difference at this secondary stage will be that there will be a need to deal with more mature interests and more subtle judgements, and to make more explicit the connections between what is done in one subject and another.

90. There are some teachers who will say that nothing has been stated so far which is not heavily obvious; to them we would reply that there are not enough schools in which these things happen. There are others, including perhaps some parents, who will feel that a target is being set which is quite unattainable by average pupils. Our answer to them is that there are schools in which it is attained, and there ought to be more.

91. In Part Two of this report we are concerned with the detailed content of the school curriculum. We have begun with this general thesis, because discussions of the educational objectives too easily lose themselves in the weighing of rival claims between this subject or that, or in emphasis on the practice of basic skills at the cost of excluding all variety or relevance of interest. We come back to the starting point of this chapter, in affirming that at present many of our boys and girls are educationally undernourished.

92. Some of them are also underestimated and under-employed, in the sense that their occupations in school commonly make insufficient demand on them, and that the total time they actually spend in educational work of any kind may be too little for their age and needs. We shall come back in chapter 6 to the length of the school working day, the need for homework—though not necessarily of a conventional kind—and the role of all those activities which are called extra-curricular; but it may be useful to say at once that we foresee the need, especially as older boys and girls stay on at school, to extend considerably the provision for activities outside the formal lesson programme, and to draw a less sharp line between what is learned in and what is learned outside the classroom.

RECOMMENDATIONS

(a) Basic skills in reading, writing and calculation should be reinforced through every medium of the curriculum. (paras. 76, 88, 89.)

(b) More demands should be made on the pupils, both in the nature and in the amount of work required. There is a need to stimulate intellectual and imaginative effort, and to extend the pupils' range of ideas, in order to promote a fuller literacy. (paras. 77–82.)

(c) The value of the educational experience should be assessed in terms of its total impact on the pupils' skills, qualities and personal development, not by basic attainments alone. (paras. 83, 84.)

CHAPTER 5

Finding Approaches

"The work of the school must not seem, as perhaps it still does, the antithesis of 'real life'."　　　　　　　　　Report of the Hadow Committee, 1926.

93. A great deal of the evidence presented to us urges that our pupils would respond better to work which is more "realistic" or more "practical". The advice is in an honourable tradition. The view of the Hadow Committee, and of others before and since then, that the schools should provide "an education by means of a curriculum containing large opportunities for practical work and related to living interests", has in some respects long been accepted. Secondary modern schools, and before them many of the senior schools, have for many years given a substantial amount of time to "practical" subjects in their programmes. The schools in our survey were markedly better off for "practical" rooms than they were for libraries, a sign that the need for the former was earlier recognized than the need for the latter. No-one now would question the need for both, in the education of all pupils, whatever their "ability": pupils are not divisible into those who need only tools and those who need only books. But life is not static, and we are still a long way from fulfilling the underlying intention of those earlier recommendations. To satisfy the definition of "realistic" and "practical" in relation to the present day, let alone the years ahead, will require work of a different scale and nature from what was formerly envisaged.

94. Under the name of "practical subjects" in the school timetable are usually included art and light crafts; needlework and cookery; woodwork, metalwork, and sometimes, technical drawing. Various other activities, such as engineering or rural studies, may be found in particular schools, according to their circumstances. (In our own discussion of practical subjects in Part Two, we have employed an even wider definition of "practical".)

95. All these subjects are capable of offering experiences of a distinctive kind, valuable in the education of all pupils. Certainly when the boys and girls come into the secondary schools, these are among the fresh experiences which evoke an enthusiastic response. Even art and needlework, which will have been known in the primary school, take on a different aspect, taught in a special room by a special teacher: the distinctive rooms and equipment are a sign of new secondary status. For the pupils who come unhappily conscious that their past inadequacies are still with them in matters of English and arithmetic, the virgin page of a new subject is doubly blessed. There are other attractions also. These subjects involve physical movement and a variety of activity, and the handling of real objects which may be interesting in themselves. They offer a chance to learn by a direct experience, rather than by a theoretical explanation alone; they may offer, in their more creative aspects, another medium of expression to those who find expression in words particularly difficult.

96. All this is helpful. But there is a danger that, in their traditional presentation, these subjects are made to exist on this capital too long. Are they able, in

the third, fourth and fifth years, to do more than keep the pupils busy as they were in the first two? Do they always do even that? They can do much more, if they are consciously used as an instrument of wider general education. But there is no guarantee that what takes place in a workshop or housecraft room will be automatically more stimulating than what goes on in an ordinary classroom; it all depends on the quality of the teaching. Unimaginative exercises can be as dully repetitive in woodwork as they can be in English. If "practical" work is to be used as one means of revitalizing the programme —and it needs revitalizing—for our pupils, something other than a larger dose of the mixture as before is needed.

97. In Part Two of this report we discuss the handling of these subjects in the classroom situation. Here, we are concerned rather with their function in the pupils' education as a whole. We believe they can indeed offer a satisfying approach to learning for many, perhaps most, of our pupils, as experiences which are worth while in themselves, as activities which can recognizably be related to "real life", and as a stimulus to effort in other learning. We also believe that some of that other learning, in subjects which are not, in conventional usage, "practical", should start more directly from the pupils' experience. In this sense the whole curriculum could effectively be made more realistic.

98. The last years at school need a unifying theme to give them coherence and purpose at a stage when the pupils themselves are growing restive. Such a theme can be found in the idea of preparation for adult life. All pupils have to grow up, and, bright or dull, most of them are only too eager to do so. A great deal has been said and written elsewhere on the early physical maturity of young people today; it is certainly quite clear, long before they leave the secondary school, that they have ceased to think of themselves as children and are beginning to reach out to the life they will lead as adults. It is right that they should. They need some reassurance that what they are spending their time on in school is taking them a step further on the way. Particularly, if they do not learn easily, they need to be persuaded that the effort is worth while. Not everything that a school tries to do for its pupils can be understood by them at the time; their view ahead, and the experience on which they base their judgement, are limited. But they can be shown the relevance to life of at least a substantial part of what is done in school and they should be expected to take something on trust. The schools are wiser than the children and the children expect them to be. So do the parents. This is nowhere more important than in those difficult areas where the whole outer environment seems hostile to education.

99. One way of marking approaching adult status is to give the curriculum a new look for the last two years of school life, and to allow the pupils themselves some choice in the subjects they study and in the kind of programme they follow. This is not uncommon now for the abler boys and girls, but in many schools would be a revolutionary step as far as our pupils are concerned. In by far the majority of schools in our survey virtually no choice or change of curriculum at all was available for any of the less able pupils. It is true that many of the schools were so hard pressed for teaching accommodation of all kinds that they could not see their way to making the kind of provision they would like to make. Others would say that, even were the facilities

available, it is impossible to devise a distinctive programme for pupils who intend to leave before completing even a fourth year, and that they are already doing the best they can for these pupils by putting them into "leavers" groups. These are very pertinent difficulties. Yet it is equally likely that failure, for whatever reason, to provide for these pupils, when special provision is being made for their abler fellows, is to confirm them in the opinion that school is not for the likes of them. It is virtually an invitation to opt out of school work, from the time in the third year when preliminary discussion of the abler pupils' plans begins to take place. Nevertheless, the experience of schools with their abler boys and girls and the valuable experiments of a much smaller number of schools in trying out new patterns of work with their less able pupils, suggest some useful lines of attack.

100. In some areas, but by no means everywhere, it is becoming the practice to offer the abler pupils a choice of courses, or programmes, of which the distinctive feature is a group of subjects broadly related to some occupational interest. Often the special studies give the name to the course—"engineering", "catering", "retail distribution", for example—although the pupils' programme will contain much else besides. We are convinced not only that such courses should be more widely available in all areas—and this implies adequate facilities for them, which many schools at present do not possess—but also that many of the less gifted pupils would respond to comparable opportunities. We nevertheless wish to emphasize in the following paragraphs that all such courses are vehicles of general education, that the occupational interest should not monopolize the whole of the pupils' curriculum, and that they should not be led to expect employment in the given occupation as a necessary consequence.

101. For the individual boy and girl, getting their first job and starting to earn their own living is probably the most momentous outward event confirming that they are "grown up". The initial thrill of this is not likely to be much different whatever the job itself may be. Well before they leave school most young people are beginning to wonder "What is it like to be at work?" and some perhaps, "Shall I be able to manage it?"—especially those who know themselves to be not very clever. The diffident ones, as well as those who are impatient to shake off the leading-strings, need to feel that school is offering them some preparation.

102. The discovery of unexpected reserves of talent among the abler pupils in the modern schools, which has been a very notable feature of those schools in recent years, would lead us to believe that a much higher proportion of school leavers than at present do so could undertake skilled work were the opportunities for apprenticeship or training available. This must be especially true of girls, of whom only a very small percentage enter employment involving any form of training. For these pupils, well-designed courses in schools which, without in any way being narrow trade-training, guided their interests and helped them to see the way ahead into further education and future training for a career, could be of great value both to the individuals concerned and to the country's economic resources. We think it vital that increased training provision should be available for such school leavers.

103. But there remain other boys and girls, who are clearly much more limited in their capacities. It is important not to mislead them into thinking

that they are acquiring qualifications for a skilled trade which they have no prospect of obtaining. And it would be dishonest not to acknowledge that large numbers of young school leavers at present enter employment which involves no skill or special knowledge which cannot very quickly be learned on the job. For them, especially, courses which made use of an occupational interest would be chiefly valuable in providing a more stimulating approach to school work and an incentive to extend their general education.

104. We suggest that for by far the majority of our pupils, courses will need to have a substantial craft or practical element, with an emphasis on real tasks undertaken with adult equipment: this will have important consequences for teachers and for buildings. But we emphasize again that in addition to providing experience in the use of tools and different kinds of materials, and the satisfaction of handling three dimensional objects, the special course work must be made to pay an adequate yield in general educational development.

105. The total amount of specific vocational content in the course will vary with local circumstances. The course must be judged by how far it constitutes a stimulating education, whether or not the pupil eventually takes up a related occupation. Equally, the range of choices in any one school does not need to be very wide. The schools cannot possibly offer courses related to all the jobs which their pupils will eventually enter, nor do they need to do so. Choice itself is important as a symbol that pupils are taking a hand in their own education, and the morale of many boys and girls will be strengthened simply by the sense that what they are doing has some relevance to earning a living.

106. There are several other considerations to be borne in mind. First, we do not think it educationally in the pupils' interest to introduce the specialized work before the fourth year of a five-year secondary course; nor do the greater number of employers appear to wish for the return of trade-training schemes beginning at the age of thirteen.

107. Secondly, a substantial amount of time should be devoted to it, sufficient to indicate that it is taken seriously, and for a satisfying level of achievement to be possible. As a corollary of taking it seriously, where special facilities or equipment may be required, as, for example, in engineering, these should be of a kind and of a scale to allow a real job of work to be done. If, particularly where the number of pupils involved is small, it is not economic to provide such facilities on the school premises then joint arrangements should be made with other schools, or more often perhaps, with colleges of further education, wherever suitable facilities exist.

108. Thirdly, the further down the ability scale are the pupils concerned, the more broadly based must be the courses which they are following. This does not mean that the courses should not have a sound craft and practical content, but that in view of the type of work which these pupils will enter on leaving school, it is clearly not possible for their school course to contain a vocational element directly related to one occupation. It is, however, vitally important that the less able pupils should feel that life at school matters to them. This can be done if the school work is related to life after school as they see it, and to broad divisions of the world of work. It should be possible to develop a school work programme embracing several crafts and practical activities which could be followed on and off the school premises for up to one quarter, or even one third of the school week. It is reasonable to suggest

that such programmes, by engendering a change of attitude, might enliven the whole approach to school of the individual boy and girl. By this the effectiveness of the school's complete teaching programme would also be improved. Something must be done at school to awaken enthusiasm for learning in these young people and we believe that a fundamental change in the curriculum would help in this direction. The vocational element must, however, never be allowed to crowd out activities dealing with other interests and knowledge and experiences, not covered by the special course. These must be taken seriously too.

109. What forms might courses for our pupils take, always accepting that there cannot, and should not, be any stereotyped pattern? In schools and areas which have for some years been providing vocationally-biased courses, mainly for their abler pupils, a wide range of occupational interests is represented. They include engineering, building and other "technical" courses for boys aiming subsequently at skilled apprenticeships in industry; catering, nursing, dressmaking and needlecraft, retail distribution and commerce courses, especially for girls. In areas where circumstances naturally favour them, there may be found courses based on rural and agricultural occupations, or, in a seaside town, courses in seamanship and navigation.

110. Some of these courses could readily be extended to boys and girls from the "average" group at the top of the ability range of our pupils; or could be modified without destroying their distinctive vocational flavour. Engineering courses, for example, at their more demanding level, are designed for able boys likely to become skilled technicians. But they can be found at more modest levels, for boys hoping to become craftsmen: and the content of such a course involving much workshop practice, technical drawing, related work in mathematics, science and English, is capable of considerable variation to suit different capacities.

111. Many of our boys are going to work with their hands, whether in skilled or unskilled jobs. Many of them already own a bicycle and soon after they leave school may hope to own a motor bike; car engines, transistor radios, tape recorders, are all within their range of everyday interests. In not so many years' time, as young married men, they will very likely be busy with domestic power tools and do-it-yourself kits, with home decorating and the building of garden sheds and garages. It would seem wholly sensible to plan courses for some of these boys centring round the use, perhaps the making, of tools; the handling and working of various types of materials; the operating and maintenance of machines. Such work could be realistic in relating its materials and examples to the dominant industries of the area; although a school would need to watch that it did not overproduce hopeful candidates for non-existent vacancies. In a single industry area, the school might think it wise deliberately to introduce the boys to a wider range of interests that they might be better prepared to seek training and employment outside the area when they are a little older. Close consultation with the youth employment service is obviously indicated in all this.

112. Not all boys will have their sights set on the same type of job. There may well be future shop assistants and clerks, as well as garage mechanics and housepainters. But within broad groups of interests, sufficient common ground can be found to provide the basis of several useful types of course.

And even though relevance to the jobs which the pupils will ultimately take up may be quite uncertain, it will often be possible to provide immediate and satisfyingly realistic applications, in projects undertaken for the school—building a greenhouse, or decorating a room or printing the school magazine.

113. On the girls' side—and the two sides are not wholly distinct—similar considerations apply. The main groups of occupations most widely taken up by girls—jobs in offices, in shops, in catering, work in the clothing industry and other manufacturing trades—can all provide the material for courses at more than one level of ability. For all girls, too, there is a group of interests relating to what many, perhaps most of them, would regard as their most important vocational concern, marriage. It is true that at the age of fourteen and fifteen, this may appear chiefly as preoccupation with personal appearance and boy friends, but many girls are ready to respond to work relating to the wider aspects of homemaking and family life and the care and upbringing of children.

114. Commercial courses present both a valuable field of interest for girls, and a problem. "Office" jobs, for understandable reasons, are highly attractive to girls; but they, and often their parents, tend to equate office work with shorthand and typing. The schools would do well to make it clear that the majority of young and moderately able school leavers who enter offices will find themselves on general clerical duties; and that changing commercial practice is reducing the market for shorthand anyway. Moreover, it is extremely difficult to extract from shorthand, unlike many of the other craft skills which may be practised in vocational courses, any general educational content or applications beyond itself. It might, on the other hand, be quite possible to justify the introduction of typewriting alone for many pupils, not as a vocational preparation but as a useful personal skill which could be practised in relation to a good deal of other work, once a modest competence was attained.

115. Some of the hardest questions arise in attempts to provide a distinctive content of work for our weakest pupils; for these boys and girls, very much below average in attainments, the object of any course must be their general personal development above all else. At the end of this chapter we include two examples of attempts to do this; we offer them not as models for imitation, but as possible pointers to some ways of attack.

116. We have concentrated so far on courses evolved around occupational interest. In suggesting that this interest should be used as an approach to secondary education we have assumed that the broad occupational pattern within our society will remain substantially unchanged, at least for the immediate future. We recognize, however, that rapid technological and social development could bring about changes in that pattern which might require further reassessment of the approaches to secondary education. But there is more to life than earning a living, and more to becoming an adult than taking a job. For some pupils, rewarding courses may be built around interests which are not necessarily tied to any occupational theme—hobby interests in photography or gardening or dressmaking or model building or sailing, for example, or in all the wider aspects of home making and marriage. We should regard it as important in any case, whatever the nature of the central studies round which much of the work of the last two years at school might revolve, that there should continue to be room for other activities: high among these we

should place imaginative experience through literature, art, music, drama or dancing, which must surely claim a place in their own right. Although, possibly, every part of the school curriculum could be made to relate to some central theme, there is no reason why it should do so and some good reasons why it should not.

117. Pupils will have personal problems of conduct and belief and need congenial circumstances in which to discuss them. As young adults, they will have to begin to learn how to manage more complex human relations, with their fellows, of the same and of the opposite sex, with older people, in their private lives and in their future jobs. They will need guidance on social manners, in every sense. They will need to acquire some awareness of a wider world beyond the limits of themselves and their jobs. They will need to be helped to understand, at whatever level of comprehension is possible to them, some of the issues of our time. Their full vocation is to grow up as people who can take their place in the world with some degree of proper pride in what they are and in what they hope to attain.

118. To attempt to provide an education which is anything like adequate to all these needs, the schools will need to call into play every possible resource. Throughout this chapter we have suggested that the idea which might give an impetus to learning and lead to more effective methods of teaching is that of preparation for adult life. We believe this to have significance for all the older pupils at the secondary stage of education, but to be especially important for those boys and girls who are at present falling short of their full potential. Very many of "our" pupils we believe to be in that category.

119. *Two examples of courses for pupils of very limited abilities.* The accounts are by the heads of the schools. (We would draw attention to the fact that both of these examples involve a complete re-thinking of the timetable and curriculum; that they make their own demands on buildings; and that they require particularly resourceful teachers.)

School A (A large mixed school, in a New Town in S.E. England)

"In September 1960 we had enough of these volunteers to make a separate (Fifth Year) form of thirteen pupils. The motives for staying on were varied. Some were immature physically and emotionally and parents were anxious that they should not be thrust into an adult society for which they were not yet ripe. Others cherished the hope of late development that would surprise us all. A few, including one under the care of the Authority, were very backward and needed the time to become literate. . . ."

The timetable was as elastic as possible with all the basic subjects under the control of the form-master (the Senior Master). There was no division into traditional boys' and girls' subjects. They followed a common course in metalwork and woodwork with a syllabus covering household repairs and "do-it-yourself" projects. Unfortunately shortage of suitable accommodation did not allow a combined cookery programme, although there was some work done together in the housecraft flat. Boys and girls followed courses in home-nursing, typewriting and commercial practice. Religious education and social studies were conducted on a discussion group basis with written work on individual projects. Physical education was also a mixed activity. This took the form of practice and training for such games as badminton and table tennis, as well as a course in ballroom dancing. The small form became a very happy unit, producing its quota of prefects and doing more than its share in the social organization of the school. Oddly enough, although not considered examination material, there were some who took single elementary subjects in their stride."

School B (A girls' school in a Midlands industrial area, with many social problems.)

"Aims:

(i) To give the girls opportunities to be socially acceptable, and to behave socially in a way which, in any community, usually falls to the most able;

(ii) To link their work with their future hope—marriage. The home, the family, the baby, the growing children, are subjects of study. Mothercraft is an essential subject if it is linked practically with real babies, nursery visits (one morning a week throughout the year) and other visits. Personal and household budgeting takes the place of Arithmetic. This is linked practically with as much actual spending, buying and budgeting within the school as can be done. Needlework, for example, becomes much more realistic when this is done on a project basis.

(iii) To link their school work with life outside, and to bring out-of-school experience into their school work.

An experiment has been tried with the really less able—the lowest 34 per cent, I.Q. generally 70–90.

They have a course consisting of 36 periods a week, allocated thus:

3 periods—Domestic Science, specially designed syllabus.
3   ,,   Visits by outside speakers from many professions and trades —e.g. theatres, branches of public health, museum and art galleries, industry, public amenities, shops, social work, police, probation work etc., followed by a visit to the appropriate centre.
2   ,,   English literature in the school library.
4   ,,   Physical Education.
2   ,,   Religious Knowledge.
2   ,,   Art or Embroidery.
2   ,,   Budgeting.
2   ,,   Mothercraft.
2, 3 or 4—Geography or history project, which is based on field work in the district.
1   ,,   The art of growing up.
2   ,,   Music.
9   ,,   Project. The class is divided into four groups of six or seven girls with a group leader. Projects vary and have to be suited to availability of staff.

Examples are:

A. *Needlework*   Group A goes out, buys patterns and material, and aims to make a garment in one week.

B. *Housekeeping*   Group B works in the flat.

C. *Research*   Group C works in the local library and museum.

D. *Know your city* Group D does window shopping; follows a local route; finds local information; collects data; visits the city; sends telegrams; makes telephone calls.

A project lasts for three weeks (not necessarily successive) and the groups change round.

Formal work of the old pattern has disappeared. There are no tests, marks, or examinations. Each girl works at her own ability level. There is close correlation between the subjects taught. There need be no lack of depth, and the scheme could be worked out at any level of ability."

RECOMMENDATIONS

(*a*) The curriculum in the fourth and fifth years at school should be such that pupils are able to see a relevance to adult life over at least a substantial part of their work. (para. 98)

(*b*) All pupils should be able in the fourth and fifth years to exercise some choice in their programmes of work. (para. 99)

(*c*) A greater variety of courses should be provided in the fourth and fifth years, many of them broadly related to occupational interests. (paras. 100–102)

(*d*) This will frequently require more advanced technical equipment and a general reappraisal of facilities for all practical subjects. (para. 103)

(*e*) Attention to imaginative experience through the arts and to the promotion of personal and social development are no less essential. (paras. 116, 117)

CHAPTER 6

The School Day, Homework, Extra-Curricular Activities

"Our students (young girls attending day-release classes in a very large firm) fall into two broad categories, (a) the smaller number who are busy people, with lives full of interest and activity: (b) the much larger group who are just rather bored with life in general. The second group are well aware of this boredom, and obviously uneasy and unhappy about it, but fiercely resent having attention drawn to it. They find every excuse for not having hobbies or worthwhile pastimes, and assure you that they are far too busy for anything other than the routine pattern of life. When confronted with the suggestions that they might in the future be faced with a thirty hour working week, and, perhaps, six weeks holiday, they looked slightly stunned, then almost scared, and finally nonplussed".   Personnel Officer.

120. A number of considerations lead us to advocate a rather longer school day for boys and girls in their last two years at school. At the age of fourteen and fifteen, the majority of boys and girls spend no more time in school than they did when they were seven. A disturbing number appear to leave school under-equipped in skills, knowledge and personal resources. A characteristic complaint of this group is that they are "bored"—with school, with life outside school, and later with their jobs. The peak in the figures for juvenile delinquency persistently occurs in the last year before boys and girls leave school. All our evidence suggests that many pupils are capable of more sustained effort, and show themselves able to respond to opportunities of a larger range of activities. The schools on the other hand find themselves short of time in which to undertake all the things they know to be profitable. Finally, young people still have to face a much longer working day when they enter employment, and some bridging of this gap seems desirable.

121. How should any extra time be used? First, to incorporate into the total educational programme many of those activities which are now called "extra-curricular". The latter word occurs in our terms of reference, and we use it here for want of a better; but our whole thesis in this chapter is that the experiences offered by these activities should form an integral part of any liberal educational programme, and that a curriculum conceived only in terms of formal lessons is unduly restricted. We think heads of schools should have the time and resources at their disposal to be able to plan the programme as a whole, with activities inside and outside the classroom as complementary parts.

122. Secondly, some of the time might be used for what is really a special form of out-of-classroom activity, "homework". The term may be a misnomer for what we have in mind, but again we use it for want of a better. Perhaps some more appropriate name may be found if the concept of what is involved begins to change.

123. The abler pupils in secondary schools are regularly required to do a substantial amount of homework, which considerably lengthens their effective working day. But large numbers of pupils, and the majority of "our" pupils, commonly do none. We are strongly of the opinion that all boys and girls would profit from undertaking some work for themselves outside what is done in lessons; we also think this work could, and for many of our pupils,

41

especially, should, take more varied forms than what is conventionally recognized now as homework. The task to be undertaken might, for instance, be making a model, or finishing some project in the art or craft room begun in school time. It might be a chance to try some new skill or craft or, for those pupils who wished to learn typing, an opportunity for intensive practice which it may be difficult to provide inside the normal school timetable. It might consist in the group viewing and discussion of a film or television programme. It might be the preparation of material before giving a talk in class, or gathering information for some group project in school: obtaining the information might involve writing letters or direct observation and note making, or visiting a museum, an art gallery, the public library or the town hall. It could be working on the school magazine, or balancing the Young Farmers' Club accounts, or mapping the route of a coming school expedition. The possibilities are almost infinitely varied, and the tasks could be purposeful and demanding but adaptable to circumstances or to the pupil's capacities. They could be made the occasion for reading, calculating, recording and discussion, without being confined to the standard written exercises which traditionally make up a great deal of homework. Some of the work of the kind we have suggested could clearly best be done, and in some cases only be done, with the facilities and equipment available on school premises.

124. We realize that there is value in the pupils doing some work at home, wherever it is practicable: this is one important way in which parents can be kept in touch with what is being done in school, and it brings them into direct partnership with the schools in the business of education. Indeed, some parents, heads assure us, are demanding more homework for their children. But many other heads, especially of schools in difficult urban areas, leave us in no doubt at all that under the conditions in which some families are obliged to live, it is asking the impossible of parents and of children to expect homework to be done satisfactorily. Even where housing conditions are good, large families and small living rooms, or the open-plan design of many modern houses and flats, may make it extremely difficult for boys and girls to have reasonable privacy and quiet in which to concentrate on their work. And some of our pupils do not find concentration easy, even under helpful conditions. Some schools and local authorities have begun to try to meet this difficulty—which exists acutely already for some of the able pupils in grammar schools and elsewhere—by providing quiet rooms for homework, sometimes on school premises, sometimes in public libraries, and teachers have often been generous in volunteering to supervise "homework" sessions. If all pupils were to do homework, there would certainly be a need to extend such arrangements. We would see them as part of a larger scheme of educational provision.

125. Most schools would agree with us in attaching importance to experiences offered outside the formal lesson programme. Already a tremendous range and variety of activities can be found. They include clubs and societies dealing with all kinds of interests: photography, stamp collecting, chess, model-making, boat building, gardening, angling, athletics and sport and games of all kinds; music, including orchestras and choirs, drama and film making—the latter taking very ambitious forms in some schools. There are enthusiastic groups studying local history or a foreign language preparatory to a trip abroad. There are plays and concerts, dances and conferences with neighbouring schools, and a host of enterprises which take place mostly in holiday

times or away from the school premises—visits, expeditions, camps, holiday journeys and residential courses, including, among most recent developments, educational cruises. The list reflects largely the variety of interests and enthusiasms of the teachers who voluntarily direct such activities; it is also an indication of the support and encouragement given by the local education authority and by the pupils' parents.

126. School activities are not merely devices for keeping adolescents off the street, although in some streets it may be very desirable that they should. There are many positive reasons why "extra-curricular" provision is important. For the individual boy and girl, it can mean the discovery of new interests. Some they may carry with them into adult life; others will vanish as quickly as many adolescent enthusiasms naturally do, but there may have been profit as well as pleasure in the experience. It is often a chance for the odd-man-out to come into his own, among the staff as well as the pupils, revealing an unsuspected talent; and for some of our pupils, especially, there may be a gain in confidence from being a member of a much smaller social and working group than is normally possible in class.

127. For the school as a whole, there is a strengthening effect, in bringing together pupils of different ages and abilities who may never work together in lessons; and in teachers getting to know their pupils in a different, more intimate companionship. The gulf which almost inevitably exists in class between teacher and taught, when the pupil is conscious of his lack of knowledge and skill in, say, mathematics, may be bridged when two enthusiasts indulge their hobby in the Brass Band. We quote from an account of a school visit made by some members of the Council.

"The most remarkable feature of the school was its vigorous musical life. The headmaster throws himself wholeheartedly into this . . . because he has a great belief in music as a communal activity which brings together not only members of his staff and boys, but also the staff and girls of the sister school on the same site. Together they run a mixed school band and a mixed choir . . . . I watched the head give a trombone lesson to a little group of four boys from the lowest second year form. He obtained from them a remarkable degree of concentration and hard work inspired by enthusiasm. Some of the academically least able boys find a place in both the choir and the band. The present second cornet, who is well down in the bottom fourth-year form, is on the way towards being a professional bandsman".

128. There may even be material gain for the school. More than one school has had a swimming bath built largely by the joint efforts of pupils and staff in their own time, often with considerable help and financial backing from a parent-teacher association. The head of a school in our sample describes, as "an indication of a friendly discipline in a self-help project", the building of an £800 sports pavilion, equipped with showers, by the senior boys and staff, in the evenings and weekends.

129. We share with many teachers a strong belief that "extra-curricular" activities are not merely extras, in the sense of being pleasant but marginal to the main business of learning, although in terms of healthy pleasure and fun alone they would be important. Perhaps in the general sphere of social education, nothing could be more valuable to boys and girls growing up,

than to learn how really to listen to each other, to argue robustly but with reason and good humour, and to tolerate differences of outlook without personal ill-feeling. Opportunities for experiences of this sort occur particularly easily through informal discussion in school clubs and societies. Some activities can provide direct extensions and illumination of what goes on in the classroom; and for our pupils, particularly, by generating a new impulse to learning, they may actually result in an improvement in basic attainments. The pupils who plan and write their own script, and shoot, process and edit their own film in a school club, are bringing into play applied skills in English and science and mathematics, as well as exercising their perceptions and judgement. Just as the pupils who go for the first time to a theatre or to a museum or into the countryside, in the company of someone who can help them to formulate their impressions, may become more articulate, as well as more knowledgeable.

130. Some of our evidence contained salutary reminders that visits cannot be guaranteed to produce the desired effects. "They were fond of taking us on absolutely boring visits to the British Museum", is what one girl remembered of the teachers' well-intentioned efforts. The headmaster of a new secondary school serving a poor district tells the following story of an incident which occurred a few days after the pupils had made their first visit to a London theatre.

"There was a loud bang on my study door and in walked unannounced a lady, clutching a paper bag. 'I have brought these' she said, and shot on to my desk a number of opera glasses—'I found my Charlie with one of these and when I asked where he got them he said he bought them at the theatre by putting sixpence in a slot in front of his seat. I didn't believe him and asked who else had got them so I've been round the houses and collected them because we don't want our nice school to have a bad name, do we?'".

Perhaps in the outcome something was learned after all.

131. The general case for a vigorous "extra-curricular" programme is strong. But whereas one head can write "After school at night the premises are full of boys indulging in all sorts of purely voluntary activities . . .", another describes her "grief and disappointment" at the meagreness of what it is possible for her school to offer. Evidence from our sample shows great disparity between school and school. The reasons for lack of provision vary. Where the pupils travel long distances from scattered areas, transport can present formidable problems. The nature of the school accommodation is another obviously limiting factor, and a large, new school with hall, gymnasium and good facilities for art, crafts, music and sports can be expected to offer much more than an old school in poor and cramped quarters. But the differences are not simply those of town schools and country schools, new schools and old schools, or of large schools and small schools.

132. Some of the most often quoted difficulties centre on staffing:

"We have few clubs and societies here, because my staff have no roots, or travel long distances; or have home responsibilities—husbands, children, aged parents."

"Apart from games and athletics, there are no continuing school clubs or societies . . . half the staff are married women with homes to care for, some with small children to collect from nurseries or schools."

"The school has few societies, notably in sport and music. The contribution in other directions is less than I should like—this is due to the fact that many of the men do extra teaching of some form or another in the evening, and that many of the married women have commitments at home."

"There appears to be a greater pressure of other interests which prevents teachers giving wholehearted attention to preparation, marking and out-of-school activities. These are earlier marriages with consequent domestic responsibilities: remunerative occupations out-of-school . . ."

"A good deal of wasted effort is caught up in the attempt to interest the less able via societies and clubs; they seem no sooner launched than a change of staff renders the spade work useless."

"Interest in school clubs is spasmodic. Up to this year we had a very flourishing angling club. Now, the master-in-charge contemplates marriage and the club is defunct. Similarly the P.E. club."

133. These comments, typical of many, come from the heads of schools in different types of area and in different parts of the country. Although they could be more than matched by the reports of full and successful out-of-school programmes, we quote them at some length to indicate the nature of the difficulties which occur.

134. To this inequality of the school situation must be added the inequalities of the outer environment in which boys and girls spend their time away from school. That the older industrial areas, with poor housing and few outdoor spaces, are at a disadvantage may be expected. What is not always realized is that some of the large new estates, although the housing amenities are good, may have few recreational facilities for young people or adults. In such neighbourhoods, as for rather different reasons in "slum" areas, the school may have an important socially educative rôle in the community.

135. From all this we conclude that extra-curricular activities ought to be recognized as an integral part of the total educational programme, and secured where necessary by administrative provision. Several things follow: first, the school programme needs to be envisaged as a whole, with "curricular" and "extra-curricular" activities planned as complementary parts. Secondly, the regular school day should be conceived as extending beyond the nine-till-four limits. Thirdly, adequate account of this must be taken in the design and equipment of buildings. Fourthly, and most crucial, the implications must be recognized in assessing the total staffing needs of schools.

136. We have come somewhat reluctantly to the conclusion that if the school day is extended, some element of compulsion will have to be introduced into what are now voluntary activities. Otherwise, it will be impossible to plan the programme as a coherent whole, or to estimate the total needs in terms of staffing and facilities, and hence to justify additional expenditure. If school premises are regularly to be available over longer periods, with adequate supervisory staff in attendance, it becomes essential to know whether twenty customers or a hundred and twenty are normally to be expected. Moreover, many school buildings are used by evening institute and other adult and youth groups, and the total demand on the premises must be taken into account by the responsible authorities in their planning. It would undoubtedly be a pity if school clubs had to lose their essentially voluntary nature, but this would be partly offset by the fact that many schools would be able to offer a

much wider range of regular activities than they now find possible; and a large element of personal choice could be preserved for pupils within the general requirement to take part in this side of the school's life. There is, too, to be considered the fact that some of those pupils who live in the most adverse environments, and who most need to be guided into healthy recreational pursuits, will not take part if these are on an entirely optional basis. In their case, the pressures of the area and of their homes may be all against the extension of educational activities, and just as, without the formal raising of the school leaving age, these are the boys and girls who will continue to leave at fifteen, irrespective of their abilities, so they are the ones who will have least to do with additional school activities, unless some definite requirement is made of them. At the same time, if the school day is to be lengthened at all, the schools must face an even more urgent responsibility to see that what goes on both in lessons and after them is genuinely rewarding: there is no point in merely extending the period of boredom.

137. A start might be made by requiring all pupils in their final two years of school to stay on for one or two "extra" sessions a week, for any activity of their choice, and the choice could be very wide. They could be encouraged to stay on at other times to do their homework, to work for themselves, or to take part in additional clubs or societies or in occasional general sessions which brought several groups together socially. If the habit grew, and a pattern were established of a generally longer school day, then there would be opportunity for greater flexibility in the planning of the "day" and the school timetable as a whole. Many sporting and athletic activities, for example, might be transferred to the early afternoon, especially in winter time, and some lessons take place in the later session. This would indeed be a blurring of the edges between the two parts of the educational programme, and would in some ways bring the county school nearer in the shape of its working day to that of the independent boarding schools. There would be ample scope for variety and experiment.

138. We have not felt it wise to specify the precise way in which the working day should be extended, because there is an obvious need to experiment with different patterns according to the local situation and the circumstances of the individual schools. Depending on the distance the majority of pupils live from their school, they might stay straight on at the end of the afternoon, with perhaps a short break for tea which they could very well organize largely by themselves; or they might go home for early tea, changing out of school uniform if they wished, as a mark of greater informality, and return later, to clubs and societies which in this case might extend into the early evening. Where the latter pattern was preferred, it would often be possible for boys and girls who had only just left school to continue with the sports or music or drama or handicraft they had enjoyed, at least for a year or so until they had had time to form new friendships and find new outlets for their interests in more adult groups. Putting older pupils, and young ex-pupils, into touch with local adult organizations clearly ought to be one of the school's objectives and where school premises are also used for evening institute, youth club, or similar activities, some overlapping would not necessarily be a bad thing. The experience of the Cambridgeshire Village Colleges has shown that suitable provision for schools, youth groups and adults on the same premises is practicable.

139. Within the agreed general policy of the local education authority, a large measure of responsibility and discretion should be left to the head for evolving a programme best suited to the pupils and the local circumstances. In some cases, a group of neighbouring schools might work out a joint programme, pooling their resources. This could have especial value for adjacent, single-sex schools, bringing boys and girls together for some activities.

140. Written evidence we have received, as well as discussions with witnesses, leads us to believe that in some areas local education authorities and schools would be willing to experiment with the idea of a three-session day; that is, there might be two sessions, morning and early afternoon, corresponding to the existing formal school day; and a third session in which, on any one day, a substantial number of pupils would be on the premises engaged either in some piece of individual work or hobby, or taking part in various informal group activities. In addition, there would be many possible extensions of this to activities under the aegis of the school taking place elsewhere than on the school premises. We think it highly desirable that official encouragement— including financial support—should be given to some experiment. From a few pilot schemes, preferably in areas of different types, the possibilities and costs could be tested, and some policies formulated for more general application.

141. A decisive factor in any scheme would be staffing. Under the present system, many schools have been extraordinarily lucky in the generous voluntary service of the teachers in out-of-school hours. But, as our examples have shown, by no means all schools are as fortunately placed, and extra-curricular activities sometimes founder altogether for lack of people to lead them. We acknowledge the real difficulties which the schools face, but we do not regard the difficulties as insuperable. In our opinion, and we believe in the opinion of the large majority of teachers, these activities represent a proper part of the teachers' professional responsibilities in the education of their pupils, and we do not accept, for instance, that married women cannot be expected to contribute. Indeed, some schools assure us that married women members of their staff give invaluable service in this field. Married women with small children represent, we recognize, a special category of teachers for whom exceptions ought reasonably to be made.

142. At the same time, we realise that to extend extra-curricular provision for all pupils on a large scale, particularly if the school day developed on a three-session pattern, would in some schools be to risk placing an intolerable burden on those teachers who are already doing most, unless staffing resources were supplemented in some way.

143. It is clear that the total number of staff needed for one kind of educational activity or another would be greater. That, in a time of continuing and acute teacher-shortages, must give us pause. But there might be room in the educational scene to draw far more on the special knowledge or skills of persons outside the school. Just as we should see some advantages, in bringing into the formal school programme people with particular talents and experience—nurses, social workers, people from commerce and from industry—to contribute from time to time to courses for older pupils, so we think that in the extra-curricular programme there might be even more room

for enlisting individuals with special interests. If a group of boys and girls wants to take up photography or badminton or learn a musical instrument, persons other than qualified teachers may be well capable of instructing and inspiring the group. We might be able to supplement our valuable short-supply teachers with other activity-leaders, and at the same time effect a helpful interchange between the schools and the general community.

144. We note also with interest that in different parts of the country experiments are taking place in joint appointments of teacher/youth leaders or teacher/wardens, who are attached to the school staffs and who spend part of their time teaching in school, part of their time working with young people in the evenings. These are developments which might foreshadow a more flexible teacher's day and a different range of responsibility for some members of the staff. Quite apart from any possible reorganization of the school day, we think it highly desirable that over the next few years thorough-going experiments in this type of joint appointment should be tried.

145. We recognize that the proposals contained in this chapter carry many implications for the total staffing resources of the schools, for conditions of service and for salary structure. Increased financial expenditure would certainly be required. The complex problems involved call for expert investigation in consultation with the professional bodies: we consider that such an investigation should be urgently undertaken.

146. There are many implications also for buildings and equipment. The designs of schools would have to allow for more continuous and intensive use of the premises in many instances. Social and recreational areas would assume a new importance, and have to be provided on a more generous scale than has been usual in the past. School provision would need to be planned in even closer conjunction than it now is with provision for other youth and adult needs. Closer administrative and financial co-operation would be required between the various authorities concerned with all the aspects of education and the social services.

147. Any local scheme would need to take careful account of existing youth service provision in the area. We do not regard any of the suggestions we have made as essentially setting up rivalries between school activities and those of other organizations for young people. In our own survey, rather more than half of all the boys and girls belonged to no club or society of any kind, whether school-based or organized by an outside body. Without advocating mere gregariousness as itself a virtue, it is safe to say that the total provision for organized activities for young people of this age group could with advantage be increased. Secondly, although a measure of overlapping between what a good school can provide and what a good youth club can provide is no disadvantage, in the main, the contributions of the two will be complementary rather than identical. Many young people, at different stages of growth, feel the need for support by belonging to groups of different kinds at different times. In addition to all the range of out-of-school activities which a good school can offer, there is probably always a need for contacts of a different kind for some pupils—particularly those who have not felt themselves successful in school.

148. Where schools and separate youth organizations share premises, there is everything to be said for the maximum informal consultation between the

two, and for mutual assistance and consideration. Just as, if central recreational facilities under the youth service were being planned, it would be desirable to take account of the interest and needs of schools in the immediate area. Some of the staffing experiments we have advocated would tend to make for generally easier co-operation between the two services concerned with young people.

149. We ought not to close this chapter without reference to an extra-curricular development which a great deal of our evidence confirms is specially significant for our pupils. That is, the experience of living away from home for a short period, in a fairly small and intimate group, and in a novel environment. This is variously achieved through school journeys and expeditions, camps, or residential courses of different types, lasting, generally, anything from a weekend to a month. In an earlier chapter we noted with admiration the enterprise of many schools in this respect. It is not our purpose to describe here in detail all that takes place; but to draw attention to the particular values that such experiences may have for the pupils for whom we are especially concerned. We not not doubt their value for all pupils.

150. The residential courses (and we use this term here to refer to all residentially based activities) take many forms. Some of them lay great stress on strenuous, outdoor, physical activity: some schools successfully combine courses of this kind with work in school for the Duke of Edinburgh's award scheme; and one school known to us in Scotland integrates an "Adventure Course" with its normal curriculum. Other courses are based on field studies of local plant and animal life, geography, geology, or history. Others again may aim at introducing young people to new recreational interests—in art or music or drama, as well as in sports. And the shorter courses often take the form of conferences, dealing with a range of subjects and interests most likely to be of value to young people just before they leave school, including preparation for the transition to work. Variety is to be welcomed. Not all pupils' needs or interests are the same, and there would be nothing at all to be gained from uniformity.

151. Most, however, of these undertakings have important features in common. By introducing boys and girls to fresh surroundings, and helping them to acquire new knowledge or try their hand at new skills, they provide a general educational stimulus. Many pupils, including some who were far from successful in normal school work, seem to come back with a new zest for everything they do: one headmaster described girls returning from a three-weeks' residential course as "having a sort of glow about them". And we have been interested to see, in a group of case-studies made available to us by one local education authority, that both the parents and the first employers of boys who took part in an exacting course in their last year at school subsequently remarked at their confidence and responsible attitudes.

152. There is little doubt that many pupils benefit from these experiences in their personal and social development. This is partly the direct result of living continuously in a small community: the less able and the more diffident pupils under these circumstances are encouraged and even obliged to play a more significant part than may normally be possible in the much larger community of the whole school. And in residential, even more than in other out-of-school activities, pupils and teachers enjoy a closer companionship.

For the pupils who come from difficult home backgrounds and live in socially deprived neighbourhoods, these can be opportunities of special help. Girls, in particular, are often desperately anxious for guidance in matters of speech and behaviour, in dealing with everyday social situations and personal relations. For some, the mere fact of abstracting them from their normal surroundings is of great significance.

153. We have tried to gather information, with the help of many local education authorities, as to the scale on which residential provision of any kind exists, and is used, throughout the country. Although we have received many helpfully detailed replies, it has proved impossible to arrive at any picture of the national situation. Local policies vary greatly, as between providing residential centres owned and maintained by the authority or leaving the schools to make their own arrangements through outside organizations. Costs to the providing authorities and to the parents also vary. The courses may be staffed by teachers from the schools, by permanent wardens at the centres, or by a mixture of both; some authorities, but not others, provide additional supply teachers for the schools, to replace members of the permanent staff who are away with a group of pupils on a course.

154. We could arrive at no approximate estimate of the total numbers of secondary pupils in any one year who participate in residential courses of any kind, or of the percentage of their age group they might represent in any given area. Least of all could we discover what proportion of "our" pupils, as opposed to the academically more able boys and girls, actually took advantage of the opportunities available. But the impressions of a good many heads of schools suggested that, although the less able pupils were encouraged to participate, they generally did so in much smaller numbers. We noted, however, with equal regret, that some heads, while being keen to send their least able boys and girls, were reluctant to allow other pupils to miss even two or three weeks of normal school, because they were potential examination candidates—even though in some cases, the examination in question was more than a year away.

155. It was not possible to estimate how far provision matches demand— partly because demand itself is stimulated by the opportunities available. It was notable that some of the authorities who already appear to have the largest and most wide ranging schemes are also those who are planning to extend their provision to meet an ever-rising demand. One such authority has announced that "convinced of the value of short-stay residential courses, the Committee have asked for arrangements to be made so that, in the course of his secondary school life, every child in the county has the opportunity of at least one short-stay residential course." Another envisages ultimately establishing a number of "boarding annexes" in different parts of the country, each assigned to a group of day schools; they would be used then not so much as centres for special courses, as regular extensions to school life.

156. We welcome these developments. We also consider it most desirable that as soon as possible a joint survey be undertaken by the Ministry and the local education authorities to establish accurately the scale on which provision is already available; how far it is meeting existing demand; and what costs would be involved in extending the provision to a much larger number of pupils, whilst preserving the variety of opportunities which is clearly so

valuable in itself. We are in no doubt at all that many more boys and girls, not least among our pupils, could and would, respond to additional educational experiences of this kind.

RECOMMENDATIONS

(a) The hours spent in educational activities should be extended for pupils aged fourteen to sixteen. (para. 120)

(b) Some form of "homework"—liberally interpreted—should be required of all pupils. (paras. 122 and 123)

(c) "Extra-curricular" activities should be recognized as an integral part of the educational programme and secured where necessary by administrative provision. (para. 135)

(d) Some experiments by local education authorities and schools in different types of extension of the school day, including a "third" session in the late afternoon and early evening, should be encouraged by the Ministry. (para. 140)

(e) The total demands on the staffing strength of the schools, and the possible implications for conditions of service, should be reassessed in light of these developments. (paras. 142, 143, 145)

(f) There should be more experiments in joint appointments of the teacher/ youth leader type. (para. 144)

(g) The design and equipment of buildings should allow for extended use, including that by other educational and social services. The closest co-operation is needed between all the authorities and agencies involved. (paras. 146, 149)

(h) A joint survey should be undertaken by the Ministry and the local education authorities to establish accurately the scale on which provision for residential courses of all types is available; how far it is meeting demand; and what costs would be involved in extending the provision to a much larger number of pupils. (para. 156).

CHAPTER 7

Spiritual and Moral Development

"It shall be the duty of the local education authority for every area to contribute towards the spiritual, moral, mental and physical development of the community."

Education Act, 1944

157. The nearer we got to the boys and girls on whose education we have to advise, the more it was brought home to us that Parliament gave the schools a difficult but not an impossible task when it told them to foster their spiritual and moral development. We learned that those who tried with sincerity and ability to do this found that they were not only fulfilling a statutory obligation, or discharging a social responsibility; they were meeting a felt personal need of their pupils. Most boys and girls want to be what they call 'being good' and they want to know what this really implies in the personal situations which confront them. This is difficult enough, but it is not sufficient. They want also to know what kind of animal a man is, and whether ultimately each one of them matters—and, if so, why and to whom. And they want to be told the truth. "It is no use", we were told in discussion, "putting up a smoke screen and retiring in flight behind it". The teacher who is not prepared to expose himself in honestly grappling with these ultimate problems had better leave them alone. His lessons must carry conviction. This is not the same as trying to convert his pupils. Above all, they don't want to be "got at".

158. The best approach to this subject is perhaps to look at the problem as it confronts a typical county secondary school and consider how it can best be tackled. In Church of England or Roman Catholic voluntary schools the situation will be markedly easier in some respects, but not in all. In county schools the first factor to be reckoned with is that the staff will probably be divided in their philosophical and religious allegiance. Some will be committed Christians. True, they will be of various denominations; but this is much less likely to affect their working together in the schools' part of religious and moral upbringing than would have been the case a generation ago. Other teachers may well be definite agnostics or "scientific humanists". Between these two committed groups there will almost certainly be a middle range of teachers who may not be very sure of what the Church believes, who may not necessarily believe all that they remember of what they themselves were taught, but who gratefully acknowledge their Christian heritage and are anxious that it should not die with them. In all this the secondary school staff room is not very different from any group of Englishmen in the middle of the twentieth century.

159. The second factor to reckon with is the questioning spirit of adolescence. This does not mean that there are no questions in primary schools and in the lower forms of secondary schools. They abound, but they are of a different nature. They are asked in order to acquire information, not to display or to resolve intellectual doubt. Boys and girls who used to ask enquiringly "What do we do?" or "What's that?" now commonly react with "Why should I?"

or "How do you know?" to much of what they have loved and practised in the past. They become increasingly aware of the differences of opinion between adults, and of the gulf between practice and profession. The border-line between cynical disengagement and constructive questioning is narrow. Sooner or later most boys and girls will pass from the acceptance of childhood through one or other of these attidudes on their way to their adult position. This happens rather earlier perhaps in modern than in grammar schools partly because their pupils come at a younger age into immediate contact with the unsheltered world outside school and home. It is a major task to steer this new doubting spirit into positive and creative channels, avoiding the trucu-lence of "couldn't care less".

160. The third factor is the confrontation between the two communities—the adults in the staff room, the adolescents in the class rooms. For better or for worse it is from these adults that these adolescents learn. The staff of the school is the largest group of adults they meet; it comprises those most obviously set in front of them as guides into the world of men. Teachers can only escape from their influence over the moral and spiritual development of their pupils by closing their schools. As long as they teach at all, whether they give formal lessons or not, they teach by the way they behave, by what they are. That is why one of the absolutely essential qualities of a teacher is integrity.

161. The fourth factor is the contrast that may exist between the standards accepted and practised at school and those which boys and girls will meet later on at work and indeed meet already as they purposely lose themselves among their older contemporaries in their life out of school. The young, though they hate to be told so, are born conformists. They conform easily to the pattern of school life, and if it is a good school this is a pretty sound pattern; they conform just as easily to the pattern of their leisure time activities—which may be good or bad, but will certainly be different. In this difference of standard between the multiple worlds of which we are all citizens lies a limiting factor to what a school can do. Its influence may well be only temporary, having no carry-over, unless it succeeds in making clear to its members that the standards it sets, and often in large measure achieves, are just as relevant to the whole of life as to the part which is lived within its walls. There is no automatic transfer of values; boys and girls need to be convinced that what applies in school ought to apply in all human relations. The Education Act wisely sees the duty of schools as being "to contribute towards the spiritual and moral development of the community", and not to provide it. Theirs is a limited, though a vital rôle and they are neither the community nor the church. Society must not look to the schools to solve its moral problems, but it expects and gets from them an important contribution towards their solution. The fact that school life is longer than it was and extends far beyond childhood in a way that it used not to do makes their con-tribution potentially bigger and more important than before.

162. A school which takes its responsibility seriously will not just leave to chance the working out of its influence over its pupils. It will have a policy, and will try to bring all its resources to bear. Very high on the list must come the corporate life of the school. In its most intimate form this means the way in which its members behave to one another. The assumptions on which staff

and pupils meet—friendliness or hostility, for instance, grudging legalism or generous helpfulness—show themselves in speech and gesture and conduct. A school where the assumptions are positive is likely to be one in which staff and pupils share many out-of-school activities together. Games, dramatics, music, school journeys, all play their part. Many schools, and we believe an increasing number, go further and encourage their members to undertake active personal service for the community. Many of the schools which were included in our survey told us of such activities, usually for the benefit of the old or the sick. All find that boys and girls of less than average intelligence may well be of more than average helpfulness.

163. However diverse the staff may be in their philosophical alignment all will approve of such positive well doing. Inside the classrooms, too, there is much common ground which Christian and agnostic may travel together. Christian ethics after all owe much to Aristotle as well as to Judaism. Orthodoxy finds no difficulty, but rather support in the concept of a natural law. History and geography, literature, civics, science, all play their part in forming the moral outlook of boys and girls, and through all these subjects the whole staff, irrespective of religious affiliations, can make a united contribution to both the spiritual and moral development of the pupils. It can open their eyes, enlarge their understanding, enlist their sympathy so that they will not be blind to the colour bar, deaf to the cries of the hungry or aloof from the loneliness of neighbours. Boys and girls need to approach all situations with moral sensitivity as well as intellectual understanding; this is partly a matter of preserving the innocent perceptions of childhood (this is not to say that all the perceptions of childhood are innocent) and partly of directing the questioning of adolescence towards personal motives and social responsibilities.

164. It is at this point that a secondary school in the mid-twentieth century may run into difficulties which it cannot solve by itself. Society itself is divided. Everybody agrees that all human situations require to be faced with moral sensitivity. Those personal situations which most perplex adolescent boys and girls are, however, situations about which there is no universal contemporary agreement. The challenging feature of their lives is now the sexual instinct which is at its most potent in these years. A hundred years ago nearly all good men would normally have given the same answers to the problems which beset the young immediately in their courtship habits and prospectively in their conception of the marriage relation. Today Christians and many agnostics would still agree in their attitudes, but it would be stupid to deny that there are profound differences in society about pre-marital intercourse and about the permanence of marriage, or that these must be reflected in many staff rooms. Tensions there must be if the questions of boys and girls are heard and answered and not suppressed—tensions, perhaps, within the staff of a school and tensions between school and home. We can only say that we believe it to be wrong to leave the young to fend for themselves without guidance, and wrong to conceal from them (as if we could) the differences on this issue which separate men and women of real moral sensitivity. For our part we are agreed that boys and girls should be offered firm guidance on sexual morality based on chastity before marriage and fidelity within it. We believe, too, that this is predominantly the standpoint of the schools. It is also important that boys and girls should realize that "going off the rails" does not involve for Christians losing the fellowship of the church,

still less of forfeiting the love of God. There are other, and often graver, sins than those against chastity.

165. Simple moral teaching is, then, not the plain, straightforward thing that it may have been in the past, and that it still is in the main in the primary school. The same kind of difficulties arise when schools try to foster the spiritual development of boys and girls. These difficulties also spring from the differences which divide good men. True, there is a general spiritual awareness that all teachers would wish their pupils to develop. Many subjects wisely and imaginatively taught sharpen the perception of more than utilitarian values. This is an important service, and many of us recall with gratitude men and women who in our adolescent years introduced us to poets who gave words to what was in our hearts but which we did not know was there until we heard Homer "speak out loud and clear". The greatest themes, and the very greatest expressions of these themes, are not the preserve of the intellectually gifted; they are universal themes and universally communicable. So far there is agreement: this kind of spiritual development is hindered only by the fallibility of teachers and that coarsening and timid defensiveness in which men take refuge from the total response that greatness demands.

166. But no Christian could for a moment rest content with an education which brought men face to face with a crucifixion but not with Christ. Religious instruction in accordance with any local education authority's agreed syllabus is instruction in the Christian religion.[1] At once the subject becomes difficult and controversial. Not all teachers, not all parents, are Christians; some are avowedly opposed to religion; some feel that religion is only for children and some that it is only for adults—in the sense that boys and girls ought to be free to make up their minds when they grow up (this need provoke no dissent), and that therefore they ought not to be influenced one way or the other before they come to years of discretion (a corollary which Christians would neither accept as logical nor believe to be practicable). Some schools faced with this dilemma take refuge in equating Christianity with simple moral instruction. But, as a teacher remarked when she found the sixth beatitude turned into an injunction against writing on lavatory walls, "religion is not about 'not writing on lavatory walls'". Some schools still reduce religious instruction to simple Bible reading with as little comment as possible—a sure way of losing the attention of most boys and girls. Some turn it into ancient history with as big or as little a claim on the attention of the average adolescent as any other period remote in time. We sympathize with the bishop who told us that he would scream if he saw any more camels on class-room walls. Faced with such evading tactics some Christians have felt that the 1944 settlement was a mistake and that no good could be expected of agreed syllabus religious instruction.

167. We believe that they are wrong because we believe, and have good reason to do so both from our own experience and from the evidence given to us, that such practices are far from typical of what happens in secondary modern schools. The best schools give their pupils something which they do not get

---

[1] So it is, of course, also in the great majority of voluntary schools. But we are glad to know that there are a few voluntary schools in which Jews are brought up in their own faith, and that there is provision in county schools for pupils not only to be "excused" religious instruction, but "withdrawn" for teaching in accordance with their parents' faith where this is asked for.

elsewhere, something which they know they need when they receive it, though
they had not realized the lack before. We believe that this can be, and usually
is, given in a way which does justice to the mixed society in which we live,
recognizing the range and degrees of religious belief and practice to be found
in it, and respecting the right of the individual conscience to be provided with
the material on which freely to decide its path.

168. Boys and girls are the first to demand that teachers should know what
they are talking about. What does this mean in religious instruction? What at
least one apprentice wanted may be inferred from a discussion recorded
during a day-release period in a steel works. "You said about teachers in
school; did they explain, you know, after-life and that to you, you know?
They're in no position to explain it because they perhaps know as little as
you do about it. You see a minister knows what he's talking about, I don't
think a teacher does. At least he does perhaps about maths, but not about
religion, because he's the same as us, unless he's a right and religious man . . ."
This boy, and there are many like him, demanded both "knowledge about",
information, and also "knowledge of", experience. This is because religion
is concerned with the relation between man and his Maker, with a personal
relationship. Out of the experience of being loved—which alone, as the boy
in "A Taste of Honey" realized, makes us capable of loving—springs the
motive power of Christian living and, more abstractly, of Christian morals.
It is this which makes Christians try to behave as they (and many humanists)
think men should behave, and makes them willing when they fail to try again.
The 14 and 15 year-old boys and girls with whom we are concerned may
perhaps perceive religion as a personal relation more clearly than their abler
brothers and sisters just because they find it more difficult to frame concepts.
They have no temptation towards merely clever theorizing. They instinctively
feel that Adam Bede was right in saying: "I've seen pretty clear ever since
I was a young 'un, as religion's something else besides notions. It isn't notions
sets people doing the right thing—its feelings. Its the same with notions in
religion as it is with math'matics—a man may be able to work his problems
straight off in's head as he sits by the fire and smokes his pipe: but if he has
to make a machine or a building, he must have a will and a resolution and
love something else better than his own ease." (Chapter 18).

169. If boys and girls are right in wanting this double kind of knowledge
about religion, it follows from our mixed society that they would not expect
all teachers in secondary schools to give religious instruction. In most schools
today this does not happen. If the apprentice whose opinions we have quoted
were to revisit his old school the chances would be more than five to one
against his finding every form master taking his own form for religious instruction as they used to do in his time. The Education Act rightly provides that
nobody may be penalized for not giving religious instruction; the practice of
secondary schools is increasingly directed to seeing that nobody need feel
awkward if he says he would rather not. We are in fact rapidly moving towards
a system of specialists assisted by volunteers who take one or two forms each.
Well qualified teachers are necessary because sound objective "knowledge
about" is essential when it comes to teaching upper forms. A teacher cannot
help his pupils unless he can put into words their ill-formulated problems and
show them how Christians would set about solving them. He must know his
Bible and its teaching, he must have thought about the relation of religion,

and religious knowledge, to other fields of human activity and ways of knowing. A teacher may be a perfectly good church warden if he has solved his problems for himself in the terms which these presented themselves half a generation ago, but on this basis alone he would not be adequately equipped to give religious instruction. For this his scholarship must be up to date, and he must move on the Christian frontiers of today.

170. Such men and women are not easy to find. The Ministry's supplementary courses have for a good many years provided a steady flow of people who are already teachers and have since acquired the special knowledge required for this work, but the supply is by no means adequate. Appropriate provision for professional training would help schools to make more effective use of ordained ministers of religion who for some time past have been recruited as specialist teachers. The scarcity value of well qualified teachers has caused them frequently to be used for this purpose and nothing else. This may well be inevitable but, like most solutions in an imperfect world, it brings its own difficulties. If boys and girls are right to demand that their teachers should know what they are talking about, teachers are equally right to demand that they should know whom they are teaching. This is especially true in the field of religious instruction, and inside this field for teachers of the less articulate. Questions will not be asked if the pupils feel they do not know their teacher; they cannot be properly answered unless the teacher can get behind the fumbling words to the real problem that puzzles the pupil.

171. Finding the right words is as difficult and necessary a step in religious knowledge as in any other kind of learning. Without it thought is impossible. The fact that the difficulty increases as ability declines underlines the importance of good teaching and good teaching conditions for the boys and girls with whom this report is concerned. From the pupil's point of view the situation is not likely to be fruitful if religious instruction is given for a mere 35 or 45 minutes a week by a teacher he never sees at any other time; from the teacher's point of view the situation is equally bad if he has to teach 600 or more different boys and girls each week. Both these situations exist and are not uncommon. We should not tolerate them in any other subject. Least of all are they tolerable here. At the beginning of this chapter we spoke of the schools' task as being difficult but not impossible. It will only become generally possible when there is a better supply of properly qualified teachers, and when schools employ them in such a way that all boys and girls have enough time in which to pose their problems and consider their solution.

172. For over a hundred years the differences between the Church of England and the Free Churches made religion an almost impossibly dangerous subject to tackle in what would now be county schools. The 1944 Act in its religious settlement was based on faith that these differences could be resolved in such a way that they would not interfere with a real Christian education in county schools. That faith was justified. Every agreed syllabus has to receive the unanimous endorsement of the religious denominations taking part. In every case this has been forthcoming—a remarkable achievement of which too little has been heard. Unfortunately from a teaching point of view the syllabuses are less satisfactory, especially where the interests (and interest) of less able children are concerned. The general approach has been to start from Bible study—itself a difficult literary and historical art once the simple story-telling

stage is over. From this source teachers are expected to build up by inference a general body of Christian teaching. This is to go a very long way round for most of the boys and girls with whom we are concerned, and many of them get lost on the way. It can indeed produce the state of mind which one head-mistress recently found among her girls. They believed the Bible to be true but unimportant for them, though they recognized that it probably was important for people like her.

173. It is unlikely then, that teachers left to themselves, would choose a literary and historical approach which might suggest to the less intelligent that the Bible belongs to the past and has no contemporary significance. They would be more likely to adopt the kind of case study methods leading back to the Bible from present day problems which the Student Christian Movement in Schools has shown to be successful in secondary modern schools. Nearly all boys and girls ask questions such as, "What happens to people when they die?", "How can God allow babies to be born deformed?", "Is mercy killing justified?", "Why is it that I'm often meaner to people I love than to those I just don't care about one way or the other?", or "What's the good of praying if everything can be explained by science?". They need to know what answer the Christian faith gives. This ought to be given in the most direct and plainest way possible. If such changes in method involve a fairly general revision of agreed syllabuses, we shall not be surprised. After all the school life of not very clever boys and girls is a good deal longer now than it was when most agreed syllabuses were drawn up and it will be longer still when the school leaving age is raised.

174. We have seen that the corporate life of the school is a potent instrument in the moral development of the pupils. So is its corporate worship in their spiritual development. We have visited many schools and taken part in the morning assembly. Sometimes we have found that on the particular day of our visit the school was divided into smaller natural communities—it may be the younger boys and girls separated from the elder, or the members of one "house" worshipping together. Normally, of course, the whole school has been together, realizing as perhaps nowhere else its essential unity. We can say with conviction and gratitude that we have very often been impressed by the reality which has marked these services. Corporate worship is not to be thought of as an instrument of education—though it is that—but as a time in which pupils and teachers seek help in prayer, express awe and gratitude and joy, and pause to recollect the presence of God. We admit we were surprised when one of our number told us that new entrants to industry whom she interviewed soon after their induction period frequently told her that what they missed most now they had left school was school prayers. Reviewing our own experience and the evidence we have received, perhaps we ought not to have been surprised.

RECOMMENDATIONS

(a) Religious instruction has a part to play in helping boys and girls to find a firm basis for sexual morality based on chastity before marriage and fidelity within it. (para. 164.)

(b) The schools have a duty to give specific religious instruction, which is more than general ethical teaching. The essential conditions for doing this are an improved supply of suitably qualified teachers and an adequate time allowance in the schools. (paras. 166, 169, 171)

(c) Local education authorities should consider a review of their Agreed Syllabuses to determine whether adequate provision is made for the needs of the older boys and girls of average and below average ability, and whether they leave sufficient scope for the teachers to develop methods which start with the actual problems which the pupils have to face. (paras. 172, 173)

(d) We reaffirm the value of the school act of worship as a potent force in the spiritual experience of the pupils. (para. 174)

CHAPTER 8

The School Community

"He was the first adult I'd ever met . . . who didn't come the adult over us, didn't use his strength, and won us over by persuasion."
                              Colin MacInnes, *"Absolute Beginners"*.

175. The previous two chapters dealt with certain features of the school's communal life, the shared activities and the spiritual influences. In this chapter we are especially concerned with the relations of boys and girls with their teachers as reflected in discipline and care for the pupils' personal welfare. The heads of schools in our survey have supplied much of the evidence; and a collection of essays by girls who have recently left school at fifteen has supplied the pupils' view. (These ex-pupils were from many different schools, none of them in our survey.)

176. Since young people are often under fire these days over matters of behaviour we asked the heads to write to us fully and frankly about general standards of conduct, and about the forms of discipline used in school and, as far as they knew, at home. We are grateful for the thoughtful answers we received. Mindful of the warning of one correspondent that " it is treacherously easy for people who have never had to control groups of children" (though some of us have) " to tell teachers how it ought to be done", we are glad to be able to draw extensively on the experience of the teachers themselves.

177. Heads are quite emphatic that by far the majority of boys and girls, in or out of school, give no cause for anxiety about their general standards of behaviour. Restraints have to be imposed on natural boisterousness, but most pupils, though cheerfully outspoken and less in awe of adults than earlier generations, will accept such restraints and see their point.

"Ninety-nine per cent accept the rules."
"We have a picture in our minds of 600 or so boys and girls who are reasonably behaved citizens, ten to fifteen who are usually law abiding but can be tempted into amoral behaviour, and a small number of amoral children, maximum six at any one time."
"Ninety-six per cent respond cheerfully to a friendly authority, if administered with obvious justice."

Many deplore what they feel is a common misrepresentation of young people's attitudes.

"For all the ballyhoo in the newspapers, I am sure that children are kinder, more tolerant, and have a far wider understanding than they used to have."
"The young people at this school seem to me to be, on the whole, well adjusted and integrated. They help in the home—sometimes perhaps more than they should, or than girls once did—but this is a natural development when both parents work. In this direction they seem more mature than their counterparts of ten-fifteen-twenty years ago. They seem more mature in other ways too. They baby-sit, some help old people, they ask questions about people in general, and are interested enough to want to know the

60

answers . . . They like cheerfulness above all qualities, but admire thought-fulness and kindness too . . . They intensely dislike any signs of self-righteousness and superiority in adults. They also appear to see through people who give them advice and codes of behaviour which they themselves do not follow."

178. Some heads are bitterly angry about the harm done to secondary modern schools by grossly exaggerated accounts of indiscipline—which often make it very difficult to recruit staff. On the other hand, they do not disguise their concern about the behaviour of a minority of pupils. Here, a distinction has to be drawn between the deliberate flouting of rules and generally anti-social behaviour in school, and misconduct outside school which is liable to bring the delinquents before the courts. Estimates of the size of the first group vary from one to ten per cent of any one school's pupils, the higher figure appearing in relatively few schools and almost exclusively in problem areas. The second group, of those who are, or who seem in grave danger of becom-ing, delinquents in the technical sense, is very much smaller, and again, they are closely associated with problems of abnormal home conditions. Emotional disturbance is often associated with delinquency. The majority of delinquents are of poor intelligence, but there are able boys who get into trouble because of their desire for excitement. The apparent association between poor intelli-gence and delinquency may partly, at least, be explained, as many of the heads who wrote to us suggest, by the fact that it is the stupid who get caught most easily. Delinquency in the technical sense is far more common among boys than girls.

179. On sexual behaviour, very little anxiety is expressed about boys under sixteen still at school, or about the relations between girls and boys in mixed schools. For the most part they are said to get along amicably enough with their largely separate lives. The markedly earlier maturity of girls compared with boys of the thirteen-to-sixteen age group is probably significant here. Where individual boy and girl friendships do develop among the older pupils, this is sometimes found to have a steadying rather than harmful effect. There is concern, however, about the relationships of some girls with older youths and men outside school. Most heads acknowledge that they simply cannot assess the size of this problem; some incline to think it is smaller than the girls' loose chatter and outwardly precocious behaviour often suggests. Of those girls who come before the courts as in need of moral care and protection, many, though not all, have distressing histories of neglect and instability at home. But apart from these extreme cases, too many girls appear to go their way without supervision by their parents. Girls' schools in particular are conscious of their need to give positive guidance, and stress the value of having married women on their staff willing to discuss sexual behaviour frankly with their pupils. Many parents for their part seem only too glad for the schools to relieve them of a responsibility they find difficult.

180. Again and again, the rôle of the parents and of the home is stressed. Since the majority of pupils cause little or no anxiety, it is to be expected that the majority of parents are careful of their children's well-being. And so the schools testify.

"We have reason to be grateful for the home influence of pupils in this school."

This is not necessarily confined to "better" neighbourhoods. One head, in an old industrial district, which he describes as "a typical Coronation Street area", affirms:

"I feel that the large majority of parents are doing their best, and that there is a wholesome atmosphere in the homes."

School and local community are closely identified.

"We are very much involved in whatever happens to the children and their parents—if they are in trouble, so are we, and we share their joy as well." He adds, however, "the parents are often over-generous in material things, and under-generous in giving their time to their children."

And this is echoed from another school, this time in a small country town:

"The parents are fond of their children and go to great lengths to provide them with the things they want—football boots, uniforms, bicycles, pocket money . . . but it is not generally their custom to be with their children very much, certainly at this age, and the children tend, therefore, to be largely unsupervised. Nobody worries very much unless the child gets into trouble of some sort.'.

Another head finds this particular lack, of parents and children spending time together, especially common among the less able pupils:

". . . as one examines the backgrounds of these pupils, descending from the able to the less able, the more one finds them being left to their own devices. At the bottom . . . they appear to be quite independent, but not knowing what to do with their independence."

181. Many heads are concerned at the number of boys and girls who go home to an empty house, and suggest that the harmful effects of this on adolescents are not recognized because they are not so obvious as with younger children. There is no easy solution to this, at a time when more and more married women are taking jobs outside the home and are being urged to do so in the national economic interest; but this evidence directly reinforces, in our opinion, the need for providing more activities under the aegis of the school over a longer school day.

182. Boys and girls left continually on their own tend to get into more or less serious mischief. Sometimes there appears to be no tradition in the area of family life, in the sense of parents and children doing things together, although the children may be physically well cared for.

"Some girls are given three and sixpence to ten shillings a night to 'clear out and amuse yourself'."

Often, the majority of mothers are working, fathers may be on shift work and there are very few waking hours in the day when adults and children can spend time together. A mother's absence sometimes puts too early a responsibility on the girls.

"In many homes where the mother is in full-time employment, older girls almost take charge of the home and of the younger children. They often make decisions in the absence of parents, who then cannot understand why they refuse to accept their authority when they are with them."

With this we can match the description of the normal start to her school day by a fourteen year old girl in one of our problem areas. She wrote the account as part of her work for her English teacher, and was not apparently conscious of particular hardship.

"Getting Up"

"At a half past four every morning the alarm clock goes off. Then I know its time to get up. I get dressed and then go down into the coldness. First of all I put on the kettle. While that is boiling I make the fire. I make my father's porridge and shout him up for work. When he's gone I get my sister up for work. When she has gone I clean up then get ready for school. After that I shout my brother up and help him to get ready for school. Then I call my mother up."

183. "Discipline varies considerably, but real difficulties in the school occur only when the home and school are at cross purposes and the child attempts to play one against the other."

A conflict of standards operates to the child's disadvantage. Schools, for example, vigorously prohibit smoking and disobedience usually incurs the severest penalties. Some parents not only give their children cigarettes as a bribe for good behaviour at home but also resent the restrictions at school.

"If he's not smoking yours and he's not smoking mine, what business is it of yours anyway?"

Truancy may be condoned, or deliberately encouraged, and the official process of following up the offenders sometimes operates too slowly. Eventually the cases come before the courts, and the parents are fined, but the children meanwhile have missed long stretches of schooling—fourteen weeks in one example quoted to us.

184. Nevertheless, inside their own walls the schools have to devise a pattern of discipline to regulate their special community. Most of them see it as a dual task of maintaining order, and of providing positive incentives to good behaviour, with opportunities for individuals to exercise personal responsibility.

"The school believes, if it is to work efficiently and smoothly, that there must be order, but that if this is secured by repression and excessive regimentation, then it has failed in its aim to train for life."

Discipline should consist in helping the pupils "towards a lasting self-discipline, rather than a system of regimentation, whistle blowing and shouting". But the same head points out that overcrowding and old and inconvenient buildings with narrow corridors can often oblige schools to regiment movement far more than they would choose to do.

185. The commonest penalties for offending against the school's code include detention (much disliked by pupils), loss of House points, and being "put on report", i.e. having to report and show work at regular intervals to the head. Among constructive attempts to fit the punishment to the crime, are playground litter duty, for those who are careless and untidy in the use of the school buildings, and contributions towards repair and replacement of damaged property.

186. We asked about corporal punishment for the age-groups of pupils with whom we are concerned. Many heads have written most thoughtfully on this, some expressing firm convictions, others doubts. We are bound to record that nearly all find it necessary to retain corporal punishment as the ultimate sanction for boys. It is rare in girls' schools, though it exists, and in practice appears to be very seldom applied to girls in co-educational schools. Many heads stress, however, that they regard this ultimate deterrent as effective only if it is used exceptionally; that they are finding less and less need to

resort to it; and that they look forward to a day when it will cease to be needed altogether.

"The availability of corporal punishment is an absolute necessity in schools of this type. Without this resource . . . a few children would jeopardise the future of many . . . I do not relish or indulge in corporal punishment, but children know it is available if they force me to use it—such occasions are now rare."

"I prefer, and I am sure most children prefer, punishment to be swift and fair and no longstanding memory of it on the part of the headmaster apparently retained. Obviously I am a firm believer in corporal punishment, although I must admit it is very sparingly used here."

"The discipline of the school . . . is firm but not repressive. Corporal punishment is virtually non-existent in the school, especially in the senior half. The application of sanctions, e.g. non-membership of clubs, not being allowed to travel with school teams etc. is the most effective weapon, but immediate physical punishment is the only effective weapon with a small minority of the younger ones."

"The attitude of the boys and the staff towards corporal punishment is healthy . . . All the staff try to minimise its use, and their efforts in this direction have been highly successful but they are very dubious about discipline if this sanction is withdrawn." The same head stresses that the attitude of ninety-five per cent of the boys, in a slum industrial area, "is one of tolerance and co-operation within the limits of their responsibilities at home."

"Corporal punishment is used as a last resort for the deliberate breaking of school rules after clear and sometimes frequent warning has been given . . . Generally, corporal punishment can be very effective in curing minor misdemeanours, such as persistent late-coming, minor damage to school property etc., when the recipient has had several warnings and realizes himself that he is only getting his just deserts. In these cases, the punishment acts like a short puff of breath on a candle flame, but for more serious offences whose causes are deeply rooted and complex, corporal punishment can act like a rush of air through a furnace and does more harm than good."

"I have discussed corporal punishment with the staff and they agree unanimously that no useful purpose would be served at all by resorting to it. They also feel much harm could result from using it. I myself could not use a cane under any circumstances; I should feel myself to be losing all dignity and to be thereby at a complete disadvantage."

"Corporal punishment is a very last resort and I look forward to a time when it will be extremely rare. In many cases its effectiveness is doubtful because, like an anti-malarial pill, it is so often a suppressive, not a cure."

Many agree that while it is sometimes effective and acceptable with younger pupils, it is much less effective with older adolescents. They have even more doubts if the pupils concerned are from homes where physical violence is familiar, and stress the need to recognize that some anti-social behaviour reflects serious emotional disturbance.

"Punishments do not work when the misdemeanours are the outward and visible sign of a maladjusted, dull or emotionally disturbed child."

187. But perhaps some of the most illuminating comments are on the kind of situation which leads to serious indiscipline. Many of the heads who most firmly defend their need to resort to corporal punishment also freely acknowledge many cases of indiscipline need never arise, if only they had smaller classes and more experienced teachers. As it is, rapid changes and shortages of staff may lead to young, inexperienced teachers being asked to take large forms of fourteen and fifteen year-olds. If, in addition, the group is made up of rather dull pupils whom it is far more difficult to interest, a situation can very quickly develop in which the head is bound to intervene. Unlucky conflicts are not confined to inexperienced teachers; there are some seasoned teachers, as one head ruefully admits, who "positively create problems" by their lack of perception and inability to make effective personal contact. Our evidence is emphatic that large classes, especially in cramped or over-crowded rooms, intensify the problems of discipline and demand especially skilled and experienced teachers.

188. The views on school discipline expressed by the recent leavers provide an interesting comparison. First, some of their most intense dislike is directed at relatively minor matters, especially rules over uniform. These are an irritation to the majority of the girls although a few speak of uniform with approval.

"We were made to have a maroon uniform which I really detest."

"Quite often before entering the buildings in the morning we would have to stand in lines, while the head marched up and down checking our uniform. You could say we were like guards being inspected by the major."

"The rules were quite strict about silly little things for instance the size of the check on our summer dresses."

"Girls of fifteen even seventeen not being allowed to eat a sweet or even be seen in a sweetshop in school uniform."

"Our uniforms left much to be desired. Ugly, big-knotted ties and a shocking colour of bright red for jumpers. And those hats. I really felt ashamed to walk down my street with it on."

Since our commentators were all girls, perhaps it is to be expected that they felt strongly over appearance, although clearly a question of adult status enters into the matter as well. But the statistics from our own survey confirm that among both girls and boys, the wearing of uniform is evaded by many of its older pupils, and especially by the fourth year pupils in the lower ability ranges.

| | | Position in Fourth Year by Ability | | | |
		Top Quarter	Second Quarter	Third Quarter	Bottom Quarter
Percentage of pupils NOT wearing uniform in schools where it is expected in the fourth year	Boys	20%	34%	44%	52%
	Girls	10%	19%	23%	36%

189. Apart from uniform, there is a general dislike of what they see as an excess of trivial rules, but an equally intense dislike of disorder and inconsistency.

"There were so many rules that no one could ever remember them, but no actual discipline as such. No two teachers were alike. This left us in a state of perpetual unbalance."

They agree completely with the heads in feeling that much discontent arises from a combination of young and inexperienced teachers, too large classes, and too frequent changes of teacher.

> "I think that what went wrong with us, our teachers were so young they could not control us."

> "I never liked the young women teachers we had. Some of them were not much older than us and it seemed a bit silly. I much prefer the older teachers who know how to teach."

> "It was not so much a case of ignorance as that they could not put the subject over properly or they did not explain."

> "There was always a change of teachers in my form. That's the reason most of us were uninterested and glad to leave."

> "Teachers came and went like water."

190. We asked, especially, about incentives which proved effective with our pupils. Many heads stress the need for a public word of praise and recognition, wherever praise is due, (with the corollary that "shortcomings in work and conduct are better dealt with individually and privately"). Many urge the importance of ensuring that the less able pupils have their share of the best facilities and equipment and of the best teachers:

> "Perhaps the most important thing is to make it clear that the less able youngsters (and the fourth year leavers) get a fair share of the best staff, the best rooms, the most interesting, e.g. practical, subjects, special jobs, etc. To this end my Deputy, my Senior Master and myself each teach the fourth year leavers and the third year lower forms pretty substantially."

Not all schools manage successfully to apply this principle of giving manifestly equal treatment. And it is frequently acknowledged, regretfully, that the brunt of staff changes and handling by temporary or unqualified teachers often has to be borne by the groups of "ordinary", average pupils, whereas the very bright and the extremely backward tend to have their special needs safe-guarded.

191. The majority of schools make use of House systems, with awards for good work and behaviour as well as for competitive sport. A few large, new schools exist whose buildings have been designed on a House basis, and in which the House units can operate as small communities in themselves, with a physical identity. But this is exceptional, and the typical day school operates its Houses despite, rather than aided by, its buildings. Most schools still clearly feel that this is an effective way of developing group loyalties or providing opportunities for service; just a few have doubts as to how far older pupils who are within sight of leaving may really feel involved in what are inevitably somewhat artificial institutions.

192. We have to acknowledge with many of the heads that there appears to be no universally effective incentive. What "works" is often a highly individual matter. It depends essentially upon a relation of mutual respect between a pupil and a particular teacher, and on the pupils feeling that someone is personally interested in their progress. So the pupils confirm.

> "In my last year I had a very nice form mistress who treated us more like girls who were on the verge of leaving school and going out to work and we got on very well together."

"There was only one teacher I got on well with. In fact I got on so well with him that I wrote him a letter telling him how I was getting on with my job. I think I got on alright with him because he took a keen interest in my work and if ever I could not do the work he use to come and assist and explain it to me. This made me even keener to work hard, as I think it would any-one."

"Most of our teachers were very understanding. If ever you needed help and advice they were only too willing to help you."

193. The personal touch counts for even more in the matter of welfare. Good schools everywhere have traditionally made it their business to look after their pupils personally as well as to teach them in lessons, but this aspect of education is demanding increasing thought. There are more very large schools, and the need to have some system for making sure the individual pupil is not lost sight of is more pronounced. There is much more frequent coming and going of staff, and therefore less likelihood than there once was of an accumulation of knowledge in the staff room not only of all the pupils in the school, but often of their brothers and sisters and parents before them, and indeed of the whole neighbourhood. It is, too, becoming apparent that there may be a great deal more to learn about individual boys and girls: the causes of lack of progress in school may be personal and complex, not to be assigned simply to limited intelligence or poor teaching.

194. Schools tell us of systems, some of them very thoughtfully elaborated, of tutors or form teachers or Housemasters, and of regular staff meetings to discuss the problems of individual pupils. As we see it, there are two basic needs to be met, by whatever arrangements a school finds practicable in its circumstances. One is to ensure that sufficient factual knowledge is built up of the background and general circumstances of the individual pupil. The other is to try to ensure that as far as possible any boy or girl will have a natural confidant to turn to. This is more difficult to achieve, because questions of mutual confidence and personality are involved, and the most efficient system cannot guarantee that pupil and appointed tutor will naturally like each other. (Or that the tutor will still be there in a year's time.) The pupils turn instinctively for personal support to some particular teacher who is sympathetic, whether or not he or she has any official tutorial status.

"One of the lessons I enjoyed was French. The teacher who took us was most understanding, and if I had been in trouble of any kind he would have been the one I would have gone to."

"If it hadn't been for the games mistress I would have left home at one time, but she made me see reason."

195. Most schools see value in creating a corps of prefects and monitors, which sets an example of service and provides opportunities to exercise leadership at many levels. The non-prefects are not always impressed:

"The school was over-run with prefects and monitors who could not control the rest of us and were wasting their time."

"Prefects were mostly fake."

A few heads suggest that a less authoritarian organization may be more appropriate to present day concepts, and are anxious to find ways in which all the older pupils can be given personal responsibility.

196. One way may lie through community service projects. Our evidence describes not only fund-raising activities for charitable causes, but also sustained enterprises in the local community involving planning, organization, and imaginative effort by groups of pupils. Some examples quoted include voluntary assistance in the local hospitals, decorating a community centre, making and repairing toys for nursery and infant schools and individual service in schemes for helping elderly or invalid persons: "they shop, fetch medicine, exchange library books, and just visit and cheer the aged with their youthful gaiety". There is a double value, in the usefulness of the service itself, and in the satisfaction of the boys and girls concerned in doing a real job. The pupils who are restive and feel themselves out-growing the interests of a purely internal school society may especially respond to these more adult responsibilities. One headmistress writes:

"there have been girls going through a difficult time, and we have found a spell away from school in quite different surroundings has worked wonders. I have a strictly unofficial working arrangement with three infant and nursery schools in the neighbourhood where there are very understanding headmistresses. A troublesome girl can become a most reasonable young lady when helping to tell stories at dinner time to infants, or helping to serve meals or to dress and undress young children. Most important of all, when she has had the status of a young adult for a few weeks she seems to gain in poise and confidence in herself, which halts the downward trend."

197. We find ourselves coming back and back to this need to make some gesture of recognizing the more adult status of the older pupils, even those who are troublesome or not very bright, and who do not seem responsive. It is not easy to contrive, even socially, inside most school buildings. The head of a large comprehensive school comments:

"We still have to improvise social accommodation in premises primarily designed for instruction and not for being lived in."

The introduction of more "social" areas and common rooms for the older pupils could have long term educational consequences.

198. Another factor which can make for difficulties in giving more privileges to the older pupils is the wide age range in secondary schools. As long as the majority of pupils have been leaving at the age of fifteen, inevitably the weight of the modern school population has been at the younger end. And although there is no single or common age, in years and months, at which the break between childhood or adolescence may be said to begin, certainly the fourteen or fifteen or sixteen year-olds are very different persons from the eleven or twelve year-olds. We see some advantages in a more homogeneous adolescent community, and are glad that the Minister has invited the Council to undertake an enquiry into the whole question of the age of transfer from primary to secondary education.

199. We have tried to let the teachers and the pupils speak for themselves. What they have to say leads us to the following conclusions. Most schools clearly have the welfare of their pupils very much at heart. The problem of serious indiscipline is relatively small, and most intractable in the areas where the social forces outside are working against the school. But at a less serious level, some of the older boys and girls, especially among the academically less successful, are impatient of what seem to them childishly trivial "rules";

they have a deep need for order, but are irked at the contrast between the independence and often quite heavy adult responsibilities which some of them know outside school, and their lack of status in school, even though they acknowledge the personal kindness of many of their teachers. They are not necessarily grown-up or logical in the reasons which weigh heavily with them: "I left school at fifteen because of all this discipline and because the school uniform was navy blue" is a not untypical statement.

200. Anything which can serve to emphasize the status of the older pupils is to be welcomed here, in the context of the work, in the design of the buildings, and in the internal organization of the community. We recognize the value many schools continue to find in traditional forms of social organization, but think they would be wise to seek also other ways of distributing responsibility. "Training for Leadership", except in very limited spheres, becomes an increasingly difficult principle to apply to the education of large numbers of boys and girls who almost by definition are not outstanding, and who are generally much less likely to become members of an élite at school or afterwards. It may be that learning to become a reliable member of a group of equals is, for many, a better general preparation for life. It is notable that in the world of adult employment more and more industries seem to be splitting up responsibility and placing an emphasis on team work. In the youth service, the "self-programming" group reflects the same trend. As larger numbers of older pupils remain longer at school, more subtle systems of sharing responsibility and developing initiative may have to be found. Community service projects appear to offer particularly satisfying possibilities.

201. We share the disquiet of those heads who feel that corporal punishment is likely to delay, rather than promote, the growth of self-discipline, and that it is humiliating to staff and pupils. We especially deplore such punishment for older adolescent girls, and the experience of many girls' schools, not all in "easy" areas, confirms that other sanctions can be effective. We realize that the presence in a school of even one or two exceptionally difficult pupils can have a quite disproportionately disturbing and disruptive influence. No blanket recipe for dealing with these cases is possible, since treatment has to be related to the individual situation. Sometimes, removal to entirely new surroundings may be in the best interests of the pupil concerned and of the rest of the pupils affected—perhaps by transfer to another school, with mutual agreement between heads, or to special schools or classes for the maladjusted. Sometimes a normal boarding school may offer a solution for pupils who cannot be helped except by removing them entirely from their home environment. There are dangers in making it too easy for schools to get rid of their misfits, and we do not think removal ought to be resorted to except in extreme cases; but where the interests of everyone concerned require this, some simplification of administrative procedure is desirable.

202. The schools also need the support of every other administrative agency which deals with adolescents still at school. Our attention has been drawn particularly to difficulties of dealing with the hard core of truancy, despite the strenuous efforts of Educational welfare officers. Evidence from two local authority areas, of contrasting types and in different parts of the country, indicates that often when the cases come before the courts nugatory fines, even for persistent offences, may confirm the parents in their belief that

school attendance is not important.[1] It is essential that magistrates should appreciate that in this exercise of their function they are part of the educational system and have the responsibility to support it.

203. It seems clear that even in good buildings and a generally healthy school, large classes, rapid turnover of staff, and too many young and inexperienced teachers may undermine orderly working and cause the less able pupils to give up trying. In physically cramped buildings in slum surroundings which offer no other outlet for youthful energies, the situation may become explosive. All that was said in chapter 3 in relation to the slum schools is confirmed again here, on the need for improved buildings and for incentives to make good teachers stay.

204. The schools cannot do the job alone, and parents cannot delegate their responsibility for guiding their children. Many situations would be helped simply by the schools knowing more of the home circumstances and the parents knowing more of what goes on in school. All existing links, such as parent-teacher associations, open-days, invitations to school functions and concerts, conferences, regular school reports, and most of all, informal conversations between teachers and parents, are extremely valuable. But there is a percentage of homes—and in some districts, a majority—which such arrangements do not touch. In dealing with these problems, the schools, and the parents, need special help. There may be a strong case for having additional members of staff who have special responsibilities for home visiting, and who act as liaison officers with all the other medical, welfare and child care services in the district. This also implies a need for teachers whose training has included some realistic sociological studies.

205. Positive guidance to boys and girls on sexual morals is essential, with quite specific discussion of the problems they will face. We include in the appendix to this report an account of how one school sets about this task. Advice to the parents on dealing with the problems of their children's physical and emotional adolescence may be equally needed, and should be easily available, whether through the school or through the health and welfare services.

206. In the general context of sex education in the widest sense, we think it important that boys and girls should have opportunities to meet members of the opposite sex in a helpful and educative environment. This is not to advocate co-educational schools to the exclusion of others. Some single-sex schools successfully run joint recreational activities with neighbouring schools, so as to bring boys and girls together for orchestras, choirs, drama, debates,

NOTE [1] As one of our contributors points out:

"The value of the pound is less than one-fifth of what it was when the Education Act of 1900 made twenty shillings the maximum penalty, yet it is still the maximum for a first offence, and many Courts do not even impose a fine of that amount. Although the maximum fines for second (£5) and subsequent offences (£10 and/or one month's imprisonment) were increased in 1944, Magistrates' Courts are still reluctant to use the power Parliament has given them." In this area, only 4 out of 264 prosecutions over a given period for third or subsequent offences resulted in the imposition of the maximum fine.

In the other area cited an investigation of court decisions over the period of a year showed that:

only 8 out of 95 second offenders paid the maximum fine of £5.

only 4 out of 100 third offenders paid the maximum fine of £10.

None of the 80 offenders appearing for the fourth or subsequent time was given the maximum fine.

conferences, dances and social gatherings of many kinds. Others again encourage their pupils to join mixed youth clubs in the area. The important point is that schools of whatever type should recognize the need and contrive to provide appropriate opportunities.

207. In matters of personal welfare, the most natural advisers of most boys and girls are their parents, but care on the part of the school to build up knowledge of the individual pupils, and personal supervision by some member of staff, cannot be other than helpful. Much depends on thoughtful and efficient organization, but even more fundamental are the personal relations which exist between teachers and pupils. We leave the last word with a head:

"The great thing is to like them. If you don't, they'll know instinctively and you'll get nowhere with them."

RECOMMENDATIONS

(a) Every effort should be made to emphasize the status of the older pupils, through school organization and in the design of school buildings. (para. 200)

(b) We welcome interest in developing group responsibilities, and see a particular value in community service projects. (paras. 196, 200)

(c) Corporal punishment for the older pupil is likely to delay, rather than promote, the growth of self-discipline. It is humiliating for both the pupils and the staff. We especially deplore such punishment for adolescent girls. (para. 201)

(d) There is urgent need to strengthen all existing links between home and school, and in difficult areas to create new ones, as, for example, in the appointment of members of staff with special liaison or home-visiting responsibilities. (para. 204)

(e) Positive and realistic guidance to adolescent boys and girls on sexual behaviour is essential. This should include the biological, moral, social and personal aspects. Advice to parents on the physical and emotional problems of adolescents should be easily available. Schools of whatever type should contrive to provide opportunities for boys and girls to mix socially in a helpful and educative environment. (paras. 205, 206)

(f) It is of the greatest importance for schools to build up a knowledge of individual pupils and to devise some system of supervising their personal welfare. (paras. 193, 194, 207)

CHAPTER 9

Going out into the World

"I couldn't believe it, you are at school and suddenly you are at work, and there are years before you are 65".   *"Home, School and Work". M. Carter.*

208. Schools cannot prepare their pupils for everything that may lie ahead in all those "years before you are 65"—or beyond—but they can make the world a slightly less confusing place for young leavers. Many conferences and courses and publications in recent years have been concerned with the transition from school to adult, working life, but there is still much to be learned about effective forms of preparation, especially at the level of our pupils. All boys and girls need guidance, but the youngest and less well endowed school leavers need it especially.

209. The school can help them in several ways. It can give them, just before they leave, an extra polish intellectually, in their skills and previous learning; and personally, in attention to speech, health, dress, deportment and social behaviour. A short residential course at this stage could serve a useful purpose, although this is not, as we indicated earlier, the only type of residential course which we hope will be available to the pupils. The school can see that they have factual information for immediate needs, and some clues as to where to turn for it in the future, in connection with employment, further education, and personal interests. And it can begin to enlarge their understanding of the wider world, so that as adults they may take a more satisfying part in it.

210. As we see it, the school programme, in the last year especially, ought to be deliberately outgoing. This means taking the pupils mentally and often physically beyond the school walls. It also means bringing men and women from the world outside the walls into the school. It almost certainly demands a greater flexibility in the timetable and in methods of study. And it may require more time than is normally available inside the conventional school day.

211. Apart from any special innovations in the programme, the more any lessons can be given a realistic and adult reference, the better. It may be in examples of industrial applications in science or in handicraft; or in problems in arithmetic which deal with wage packet deductions or hire purchase or value-for-money on consumer research lines. Discussions in any of the humane subjects may tackle personal relations—on the job, as well as in private life; or begin to reveal, even at a very modest level of understanding, how aspects of government and economics and social justice touch us all, and that society is not simply divided into Us and Them.

212. Boys and girls growing up in a welfare state, for instance, ought to know how the social services are paid for and how they operate locally. They ought also to realize the continuing need for sensible self-help and for voluntary assistance to those unable to help themselves. If the school is one which engages in community service projects, these ideas will not be unfamiliar.

But we note, for example, that a church organization which has held confer-ences for some 2,000 school leavers records "We have yet to meet any sugges-tion that any of their own money should be used for charitable or humani-tarian or religious purposes, on a budgeted basis".

213. Civics, current affairs, modern history, social studies, whether under those names or not, ought to feature in the programme. They need sensitive handling if they are not to go sadly awry.

"Our current affairs lesson was horrible. We had to sit and listen to the teacher preach about what she believed."

"History was all right at the beginning, but when I got to the beginning of the fourth year we had nothing but politics, politics, politics."

"But when they say to you 'What do you think?' well, there's nothing to say and you begin to dread discussion lesson in case he asks you for your opinion and you don't know anything about the subject."

"What with politics and ban the bomb English lessons were right crummy."

Above all, they need lively presentation in terms of people and events, if they are not to seem arid abstractions to most boys and girls. Again, taking a close look at the immediate environment can be rewarding, in discovering how the world locally earns its living and enjoys its leisure. But some environments are the reverse of stimulating, except to the sociologist, and the important thing may sometimes be to lift pupils' eyes beyond the local horizon.

214. Television has made this notably easier to do than it once was, and perhaps the main strength of school television as a new resource at the disposal of the teacher lies for our pupils in its power to extend their know-ledge of the contemporary world and enlarge their sympathies. A television programme in the field of geography, or current affairs or vocational guidance makes its impact in sharp and concrete terms. It has the prestige of a medium that belongs to the outside world; and although it is necessarily a one-way communication it can serve all the more effectively as a basis for discussion in so far as it is an experience shared with the teacher, and not immune from criticism.

215. Films similarly offer a teaching medium with some of the same power as television to enlarge the pupils' world, coupled with the advantage of being more readily available for use at any time. The films made for television broad-casting itself and the recorded programmes set a high standard, and some of this material ought to be available for use by the schools—the more so as many schools as yet lack the receivers to take television programmes direct. At a recent survey there were only 5,000 television sets in schools as com-pared with 30,000 sound radio sets.

216. At home, boys and girls, like their elders, spend rather more than two hours a day on an average watching the television screen. It is not surprising therefore that they often have a wide and miscellaneous store of items of information gleaned in viewing. True, the knowledge may be shallow and lack coherence, but this is where teachers can help. Many a pupil now sees skilful documentaries or looks in at interviews who would never come near such information in books or sober magazine articles. Similarly, films and plays and ballet are seen of a kind and quality not often available locally. Furthermore, it is not too much to say that when these pupils leave school, television will be for most of them the most important source of knowledge

about the world outside the confines of their own experience; of enjoyment
of the arts; of acquaintance with the full range of human personality, and of
contact with ways of speaking and thinking other than those of their own
social group. We believe that teachers should reckon with these facts, and
that their own training should help them to take account of television as a
social force, as well as offering them some preparation for the proper handling
of school broadcasts in sound and television.

217. The ultimate response of the pupils to television and the other mass
media will depend on the whole of their education. Nevertheless, not only
through television, but in a very large field of popular culture—music, films,
theatre, journalism—pupils can learn, with guidance, to sharpen their perceptions. In this way they not only widen their range of interests, but are
helped to take a more intelligently critical view of what is available. Exercising
their own judgement on experiences well within their comprehension is an
important piece of general training for our pupils.

218. One of the memorable things that broadcasting can do is to bring men
and women of outstanding achievement into direct contact with the young
people in the classroom. We hope also that as part of the ordinary school
programme many interesting persons may be drawn into the life of the school,
although we realize that it can be difficult to find people who are at ease with
adolescents and able to communicate their experience. We are thinking here,
however, not of formal lectures, nor of the talks which form part of the specific
programme of vocational guidance and to which outside speakers commonly
contribute now, but of small, informal discussion groups, dealing with matters
of interest arising out of normal school studies in which the visitor would take
part along with the teacher; or of using local expert skill, in a sport, say, or
music, or gardening or photography, in connection with "extra-curricular"
activities. Men and women from overseas; a local councillor; a supervisor
from a large store; former pupils who have been out earning their own living
for a few years; a hospital almoner; a policeman; a journalist; people connected with the youth service and with further education—all these and many
others might be found in any neighbourhood, and be invited to share their
direct experience with the pupils.

219. One of the virtues of such contacts would lie simply in providing opportunities for ordinary adult conversation. Some of the boys and girls with
whom we are concerned have very little experience outside school of taking
part in, or even hearing, sustained conversation on matters of general, adult
interest. In their homes, many parents seem not to talk about even their work
in front of their children, except perhaps to grumble. A headmistress tells us
of fourteen-year old girls who had no idea what jobs their fathers and mothers
did every day; and youth leaders confirm that girls, especially, respond gratefully to adults who will talk with them on equal terms.

220. As well as meeting visitors in school, the pupils themselves need to go
out and explore. Sometimes, they may go as small teams carrying out a
particular investigation. At others, they may be taking part in a series of
visits planned to give them glimpses of different types of industry or to take
them to places of cultural interest. Always they will need good preliminary
briefing. Many schools do already arrange excellent programmes of this kind,
but there is room for more experiment in this field, especially in relating the

experiences of the visits more closely to the rest of the work in school. The pupils themselves ought to be brought in as much as possible to the initial planning and organization and making of arrangements. In the management of themselves and their contacts with other people outside the familiar school situation, and in the subsequent presentation of their experience, they can learn much, quite apart from any specific information they may have acquired.

221. One source of outside experience on which to base studies in school could be community service projects such as we have discussed earlier. Another ready to hand, but seldom put to use, is the spare-time employment which many pupils obtain for themselves. In our sample, forty-two per cent of the fourth year boys and fifteen per cent of the girls had an out-of-school job. Such work is not likely to have much bearing on the kind of employment they eventually take up—a great many schoolboys, for example, do paper rounds—but it can give a taste of the authentic discipline of a real job. We are not in the least recommending that all pupils should be encouraged to take part-time jobs: but if considerable numbers are doing so anyway, teachers might as well take account of the fact and help the pupils to make useful sense of the experience.

222. Another possibility which some other countries are examining is deliberately to provide limited experience of different kinds of employment, on a release-from-school basis, inside the educational programme. In Sweden, sample work-experiences have been introduced into the educational system, as part of the process of vocational guidance. In the U.S.A. it has been possible for some years for High School students, older than the boys and girls we have in mind, to work under supervision in offices and business establishments, and to have this credited towards their graduation. In this country, short "works courses" in holiday time have been available for some years to sixth form pupils from grammar and independent schools. We have been interested to realize that some limited experiments in this direction with younger pupils have also been introduced, on purely local initiative.

223. We have had a number of examples, all quite separately sponsored, brought to our notice, of schemes in which schools, the youth employment service and groups of firms have co-operated in various ways. Girls have made extended visits to shops or offices, intensively for a fortnight or in a series of half-day visits spread over a term. Boys have attended factories on Saturday mornings. In a scheme organized through a Rotary club, pupils of sixteen and seventeen have spent a week with firms, covering eleven different types of occupation between them. Another school is at present engaged in arranging for small groups of pupils to pay extended observation visits to particular firms, and in one case to participate in some of the activities of the training school there.

224. In all the examples brought to our notice, the experience has been designed as part of a wider programme of general preparation for school leavers, rather than as an introduction to any specific field of future employment. The intention has been to present a closer view of the world at work than is possible in the more usual brief visit, and to give the pupils some sense of being out on their own, although the schools have been in close contact with the shops or offices or firms concerned, and members of the school staffs have visited the pupils. It is hoped that the experiences which the pupils bring back with them will provide useful matter for discussion and evaluation.

225. We have not seen any of these schemes in operation—some have been single, short-term experiments only—and we cannot therefore offer any opinion on their effectiveness in providing an additional stimulus to boys and girls in their general school work. We record them, nevertheless, as examples of efforts by the schools to inject an element of realism in the content of the final year's course.

226. The schemes are a long way from the elaborate work-experience programmes of the Swedish pattern, and rather different in their objective. We do not suggest, even so, that they are likely to become practicable or even desirable for the large majority of boys and girls, but, clearly, the older the pupils concerned, the easier it becomes to envisage extensions of experience outside the school. An accumulation of more information on tentative experiments in this field would be useful, together with a study by the Ministry of Labour, industry and the trade unions, and the education authorities, of the legal and safety issues which would be involved if any extension of these ideas were contemplated when all pupils are at school till at least sixteen.

227. The novel aspect, and some of the potential difficulties, of schemes of the kind described lie in their being related to commerce and to industry. But these are not the only fields in which pupils have engaged, or could, in responsible activities away from school. There are many possibilities: work on a farm, for example, as an extension of a rural studies course; helping in a local children's home or in an infant or nursery school; observing and assisting in a hospital, suitably selected; or possibly quite different enterprises, like spending two or three days behind the scenes at the local civic theatre, helping with costumes or scenery or the ticket office. Most projects of this sort could only be carried out by a few pupils at a time, but related to a larger programme they might encourage the pupils to see some relevance in their school work to the interests and work of the adult world.

228. One of the things boys and girls ought to know, and be encouraged to want to know, is how to continue their education, formally and informally. They need to know about further education, not just as a pamphlet on local courses, but in fairly concrete terms of what sort of things you do, and where, and with what objectives. They need if possible to have visited some of the local institutions, and to have met some of the staff and students. Open days in colleges of further education arranged specially for the benefit of local schools are not unknown, but could happen more commonly than they do. And reciprocal invitations could be made more often to further education staff and principals to visit the schools.

229. There could be a positive advantage, where conditions and facilities are suitable, for some pupils, in attending a college of further education for some part of their course in the last year and thereby having a ready-made link for the future. This already happens in some areas, sometimes for lack of adequate facilities in the schools, but sometimes by deliberate policy. Where such arrangements are made, they are much to be preferred on a group rather than on an individual basis. Otherwise, there can be many problems of fitting a few school-age pupils into classes intended for older, adult students, and the content of the course is less likely to be suited to the pupils' needs, or sufficiently related to the rest of their work at school.

230. Some boys and girls will be helped by knowing about further education at very much humbler levels. For example, pupils at the lower end of the ability range quickly lose their grip on reading skills, if they have no compulsion to practise them once they have left school. And they probably do not worry much about it immediately, but a few years later may suddenly realize they are miserably handicapped, in their work or in their private lives. They can be helped, in many evening institute classes, but the difficulty is always how to make the existence of these classes known to those who need them.

231. In addition, there are all the recreational activities offered by evening institutes, youth clubs, sports organizations and adult societies, which boys and girls should at least realize exist. They should know where to turn, when they are ready to take up a new interest or want to continue an old one started at school. And the below-average pupil may not find it easy to obtain this kind of information for himself, or summon up enterprise to take the first steps, without previous encouragement. Possibly the schools could do a useful job in preparing a simply annotated hand-out for school leavers, giving the names of persons, places, and organizations which boys and girls, and their parents, might at some time be glad to know about.

232. Some elements of continuity at the point of transition are likely to be helpful. Young school leavers may be exhilarated at their new wage earning status, but they will often need information, guidance, and a degree of moral support. The youth employment service attempts to provide this, but its resources are limited; large firms can help through induction courses and by means of supervisory and welfare schemes, but, although we have not been able to discover any sources of exact information on the size of firms entered by the younger and less able leavers, it is certain that many of them start work in firms too small for such provision to be possible. While recognizing that many youth employment officers regard their work as primarily a social service, we think there is room for further developments in regular advisory and welfare services and particularly commend a useful experiment recently carried out by one local education authority, whereby a voluntary social worker was attached to a school to establish contact with the girls before they left. Subsequently she continued to visit them at home during their first year of work and was freely available for consultation. This supplementation to the normal review process conducted by youth employment officers seems to us a particularly useful venture.

233. We have said little so far about the more formal processes of vocational guidance, operated jointly by the schools and the youth employment service, because there has been a number of recent publications on the transition from school to work. Generally speaking, there has been more development here than in the other aspects of preparation for leaving school. A whole team of adults may be available—head, youth employment officer, careers master, other teachers, housemasters, personal tutors—who between them can help boys and girls get a clearer picture of what the world of work is like. In large schools it may not be fanciful to look forward to a stage when there is a full-time counsellor available to advise the pupils throughout their school course and to prepare them for going out into the world. One significant aspect of vocational guidance work is that, apart from its importance in its own right, it provides a natural and acceptable means of keeping personal contact with older adolescents and unobtrusively supervising their general welfare.

4

234. We are glad to see that the youth employment service has been increased in recent years so that the officers can now give more time to individual pupils whom they are advising about careers and opportunities for further education. A good deal remains to be done, however. For instance, the law restricts the information about their leavers which headmasters may give to the youth employment officers. This particularly hampers them in interviewing our pupils many of whom will not have external examination results and other objective assessments to help them. There are also too many secondary modern schools which have no careers teachers.

235. It is surely important that there should be at least some one member of the staff whose special business it is to be knowledgeable about employment and further education, to organize reference and display material, and to make the essential liaison between school, parents, youth employment service and employment. It is important, too, that such a member of staff has a teaching programme which allows time to do these things. It may be even better, if he or she is the leader of a team of teachers—as is essential in a very large school. The more members of staff involved, the more useful knowledge is likely to percolate through the school; and it could obviously be an advantage to associate with the vocational guidance work some teacher who is well used to dealing with the less able pupils, and who will appreciate more readily what extra help they may need in sorting out the information available. Some heads are responsible for careers guidance themselves, and do it very well. But apart from the heavy demands this makes in all but very small schools, there is advantage in the knowledge accumulating in the staff room rather than being confined to the head's study.

236. In many areas schools arrange careers conventions in conjunction with the local youth employment service whose officers can suggest local organizations which might be approached to provide speakers, exhibition stands, or representatives who can give parents information on the day to day work in their own occupations. Rotary clubs have been particularly helpful in many areas, but it is important that there should not be undue emphasis on those occupations which require more formal education than our pupils are likely to achieve. A commendable feature has been the provision of examples of various local crafts and trades with young workers actually operating the machines or carrying out the processes in the school hall.

237. A major problem is how to ensure that the teachers themselves, apart from having the right contacts and the necessary sources of information, really understand the work situation as their pupils will meet it. Late entrants to the teaching profession who have themselves done other jobs will have a useful contribution to make here, but these will always be a minority of teachers. Our pupils, especially, present a difficulty. Where the older and abler pupils are going on to careers involving higher education and training, at least the initial stages on the road will not be unlike what the teachers have known themselves. It is more difficult for the teacher to become familiar with the commercial and industrial situation as it will be encountered by the young school leaver, although the vacation work done by students in training and the general encouragement now being given by the training colleges to gain wider working experience will be most valuable in this respect.

238. There would seem to be a strong need for many more courses and conferences for teachers which would bring them into contact with representatives of industry and further education institutions in their area. The youth employment service might develop important liaison functions in this connection, and would have need itself of additional resources of staff.

239. A most promising recent development has been the decision of the British Employers' Confederation to promote pilot "Introduction to Industry" schemes for serving teachers, with the possibility that some similar provision may be attempted for student teachers in training. Under such schemes it is suggested that selected teachers may spend a block period of two or three weeks, or a series of days spread over a period, with a particular company. Any experiments which are established should obviously be welcomed and watched with interest.

RECOMMENDATIONS

(a) The school programme in the final year ought to be deliberately outgoing—an initiation into the adult world of work and of leisure. (para. 210)

(b) The special function television and film can have as sources of information and stimulus needs to be more fully recognized, both in the equipment of schools and in the training of teachers. In particular:

i. The broadcasting organizations should pay special attention in their plans for the extension of school television to the great value of the medium in the education of "our" children, and to their special needs.

ii. Local education authorities should base their development plans on the concept of television receivers as necessary equipment for the education of our children.

iii. Training colleges and university departments of education should include in their courses some consideration of the significance of films and television as social and educational forces, as well as some preparation for the proper handling of school broadcasts in sound and television. (paras. 214—216).

(c) Experiments enabling some pupils over the age of fifteen to participate to a limited extent, under the auspices of the school, in the world of work in industry, commerce, or in other fields, should be carefully studied (paras. 222—227).

(d) All links with, and knowledge about, the youth employment service, further education, the youth service and adult organizations need strengthening. (paras. 228, 231, 233, 234)

(e) Schemes for augmenting the personal advisory and welfare service to young school leavers should be encouraged. (para. 232)

(f) All secondary schools need teachers with special responsibilities in careers work and adequate time and facilities to do it effectively. (para 235)

(g) Courses, conferences and schemes for enabling teachers to gain some familiarity with industry are much needed. (paras. 238 and 239)

CHAPTER 10

Examinations and Assessments

240. Boys and girls who stay at school until they are sixteen may reasonably look for some record of achievement when they leave. Some form of leaver's certificate which combined assessment with a record of the pupil's school career would be valued by parents, future employers and colleges of further education and should, we believe, be available to all pupils who complete a full secondary course. We are interested to see that a similar recommendation is contained in the report of a recent Working Party in Scotland[1], although we do not advocate any specific style of certificate such as is suggested there.

241. An assessment of the pupil by the school is essentially what we have in mind. Unfortunately, one of the most sought after forms of assessment, though one that is often misunderstood, is a public examination. We say unfortunately because we are convinced that for large numbers of the boys and girls with whom we are concerned public external examinations are not likely to offer a suitable means of assessment. Since we first began to consider our brief, the Minister has approved the proposals of the Beloe Committee for a whole new system of secondary examinations which will begin to operate in 1965. It will involve the teachers in new tasks, and create a situation in the working of the schools which is bound to affect all pupils in some degree, whether they are examination candidates or not. We think it important that the general public, especially parents and employers, should be kept well informed on the changes that are taking place and that they should understand the nature and the limits of the proposed examinations.

242. Many details about the new scheme are still uncertain, but some basic features can be stated. The examinations will be regionally not nationally organized. There will be room for local variations in the kind of papers set and for different methods of assessment or marking. The examinations will be open to pupils in the fifth year of a secondary school course. They will be different in character from existing G.C.E. examinations, and aimed at a band of candidates extending from those who just overlap the group taking the Ordinary level of the G.C.E. examination to those who are just below the average in ability. The new examinations are intended to be of such a standard that pupils above the average in general ability could hope to be successful in four or more subjects, while pupils a little below average might manage single subjects. Any pupil who is successful in one or more subjects will obtain a Certificate of Secondary Education.

243. Some points need particular stressing:
    (a) These examinations are not intended for all boys and girls.
    (b) The schools will be responsible for deciding whether or not it is in the interests of any pupil to enter for any public examination. No school is obliged to present any candidates and no pupil is obliged to enter.
    (c) Despite its title, the Certificate of Secondary Education will not by itself symbolize the satisfactory completion of a secondary course;

[1] "From School to Further Education" (H.M.S.O. 1963).

possession of a Certificate, or lack of one, will not necessarily be a measure of success or failure in school.

244. We are convinced that for a substantial number of pupils public examinations would be entirely inappropriate, and for a considerable number of others they would be appropriate over only a small part of their school work. In other words, we do not think that external examinations will provide a valid major incentive for many of the pupils with whom we are concerned. A longer school life will need to justify itself in other terms.

245. The general case for and against examinations has been set out both in the Crowther report and in the report of the Beloe Committee: we do not propose to repeat the arguments here. We accept the testimony of many schools that the introduction of G.C.E. courses has stimulated their abler pupils to hard and enthusiastic effort, and that success has strengthened the morale of pupils and teachers alike. Similar claims will no doubt be legitimately made for the newer examinations when these are established. We likewise strongly endorse the warning that the tendency of examinations to limit freedom in the curriculum and to restrict experiment could be especially harmful to pupils in the lower ability ranges, at a time when freedom to experiment with new educational patterns is most needed. We would reiterate the statement of the Crowther report:[1]

"In some subjects a good modern school education seems to us very difficult to reconcile with an external examination. If it is right, and we believe it is, that the approach to knowledge should be as little abstract as possible for boys and girls of ordinary ability if full use is to be made of their environment, then a good deal of the approach to history and the social sciences, to geography and to biology will be dictated by the character of the place in which the school is. In practical subjects also, the right teaching approach does not lie through a series of graded exercises standing by themselves, which is what a large-scale examination tends to encourage, however much the examiners may wish to discourage it."

246. Since, however, examinations are undoubtedly here to stay, and as time goes on the tendency is always for more rather than fewer pupils to be involved, we must seek means to minimise the more adverse effects. "Examinations Bulletin Number 1" of the Secondary Schools Examination Council, emphasizes the possibilities for experiment within the new scheme. Particularly valuable for the less able pupils would be the inclusion in the final assessment of "course work"—that is, work done during the year by the pupils as part of their normal assignments. Pupils who do not give of their best in the strained and artificial circumstances for examination, but who could work responsibly when not flustered or harassed by strict time limits, would benefit from such a provision. Some types of work, in the crafts for example, would lend themselves more easily to this treatment, but the difficulties of including other work would not be insuperable.

247. Another feature which we should welcome would be an emphasis on oral work. Any test of the pupils' attainments ought to include their command of spoken English. Although the techniques of examining will need careful exploration, the tape recorder has made it possible to contemplate an assessment of the pupils' performance in the ordinary classroom situation: they might,

_____
[1] "15 to 18" paragraph 127.

for example, be recorded giving short prepared talks to the class group, and afterwards engaging the group in discussion. If this kind of examination practice led to schools paying more attention to oral work this would be one case where examinations were educationally beneficial.

248. Thirdly, we hope some means may be found to take account of the teacher's opinion of the candidate, especially where this may be at variance with the examination performance. Many other European countries do accept the principle of referring to the special knowledge the teacher has of the pupil—just as they also commonly include oral work as a recognized part of examinations.

249. The Certificate of Secondary Education will be based on a fifth year examination. The returns from our own schools survey showed that fifty-seven per cent of the modern schools were taking in 1961–62 some form of fourth-year examination, and that thirty per cent of the boys in the lower half of the ability range in those schools, and thirty-four per cent of the girls, were fourth-year examination candidates. All the arguments against fourth-year examinations have particular force in relation to the less able pupils, even though the examination in some cases may have been a bait to persuade the pupils to stay an extra term or two. As long as boys and girls are leaving school after four years, there is little time available anyway in which to attempt the more adult work which we have been urging; the demands of an external examination at that stage would impose a further limitation. When the school-leaving age is raised to sixteen, the natural tendency will be in any case to take whatever examinations are thought to be appropriate at the end of the school course, i.e. at the end of the fifth year. Meanwhile, we stongly urge that schools should not enter pupils for external examinations before the fifth year, and that they would be well advised to look forward to a future situation in which the minimum secondary school course must be planned to the age of sixteen.

250. Over the next few years, the schools will be exceedingly busy with the problems of devising and operating examinations of a kind and on a scale which they have not known before. The responsibilities of the teachers will be heavy. The more seriously they take those responsibilities, the greater will be the danger that their energies will be diverted from non-examination work and from the educational needs of their pupils as a whole. For those pupils who are only slightly, or not at all, involved in the external examinations, it will be more than ever urgent to experiment with interesting and demanding forms of work, if they are to be convinced that what they are doing is of any consequence.

251. Historically a good deal of prestige has attached to external examinations in the non-selective schools. The schools have been anxious to do fairly by their abler pupils, and their success, particularly with G.C.E. courses, has helped to strengthen the confidence both of parents and of the teachers themselves. There has been a tendency for the "examination forms" to acquire a disproportionately high status, unless the schools have been particularly sensitive to this danger. It may be that this exaggerated regard for examinations will disappear as examinations of one kind or another become more commonplace. On the other hand, the more pupils who enter for examinations, the greater the risk of creating a sense of rejection among the dwindling

numbers of those who do not. If the schools are not to have a seriously depressed class of pupils on their hands, they will need to give a more positive, distinctive character to the programmes of these non-examinees.

252. Here, a choice of subjects or of courses with some unifying theme such as we have urged earlier; projects which include some short-term but intensive work, the object of which is clear to the pupils themselves; a deliberate policy of giving publicity to these activities in the school and among the parents; even the simple matter of giving a distinctive title to the form or the course, will help to maintain morale as well as interest. Most boys and girls are able to accept realistically differences of ability among themselves; it is not the fact that they all cannot attempt the same work, but the realization by some pupils that what they are doing is not valued by the community, which is most likely to produce a sense of rejection, apathy or hostility.

253. When classes contain a mixture of pupils, some of them entering for examinations in some subjects, and others not, a real teaching problem will arise. Where numbers allow, separate examination and non-examination sets drawn across two forms may be the best answer. Where this is not practicable, much organizational skill will be demanded of the teacher to ensure that the non-examinees do not merely trail along on a syllabus which is geared to examination requirements. The difficulties are probably less in craft subjects, where work is on a largely individual basis, than in subjects like English and history, where set reading or periods of study may be involved. The selective schools have had some dispiriting parallels, in the pupils who "drop" a G.C.E. subject half-way through a school year, and who then remain nominally in the class, merely filling in time till the end of the year.

254. For all pupils, balance is needed between those activities which are examined and those which are not. No pupil, however able, ought to be occupied exclusively with examination work, or to feel that time and energies spent on anything else are wasted. Still less ought the pupils who attempt only a small amount of examination work to feel that this is the only part of their course that counts. Subjects like religious instruction, literature, art and music could be particularly affected, or activities like class discussion, whose value generally does not lie in any measurable results. The attitude of the head and of the staff will be decisive here. Only if they show that they value parts of the curriculum that are not examined or examinable will the pupils value them also. They may show it in various ways—by ensuring, for example, that the heads of department take some non-examination work, and by encouraging public displays, exhibitions, and activities such as concerts and plays and conferences, whose interest lies in themselves. A pupil's programme will be justified only if it makes educational sense as a whole, whether it is subject to external examinations or not.

255. If the schools are to act wisely over this, they will need understanding support. They will need to be free of external pressures to put as many pupils as possible through as many subjects as possible, as a matter of local prestige. We should deplore, for example, any practice of publishing lists of external examination results, thereby indirectly promoting local competitive rivalries which would tend to reduce the freedom of action of individual schools. And we should strongly champion the right of any school to abstain altogether

from public examinations if the head and staff were convinced that the best interests of the pupils required this.

256. We believe that the support of parents will generally be given, if the schools and local education authorities take parents sufficiently into their confidence about what is happening. There is evidence now that parents are increasingly willing, and even anxious, for their children to stay on at school, without any special bait of examination certificates, if the school has a real policy for the less able pupils and makes it known. Parents and the general public must be kept well informed if some dangerous misconceptions of what the new examinations and certificates stand for are to be avoided. Examinations, however carefully organized, are at best rough-and-ready measuring instruments, useful enough, as long as their limitations are appreciated.

257. The hope is expressed in Examinations Bulletin No. 1 that all concerned with the C.S.E. " will do all they can to secure a wider understanding among parents and users of the Certificate of the limitation of public examinations", and that "they will encourage users of the Certificates to seek other evidence of the qualities and potentialities of school leavers". Similarly the Beloe Committee expressed the hope that while employers and those concerned with selection for further education courses will obviously find the information contained on examination certificates useful, they will treat this as "only one piece of evidence among others, notably school records". The youth employment service can be of valuable assistance here, both in urging employers to pay attention to the schools' assessments and in advising the schools on the kind of information and the manner of presentation which is likely to be helpful to employers. In the field of further education, too, there is a double need for information, both in the selection of a boy or girl for a job which may be associated, we hope increasingly, with a course of training or part-time education; and in direct selection for courses by further education institutions. Here personal links between the college principals and the schools are essential.

258. For many pupils, "other pieces of evidence" may be the most important: employers, as one headmaster reminds us, "do not always want clever people". Other qualities, whether in employment or in private life, may count high: patience and persistence in seeing a job through, for example, where care matters rather than speed; general attitudes to learning, rather than performance in a single test; honesty, cheerfulness, pleasant manners and an ability to get on with people.

259. For the more personal qualities, we doubt whether any public document is desirable, although some schools have told us of interesting experiments with "character certificates" which they find have an incentive value for all their pupils in the last year at school. We should feel some reluctance for sixteen year-olds to be saddled with a permanent record of their past inadequacies. Entry into employment or into further education is for some boys and girls an opportunity to start afresh. In general we should feel that the best means of conveying purely personal information about the pupils, where it is legitimately requested, is still in confidential letters from the head, and that this will be easier where contact between the schools and the neighbourhood is close.

260. There is, however, other information about the pupils' work and progress, and general participation in school life, which might usefully find a place in a purely internal leaving certificate such as we proposed at the outset of this chapter. And here, despite experiments by some schools, we believe important work remains to be done in discovering the best form and manner of supplying the information. We can see the certificate meeting several needs. For the pupils who have taken no external examinations, it could contain some assessment of progress based, perhaps, on the whole final year's work at school, rather than on one examination. For other pupils, it could supplement the Certificate of Secondary Education by recording what studies had been followed other than in subjects externally examined. Or again, since the introduction of elective "courses", such as we advocate, may involve the dropping of some subjects entirely from the beginning of the fourth year, the pupils might find it helpful to have on record that they have followed a basic course in school for at least three years in a subject which does not appear in the final course or in any external examination certificate.

261. We see no simple formula offering clear-cut policies to the schools for dealing with examinations. In as far as the teachers are able to assume fully the opportunities and responsibilities that are offered to them under the new Certificate of Secondary Education proposals, they have it in their power to shape the examinations which will inevitably assume importance for large numbers of boys and girls, rather than to allow education to be shaped by the examinations. But the more pupils there are who acquire examination certificates, the more squarely the schools are faced with a duty to deal faithfully with the rest—a very substantial number of boys and girls. Living sensibly in a world which prizes examinations means taking the mystique out of their results, and making education worth while to the unexamined.

RECOMMENDATIONS

(a) All pupils who remain at school till the age of sixteen should receive some form of internal school leaving certificate. This need not follow a uniform pattern, but local consultation between schools, the youth employment service, further education and employers would be helpful in arriving at a form most likely to be useful to the pupil. Such a certificate for some pupils would include a record of achievements in public examinations. (paras. 240, 260, 261)

(b) No pupils should be entered for any external examination before the fifth year; schools should look ahead to a situation in which all pupils will be in full-time education to sixteen. (para. 249)

(c) In relation to the new public examinations for the Certificate of Secondary Education, each school has an individual decision to take. The new system offers a tool for teachers to use where and as they judge appropriate. It should not be allowed to shape the whole education offered by the schools. (paras. 250, 255)

(d) We are convinced that many of the pupils with whom this report is concerned ought not to be entered for public examinations; and that for all the pupils a substantial part of the curriculum should be unexamined. (paras. 244, 254)

(e) For those pupils who do enter, we hope that oral work, "course" work, and the teacher's assessment will play a significant part in the new examinations. (paras. 246–248)

(f) There is urgent need to keep parents and the general public, especially employers, well informed as to the nature of the new examination schemes. (para. 256)

Great threat for non-examinees to be
dis-regarded & not counted as
important. Too great a stress
laid on examinations & thus
enjoyment is taken out of subject
if it has to be learned as a
matter of course.

CHAPTER 11

Building for the Future

262. It is no part of our task to elaborate a blue print for school buildings, playing fields and equipment. Nor would we wish to do so at a time when there is need for bold experiment in the content and methods of education for many pupils in the secondary schools.

263. We cannot, however, ignore the physical environment of the schools. Educational experiment has usually taken place in buildings designed to meet past or current educational ideas, rather than those which it is the object of the experiments to test or develop. This has inhibited experiment, and made the results difficult to interpret. In our view, the nature of the new educational solutions that are needed will involve major alterations in current school design.

264. This is clear from much of the evidence we have received. This unquestionably challenges the accepted curriculum and teaching methods, and consequently and inevitably, the accepted design of the accommodation. For example:

"A change in physical environment, a change in curriculum and a change in educational approach . . ."

"Secondary school buildings will need to be specifically designed for a more informal and less academic approach . . . There seems little doubt that the existing subject curriculum and traditional timetable are not meeting fully the needs of pupils of average and less than average ability."

" . . . and the necessity for research and experiment in this field is emphasized".

"Is it even clear, for instance, that the traditional sort of school day . . . is necessarily the right sort of pattern for the group we are now discussing?"

" . . . More could be learnt from the curriculum and methods used in good special schools and classes."

"The teachers' job with this age group should be accomplished through group work and elective study."

" . . . releasing them for one day each week to work in a technical college."

"Workshops designed in a new way and in new groupings."

"These practical rooms need not be very large, because they should be used only by small groups."

"There still remains a great deal of scope for extending education outside the school buildings."

265. This evidence needs to be read against the background of our own survey of existing school buildings. The detailed results of this survey are given in chapter 25. But there is one important point that needs making here. About four-fifths of the schools in the modern school sample fall short of the currently accepted standards, and these are the standards which we regard as inappropriate to the needs of the pupils with whom we are concerned. We draw attention in particular to the fact that less than two-thirds of the schools

have a library room of more than 500 sq. ft.; over half the schools have no provision of any kind for music; a third of the schools have no proper science laboratory; half the schools have no gymnasium, or, even if allowance is made for small schools which may have suitable halls designed to serve also as gymnasium, two-fifths of the schools are left with no gymnasium and no compensating facilities in the size and equipment of the hall. There is a general shortage of teaching spaces and of large classrooms. In addition, a quarter of all the schools in the sample are both poorly accommodated indoors and seriously deficient in playing field provision out-of-doors.

266. We recognize that this situation may be thought to pose an impossible dilemma. On the one hand, it can be argued that if so many schools fall below current standards, and some of them far below, all available resources should be concentrated on meeting those needs, without for the time being attempting to substitute different and probably more expensive standards. On the other hand, it can be argued with almost equal force that it would be educationally wrong, and an unwise use of resources, to build or remodel so many schools to meet yesterday's needs.

267. In our view, this dilemma must be faced and resolved. We believe that it can be, but only by creating new knowledge on which to base the necessary judgements on the size of the building programme needed to meet current and future requirements, and on the timing of changes in building policy. Accordingly, we believe that a boldly experimental approach is needed not only to establish educational needs, and the means of reflecting them in a new physical environment, but also as a basis for formulating future policy for school building. Nevertheless, we do not think that generations of school children should be condemned to existing conditions until experiments have continued long enough to establish new standards.

268. Fortunately, the Development Group of the Ministry's Architects and Building Branch were already thinking along similar lines, and we are grateful to the Ministry for making available to us the Diagrams and Comment which follow. We found that these illustrated very well some of the ideas we were forming and we decided to include them in our report; but the Ministry is continuing its investigations and neither we nor it should be regarded as committed to any particular solutions. None of the diagrams which follow is intended as a fully developed design for part of a complete school. Nor do the diagrams together set out to cover all aspects of a school's work and activities.

Some examples of an experimental approach supplied by the Development Group of the Ministry's Architects and Building Branch.

    I. The diagrams are an attempt to give architectural application to the following assumptions:

        (*a*) that for part of the time some pupils will be out in the adult world on their own;

        (*b*) that the time they spend 'on the campus' will be so arranged that they will be able to carry through a particular job of work, or pursue a particular interest with reasonable continuity—i.e. that the day will not be fragmented into 35 minute particles;

(c) that they will have a personal interest and concern in the actual running of the community and the actual maintenance of the grounds and buildings;

(d) that each will have some degree of choice in the work he or she does;

(e) that it will be hard to draw firm demarcation lines either between subjects or between the practical and the academic;

(f) that for part of the time pupils will work individually on both practical and reference studies, but with experts and helpers always available; and for part of the time in groups of varying sizes (half a dozen or so for special coaching; 15–20 for a discussion group; 50 or 60 listening to a lecture or watching a film),

(g) that clubs and societies will form an integral part of the educational course;

(h) that each person, as well as belonging to a number of working groups and societies, will also be a member of a social club, the organization of which will be partly the responsibility of the pupils;

(i) that the staff will consist of an interesting mixture of teachers who have come through the normal grammar school/training college or university channels, and other qualified teachers with a variety of backgrounds. In addition, they will be supplemented by occasional help from expert outside persons, and by visiting speakers and discussion leaders— perhaps an industrialist, a politician or a minister of religion, for instance.

(j) that the staff will work in small groups, each with a modest H.Q. of its own, and each responsible for the pastoral care and the individual work programme of a number of the pupils. There will also be accommodation for the staff as a whole, to enable its members to meet regularly both formally and informally, and to preserve the sense of unity and corporate responsibility for the working and social life of the school.

(k) that the pupils will similarly be divided into socially identifiable groups, each with accommodation reflecting in some way or other the group's identity, and each with a stable relationship with one or more members of the staff.

II. *Diagrams* 1, 2 *and* 3 are all examples of ways in which the accommodation might provide for a move away from the traditional division of the curriculum into separate subjects, towards an approach to teaching in which different activities are viewed as facets of the whole, with each facet informing and vitalising all others.

III. In the Centre shown in *Diagram* 1 there is a group of teaching staff who are responsible for a variety of work connected with sciences and crafts. Here there are pupils working in groups of various sizes, or individually. Some are engaged in craftwork—woodwork, casting, glazing, soldering, clay-modelling, carving. Others are making scientific investigations, both indoors and out. Others are engaged in work connected with the grounds and buildings. Some are drawing and designing; some are reading reference books; some are writing up reports and sorting out material. All are involved in a mixture of practical skills, reference, writing or drawing.

IV. To the right, as one enters, there is a shop window displaying some of the things designed and made here (more are exhibited inside, with full working drawings and reports). Behind this is a small pottery and modelling studio, opening onto a covered area for carving. The central circulation area provides a visual and physical connection between the various workshop areas to the right, the reference and design areas to the left, and the indoor and outdoor spaces for science.

V. There are groups of people working in the studios, group rooms and drawing bays, as well as in the workshops and laboratories. A few people are mending machinery in the large covered area which links the wood shop, the construction shop and the groundsman's office. (Others are out constructing a tennis court or a building with quantities, calculations, scaled drawings, reporting, etc. included as part of the job). There is a group in the construction shop setting out the frame of a garden shed with full-size details chalked on the wall. There are also a few working in the garden and the greenhouse.

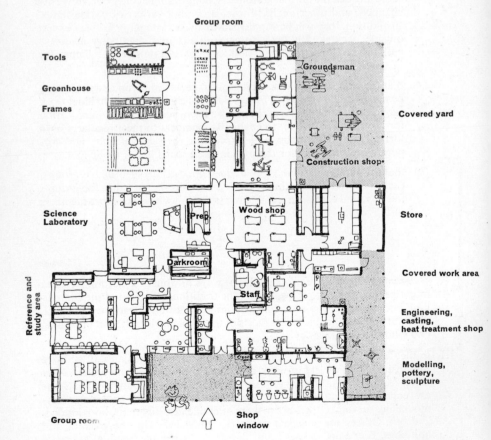

DIAGRAM 1
Science and Crafts Centre

VI. The simple flat-floored drama room shown in *Diagram* 2 is not a theatre (although tiered seating could be set up for a small audience on folding platform units), but a setting for everyday dramatic activities where experiments are made in different forms of action and movement, lighting, and scenic effects. Costumes and properties can be designed and made in the adjoining studio, which is equipped for light craftwork, drawing and painting. It is planned round a central materials store and service unit, and has large uninterrupted wall surfaces for murals and displays. These two spaces are higher than the rest, with galleries over the low curtained recess and drama store, thus providing additional space for storage, experimental lighting, equipment and acting.

VII. Off the studio are several reference and seminar rooms for small group or individual work, one of them with projection facilities, another with reference books and periodicals. There is, also, a small sound, lighting and television studio where record playing, sound effects and radio equipment can be used, and in which there is also a simple television camera channel.

VIII. Much of the musical work has links with the drama and movement. For smaller orchestral or choral work the music room is appropriate, but on occasions the drama studio is used. In addition to the practice rooms are small listening booths wired up for tape-recording and record playing. There is also a store for instruments.

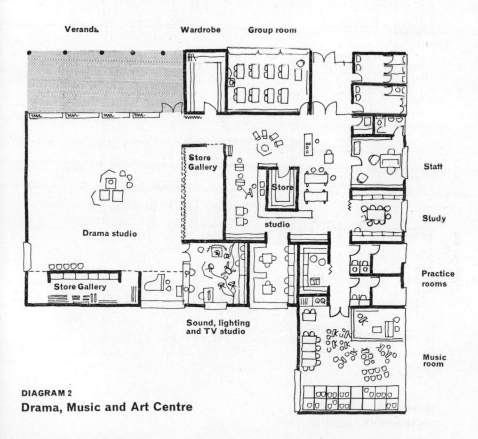

DIAGRAM 2
Drama, Music and Art Centre

IX. In the centre shown in *Diagram* 3 a wide range of crafts can be pursued. The various studios surround a small open garden court for outdoor work and display, and each studio leads out to a veranda for work under cover. At the entrance there are areas for display. To the right of these is a small room for group discussions and the reading of reference books. The five studios are inter-connected by common work areas, but at the same time a measure of separation is provided for the specialist equipment. Thus the bay for blockmaking and printing leads to the drawing and painting area. This in turn leads, through folding doors, into the textile studio designed for fabric printing, weaving and embroidery. Continuing ant-clockwise there are areas offering wide scope for three dimensional work including the use of woods, metals, plaster and clay. Storage is provided for small equipment under benches, in cupboards and drawers, and there are store rooms for the large quantities of materials and work which accumulate wherever there is lively craft work in progress. Such a centre might offer courses both to pupils and and adults, and local craftsmen might be part-time members of the staff.

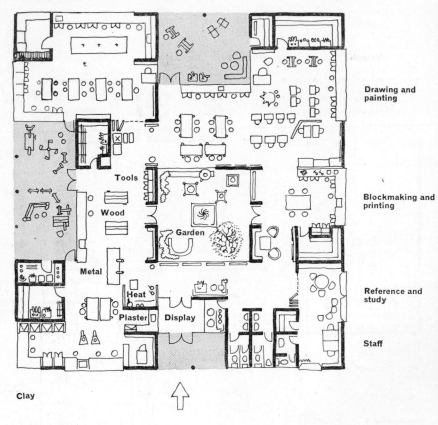

Textiles studio

Drawing and painting

Blockmaking and printing

Reference and study

Staff

Three-dimensional workshop

Tools

Wood

Metal

Heat

Plaster

Display

Garden

Clay

DIAGRAM 3
Arts Centre

X. *Diagram* 4 is an example of one of the ways in which accommodation might be provided for the younger of the pupils with whom we are concerned. It provides clearly identifiable homes for the pupils and their teachers, without either imposing or making impossible the traditional pattern of one teacher to one class; but it is assumed that a small group of adults together plan the varying patterns of work and recreation. It also provides a social centre for the group as a whole, and many and varied opportunities for using whatever approach to teaching is best suited to capture the interest and imagination of the pupils.

XI. As one approaches this Centre across the paved garden court one sees that the accommodation is divided broadly into three inter-communicating parts: to the left and right a series of spaces designed for groups of roughly 100 or 120 children; and straight ahead a common room and lunch area overlooking the veranda and garden.

XII. The working areas on either side consist in principle of a central work studio and resource area, connected to rooms of varying size and character which can be adjusted for different kinds of groups. In these rooms there are areas in which a few people can work on their own, low window seats and working surfaces, plenty of storage and display space, and small bays for the teachers' records and equipment. In addition, the staff office near the entrance is also suitable for small group work, special coaching or meetings. The central studio has sinks, study bays, workshop facilities and- most important- a resource store designed for a rich display of materials and objects to encourage creative work.

XIII. Such a working and social centre can provide opportunities for a broad approach to learning, in which both theory and practice can be mixed in varying degrees. It has elements in it both of the formal classroom and of the workshop, craftroom or laboratory. Whereas new techniques and skills will be acquired in more specialized accommodation elsewhere, individual exploration and improvisation will be encouraged here.

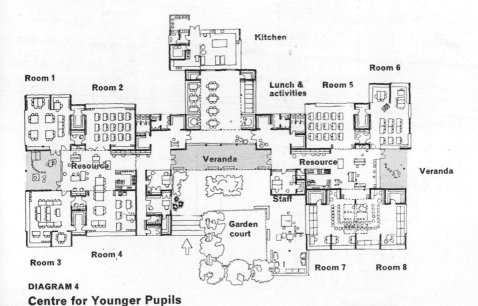

DIAGRAM 4
Centre for Younger Pupils

XIV. *Diagrams 5 and 6* are examples of possible ways of meeting some of the needs of the young adults at the top of the secondary schools, and of those who have just left, on a basis designed to build bridges between the world of the school and the world outside.

XV. This club house shown in *Diagram 5* is primarily a social centre for older pupils and adults, but it is also used for teaching and study purposes. There are three parts to it: on the right, the social, study and dining areas; in the centre the games room; and on the left the home management centre, over which is a small visitors' bedroom wing for lecturers, students, exchange visitors from abroad, or possibly a member of the staff or a few of the pupils. In the right hand block there are some older pupils helping in the main kitchen and dining room with the preparation and serving of lunch—as a preliminary to possible further training in catering. They have a smaller, separate room where they can work on their own. Others are running the shop and snack bar. Others again are working in the group study room off the common room.

XVI. Across the veranda in the home management centre, the staff group includes the visiting nurse, doctor and social worker, and others are called in from time to time. The people here are concerned with the study of health, family and community. There is again a mixture of book work and practice—but the practice includes real situations. Some people are running the visitors' wing upstairs and the small dining room and kitchen: they entertain visitors and order supplies, look after the services, laundering and equipment under the guidance of the housekeeper and caretaker. Some are learning about maintenance, repairs and services in the home workshop next to the boiler and meters. Others are dressmaking or making curtains for an old peoples' home. A few are typing reports and accounts. At certain times there are films, television and discussions in the larger central area. The first aid unit is here and beds are available for those feeling unwell.

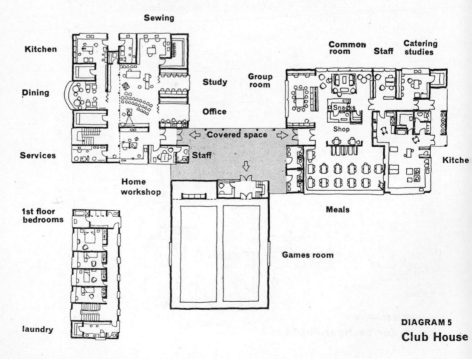

DIAGRAM 5
Club House

XVII. *Diagram* 6 shows a less elaborate centre, designed primarily as a common meeting ground—a centre for which perhaps 120 or so young adults at the top of the school might largely assume responsibility. It consists of three parts: a central entrance space with a snack counter; to the right the lavatories (with a powder room for the girls), and lockers for all personal belongings; to the left, three common rooms. Two of these are connected by sliding folding doors so that a larger space can be made available for a dance or a lecture. Each room has window seats in bays for small conversational groups, shelves for books and magazines, individual study or writing places, comfortable chairs, carpets and curtains. In addition there is a small office for committee meetings and administrative work. This setting is designed to provide a common ground between the oldest pupils and their friends in the adult world.

XVIII. We would emphasize that none of these diagrams has been prepared as part of a fully developed design for a complete school: they are included simply to illustrate the ways in which architectural thinking ought to go hand in hand with, and to contribute to, the study of the educational problems to which we have drawn attention. Moreover, the Diagrams are all firmly rooted in the educational ideas and practice of teachers who are now grappling with the problems with which we are concerned, often with little or no help from their physical environment."

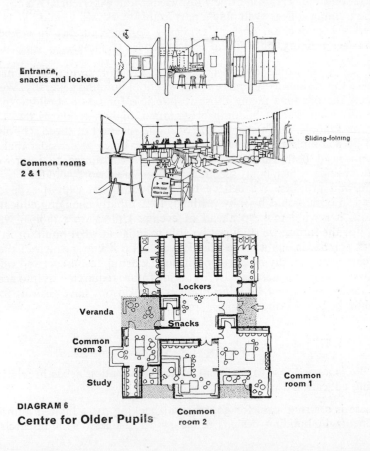

Entrance, snacks and lockers

Sliding-folding

Common rooms 2 & 1

Lockers

Veranda

Snacks

Common room 3

Study

Common room 1

DIAGRAM 6

Centre for Older Pupils

Common room 2

269. The Council would urge that the main need is for bold educational experiment in which the development and testing of new educational ideas will recognize the intimate relationship that exists between the physical environment and educational possibilities. The building should both reflect and enhance the quality of the school's work: it cannot do so unless educational aims, and the environment within which they are to be realized, are considered together as aspects of the total purposes of education.

270. The experiments which we have in mind should not therefore be confined to one or two aspects of the curriculum, or one or two experimental school buildings. We wish to see a much more comprehensive approach, in which all aspects of the work of the schools will be studied in a context which ensures that building design will both inform, and be informed by, developing educational ideas. While therefore we certainly consider that a limited number of experimental projects involving whole schools should be mounted with government support, as part of the further studies which we recommend elsewhere in this report, we should also like to see a major development of local initiative. There are many opportunities available within the present building programme, and within current cost limits, to provide buildings designed to test and develop new educational ideas. And even where such projects have to be limited in scope, they may none the less make an invaluable contribution to the creation of new knowledge and experience. We also hope that the training colleges will play a part in this work: we should like to see a number of experimental projects explicitly designed for use in connection with teacher training, both initial and in-service training.

271. Finally, we would emphasize that we are not urging the immediate raising of the cost limits per place for new school building generally. We fully recognize the dilemma facing those responsible for school building policy: within any given size of building programme, higher standards must mean fewer new schools, and a slower rate of modernization of those schools that do not need complete replacement. At the same time, we consider that there is urgent need both for a major rebuilding programme to improve the conditions under which many secondary schools now work, and for a series of experimental projects. We believe that the additional capital expenditure involved in both would be fully justified. In a rapidly changing educational situation, it is vital to keep ahead of events. Unless we establish what is needed for the future, we shall not be able to judge at what point, or in what respects, standards ought to be raised: we shall not know which of the new needs can be met simply by a redisposition of existing resources: and we shall not know what opportunities exist for taking future requirements into account in the design of current building projects. We do not have to wait for the millenium before making a start.

RECOMMENDATIONS

(a) There is a need for reassessment of accommodation needs in relation to changing educational patterns. (paras. 263, 264)

(b) There is a strong case for government backing for a limited number of experiments in building design, to be associated also with research into

educational methods, teacher training, and the pattern of the school programme. These should start now, to provide information for future large
scale development. (paras. 267, 269–271)

(c) The improvement of conditions in existing schools should not be delayed
while experimental designs are tried out. We draw attention to the functional
deficiencies of many schools in our survey, particularly in relation to the
inadequate provision of practical rooms, science laboratories, libraries, and
in the size and design of classrooms. Some of these deficiencies which are
due to overcrowding in otherwise good modern buildings arc relative, and
could be relieved. But other buildings, particularly in slum areas, are so
totally inadequate as to require urgent replacement. (paras. 265, 271. cf. also
Chapter 25)

*Attention is drawn here also to other points relating to buildings appearing in
the report:*

(d) Few schools at present have adequate facilities for the social needs of
older pupils. Extended extra-curricular programmes are likely to make increased demands on buildings in the future. (Chapters 6 and 8)

(e) In the evolution of new designs, the neighbourhood needs of the community should be considered, especially in heavily built-up areas. (Chapter 3,
paras. 71, 73; Chapter 6 paras. 146–148 and Chapter 17, para. 409)

(f) Due provision should be made in all schools for developments in educational methods requiring new equipment or the more extensive use of existing
types of equipment, including all audio-visual aids. (Chapter 9 paras. 215,
216 and Chapter 19, para. 496)

CHAPTER 12

The Teachers Needed

272. Whatever happens in the schools depends on the men and women who staff them. Imaginative accommodation, modern equipment, skilful organization, a determined attack on social and economic handicaps—all of these are necessary to progress, but the key figure remains the teacher. This fact is confirmed again and again by the remarkable achievements of some schools in the most adverse conditions, and by the evidence that boys' and girls' behaviour, confidence and attitude to work can all be shaped by successful relations with individual teachers: what ultimately counts is a person.

273. In the teaching situation success depends on more than having a kindly and sympathetic interest in young people: most men and women who choose the teaching profession as their career can be counted on to possess that; control is required also, and knowledge, which the pupils respect, and the professional skill to transmit that knowledge to boys and girls whose own manner and means of learning may be different from the teacher's own.

274. That is why in this chapter we find it necessary to consider both the work of the teachers in the schools and the implications for professional training. In doing so we do not wish to appear to be entering into questions of detailed planning which are properly the concern of the National Advisory Council on the Training and Supply of Teachers: but we do feel bound to draw attention to those aspects of training which particularly affect the educational problems at issue.

275. For many years much anxious calculation has gone into questions of teacher supply. We believe no less anxious consideration must be given to the question of demand: not simply how many teachers are needed, but what kind of teachers, with what professional and personal resources, do the schools require to do their job? To ask this question is realistic, even in face of the formidable prospect of continuing shortages: one way to mitigate the effects of the shortages is to make sure that the teachers who are available are equipped to tackle the job which requires to be done; ways to improve supply are to widen the basis of recruitment and to make the work attractive by showing that it is personally and professionally satisfying in its demands.

276. Here we must urgently draw attention again to the special difficulty of securing and retaining good teachers, for schools of all kinds, in slum, heavy industrial and other ill-favoured areas. The children of these areas, because of their surroundings, are severely handicapped at the outset of their education, and they stand in need of especially gifted teachers. In these times of teacher shortages, however, to which we see no early end, highly gifted and experienced teachers can choose where they will work; and, although some with a strong sense of vocation fortunately do choose to work in the least attractive areas, many, understandably enough, do not. These areas in consequence tend to have more than their share of teachers who cannot secure other appointments, coupled with a formidable turnover of teachers who are only there until they can move elsewhere.

277. This problem of uneven distribution of highly qualified and experienced teachers will not be solved merely by increasing the general supply of teachers. The Crowther report drew attention to the serious difficulties, and made a recommendation:

"The bad areas, which pay more than their fair share of the price for a shortage of teachers, need a direct attack on their problem. There should be an attempt to discover by experiment whether financial incentives to teachers to serve in difficult areas would be effective" (para 658 (k)).

The problem has remained unsolved and still largely unrecognized. Until it is solved, large numbers of boys and girls, including many of those with whom we are particularly concerned, will continue to be penalized by the accident of their environment. For this reason we have already recommended, in Chapter 3. that a Working Party on the slum areas should investigate ways of staffing the schools satisfactorily, and we hope that it would offer solutions applicable to ill-favoured areas in general. We include as an appendix to this report a paper submitted to us in evidence which reached us too late for discussion with the appropriate professional bodies, but which suggests one way of grappling with the problem of the deployment of teachers. We can at present see no alternative to some solution involving the recruitment of a special body of teachers who are ready to go where they are needed in return for financial compensation, whether under schemes centrally operated through the Ministry or by groups of local education authorities working on a consortium basis. What is quite certain is that this is a matter of urgent educational concern which must be faced.

278. One of the problems, as many heads assure us, in finding teachers for our pupils is just the lack of a sufficiently attractive professional image. Most people enjoy teaching the abler pupils : the response is quicker and surer, interest is more readily established and maintained—and discipline the easier for that reason—and the teacher welcomes the sense of intellectual challenge. Teaching the very backward is also attractive in a different way: the teacher is often moved by a deeply compassionate desire to help those pupils who seem to be heavily handicapped, the dependence of the pupils can lead to a particularly close personal relation, and even their slow progress is a proper source of professional pride. It is the pupils in the middle, the majority of our pupils, and indeed the majority of all boys and girls, who excite the least professional interest: too often seemingly rather dull pupils get rather dull teaching, with equally dull results.

279. In discussing the teaching demands made by our pupils, we should make it clear, though we hope the implication is plain throughout the whole report, that we are not designating any special corps of teachers for "average and less than average" pupils. We are concerned with the majority of teachers in the non-selective schools, in which our pupils constitute the majority of the pupils. Any system of training or of appointment which would tend to create in a school separate categories of staff or of pupils is to be avoided; and any students who are proposing to teach in secondary modern and comprehensive schools should include in their training some study of the pedagogic problems presented by our pupils. Similarly their training ought to be preparing them now for the new situation which will exist when all our pupils are in school till the age of sixteen, with the many implications that will

have for the nature of the curriculum and of the relation between teachers and older pupils.

280. Many heads have stressed that for the sake of morale all pupils should feel that they are enjoying a fair share of the school's resources, whether in special facilities or in teachers with special knowledge and experience, in science, for instance, or the craft subjects or physical education. Equally, heads of departments in subjects such as English or mathematics should contribute to the teaching widely throughout the school. They obviously cannot teach all the pupils every year, but their work ought to be so disposed over several years that they meet different ability and age groups, and thereby acquire a cumulative experience of the teaching problems of their subject which they can discuss with other members of their departments. This principle will be especially important to preserve in face of the growth of public examinations in secondary schools, since the time and energies of the senior staff are likely to be in heavy demand for examination work. It is frequently urged that teaching average pupils requires more than average professional skill; what is not so often noted is the intellectual challenge to the teacher presented by these pupils, with whom, even more than with the most able, he has to act as mediator and interpreter of his subject.

281. Only the most backward pupils—the lowest ten to fifteen per cent perhaps of the whole ability range—probably ought to be singled out as a group to be taught for the larger part of their time by one special teacher. Even here, we think it in the pupils' interest as they grow older that they should rub shoulders with their abler fellows, as they will in the world outside school, and get accustomed to working with a greater number and variety of teachers. As for the teachers, even those most dedicated to the care of backward children ought from time to time to have the personal stimulus of undertaking a wider range of work.

282. Given, then, that most of the staff of the school may be expected to take some part in the teaching of our pupils, what qualifications and resources will the teachers need, to provide the kind of programme which we have suggested elsewhere in this report as desirable? In particular how can greater coherence over the curriculum as a whole be contrived, and a larger craft and practical element be included? One way of giving coherence is through continuity of contact with particular persons. The school can attempt this by various means, socially, for example, through tutors and housemasters, or through form teachers to whom real supervisory responsibilities are delegated; in the classroom, by ensuring that there is some continuity from year to year in the persons who teach particular groups of pupils—and that the groups do not get reshuffled too frequently; and most commonly of all, perhaps, by arranging that some one person teaches the group often enough to establish a close personal relation with the pupils.

283. The traditional, and still valued, method of supplying this last kind of continuity is through a form-teacher who takes the form for a substantial part of its work. In practice, this has usually meant that the subjects which were regarded as "not specialist"—religious instruction, English and mathematics, particularly—have been assigned to the form-teacher, with the grave disadvantage that, despite some excellent work, these subjects have too often

been handled with an amateurism not accepted in other parts of the curriculum, and they have been among the least well taught. Yet they constitute what many people would regard as the essential core of general education.

284. While we accept the form-teacher principle, we urge more widespread re-thinking of the basis on which form teachers are assigned. It is enough that they should be capable of teaching with confidence and competence some two or three subjects which, together, would give them a substantial amount of time with a particular group of pupils: but there is nothing to be gained by a teacher taking his form in subjects of which he knows too little to teach effectively. There seems no logical reason why the "form" subjects should be confined to the range which is still traditional in many schools. More useful groupings, and more manageable from the teacher's point of view, might be subjects which were related in some way. Typical combinations might be English and social studies; English, drama, art; English, religious instruction and social studies; biology and rural studies; biology and geography; geography and mathematics or science; science and housecraft; housecraft, art and needlework; mathematics, technical drawing and handicraft; music, drama and physical education. There are many other possibilities. The starting point should be the range of subjects and interests which one teacher can reasonably hope to handle, not an unwarranted assumption that some subjects are inherently "form" subjects. We have stressed elsewhere the unsatisfactory situation that often arises from this assumption in religious instruction and in English.

285. We think it reasonable and desirable that the majority of teachers should, in addition to offering one major subject which they are competent to teach at all levels in the school, be able to contribute to the teaching of at least one and preferably two other subjects over a more restricted range whether of age or ability. In suggesting possible groupings of subjects, we have deliberately included housecraft, handicraft, art, music, drama and physical education, the traditionally "specialist" subjects. We believe the schools require more teachers whose pattern of qualifications cuts across the conventional divisions of "specialist" and "non-specialist", "practical" and "academic" subjects. A school so staffed would be capable of a more flexible organization; could offer many of its pupils more choice and variety in crafts and other practical work and physical education; and be less at the mercy of staff changes, which at present bring a whole department to a standstill if the one "specialist" departs.

286. We are convinced that many men and women could, with training, including intensive short courses for teachers already in service, make a most useful contribution as assistant members of a "subject" team, as well as making a major contribution in their chosen main subject, and that many would welcome the chance of combining more freely than is now possible subjects of different types. For example, some men whose main subject is science or mathematics, with a personal interest in woodwork or model making, might more readily develop a useful competence in handicraft than they do in teaching English as a general form subject; many married women teachers could surely acquire with little difficulty sufficient professional techniques for teaching junior housecraft, and could combine it very effectively with a main teaching responsibility in, say, social studies or English; and

many young men and women would be ready to help with a variety of recreational sports and athletics, given some basic training. The enlarging of some "practical" departments would have advantages for the main specialist teachers also: the housecraft teacher, for example, who is often isolated in her "specialist" room from the rest of the life of the school, could more easily be released to do more wide-ranging work with the older pupils in household science or child-care studies. And not least important, from the pupils' point of view, the chances of one side of the curriculum consciously reinforcing another would be markedly increased.

287. We conclude that many more general training colleges should be able to offer housecraft, handicraft, science, art, music, or physical education at an appropriate level to students who are not aiming to become main specialists in these fields but who would be interested in acquiring a teaching competence at a subsidiary level; and that short, intensive courses over a similar range of subjects should be available nationally or locally for serving teachers. The "specialist" colleges similarly would need to offer a complementary range of subsidiary subjects on the non-specialist side. We realize that there are many implications here for the policies on which training colleges are staffed and equipped, and indeed, for the sixth-form curriculum of grammar schools, from which teachers are recruited, but we believe these should be seriously examined in the light of the apparent staffing needs of the schools and the educational interests of large numbers of pupils.

288. In the schools we should hope to see teachers working even more closely than now as teams; not only in relation to the teaching of a particular subject throughout the school—and the head of department's function would become even more significant under the kind of staffing pattern we have suggested—but also in relation to the total curricular programme of particular groups of pupils. The form-teacher, as re-defined, might have a key role as co-ordinator of studies. No one person can hope to possess all the skills, knowledge, and personal qualities required to supply the needs of a group of older adolescents, if their experience is to be varied and demanding as it should be, but there must be some means for ensuring that the experience is not too fragmented, and that important knowledge about the pupils is shared by all those who teach them. This is not to advocate the artificial straining of one subject to relate it nominally to work in another, but simply to urge that all the teachers concerned with a group of pupils should be aware of each other's work. In senior co-ordinating roles some valuable members of staff might qualify for graded posts who would not be eligible for posts as heads of subject departments. We see salary and promotion incentives of this kind as more acceptable than posts specially allocated to teachers of average pupils, which would tend to create a separate class of teachers.

289. The more points of contact teachers have with their pupils, the better the chance they have of establishing successful personal relations. All that we have said earlier in relation to the value of extra-curricular activities applies here, and the suggestion that more teachers should be able to make some contribution in the field of art, crafts, music and physical education has added force, in that these are subjects particularly likely to lead to informal, recreative activities outside the lesson programme.

290. We note with interest the growing practice in training colleges of encouraging students to gain experience of working informally with young people in the neighbourhood, by service in youth clubs and societies, and by assisting with school journeys and camps. These seem developments worth fostering as a regular part of teacher training, for two reasons. First, because it will help the young teacher to recognize the significance of the social and recreational side of the school's life, and to participate more readily in it; secondly, because these contacts with young people will provide a useful background to the sociological studies which we believe should be part of any general training course.

291. Such work as has been done in the study of social and environmental influences suggests that the learning difficulties, including the linguistic, of many of the pupils with whom we are concerned can be related to home background. And for some pupils the relation would seem to be very close indeed. Much investigation remains to be done, both in establishing the nature of the educational difficulties and in developing teaching techniques for dealing with them; we believe experiment in teaching techniques, based on the findings of research, is needed, and that some of this might best be undertaken by a training college in association with a specially staffed experimental school.

292. Apart, however, from these special enquiries, all teachers in training should have some introduction to sociological study, such as many colleges now offer, in order that they may put their own job into social perspective and be better prepared to understand the difficulties of pupils in certain types of area. They need, we suggest, some straightforward courses in recent social history; a study of the family and its changing function and structure in present day society; and guidance in understanding the current literature of sociology and psychology and the implications of research results. Some students may need to examine their own social preconceptions. It cannot be assumed, for example, that teachers with the same social and economic background as the pupils they teach will automatically have more insight into their pupils' difficulties; in so far as the teachers' own educational progress may have been untypical of others in their circumstances, they may even have less sympathy with environmental difficulties.

293. We have already indicated that we consider the greatest possible liaison is desirable between the schools, the youth service, the youth employment service, and all the social and welfare services which deal with young people, extending to some joint appointments of the teacher/youth-leader type, or, in difficult areas, to teacher/social worker posts. Liaison would be easier if it were possible to provide joint training facilities for teaching and the social services, including the youth service and the youth employment service.

294. Training courses of this kind might appeal to school leavers who do not necessarily want to teach, although they are interested in work with adolescents. We recognize that one of the problems of providing joint facilities is the inevitable disproportion between the numbers of future teachers and the students who wish to enter the social services. To be effective, joint training courses would need to be concentrated in one or two colleges, and in colleges which train a substantial number of students for secondary rather than primary work. Because, however, of their special bias, these colleges might develop strongly on the side of sociological studies and provide eventually a source of future college tutors and research workers in this field.

295. What we have advocated in relation to the recognition of vocational interest in school work, and the preparation of pupils for adult working life, requires that many of the teachers themselves should have experience of the industrial situation. Schemes such as we have referred to in Chapter 9 for introducing selected teachers to industry by a series of concentrated visits or studies deserve encouragement; and there is need of more machinery by way of conferences or courses which bring teachers and the youth employment service and industry into closer consultation.

296. In this connection, men and women recruited to teaching after experience in other kinds of work may have a special part to play. But mature persons, with experience of a world outside school, may also have a valuable contribution to make in the personal education of adolescents. Older, married teachers, for example, can often handle the problems of sex education more easily than younger members of staff. We strongly urge the further expansion and permanent retention of day training schemes with mature entrants and enquiry into how these schemes may be made financially more attractive to older men and women, with family responsibilities, who may be relinquishing a considerable salary in other employment to take up teaching. Greater generosity in grant arrangements may well be justified here, in that many of these older entrants will subsequently give a long period of service, whereas many young students, particularly women, leave the profession within two or three years of completing their training.

297. We do not overlook the fact that many young women may be expected to return to teaching at a later stage in their lives, and should, indeed, be encouraged to feel that they have some moral obligation to do so. It is essential to recognize that the changing pattern of society, with the trend towards earlier marriage and child bearing, is compelling some changes in the structures of the professions and in the rhythm of professional careers. Every means of making it easy for the married teachers to return to the profession ought to be examined, including, for example, the provision of refresher courses with full salary paid from the beginning of the course; and since many women will be prepared to serve part-time though not full-time, the possibility of making part-time service more attractive in terms of increments and pension rights should also be investigated.

298. Whatever arrangements are made to recruit or bring back older men and women to the profession, the main source of teacher-supply is bound to be the young entrant who makes teaching a first choice of career. The young probationer teacher faces special problems in relation to some of the pupils with whom this report is concerned. Teachers are needed who are able and willing to meet boys and girls on more adult terms, and who yet can preserve a necessary authority. If the pupils are also of limited abilities and difficult to interest, the task may well be beyond the skill of a very young and inexperienced teacher—our evidence argues it often is. As a general rule, we think probationer teachers should not be given the older and less able groups, and that the probationary year should be treated as a year of continued training and guidance, for which the head of the school and the senior members of the school staff have a major responsibility. We should also welcome more schemes whereby the schools and the more experienced members of staff were drawn into direct partnership in the training of students.

299. So far, we have implied throughout this discussion that the teachers will be receiving their training in training colleges. We have done so deliberately, because we are convinced that the kind of training the colleges offer, that is a "concurrent" course in which the personal higher education of the student is combined with pedagogical studies, is likely to provide the most suitable professional preparation for teaching most of the pupils with whom we are concerned. We are also aware that current policies require the colleges to concentrate on the training of primary teachers, and that in the immediate future only a minority of teachers with this type of training, mainly specialists in certain "shortage" subjects, will be available to the secondary schools. While we recognize the serious teacher shortage which the primary schools face, we are concerned lest an emergency measure which does not rest on any positive assessment of the needs of the secondary schools should be retained as long-term policy.

300. It was for this reason that at a fairly advanced stage of our deliberations we requested the Minister to make known our views to the Robbins Committee. The letter is included as an appendix to this report. Briefly, it argues that a "concurrent" training, which includes a prolonged study of child development combined with a study of a range of subjects, is more likely to produce effective teachers of less able pupils than the existing "consecutive" pattern of graduate training which consists of a more specialized course followed by a much shorter period of professional training. We realize that many changes may be contemplated in the future in the relative rôles of the training colleges and the universities, and indeed that altogether new types of training institution may emerge. We are not concerned with types of institution, or with the title of the qualification which trained teachers may eventually claim, but with the preservation of a pattern of training which we are convinced has marked value for the future teachers of large numbers of boys and girls.

301. It is clear, however, that if current expectations are fulfilled, not only will university graduates, as opposed to concurrently trained teachers, enter the secondary schools in increasing numbers, but also many of them in the near future will be without any kind of professional training. We view with extreme concern the prospect of large numbers of teachers without any training in the craft skills of their profession, whose own educational experience will have given them very little insight into the learning difficulties of many of the pupils they will teach. We echo the statement of the National Advisory Council on the Training and Supply of Teachers, in its Eighth Report:

> "Here (in the primary and secondary modern schools) teaching methods and techniques, with all the specialized knowledge that lies behind them, are as essential as mastery of subject matter. The prospect of these schools staffed to an increasing extent by untrained graduates is, in our view, intolerable."

302. We therefore urge that a training requirement for graduates be introduced at the earliest practicable moment; that meanwhile the conditions of training, including the financial inducements, be reviewed, in order to make voluntary training more attractive; and that there should be an emergency programme of in-service courses to help the untrained graduates equip themselves better to deal with the teaching problems they will encounter.

303. We are convinced in any case that the content of many graduate training courses should be re-examined, and the inclusion of some introduction to sociological studies and the possibilities of work in practical subjects be considered. Graduates who are likely to be teaching in secondary modern schools ought to do some part of their teaching practice in those schools; and we believe that the training colleges with their experience of work in this field could have a valuable part to play in the training of these graduates.

304. We have found an incursion into questions of training unavoidable, because these ultimately affect the teaching resources of the schools. But whatever training provision is made, there remains the need to persuade students that teaching our pupils is personally and professionally rewarding.

305. We believe that many students may have been deterred from entering the secondary modern schools, by a false image of indiscipline and of work which held small promise of intellectual satisfaction. On discipline, the evidence presented to us demonstrates convincingly what those in daily contact with the schools have always known: that by far the majority of schools are healthy and orderly communities, and that the number of schools where serious disciplinary problems arise has been grossly exaggerated. The difficulties of particular schools and pupils are formidable, and must not be minimized, but they are not characteristic of the secondary modern schools as a whole.

306. Reassurance about the possibilities of the work may be even more necessary. A young teacher may expect to manage his classes more confidently as his experience increases, but if he is as lively-minded as we hope our teachers will be, he will be looking for a prospect of growth in his own intellectual experience. It is there for the taking. There is evidence that our boys and girls, properly taught, can reach much higher standards than is commonly assumed. They need an intellectual and imaginative diet which goes far beyond the routine skills in English and arithmetic, and, if they are fully to benefit from it, they need teachers who have a deep insight into the subjects they teach. Teachers, for example, who are going to present literature to our pupils must themselves be widely read and sensitive in their own responses. The fact that few, if any, of their pupils will ever read so widely or so deeply makes the rôle of the interpreter more, not less, exacting. In all subjects, to make the connections with the world outside school demands constant alertness and frequent additions to the teacher's own stock of knowledge and understanding. In relation to those pupils whose potential ability may be masked by environmental and, particularly, linguistic handicaps, here is a largely unexplored territory; the evolution of practical teaching techniques will demand the highest professional skills, and might contribute to a major break-through in learning. It is work which can only be done empirically in the classroom, and which, we hope, may qualify for support by research grants. Finally, the provision of a longer school life for all boys and girls will create a new situation, calling for teachers with imagination and energy. These seem to us personal and professional challenges to which able men and women will respond.

307. There is one further point which has been well made by one of our contributors to evidence:

"For very many teachers conditions of service are as important as monetary awards. Fatigue is already a serious and continuing difficulty to many of the best teachers. If teachers are to bring to the kind of teaching we are now envisaging, the power to devise and carry through original schemes of work, if they are to organize a variety of purposeful out-of-class activities in the evenings, at weekends and in the vacations; if they are to develop close contact with the homes and with the employers; if they are to devise and conduct local and area schemes of assessment; if, above all, they are to know their young people thoroughly and to exercise considerable personal responsibility for them—if they are to do all these things and yet retain the freshness and vitality which is essential for successful work with young people growing up—then they must have time to do all these things and adequate ancillary help of many varieties must be provided."

Schools will increasingly have need of more resources of non-teaching ancillary staff, in connection with clerical work of all kinds, the servicing of workshops, craftrooms, laboratories and rural science departments, and the maintenance of costly audio-visual equipment; and there well may be a case in large schools for appointments combining the duties of school matron with those of domestic bursar. It is sound economy to expend money on these and similar services and thereby conserve the mental and physical energies of the teachers for the exacting job we hope they will be highly trained to do.

RECOMMENDATIONS

(a) The training of teachers should include preparation now for the new demands that will be made on them by the raising of the school leaving age. (para. 279)

(b) The training colleges should be equipped and staffed to enable students to teach pupils of secondary age in a main subject and in at least one, preferably two, other subjects; with the possibility of a choice of subjects which cuts across conventional divisions of "practical" and "academic". Facilities in other institutions e.g. art colleges or technical colleges, might be used to supplement training college resources. (paras. 285–287)

(c) More flexible use should be made of the system of graded posts to provide salary and promotion incentives for teachers who may not be eligible for posts as heads of subject departments but who have a valuable contribution to make in the work with "ordinary" pupils. (para. 288)

(d) The training of all teachers should include sociological and environmental studies, with special reference to the problems of pupils in culturally deprived areas. (paras. 290–292)

(e) There should be expenditure on research in training colleges and departments of education, to include the setting up of a special type of training course in association with an experimental school. (para. 291)

(f) One or two joint training courses should be established, for intending secondary school teachers and for students intending to enter other social services. (paras. 293–294)

(g) The recruitment of persons from other fields to teaching, and schemes for introducing selected teachers to industry, should be strongly encouraged. (para. 295) (*h*) We urge the expansion and retention of Day-Training schemes for older students, and re-examination of grants. (para. 296)

(*i*) The policies on which the teacher training programme is based should be reconsidered, to ensure that a substantial proportion of intending teachers in secondary schools will have training of the "concurrent" pattern. (paras. 299–300)

(*j*) A training requirement for graduates should be introduced at the earliest practicable moment, and a date announced in advance. (para. 302)

(*k*) As interim measures, an emergency programme of in-service courses should be instituted for graduates and other teachers who have obtained qualified status without training, to help them deal with the problems they encounter in the schools; and the content and conditions of the training course for graduates should be reviewed, in order to make voluntary training more attractive. (paras. 302–303)

(*l*) Schools should have more ancillary help of various kinds. (para. 307)

Plate 1. Typical Schools in Typical Neighbourhoods
(a) (*above*) Spacious grounds in a new housing estate
(b) (*below*) A cramped site in an ageing urban area

Plate 2. Welcome to Visitors
(a) (*above*) The headmaster's door in an old boys' school
(b) (*below*) The entrance to the neighbouring girls' school

Plate 3. The library in a large new school.

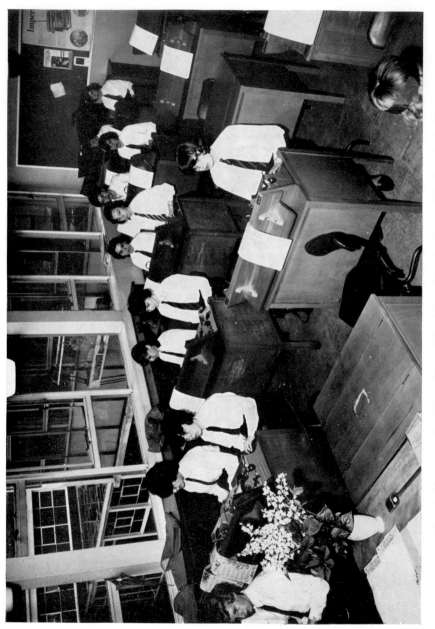

Plate 4. Classroom Conditions. These girls might well be the sisters of the boys in the plate below for this new school serves the same district

Plate 5. Classroom Conditions. Note the boy on his knees in a desk too small for him; the thin wooden partition, the lack of storage and bookshelves

Plate 6. Physical Education. The good conditions in this modern gymnasium help the staff to secure a good turnout by the girls.

Plate 7. Physical Education. This narrow space serves as assembly hall, dining room, gymnasium and main corridor. Glass partitions separate the classrooms from the hall. They are not sound-proof.

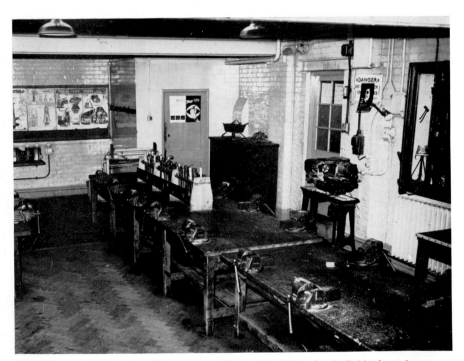

Plate 8. (*above*) A modern laboratory with good facilities for individual work. (*below*) Makeshift accommodation. An improvised workshop in an undersized room.

Part Two

The Teaching Situation

Foreword

We have drawn freely on the experience of others in putting down in this part of the report our view of the most effective way to set about the education of the boys and girls with whom we are concerned. Those who have helped us are not, of course, responsible for the use to which we have put their wisdom and none probably, would agree with all that we suggest. Nevertheless this part of the report is essentially what Lord Wavell called his anthology of poems, "Other Men's Flowers".

CHAPTER 13

What Should "Secondary" Imply?

308. Boys and girls going to a secondary school for the first time are normally keen to do their best. It is a large and strange world compared to that which they have known. There are new subjects and new kinds of equipment to attract their interest. The craft shops, the special art room, the fully equipped gymnasium or the laboratory—these are for them new and exciting aspects of school life. But at first, and often well into the second year, they remain very much the children they were in the primary school. Much of the character of their school work is still what we should call primary. They are in the collecting stage—witness the badges in their button-holes and the tattered book of engine numbers. They collect knowledge wholesale which only later will they reduce to intellectual order. They are, too, at least for part of the time still in the stage of unselfconscious imaginative fantasy. The West is still wild; the frontier open. The world is still such stuff as dreams are made on. Watch the girl in the back garden. She would infinitely prefer the real thing, but she makes believe she is exercising a horse. The wise secondary school teacher, like the wise primary school teacher, makes use of these childhood traits.

309. There comes a time, however, when childish things are deliberately rejected. Too often school and school work are included in this list. A child who has been regular in attendance at school decides to stay away—far more of the children in our survey with unsatisfactory attendance records began their truancy in the third year of school life than the second. Discipline becomes more difficult, note-books untidy, there is a struggle over uniform. Many boys and girls, of course, are not difficult like this at all, and many only for a short period, but it is frequent enough to be troublesome. One of the reasons for this rejection is that "school" has become identified in the child's imagination with an outgrown phase. There are various aspects to this rejection of school. The one we are concerned with here is the loss of interest in work. Where this occurs it is often because of a failure on the part of those who plan the work to keep pace with the developing personality of pupils who no longer accept all that comes their way; but stand back and ask, "What's it all for? What's it got to do with me?" Unless they are satisfied with the answer, their interest sags.

310. The kind of difference between primary and secondary which they seek is partly a matter of attainments, of doing more advanced work. But if this were the whole, or the main part of the story, many of those with whom we are concerned would hardly be capable of secondary work, and the promise of "secondary education for all" would be impossible to fulfil. A satisfactory definition cannot start from the presumption that all that is below a certain standard is primary while all above is secondary. We cannot say, for instance, that in arithmetic fractions are primary, but logarithms are secondary.

311. Age, of course, also comes strongly into their feelings. They are so often urged to "be their age" that it is reasonable they should demand an education which comes up to their age, and be dissatisfied with one which in their view

often fails to get as far. The trouble with chronological age is that, though it makes a clear administrative division, it is much less satisfactory as an educational one. The rough administrative definition is that below the age of eleven is primary; what follows eleven is secondary. This is as straight a frontier in time as the 49th parallel is in space. The trouble is that psychologically eleven is no longer the watershed it was once thought to be. Different people cross from childhood into adult life, or rather into the debatable No Man's Land of adolescence, at considerably different ages. Moreover many linger behind childhood in some aspects of life long after becoming adult in other ways. Physiological and psychological growth do not proceed at precisely the same pace, and community pressures may push boys and girls into a seemingly earlier social than personal maturity. In terms of age the most that we can safely say is that the frontier of childhood is crossed during secondary school life; that boys and girls enter as children at eleven and leave as young, but very immature adults at fifteen.

312. During that period boys and girls are becoming aware of themselves, self-conscious in both the good and the embarrassing implications of that term. It is possible to make good use at school of this characteristic of adolescence, and to induce them to think critically and purposefully about their work. It is this quality which is needed to give a true secondary flavour to their education. An illustration may help here. To make a pottery bowl involves considerable experience of handling clay: in getting to know empirically how clay behaves when wet or dry, and gradually acquiring skill of hand and eye in making it obey the potter's will. All this gathering of experience is learning of a primary kind whether the pupil is ten, twenty or forty years old. But the purposeful employment of this skill to produce a bowl which will serve a special purpose and look right in a particular place—and to be right in one's judgement nine times out of ten: this is secondary education. The progress from the child's first lump of plasticine at home to the housewife furnishing her house with conscious taste is a progress through primary and secondary ways of learning. A pupil's secondary education cannot begin until he has enough experience behind him to enable him to make sensible judgements on what he is doing. It does not begin until and unless he makes those judgements. It is, of course, perfectly possible for some of a pupil's work to be already secondary in character, while other parts of it are still wholly primary. There are pupils whose capacity in mathematics has brought them early to the secondary stage in that field, who yet see no more in a book than an exciting story with a good plot and plenty of opportunity for day dreaming. They have not yet developed the adult use of the imagination to enter with insight into the feelings and problems of others, but are still in the childish stage of fantasy and projection. The step forward from primary to secondary depends partly on earlier good teaching in the primary style and partly on a favourable opportunity being recognized and taken by the teachers in the secondary schools.

313. The work in a secondary school becomes secondary in character whenever it is concerned, first, with self-conscious thought and judgement; secondly, with the relation of school and the work done there to the world outside of which the pupils form part and of which they are increasingly aware; and, thirdly, with the relation of what is done in school to the future of the pupils, that is to the part they see themselves playing, or can be brought

to see themselves as playing in adult life. The first of these characteristics, the quality of self-conscious judgement, differs in kind from the other two. It describes a mental process that involves the use of reason and imagination to bring order into the world of things perceived. The other characteristics define directions in which this process must be employed, at least for the boys and girls of this report, if they are to develop the power of judgement.

314. The degree to which most of the boys and girls with whom we are concerned can exercise this sort of mental ordering is strictly limited in precisely those areas of knowledge in which the most spectacular successes of the modern world have been made. The abstract thinking of mathematics, and the concepts behind the scientific method will be beyond their reach, but they can acquire a commonsense in figure handling and a reasoned application of scientific skills to particular conditions, such as the diagnosis of electrical faults or the correct installation of a hot-water system, which involve true self-conscious judgement and are thoroughly secondary in the sense in which we have used the word. It is important that these boys and girls should penetrate as far as they can by secondary ways of learning into the world of mathematics and science. At present this is not very far. Better conditions of learning will add considerably to the distance they can go; but, compared with abler pupils and compared with their own possibilities in other fields, their journey into mathematics and science will always be relatively short.

315. The field in which it is most important that ordinary boys and girls should learn to exercise a common-sense judgement quickened by imaginative insight is that of personal relations. Their greatest service to the community, and there is none greater, will be as men and women who can be relied on to make a success of their own lives and by the quality of their living to bring up their children to do the same. This is not something which can be taken for granted or left to traditional methods of indoctrination. In a contracting world, where all men are neighbours but by no means necessarily friends, everybody needs an education of the imagination and the will to enlarge the area of his concern and acceptance of responsibility. Self-conscious judgement, too, is necessary now that private life has become a target for every art of direct and indirect salesmanship of goods, services and entertainment. In this whole field of private conduct an education which is genuinely secondary can equip the boys and girls with whom we are concerned to make right choices and to carry them out.

316. The transition from primary to secondary in most aspects of school work needs to be completed early in the period of three years from thirteen to sixteen. If the secondary characteristics are not apparent throughout most of this period, the education pupils receive will not help them to grow up because it will not be directed towards responsible adult behaviour and understanding. For real secondary education the last of these three years is decisive. By the age of sixteen most boys and girls will have had sufficient taste of adult life to know what it implies. Only if they remain at school until sixteen will they be able to bring their education and the adult world into a common focus.

CHAPTER 14

An Education that Makes Sense

317. Most boys and girls, and especially those with whom we are concerned, want their education to be practical and realistic. They feel a good deal better if they can see that it is vocational. They like to have some say in choosing what they shall learn. We believe that these four words—practical, realistic, vocational, choice—provide keys which can be used to let even the least able boys and girls enter into an educational experience which is genuinely secondary. This chapter of definitions is necessary because these four words have been so bandied about that it often appears that those who use them mean almost contradictory things. If we could have avoided them we would have done so; but we have been unable to find others which express so well the qualities which give life to the secondary education of the boys and girls of our report.

318. Time spent on "practical subjects" was defined for the analysis of our survey roughly as time spent away from the classroom and its desks.[1] It included, therefore, art and music and physical education as well as wood or metalwork, rural studies, housecraft and needlework. This yardstick will do well enough as an indication of the way our minds are working, and, which is perhaps more important, the way in which the boys and girls feel. Practical, then, when applied to work tends to mean doing something where physical skill is needed to produce ends which may be as entirely different as throwing a javelin, building a rope bridge, budding a rose, making a table, painting a picture, singing a descant or baking a cake. Usually it leads to something which can be seen or handled, though this test will not apply easily to music or drama. Apart from the sheer joy which most people feel in making something, the special importance of practical work to the boys and girls of our report is that it is for many of them both the surest way in which to achieve some success and the area in which success is best recognized by their peers and their parents. The radio works, the canoe floats, the dress fits, the top of the mountain was reached. Practical work leads not only to success which is easily recognized, but to success which is obviously worth while. A healthy and vigorous body, good food, serviceable and stylish clothes, music and art that lift man out of himself—these are indisputably things worth having.

319. The "practical subjects" have special value for less able pupils also because it is often easier to make the bridge between school and non-school in these subjects than in others. The table made at school can lead naturally to the table in the department store window; tables (and for that matter furniture in general) will be looked at with a knowledgeable and appraising eye if the woodwork master teaches his boys to see and to think as well as to make. The choir that sings in schools can sing in hospitals; the jazz group that practices in the dinner hour can play for evening dances. Here is an easy gate to one of the qualities that makes education secondary. It is in contexts like

[1] See paragraphs 639, 640.

114

these that we use the word practical; and it is for these and similar reasons that, without underestimating its value for abler boys and girls, we find it an indispensable key to providing really secondary elements in the education of the boys and girls of this report.

320. Two cautions are necessary. The practical subjects ought not to be an ivory tower in which our boys and girls take refuge, or are shut up because they are not good at words and ideas. Taught properly, they should indeed be one of the major ways by which ordinary boys and girls find they have ideas to express and acquire the words to express them. But, our second cautionary word, not all the boys and girls with whom we are concerned are practically minded. Some pupils of well below average ability are better with words than with things. This is no reason for their avoiding practical work, but it limits its usefulness as an instrument of their general education.

321. "Realistic" in our usage is a word that has a good many affiliations with "practical", but it is applied more particularly to situations in which people find themselves. Realistic stands to the classroom subjects in the same kind of relation that practical does to those carried on in the specialist art room, the craft rooms and the gymnasium. To set a class to study a carefully defined problem in human conduct and human relations into which boys and girls can project themselves and work out the various implications of different courses of action—this is realistic teaching. It is also imaginative teaching. Indeed very often the only way to be realistic is to use the imagination as an aid to responsible living, thus developing conscience from the stage of taboo to the level of insight. There is, however, an apparently contradictory context in which we use the term. It is sometimes almost equivalent to "utilizable". Much of the information, for instance, that is given in courses on citizenship or civics can seem remote and, consequently, is likely to be quickly forgotten. But if, for instance, some way is found of relating this information to a real situation with which the pupils are or want to be familiar—household budgeting, gross and net wages are obvious examples—it becomes useful information which is obviously worth acquiring. To our boys and girls "realistic" means belonging to the real world, that is to the world of men and women, not of school children.

322. "Vocational" is a dangerous but indispensable word. It rightly means all that belongs to a man's calling. That itself is no doubt an old-fashioned word, but at least it suggests that there is more to a job than money. This is recognized by the still current use of the term to describe the process by which a man discovers whether he ought to be a priest. This meaning runs the risk of being lost in the narrow context in which a course in bricklaying is no doubt rightly described as vocational education. Probably at first boys and girls only think of a subject as vocational if it involves learning to do something, like bricklaying, which is part of the way people earn their living and which is not related to school work as they have hitherto known it. They can see the point of a vocational subject and often enjoy it whether they themselves are going to take up this kind of work or not. Once they begin to clear their own minds about what they are going to do, vocational takes on for them a more precise and yet a wider meaning. They know that shop assistants, for instance, have to talk to customers; and with this knowledge the whole of English, not just some special limited "trade English", gains significance. Ordinary school

work becomes vocational. Probably the noun with which "vocational" can most helpfully be associated in a school context is "guidance". This is something which should run through much of the work in the last years at school, which should be concerned with what the young people are going to make of themselves both as young workers and in a much wider sense as young men and women. To girls especially the personal aspect of vocation to marriage is already apparent. The interest is ready made; there is an opportunity to give it depth of meaning.

323. The next step forward in life should be seen and talked about positively as going to work, not negatively as leaving school. This step needs to be prepared for in many ways through many subjects of the curriculum. Going to work means earning money, and this is important psychologically as well as financially. Both implications should be explored. Going to work means choosing between this and that opening. The choice ought to be based on knowledge of what openings there are and what the jobs are like. This leads on to weighing one kind of consideration against another—the interest of the job, the pleasure of companionship, the fatigue of travelling, the size of the wage packet, the possibilities of promotion and many more. A right choice involves self-knowledge as well as knowledge of the job—what one can do and what one can't. These are issues which a good school will help its pupils to face, and will take great care to see that they are brought forward and not ignored.

324. But what of vocational work in the narrower sense of learning a skill or a trade? Many of our boys and girls will work with their hands.[1] They will thus be engaged in activities which in a more advanced and specialized way, but also in a more circumscribed way, are akin to much that goes on in the practical subjects. Sometimes there will be a direct relation between what is done at school in these subjects and the work that is subsequently taken up. If there is, so much the better. But in the great majority of instances, there will not be. The value of the practical work at school is not thereby destroyed. It is worth its place both in general terms as part of the education of the person and also in the narrower vocational sense of providing broad experience in physical skills on the basis of which a reasonable judgement about employment can be made. The boys and girls of our report value practical work because it has vocational relevance—possibly for them, certainly for others. It may be school, but it is also real. In the last years at school the same realistic value, as we have already noticed, can be given to other subjects by vocational references without destroying their importance in their own right. English, above all, has vocational relevance to many jobs. Exact understanding of oral and written instructions and clear expression in speech can be seen to be important in many situations which boys, and even more often girls, know they will have to face. But if this was all that English had to offer it would be a stunted contribution. Going to work involves working with other people and getting on with them. It is in this matter of human relations that English has most to give.

325. Education in the junior school and in the early stages of the secondary school is like a table d'hôte meal. The subjects are there on the form time-table and are taken by all the form. There is no choice. Some secondary

---

[1] It should be remembered that industrial developments point to a reduction in manual work; and it must not be assumed that manual work is, or ought to be, hereditary.

schools continue in this way right up to the end; indeed as far as timetable making is concerned our survey shows that this is a great deal more common than the reverse and especially so where the less able boys and girls are concerned.[1] But, if we are right in the broad significance that we have given to the word vocational and to the importance of helping boys and girls to make a wise vocational decision, there should also be some element of choice about the later stages of their school work.

326. The less able of our boys and girls are good at so few school things that it is surely common sense to let them develop what strengths they have. They will then enjoy what they are doing and they will want to do their best at it. Their choice may also sometimes be dictated partly by personal reasons—the fact that they like one teacher or cannot get on with another. Such personal likes or dislikes may seem frivolous reasons for selecting an educational curriculum; but they are certainly worth paying attention to for boys and girls who find learning difficult anyhow. This is especially true during adolescence when physiological changes make tremendous inroads on personal equanimity. To provide a means of avoiding a personal quarrel or to enlist the support of a strong liking is often educational wisdom.

327. But to give pupils a sense of being free to choose does not always involve a choice between subjects or between teachers, both of which involve problems of timetable and organization which may be difficult to resolve. There is often a choice of craft or medium which can be made within a "practical subject". This can go far to meet a growing boy's or girl's desire to follow his own bent and to follow it long enough to reach some real competence. This can be just as true in physical education. On an even narrower front it is possible in the humanities. Here the division of labour involved in a co-operative project can be used to give boys and girls some opportunity of contributing their own special interests and talents to the making of a greater whole. Single lessons may also be used to present pupils with the necessity and pleasure of making a personal decision. This may involve a weighing up of the arguments for two different courses of action, which is the beginning of sound moral judgement, or a comparison of several accounts of the same event in different newspapers which provides an approach to a critical opinion. In both instances the pupils take a hand in their own education so that they feel they are being treated not only as real people who have the right to their own views but also, which is even more important, as people who have the capacity to form a right opinion. Freedom of choice is something which all adolescents claim; wise teaching and organization can help them to justify that claim. We have it in our power to change what might otherwise be brash defiance into responsible judgement.

328. An education which is practical, realistic and vocational in the sense in which we have used these words, and which provides some ground in which to exercise choice, is an education that makes sense to the boys and girls we have in mind. It should also make sense to the society in which they live and which provides their education. But if their education could be completely described in these words it would be sadly lacking. An education that makes complete sense must provide opportunity for personal fulfilment—for the good life as well as for good living. This is not, of course, a matter for a series of lessons. It is a quality to be sought, not a subject to be taught. One of the

[1] See paragraphs 643, 644.

elements involved is that which shines out when the only possible answer to the question 'why are you taking so much trouble to do this properly', is 'because I enjoy doing it'. This situation may well arise in the course of a hobby, but it may also be found in parts of school work. Wherever it occurs, it is something to be fostered—doing something worth while for its own sake is a principal aim not only of education but of life. It is within the reach of clever and stupid alike.

329. Boys and girls of average and below-average attainments may initially be attracted—we think they will be—by the approach to secondary education which we have been discussing. They are not, however, likely to persevere unless something is done to lessen their greatest handicap—that inability to express themselves which soon convinces them they have nothing to express. Any education that makes sense to them must concentrate on helping them to talk sense. Sometimes their ineffectiveness may be caused solely by poor intelligence; their understanding is not attuned to the wave length of mature talk which simply goes over their head. They need to be taught where others would 'catch-on'. At least as frequently a naturally slow mind is associated with a word-starved environment and quite often, we believe, the environment alone is to blame for a disappointing failure both to understand and to express thoughts above a childish level. It has long been noticed that country children from remote farms where there is no young companionship have a great deal of lost oral ground to make up when first they come come to school. Something of the same kind of handicap attends boys and girls as they pass from childhood into adolescence in homes where there is no intelligent adult conversation to hear. At a time when they should be reaching out in curiosity to the things their elders talk about, they may find that nothing but the simplest physical pleasures and needs are discussed. The only outside subjects of passionate argument may be the fortunes of football clubs or of pop singers. Many boys and girls may well appear to be much more stupid than they need be simply because of the inarticulate homes from which they come.

330. The remedy, of course, is not a matter of speech training or formal debates, though both may come into it. It involves the cultivation of all the means by which people express their thoughts and emotions—mime, drama, music, conversation—so that the atrophy may be overcome. A double obligation rests on the schools. They have to provide the background of conversation and exchange of information which an educated family offers, and they have to coax their pupils to take part in it. Family opinion and the verdict of those a little older than the pupils is often against what the schools try to do in this field. They are working against the grain. For this reason many failures must be expected, but success can be achieved. When it is, there is nothing which schools do which provokes more genuine gratitude. There is no gift like the gift of speech; and the level at which people have learned to use it determines the level of their companionship, the level at which their life is lived.

CHAPTER 15

Attainments and Achievement

331. An education which is practical, realistic and vocational must send boys and girls out into the world literate and able to perform simple calculations with confidence and accuracy. Such simple minimum demands present no difficulty to most children, but they are still a hard task for many of the boys and girls with whom this report is concerned. This chapter is about the simple educational equipment which everybody needs. One point cannot be made too soon or too strongly. An exclusive diet of the "Three R's" just does not work. Boys and girls brought up in this way disappoint their teachers by failing at the end to have acquired the equivalent, so to speak, of even one R.

332. But in fact restricted teaching of this kind is not what most schools do, though it is what some older people would like to see. And, partly at least because they do much more than this, standards of reading are in fact rising. The reading test which has been given at intervals since the war records a steady rise in literacy. This test is not a simple measure of ability to read; it requires for success a fairly wide and precise knowledge of words many of which belong to the kind of work which is done in secondary but not in primary schools. This is as it should be. Literacy is not a single skill, something achieved once for all with the power to translate written symbols into sounds. It involves the power to invest words with meaning, to recognize the ideas which somebody else wishes them to convey and to use them oneself to express the thoughts which without their help would remain fleeting and inchoate. "How do I know what I want to say until I've said it?" is a childish but not a foolish, remark.

333. "What I want to say" will not be the same at the age of eleven and of sixteen. What most people needed to say in 1863 was on the whole a good deal less complicated than what they say in 1963, and even more so than what they will be saying in 1983. Literacy then in its full sense is not a package deal which the primary school can hand over complete to the secondary school. It is something which ought to grow with the pupil, and go on growing after school days are over whenever new situations are encountered demanding a more developed language.

334. The gain in literacy since the war, as far as it can be measured by the reading test, is set out in this table :—

Year	Reading Test Average Score	Reading Age Gain in Months
1948	18.0	—
1956	18.9	6
1961	21.3	23

These are figures in which teachers may well take pride. But they are not the whole story, and the part which they conceal is the part with which we are especially concerned. Roughly a quarter of the modern school population aged fifteen have a reading age of thirteen years or less. One in seven modern schools, largely for social reasons, has a median reading age which is fourteen

119

months below the median reading age for all modern schools. This chapter is largely concerned with these minorities whose numbers at present leave school without reaching an acceptable fifteen year-old degree of literacy, and then rapidly forget much of what they did learn at school through sheer lack of use.

335. An increasing number of jobs require a reasonable grounding in elementary mathematics. Running a technologically advanced society requires some mathematical skill from a long line of workers ranging from administrative and professional staff to craftsmen and operatives. More competence in this field is required today from the abler boys of this report than would have been needed only a few years ago. But a lower standard of numeracy than of literacy will do as a bare minimum. For the least able it will be sufficient if they can apply the arithmetical rules, which average children have mastered by the end of the junior school, with confidence and understanding to the situations involved in running a home or earning a living in a simple routine job. Of course more than this is desirable and we believe could more often be attained than it is; but many of the boys and girls of this report will always find it hard to reach even this bare minimum standard.

336. Some ways in which the various subjects of the curriculum can best help these important minorities who find literacy and numeracy difficult are discussed in chapters 17, 18 and 19. Here, and in chapters 16 and 20, the accent is on general factors in the experience of the pupils and the organization of the school which hinder or help their development.

337. The first step is to recognize some of the consequences of poor ability. The less successful a pupil is, the more courage he needs to keep working. The temptation to give up trying grows year by year because the older he is the more clearly he realises that he will never produce as good work as abler pupils. Each term he falls a little further behind. He makes more mistakes than they do, and therefore has more practice in getting things wrong and less in doing them properly. If he is working carefully, he works slowly. He is likely to be helped with the harder parts of the work—to be told instead of having to work it out. He learns by heart, but not to use his head. His lesson books are simpler, shorter and more profusely illustrated. His written work unfortunately more often takes the form of filling in a missing word instead of writing a sentence, or drawing a picture instead of writing a paragraph, so that he has less experience of using words than his abler contemporaries although he needs more. He probably has less experience of education altogether since he cerainly has less homework to do and may very well have none.[1]

338. Some of these additional handicaps are unnecessary. There is no reason for instance, why those who are poorer at school work should give less time to it. In Chapter 6 we have argued in favour of some form of homework, liberally interpreted, for all. Many schools which have successfully introduced it have found that parents welcome it and pupils realize its necessity once they see that to do more work is almost certainly to accomplish more.

339. The second stage in our diagnosis takes us back to the beginning of the secondary school course. On the first day of each autumn term some of the ablest new comers to a modern school may still be upset because they have

---

[1] Details are in paragraphs 573, 580, 590, 596, 605 and 611.

disappointed their teachers or their parents. This is not the school they had set their hearts on. But, if the modern school is not a dead end, but has openings beyond it to higher education and to employment which used to be accessible only to grammar school pupils, this initial depression or even resentment will soon vanish. Pupils in the A stream of any school usually work hard and get on. As more and more modern schools are able to provide good fifth-year courses there is less and less need to worry about quite able boys and girls finding themselves in a dead end. They soon discover that their new school exceeds their expectations. They become a credit to it, a success.

340. The real worry is for boys and girls who never thought of a grammar school place but who started their secondary school life with enthusiasm for the new and exciting things that the modern school had to offer with its gymnasium and craft rooms, its laboratories and its library. Some of these boys and girls will soon become apathetic because they are defeated by much of their school work, and especially by that which is most directly concerned with literacy and numeracy. They soon discover that their new school falls short of their expectations. They become a failure, the boys and girls about whom the school will report that it "could do little for them". What has gone wrong?

341. One reason for failure is likely to lie in the way that the classroom subjects, and especially English and mathematics, have been taught in the first year. Moving to a new school is an unsettling process for all pupils. Often their work marks time or deteriorates for a little. This is particularly likely to happen to the less able. They are liable to misunderstand even familiar questions if the wording is slightly different from what they have been used to. They are at a disadvantage with a new teacher; and their new teacher may well be at a loss with them. He feels that he must find out what they know. On what foundations can he build? They are, therefore, tested and questioned. They get worried. What little confidence they had evaporates. They give a much poorer account of themselves than they need. Their self-esteem suffers. The teacher forms a poor opinion of their work—and justly. But need he have put himself in this position?

342. His conscientious effort to dig down to firm foundations is misplaced because it is based on a false analogy. Learning is not a neat placing of one brick on top of another. The growth of abilities is more like a rising tide which momentarily recedes only to come a little higher up the beach next time. In similar confidence the teacher needs to launch out on a little new work in English and mathematics from the very beginning even with the dullest pupils. If he does, he may gain their interest; their confidence will return and they will begin to make progress again. New work need not at first involve any new techniques. It is what the English and mathematics are about that should have the newness; the level of vocabulary and the arithmetical processes involved may remain the same provided that the subject matter is different. In the course of following up new interests or enquiries the old half-learned techniques will be used time and again, so that their use is revised in a way that is relatively painless because it is concealed. Even the simplest skills are better mastered and remembered when the mind as well as the memory is brought to bear. Revision which brings in the same techniques in different contexts often brings deeper insight or discloses new relationships. If immediate recall of some necessary process fails, then the boy who has the largest number of possible routes back to what he wants to remember has the

best chance of succeeding. The less able pupils are never likely to have as many of these routes open as clever ones have just because they work more slowly. It is important that they should have as many as time can be found for.

343. The well-intentioned simplification of the curriculum in the wrong way often persists throughout the secondary school. There is, of course, a necessary and desirable simplification to which we shall return subject by subject; but our concern is here with that simplification which refuses to go on or to branch out until the work already done is so well known that mistakes will not occur. A special form, sometimes described as a Remedial Class, is set apart for those whose progress is thus halted. Its numbers are kept small; it is usually in charge of a specially devoted teacher. There is clearly need for some remedial teaching in most secondary schools to make up for time lost through long absences, transfer from another school and other casualities which are more serious in their effect on less able boys and girls than on average pupils. But the time spent in a remedial class should be kept to a minimum. It is no good keeping boys or girls there until they have acquired a perfect memory for they will always be quicker at forgetting than their abler contemporaries. But, if they cannot remember the little they learn in a remedial class, what is the point of trying to cover more ground?

344. The answer is that their work ought not to be judged by how much they can remember and how few mistakes they make when tested at the end of a year's work. It should be judged by the quality of the work they are doing at the time it is done. The fact that most of us when brought face to face with our own children's homework have to admit that we "couldn't do that now" does not mean that it was useless for us to have been taught to do it at school. So it is on a shorter time scale with the boys and girls of our report. They will forget in the sense that they cannot reproduce their best work when they are doing an examination; but, well taught, they do not forget how to look it up again if need arises. They are better people for having had the experience of doing something even if they never do it again.

345. Well taught—and this is something which makes great intellectual and imaginative demands on the teacher—these boys and girls can get both interest in what they are doing and pride in seeing what progress they are making. Their attitude to their work is itself a sound criterion for us that their education is being worth while. But it is not a sufficient criterion for them. They need something more objective, more tangible. How is this to be provided? Clearly ordinary examination papers set to all the pupils in each year of the school course could give them no satisfaction at all. They would all be near the bottom. What they need is to measure, or rather see, the progress they have made, to compare their work today with their work last year, and not to see how well (or rather how badly) they do in comparison with their clever contemporaries. There is a sound case for preserving specimens of old written work and, after an interval, comparing it with work now being done. It is worth drawing the attention of both pupils and parents to this cumulative record, which ought to give them the courage to carry on. And if there is not evidence of progress, there is something radically wrong which needs investigation. Besides this long term review there is still, except for the least able, a use for form examinations or tests to see how well the term's assignment of work has been mastered.

346. The boys and girls of this report are, however, at their worst in written work. This does not mean that it is unimportant for them—far from it—but that it would be both depressing and misleading to assess their progress in literacy solely on what they can write. Speech is their main means of communication and always will be. Unfortunately the fact that speech is fleeting and cannot be taken home to be corrected has led to its playing only a small part in taking stock of their educational progress. The mere difficulty, too, of getting sufficient time for oral work with each member of a large class has also lead to an unhappy neglect of speech. These difficulties are now on the way to being overcome. Speech on a magnetic tape can become as permanent as writing in a notebook. It should be possible to compare some oral work done last year with some current discussion. For this purpose it is not necessary to preserve much of the past, nor something from every member of the form. A comparison of a group discussion in the second year with a group discussion in the third or fourth year should provide convincing evidence that real progress has been made.

347. In the early and middle years of the secondary course the incentives to perseverance have to be found within the school situation itself. Work that is new, interesting and realistically demanding; opportunities of looking back and seeing how different one is from the small fry of a year ago; quick help to straighten out a difficulty; simple praise whenever possible and justified— these are the means that have to be used. They go on being useful to the end; but in the last years of the course they can be reinforced by external incentives. For some of the boys and girls of this report an external examination may well provide such a target; but for most of those with whom this chapter has been particularly concerned it will not. Either the examination will not be worth holding or they will fail to pass it.

348. But there is still a real vocational incentive to work hard in order to reach some sort of a reasonable minimum standard of literacy and numeracy. There will be interviews with employers to face; many jobs involve the need to talk to the general public—and to add up bills and to give the correct change. What the school has to say about these boys and girls and their work is better given in a personal testimonial or a school leaving certificate than by an external examination. The appropriate form of external incentive varies with the ability of the pupils; but getting ready to go to work is always a valuable spur which can be used in the last year of school to call forth a strong finish to school work. It is astonishing what progress in English and arithmetic this stimulus, applied at the right moment, can produce.

CHAPTER 16

The Subjects and the Curriculum

349. What should be taught? We have already made clear the importance that we attach to literacy, numeracy and that part of religious upbringing which falls to the schools. Physical education, too, is something which all growing boys and girls need. The next three chapters are devoted to the various subjects of the curriculum as a whole. Each chapter deals with a broad field of knowledge in each of which boys and girls ought to be getting some experience all the time they are at school. If this report were about all the pupils in secondary schools instead of only half we should still hold that up to the age of sixteen nobody should go without some practical work, some experience in mathematics and science and some in the humanities. And it ought to be a sizeable share of each, not a concession to idealistic theory which sensible folk need not take too seriously. Up to this point we are rigorists. We would like to prescribe this for all pupils in all secondary schools as an obligation.

350. But beyond this point we become permissive. We would neither draw up a fixed table of information, subject by subject, which all pupils should master, nor even prescribe beyond the minimum essentials set out in the preceding paragraph a set list of subjects which all should study. A universal fixed curriculum ought to be ruled out if only because of the wide range both of capacity and of tastes among the pupils with whom we are concerned. At the bottom end of the scale it is a matter of finding a very few things in which the pupils show interest and can make progress and working outwards from them. Near the top of our terms of reference, half-way up the whole scale of ability, it is a matter of selecting from a fairly large number of possibilities those that are likely to be most valuable to the individual pupils. The selection will vary from group to group. On the pupils' side, a prime consideration will often be relevance to what they are going to do when they leave school; on the schools' side, the selection is bound to be affected by the strengths and weaknesses of the staff. An historian turned reluctant geographer, or vice-versa, is not likely to inspire pupils who take a great deal of rousing at the best of times. Both subjects can, as we shall see later, offer many of the same values. If the head decides that the cobbler had better stick to his last, we shall neither be surprised nor unduly distressed.

351. For our least able pupils, then, "subjects" hardly come into the field of possibility; for the better ones there is often no compelling educational reason why one should be chosen rather than another. Why, then, should the customary division of the curriculum into certain traditional subjects be retained?

352. First, we have in mind the convenience of readers. We hope that teachers will feel that this part of the report is about the work they actually do in school, that it is really addressed to their teaching problems. They are more likely to do this if they can recognize familiar landmarks, even if some of them are stumbling blocks. It would have been possible, but a little forced,

124

to have used new descriptive terms which avoided subject names. We might have written of verbal and plastic creative work. We have preferred to write "English" and "Art"; and, we hope, to make it clear in the text that these are concerned with more than grammar and clay and have indeed something important in common.

353. We might have grouped our suggestions round certain methods of teaching instead of round the traditional subjects, and written chapters on projects or assignments. It is not because we think a wise choice of methods unimportant that we did not do this. It is because in our view this might have concealed one of the most important aspects of any discussion of the curriculum—the subject matter that is actually taught. The traditional subject divisions may sometimes seem artificial and restrictive, but at least they have the merit of a certain precision. A boy or a girl can at least come home and say what his lesson was. This has a value which ought not to be sacrificed. Some subjects necessarily stand apart in their own right. Learning a foreign language, for instance, is not really like anything else in the curriculum, and it is almost inevitable that the word French (or German or Spanish as the case may be) should appear on the timetable. Similarly what goes on in the laboratory is almost bound to be labelled "Science", and the gymnasium is naturally the scene of Physical Education. A good deal of the curriculum is, therefore, almost bound to carry subject names. It seems to us that there are advantages in carrying the practice right through it.

354. A subject name is not only a signpost to the pupil of what a lesson will be about, it also provides a similar reminder to the teacher. It marks out in intelligible shorthand the kind of contribution he is to make to the educational programme. It also links this contribution with his own adult field of knowledge. He speaks with more conviction in this field. When he is on his own ground his pupils should feel that this lesson is not just textbook stuff.

355. Many of the abler of the pupils we have in mind will be candidates for the new Certificate of Secondary Education. This necessarily involves the examination of subject matter which is at least roughly comparable from school to school. And this in turn involves the fixing of certain limits within which the teaching will take place. It seems almost inevitable that most of these comparable areas for examination will bear the conventional subject names however unconventional the methods of examining may be, and we hope will be. But, though the conventional subject names will remain, this does not mean that the syllabus of what is actually taught should be the poor relation of a grammar school course. The teacher needs to ask himself what his subject has actually meant to him, and then think what it can mean to our boys and girls. He must undertake a radical enquiry into his own education and then plan with a free mind the best thing for his pupils, remembering that virtually none of them will carry their education as far as he has, and that most of them will stop doing anything about his subject, whatever it is, as soon as they leave school. At fourteen or fifteen he was only a third of the way through his education; they are near the end of theirs. This involves a thorough reconsideration subject by subject of what should be taught. The three following chapters have some suggestions to make about this; the general policy behind the new Certificate of Secondary Education is designed to make such a review easy.

356. This new examination is to be a subject and not a group examination, that is to say it is to be an examination in which regulations will neither prescribe the minimum number of subjects candidates can offer nor insist on certain combinations of subjects. Each subject is a unit on its own. These then are counters out of which a whole curriculum is composed in different patterns for different pupils.[1] This conception seems to us important when we are considering the needs of the pupils we have in mind. Their school week can profitably be varied not only by turning from one subject to another, but by recognizing in the timetable the different rhythm of work which is appropriate for different subjects. Hitherto their school day has been composed of a succession of thirty-five to forty minute periods varied by an occasional double period for a practical subject. By the age of fourteen, however, we think that boys and girls can well concentrate for longer than an hour and a half at a time when the nature of the work in hand makes this natural. This is often so in the practical subjects, for which longer continuous periods are often worth while at this age both in their own right and as a useful step towards acclimatization to the longer and less varied working day of industry and commerce. But any such change should only apply to a proportion of the school week. The span of attention to classroom subjects which pupils of below average ability can manage is short. Some subjects, too, like learning a foreign language, require short but frequent lessons rather than a few long ones.

357. In Chapter 20 we shall be discussing two possible ways of providing different patterns of curriculum for different groups of pupils—the method of grouped courses, usually with a vocational bias, and the method of options between subjects. In both methods subjects play an important role as the basic unit out of which the whole programme of work is assembled. Some basic unit of known content there must be if chaos is to be avoided: the traditional subjects of the curriculum, enriched as necessary by newcomers, seem to be suitable for this purpose. They are good servants, but bad masters.

358. They are bad masters if they keep themselves to themselves. They ought to support one another, to approach similar situations from entirely different angles. If one approach gets no response from a boy or girl, another may suddenly make things clear. This is one reason why we have not given separate chapters to each subject, but grouped them together in three broad fields of experience. But the various subjects should not only support each other within the field of the humanities or of mathematics and science, but there should be a good deal of cross-reference between the fields. Thus the question of hire purchase is one that may be (and should be) considered both in the field of mathematics and of the humanities. The two teachers should be aware of each other's plans and see that their pupils realize the connection.

359. The subjects are bad masters also if they think of themselves as the sole arbiters of school time. There are some important things to learn which belong to a good many disciplines but which do not bulk large enough in any one to be quite sure of a place. Room must be found for them, and this will not happen unless a member of the staff is made responsible for seeing that this happens. High on any such list of topics would be health education, which may serve as an illustration. Its biological foundations belong to science, its practice

[1] The composition of the timetable in the schools in the sample is described in Chapter 22.

and its proof lies to a great extent in the hands of the physical education department; its moral implications to the humanities; its references to home surroundings—a difficult point where smoking is concerned—belong to the head in his dealings with parents; and its setting in a school that is clean and whose equipment makes cleanliness easy belongs to the head in his relation with his governors and his administrative staff. This might be thought an exhaustive catalogue, but it includes as yet neither the school doctor nor the school nurse who speak with an authority on these matters that is often more acceptable to boys and girls than that of their teachers. Then, too, a school in which the housecraft department felt that it had no concern with health education would be sadly lacking in imagination. There is no doubt of the importance of this aspect of education to the boys and girls with whom we are concerned. No teacher would deny this. But each one of all those we have listed may well believe that somebody else is attending to it. And each has enough to do in his own department anyhow. What is everybody's business can easily be nobody's business.

CHAPTER 17

The Practical Subjects

A. IN GENERAL

360. "Practical Subjects" were roughly defined earlier as activities away from desks and classrooms, involving some form of physical skill. Clearly, any divisions of the curriculum are largely a matter of convenience of discussion. Science, not dealt with here, frequently involves highly practical investigation; drama, referred to later in the context of English, might also have been treated here; form and feeling enter into art and music and literature alike.

361. For present purposes, we have related much of our discussion to the subject names which appear on most school timetables—art, craft, needlework, housecraft, handicraft, music and physical education. But we strongly commend the introduction of other activities, as yet found in only a minority of schools, such as rural studies, photography and film-making, and the extension of existing subjects, handicraft for example, to include not only the traditional work in wood and metal but also building and engineering crafts and work with plastics. Again, certain aspects of traditional subjects may increasingly need to be developed in connection with special courses, as art, for instance, in relation to retail studies, housecraft in relation to catering or nursing or child-care. Experiment rather than conservatism is needed. We do not wish to suggest, by listing names, that all these "subjects" should feature in the programmes of all pupils or of all schools. The older pupils' need of choice, and the need of each school to build from strength according to its resources, both imply variety and selection.

362. These subjects offer creative and civilizing experiences beneficial to all pupils. In urging that they may have additional values for the boys and girls of this report, we are not indulging in the fallacy of supposing that there are two types of pupil, the able and "academic", and the less able and "practical"; but we do strongly believe that many, though not all, of our average and less than average pupils may find through practical activities a sense of achievement which can energize the rest of their work.

363. The exercise of a skill is what these diverse activities have in common; but the skill element is not their only or even their chief educational value. The pupils, and sometimes their parents, may be prone to suppose it is, especially in the workshop crafts which they like to think have a direct vocational import. Besides, it is naturally satisfying to feel yourself gaining in mastery over tools and materials and in control of your own bodily movements. When success in other disciplines is elusive, it is reassuring to know you can handle a saw or a sewing machine, play an instrument or a game, if not as well as the next man or woman at least better than you could last term or last year.

364. The pride and pleasure of a measurable achievement is considerable. So is the sheer fun in trying things out, whether it be a new recipe or first time

on the trampoline or painting a mural. There has to be room for simple enjoyment, and for light-hearted experiments which are not regarded as tragedies if they go wrong. There can be, too, an intense creative satisfaction in making and doing which is especially important for those who do not easily achieve expression in words: art, drama, and dance, particularly, draw powerfully on feeling and provide both an emotional release and a channel through which feelings can be constructively employed.

365. But these are not all the dividends. There is the advantage of grappling with a problem in a practical situation: and of learning from the discipline of the material which is different from the discipline imposed by a teacher. The English teacher may tell you that your written work is faulty, but if the piece makes sense to you, the criticism may remain unconvincing. But what can be done with fabric and wood and metal and stone is a matter of pragmatic test: some things work and others manifestly do not. The English sentence may be broken-backed but still convey its meaning: the ill-made stool collapses. Again, in the variety of media available, there are more possibilities of success; pupils of quite modest talent have more chances of finding something which they can manage and enjoy, and the resultant increase in confidence may be reflected in all the rest of their work.

366. This individuality of experience can happily be combined with group projects—indeed, a major contribution of a subject like music lies in the communal life of the school. The weaker pupils gain from association with abler companions, without being in competition with them, and all can enjoy sharing in an enterprise which is valued by the community. Moreover, most of these activities link readily with the social and recreative interests of young adults, and, if stimulatingly taught, will develop informal extensions in clubs and societies which will in turn feed back into the classroom.

367. In practical subjects, except in music and games, the size of the teaching group is commonly smaller than that of a full class. A closer relation between teacher and pupil is possible, and allows immediate comment on the work in hand which is especially helpful to the boys and girls who lack confidence or who quickly get into difficulties. While we welcome this feature of practical work, and think the maximum advantage should be taken of it by teachers, we also realize that the small teaching group would be as valuable, and sometimes even more needed, in subjects like English, in which rarely does a teacher get a chance to work with less than thirty pupils at a time, although lack of power over language may be many pupils' gravest handicap. Since the staffing prospects for many years yet seem to rule out the possibility of even the majority of lessons being taught in groups of fifteen or twenty, there should be more reflection on the priorities for small classes, and except where safety considerations are involved, they should not always be assumed to lie with the practical subjects at the expense of the rest. This carries implications for the size and design of some "practical" rooms.

368. But since the craft, handicraft, housecraft and rural studies teachers will usually have the advantage of smaller classes, and often, too, longer continuous periods of time with their pupils, they have an obligation to seize all their chances, not only to teach the special skills of their subjects, but also to reinforce the pupils' understanding of the use of language and of number, and to develop their powers of reasoning and judgement. Most practical experiences, if they are to justify fully the time spent on them, should lead to thought and

expression: they are not to be regarded as a substitute for thought for the less intelligent.

369. This requires that the teachers shall be able to appraise the general educational needs of their pupils, and that they use the technical matter of their specialist subject as a means as well as an end. It also requires that as well as being good exponents of their skills, they should be able to call on other cultural resources to draw analogies and illustrations from other fields, and be sensitive to where their subject touches on other aspects of human experience. Any craft, however useful and enjoyable in itself, ought also to lead to a consideration of other things that men have made—buildings, parks, gardens, furniture, clothes, paintings, sculpture, ships, motor cars, the pots and pans of everyday use as well as the masterpieces of art. It needs a sense of history as well as a perceptive eye on the contemporary; a feeling for the appropriateness of materials to their use; a response to colour and form and design, in the natural as well as the man-made world; a sensitivity towards the personal and social needs of human beings in relation to their environment. Few fourteen year-olds or fifteen year-olds can be expected to get so far on the strength of their time in the workshop or the housecraft room; but the teacher who can bring out the connections will start them thinking, and give them a vocabulary with which to do it.

370. Books do not become superfluous because subjects are practical. Our pupils need plentiful sources of information, simply, but not childishly, presented, to which they can be encouraged to turn for self-help. They also need sources of ideas, not to copy slavishly but to stimulate their own invention, and books which enlarge their perspectives; handsomely illustrated works, for example, on furniture, costume, painting, architecture, ballet; books which deal with the history and traditions of their subjects, in this and other countries; stories of the lives of musicians, inventors, artists, sportsmen; books which may eventually lead some of them to museum and art gallery and theatre, and widen their range of personal interests.

371. These books must be put persuasively in their way, and some must be conveniently to hand in the appropriate room, along with other reference material. But many such books are needed in the library too, to delight the casual browser and the pupils whose particular programme may not take them into the art studio or the workshop. There is a need to duplicate a good many books, and to make a point of featuring others, perhaps too costly to duplicate, in a display in the library, or in association with an exhibition of work, always with information on where to find them again. Our pupils need every inducement to read, and their practical activities ought to provide many starting points for doing so; what is to be avoided is treating these as non-bookish subjects for non-bookish pupils.

372. Closely related to the use of books is display. Most specialist rooms will need not only extensive wall surfaces for charts, posters, photographs, and illustrations of all kinds—and they ought to offer a silent lesson themselves in good arrangement and presentation—but also well designed exhibition areas for showing sometimes the pupil's own work, sometimes interesting material from other sources. Display areas are needed, too, on the main school thoroughfares where pupils going about their daily business will see attractive exhibits, well labelled and documented, and have room to stop and discuss them.

373. Another still more direct way of contributing to the general life of the school may be in work or activities specifically communal in their object—a mural for the dining-room, a lectern for the hall, curtains for the stage, playing by the orchestra for morning assembly, providing the refreshments for some social occasion. In these and many similar ways instructive experience for the individual may also enhance the school's corporate life. The knowledge that they are contributing, and the public appreciation of their efforts, can strengthen the morale of many of our boys and girls.

374. Clearly, although there are affinities between the practical subjects, they are not all equally interchangeable. Some form of physical education, for instance, ought to feature in the programme at every stage, though we hope with increasing scope for choice of activities and in the amount of time devoted to them. Music offers distinctive experiences of which too many older boys seem to be denied the opportunity, to judge from our survey. Art, the studio crafts, needlework, housecraft and handicraft form a more nearly homogeneous group within which choices are bound to be made as the pupils grow older: not everyone can, or will want, to do all of these things all the time. But there must be some initial experience on which choice can eventually be based, and it is desirable that the younger pupils should have opportunities to sample as much as possible.

375. They may even need some compulsion to do so; some of our pupils are reluctant to risk the unknown, and will say they have no interest: nor can they have, until they have given things a try. It has been put to us that in handicraft "sampling" presents difficulty as long as pupils are leaving school at fifteen: boys need a fairly solid and continuous basic course before they achieve skill enough to benefit from a choice. With the raising of the leaving age, however, this problem could be resolved. We have not labelled crafts "boys'" or "girls'", although the workshop crafts will generally be taken by boys and the domestic crafts by girls. We regret that in many schools girls are denied the satisfying crafts of rural studies. We welcome, however, the fact that some schools achieve a sufficiently flexible organization to allow boys to take cookery if they wish, and girls, handicraft or technical drawing; and where a school has vocationally-slanted courses related for example to catering or the clothing trades, the conventional divisions of boys' and girls' interests will clearly not apply.

Art and the Studio Crafts

376. Art and the related crafts, such as modelling, carving, pottery, weaving, embroidery, basketry, fabric printing, bookcrafts and leather work, are particularly helpful in the sheer variety of techniques and experiences they offer. To take full advantage of these possibilities requires more space than many schools now enjoy, and more flexibility in the shape and furnishing of working areas, to allow different groups of different sizes to use them in various ways. But given the facilities, there is the possibility of suiting almost every customer, and at many different levels of accomplishment.

377. Some pupils will respond best to a precise and craftsmanlike approach. Others, including some of the most difficult of those with whom this report

is concerned, may need a more freely emotional outlet, and find, especially through painting and modelling and carving, some means of exploring feelings which have to be inhibited in everyday life, or of vividly living out again past experiences. Here they can deal imaginatively with the real, and realistically with what is imagined. There are analogies in this with some forms of dance and drama and imaginative writing. A teacher need not venture into the dangerous realms of psychiatry to recognize that for some pupils these experiences may have a therapeutic value, and for most, a strong emotional satisfaction.

378. But art is not only a matter of the emotions, and for many boys and girls it can offer a rewarding discipline of hand and eye and intellect. Here is a training in perception and selection, a way of looking and a means of communication. Film-making is a particularly interesting example of a creative craft which combines exacting technical skills with invention, visual imagination, and selective judgement. To make people more observant of the world about them, more responsive and more discriminating, is potentially to enrich their personal lives a great deal. It also has a significance for our standards of living and the quality of our industrial products. In school, creative enjoyment will be the mainspring, and perhaps for the majority of older boys and girls who choose art subjects the work will be at a semi-recreative level. For some, however, it can clearly form part of a group of studies which will have broad vocational relevance. Design and function, decoration, display and communication, have special significance for those who may one day work in shops, in commerce, in the dress and clothing and furnishing trades, in textiles, buildings and printing; and, not least, for the future housewife.

Handicraft

379. Much of what has been said about the crafts in general applies equally to the particular crafts which are comprised under handicraft. But they bring in an extra element. A great deal of the world's work involves the use of tools and machines, and the boy in the school workshop, as well as knowing the pleasures of a craftsman, has a strong sense of being directly in touch with what is going on in industry. As far as specific technical processes are concerned, the relation is slender. But in as far as he is coming to terms with tools and materials he is right to feel that in the workshop he can do a "real" job.

380. This satisfaction may be lost, if the course is too narrowly conceived as a series of exercises, though progression there must be. It is particularly important for the less able pupil that the emphasis should be on making things, rather than on practising processes for their own sake. There are parallels here with the need in mathematics to combine repetition in practice, to strengthen techniques, with variety in the examples and applications. The examples need to be such that they are relatively free from complexities of detail, interesting in themselves, and do not take too long to complete. Some schools, for instance, have made a successful feature of toy-making and repairs, linked with a service to a children's home. Sometimes the work can directly serve some other study, as in the making of rough working models for use in mathematics and in science. There is considerable scope for the improvization of apparatus; or for the making of equipment needed elsewhere in the school—bookshelves for the classroom, tools for the garden. A "handyman's" course related to common jobs about the house and involving the

use of domestic hand power-tools, such as many of their fathers will have at home, may appeal to boys who have neither the refinements of skill nor the ambition to become professional craftsmen, and will serve a doubly useful purpose in providing safety training in the use of such tools. Some girls would gladly join in a domestically-biased "do-it-yourself" course.

381. For the really dull pupils, a high standard of accuracy and finish is no more likely in handicraft than in the rest of their work. But the end product in the shape of something which works and can be used, can give personal satisfaction; and the experience itself can, and ought, to be made the occasion of much general education.

382. For the abler pupils the vocational impulse may be strong. Many of these have a prospect of taking up eventually some skilled trade, whether or not they have any clear notion at the age of fourteen of what this may be; and while it would be a mistake to suppose that the only interest in handicraft of most boys is vocational, there is a natural tendency for them to see their wood and metalwork as a link with future employment. The schools can legitimately use this to encourage increased effort; and, if it leads to a general improvement of work, it may indeed result ultimately in better employment prospects. It will add interest too, to relate some of the subject matter of the handicraft course to the dominant occupations of the locality—rural crafts and the use and maintenance of agricultural machinery in a farming area; or the motor-engineering or ship-building or steel working of industrial areas in which many of the boys will soon be earning their living as their fathers are already. This can help to give a sense of solidarity with the home and the neighbourhood, as well as introducing a reassuring realism into school work.

383. There is room, too, to widen the scope of "handicraft" to include, for example, building crafts, which can provide the basis of a satisfying practical course whether or not the pupil is ultimately an entrant to the building trades. Particularly if the school has any bias towards rural science and animal husbandry, brickwork and cementwork, drainage, fencing, estate maintenance, the erection of useful constructions in the service of the school, will provide plenty of realistic applications.

384. A welcome development in recent years has been this general extension of craft skills to a widening range of projects. Some of them are useful to the school in its everyday life—a sports pavilion or a swimming bath, for example, although experience has shown that for the latter it is advisable to seek expert technical advice and assistance. Many link directly with out-of-school hobbies and recreations—aero-modelling and model railways, canoes and boats and camping equipment. And there are examples of schools building a permanent camp or climbing headquarters on a site they have acquired. Often, these are team jobs, including girls as well as boys, and a large part of the work may be done out-of-school, through some enthusiastic club or society, although there is no reason why such projects should not be also properly regarded as within the scope of handicraft in school. However they are managed, these enterprises have a double value for the pupils, who both gain from making the equipment and from using it in other school activities.

385. Another development lies in the growing demand for machine tools in schools, which surely makes sense—not because they will familiarize pupils with industrial processes, for the machines appropriate for schools will not

be of the industrial mass-production type; but because machines are part of the culture of our society, and their introduction in school is a way of providing a further educational challenge in the course. The use of power-tools requires thought and planning and skill, and as such extends the demands on the pupils. It also adds to variety in the work, and increases the possibilities of offering "man-sized" jobs, which most boys tackle with zest. The provision of more engineering craft courses to include work with machine tools for older pupils is a development to be encouraged. Again, this is a field in which expert professional advice both in the selection of machines and in safety precautions is essential.

386. Additional equipment and probably different workshop planning will in future be needed in the schools. It may sometimes be necessary for some pupils in their final year to attend a local college of further education for part of their course, as happens already in some areas, in order to have the advantage of specialized facilities not easily available in schools. Provided that there is close consultation between school and college, and that the out-of-school part of the course is sensibly related to the rest of the pupils' programme, this seems a sound procedure. It may widen the scope of the work, give the pupils a useful introduction to the world of further education, and confirm their more adult status as students rather than school-children. It will serve an additionally valuable purpose if it strengthens the links between schools and colleges and enables the respective staffs to learn more of each other's work. It will not, however, obviate the need to provide most secondary schools with better and more varied craft facilities.

Rural Studies

387. We referred earlier to some applications of rural crafts. In this connection we note with regret how few schools in our survey appeared to have facilities for serious work in gardening or rural studies.[1] A well developed rural studies course, which will include much besides craft skills, can offer particularly satisfying experiences, to all boys and girls, in the contact with living and growing things. For our pupils, the crafts involved in gardening and livestock keeping, linked as they easily may be with almost every part of the curriculum, may provide a motivating force in their education. The range of material is vast: flowers, fruit, vegetables and herbs; lawns, trees and shrubs; rockeries, pools and streams; greenhouse cultivation; agriculture and forest plots; rabbits, poultry, bees and possibly goats, calves, and pigs. There are dangers to be avoided; too much land under cultivation and too much stock will turn pupils into labourers and extinguish any spark of interest. And too much may be expected of the dedication of teachers, without suitable buildings and ancillary help, especially at weekends and in the holidays: such help is beginning to be provided by some authorities. Given the right conditions, rural studies can offer a wealth of rewarding experiences, both in lessons and in the many out-of-school studies to which they easily lend themselves, in the formation, for example, of Young Farmers Clubs, which have county, national and international connections. Some boys and girls will find a career through gardening and livestock keeping, but many others, town-dwellers as well as countrymen, may acquire satisfying hobbies which will continue long after they have left school.

[1] See paragraph 664.

Groud fw
C·IV

Housecraft and Needlework

388. The domestic crafts start with a built-in advantage—they are recognizably part of adult living. Girls know that whether they marry early or not, they are likely to find themselves eventually making and running a home; moreover, some quite young schoolgirls, with mothers out at work, are already shouldering considerable responsibilities—a fact which needs to be taken into account in school housecraft programmes. Although we live in an era of high standard mass production in clothes, many women continue to find pleasure in needlework, including embroidery, as a recreational as well as a useful art. Even those girls who do very little sewing themselves after they leave school will, as young wage-earners, spend a sizeable amount of their money on clothes, and as young married women they will soon be responsible for buying clothes for the family and furnishings for the home: they will need some foundation of taste, and an eye for finished workmanship and quality in materials, fashion and design.

389. Housecraft and needlework easily justify their place in the curriculum to most girls; and everything that has been said about other crafts as satisfying skills and instruments of general education applies equally to these subjects. There is ample matter for interesting basic courses during the early years in the secondary school. When in the fourth and fifth years, choices begin to operate, there will be some pupils, especially those who hope to find their future occupations in dressmaking or the catering and food trades, who will want to carry these crafts to a higher level of technical skill and make them the central parts of their programme. In a mixed school there will be boys as well as girls in this group. Other pupils may drop the subjects entirely from their formal programme, although they still may enjoy, say, an out-of-school cookery club at a recreational level.

390. Since these are always likely to be popular subjects for girls, there will also be large numbers of pupils who fall into neither of these two categories, and these set the challenge: how to provide satisfying developments of the work for relatively mature young women of fifteen and sixteen and even seventeen, who may not be of very high general ability, but who certainly need to tackle something more demanding than what they practised in the second and third form. There may also be some girls who are far from enthusiastic, because they have had their fill of scrubbing and washing-up and getting meals for the family at home; and yet they may need all the more the education a good school course can give in the wider aspects of homemaking, and in the skills which will reduce the element of domestic drudgery.

391. For many of the less able girls, it is not the straightforward, individual tasks of cooking and sewing and cleaning which are likely to defeat them, but the management of themselves and of their total time when a whole complex of tasks has to be accomplished. These pupils, especially, may benefit from the concentrated experience of running a house or a flat for a block period of time—perhaps a week and probably more than once in their last year. But if the experience is to be fully educative, they must be required to work independently, and the conditions must be reasonably realistic. To encourage independence, it is obviously better that the flat should be a self-contained unit, even a physically separate building than merely a "living area" at one end of the housecraft room, continually under the teacher's eye.

Realistic conditions are a little more difficult to ensure: real houses get lived in and untidied by adults and children and animals; a model flat which is unused, save by the pupil housewives themselves and their occasional visitors to lunch, belongs more to an ideal home exhibition than a real world.

392. There is everything to be said for inviting in a few children for the day, perhaps the pupils' own brothers and sisters, perhaps children from a nearby infants school, to feed and entertain them, play with them and read to them; something valuable can be learnt about small children as well as about housework. Or, in the design of a new school, part of the social and commonroom provision for the senior pupils might be incorporated in a house in the school grounds, maintained by the housecraft department; rooms could be used for informal group activities, with the pupils on duty acting as housekeepers and hostesses.

393. A second element of realism needs to be introduced in claims on the pupils' time. Real housewives have to take children to and from school, keep appointments, and fit in their cooking and sewing and cleaning and their own recreation with demands which are outside their control. The pupils who are least competent in managing their time need some contrived complications in their programme—an appointment to attend, perhaps a lesson or a meeting with the head; notes to make on a particular broadcast programme; some set reading to cover during the week. Sometimes, special projects might include the redecoration of a room, with all the attendant preliminary planning, although this could obviously not occur very often.

394. Schemes of this kind are being tried, and would be tried more often if more schools had suitable facilities; but improved accommodation alone does not ensure a good course, and there is room for much thought and experiment in the realistic use of housecraft flats.

395. A different approach to domestic studies which might be developed with the rather abler pupils lies in applied household science. There is a large field of topics round which a course might be built, heating and lighting, electrical appliances, detergents and polishes, natural and man-made fibres, the constituents of foodstuffs, the effect of chemical additives, the properties of aspirin and other commonly-used medicaments. Much of this study would lend itself to simple experiments and recording, and would require not a highly equipped housecraft room but something like a modestly furnished laboratory.

396. The course might include a comparative study of commercial products on consumer-research lines. And associated with it, whether under the aegis of housecraft or English or social studies, a consideration of advertisements might lead not only to a nicer appreciation of the advertisers' techniques but also to an identification of the prejudices and emotions at which they are aimed. It is a useful beginning of self-honesty to realise that standards are not wholly imposed from without, and that if advertisements contain subtle appeals to, say, material or snobbish interest, it is because they have found a response in the reading and viewing public.

397. We have not overlooked the fact that probably one of the easiest approaches, even with the most difficult girls, to more critical work in both housecraft and needlework lies in their natural interest in dress and personal appearance and social behaviour. Many schools do already successfully

make use of these interests. It would be a pity, however, if the pupils were not led beyond their purely personal preoccupations with themselves and their own concerns, to some wider concept of their rôle in life.

398. One line of advance lies in courses built round broad themes of home making, to include not only material and practical provision but the whole field of personal relations in courtship, in marriage, and within the family—boy and girl friend, husband and wife, parents and children, young and old. At the age of thirteen and fourteen few girls are ready to explore these aspects of adult life and there are some aspects for which they will not be ready till after they have left school; but older girls can be brought to see that there is more to marriage than feeding the family and bathing the baby, and that they will themselves have a key role in establishing the standards of the home and in educating their children. Married teachers who have returned to the profession after bringing up their own families can make a specially valuable contribution here.

399. A study of young children, which appeals to many girls, might include not only their physical nurture but their behaviour and emotional needs, and the relation of these to children's stories and literature. Visits out-of-school might include time spent with infants in a local school or children's home. Or again, since caring for the sick and the elderly is commonly a woman's responsibility, the school course might include home-nursing, and visits take pupils to hospitals or on errands of service to old people in the neighbourhood.

400. Some courses could usefully be designed for mixed groups of boys and girls more often than they are. Partnership in marriage, whether in household chores or in bringing up the children, is an important concept for our society. We note with interest the ingenuity of one boys' school which, lacking the focus a housecraft department might provide for studies of the family, has introduced, for pupils in their final year, a series of discussions on personal relations: many of these topics relate to family life, and are largely treated from the standpoint of the boy, thirty years on, married and with a son much resembling himself as he is now. Many of the adolescent difficulties of the boys themselves are illuminated by discussion of the problems of these hypothetical families—the responsibilities of parents to children; quarrels; pocket money; staying out late; undesirable friendships; social loyalties.

401. For both girls and boys, a range of rewarding studies can be developed, basically related to domestic crafts and interests, but reaching out both into the humanities and into science. But to do so will require teachers who see their job as more than the teaching of crafts; and accommodation for older pupils which is not necessarily conceived in terms of conventional specialist rooms.

Physical Education

402. The essential needs in physical education for many older pupils could perhaps be summed up in the words variety, choice, better facilities, and links with adult organizations.

403. Most healthy young people enjoy being physically active; many find in sport satisfying exercise, fun, comradeship, and a sense of achievement. We believe that many more could do so, who are at present underestimated and under-challenged. For some boys, particularly, self-esteem is linked with

ideas of physical strength, prowess and daring—and where appropriate outlets are lacking in overcrowded urban areas, explosively violent behaviour may result.

404. But much of our evidence is convincingly emphatic that conventional gymnastics and field games, valuable as these are for those with skill enough to perform well, are not a source of enjoyment or of self-esteem for all pupils. Boys who, as 11-year olds, punted footballs about eagerly enough, may fail to develop sufficient skill later to participate enjoyably in team games involving large numbers of players and complex tactics. Slowness of mental reaction, poor co-ordination, differences of physique and of temperament, timorousness, fear of looking foolish may all be limiting factors. Girls who out of school will energetically dance the evening away appear reluctant in the gymnastics lesson, and take whatever evasive action they can, "forgetting" their kit, feigning illness, or simply staying away. This is a matter not only of limited skill, but, frequently, of growing distaste for what they regard as childish activities.

405. There is often a marked difference here between the attitudes of boys and of girls which reflects their different physical and emotional maturity. If it is in the interest of all adolescents and young adults that they take some form of physical exercise, then there is surely a need in this country to establish for girls a much more attractive image of athletic grace and physical well-being which is reconcilable with their notions of adult interest and fashionable good-looks. Perhaps the Scandinavian countries have something to teach us here.

406. On the other hand, some of these same reluctant pupils, girls as well as boys, can enjoyably engage in swimming or dancing or some individual form of athletics, or in an easily organized game involving only a few players. Squash, skating, archery, fencing, judo have all been successfully introduced in some areas. Some pupils, girls especially, under a skilful teacher, will work in modern dance and movement lessons with an absorption they rarely show at other times in school; and they find through this activity a keen imaginative and aesthetic pleasure, such as others may discover through art or music—and indeed, all three are sometimes allied in forms of dance-drama.

407. Variety of provision, a degree of choice, both in the activity undertaken and in the amount of time given to physical education, are all desirable for the older pupils, but not easy to contrive. A major difficulty is lack of staff; specialist teachers, especially in girls' schools, are in seriously short supply, and unless they can be supplemented by other teachers, as we have suggested earlier, who can offer some form of physical education as a subsidiary teaching subject, it will be virtually impossible to provide an adequate choice.

408. Nor do premises greatly help.[1] Rather less than a third of the schools in our sample had playing field provision up to the standard prescribed by regulations, and two-fifths of the schools had less than half the prescribed acreage. Many lacked an adequate gymnasium. Only a tiny minority had a swimming bath, in most cases laudably provided largely by their own efforts ; and ease and frequency of access to outside baths greatly varied. Perhaps in any case some reconsideration needs to be given to the kind of provision which is

---

[1] Details are given in paragraphs 666–670.

most needed. Swimming, surely ought to come higher on the list of priorities. Could some more hard-surfaced areas, rather than large areas under grass, give more versatile year-round use? Would a sports-hall be more useful than a second or third gymnasium in a large school? The answers will not necessarily be the same for all areas.

409. The down-town school raises exceptional problems demanding exceptional solutions, Its pupils need, more than most, constructive outlets for physical energy and a wider range of activities to compensate for cramping environment. Either the schools should be supplemented with generous community centre facilities; or better still, the schools in crowded urban areas— the potential, as well as the actual slums—should be conceived on a different design and scale, as part themselves of a community centre serving all the social needs of the neighbourhood. It is no solution to provide detached playing fields and sports facilities miles away: the provision is most urgently needed on the spot, out of school hours as well as in school time.

410. Fortunately, not all the problems have to be solved entirely within the limits of the school premises and the school staff. One of the most striking developments in recent years has been the increase of informal out-door pursuits offered to young people, through the schools and through youth and sports organizations. Cycling, camping, rock-climbing, fell-walking, sailing, canoeing—these and similar activities have proved to have a wide appeal; and because, although challenging, they do not necessarily require the highly co-ordinated, refined skill typical of many sports and games, they may have a special value for the pupils with whom we are concerned. We have already urged earlier, the need to assess nationally the various forms of residential provision, including camps and out-door-pursuit centres, of which many have recently been opened; increased facilities would make it possible to supplement the school programme in ways we believe to be significant for large numbers of boys and girls. So too would the provision of more community sports centres in towns.

411. These out-of-school extensions of physical activity would have the advantage of introducing pupils to recreational interests which can readily be carried forward into adult life, and might go some way towards bridging the gap noted by both the Albemarle and Wolfenden Committees—the sharp break that occurs between school and membership of adult organizations, with a resultant "wastage" of young people who appear to lose interest in physical recreation altogether. The situation might be further helped if the schools, as a matter of policy, as well as a way of increasing their own staff resources, deliberately sought the assistance in some extra-curricular activities of local experts and enthusiastic members of adult clubs, some of whom might might well be found amongst the parents.

Music

412. Out of school, adolescents are enthusiastically engaged in musical self-education. They crowd the record shops at weekends, listening and buying, and within the range of their preferences, they are often knowledgeable and highly critical of performance—and the technical performance of the music they like is frequently high. They find rhythm exciting. Some teach themselves or each other to play an instrument. Transistor radios and tape recorders are

longed-for presents. From radio, television, cinema and concert hall, and for that matter, from the local chain store, music is making a continual impact. Here is a vigorous popular culture which is international in its camaraderie.

413. Yet in the schools, the contrasts are striking. On the one hand, there are the individual schools, or whole areas, where music flourishes, extending beyond the classroom to choirs, orchestras, brass bands, concerts, informal club activities, and involving many of those same boys and girls whose private out-of-school diet is "pop" records. In these schools, pupils and staff, and boys and girls of different ages and ability are brought together in co-operative non-competitive efforts, in which the less able certainly benefit from the support of their companions. The playing and singing for school worship at morning assembly; musical and dramatic productions for public performance; and cheerful contributions to an end-of-term party—by these and many similar experiences a sense of unity is fostered, and the individual's range of responses widened.

414. On the other hand, on the evidence of our schools survey,[1] music is the subject most frequently dropped from the curriculum in boys' and mixed schools; and it is the only subject in the practical group for which one single period a week is common.

415. The reasons for this weakness, where it exists, appear to be several. One is an unduly narrow conception of the subject. If the scope of music in school is restricted to choral singing, difficulties and discouragement may arise at the stage when the boys' voices begin to change, though many schools have seized the opportunity to introduce fresh types of choral music congenial to adolescent male voices. Apart from singing, however, there is much else that can be profitably be attempted: various forms of instrumental music, training in selective and critical listening with the aid of scores, a combined musical and scientific approach to the phenomena of sound, all can play their part in the scheme.

416. Another is undoubtedly a shortage of suitably qualified music teachers. Many schools are without a specialist, and others have only one, with no supporting team among the rest of the staff to help share the burden of all the activities, in and out of school, which a lively musical department ought to promote. Again, although one way—and it is certainly not the only way— of developing musical interests in school is to start from the pupil's recreational interests out of school, not all music teachers who are highly qualified themselves are able to bridge the gap between the popular enthusiasms and the much more varied and demanding forms of music to which they rightly feel the school should be introducing the pupils. It takes a particular skill to use that initial interest, and without rejecting what the young people have spontaneously chosen, to sharpen perceptions and extend capacities for enjoyment over a much wider field. To do so does not imply handing over the initiative to the pupils and accepting the music of "pop" culture, with all its commercial pressures, as the basis for a scheme of music teaching. Rather it involves the teacher in an analysis of what it is that makes the appeal of the best of that culture—the rhythmic vitality, the easily-memorized tunes, the clever harmonization and orchestration, the highly professional performances —and in the presentation of good light music which has these qualities but for

[1] See paragraph 640.

various reasons is not likely to have come the pupils' way. The teacher will also realize that a transient liking for "pop" may exist simultaneously with a capacity to enjoy far more serious and substantial music, if only the school can provide the opportunity. Something of the same problem confronts the English teacher, seeking to extend the pupil's range of reading.

417. The music teacher, however, operates at a greater disadvantage. Some will consider music neither a useful nor a prestige subject. It is especially liable to be hit by examinations in two ways. Since it is not a readily examinable subject for most pupils, it tends to disappear from the programme of the more able as examination pressures increase; and because the more able pupils cease to take it, it may lose significance in the eyes of the rest.

418. Most of all, music is frequently the worst equipped and accommodated subject in the curriculum.[1] It is only very recently that specific accommodation for music has begun to be included in the design of school buildings: half the schools in our survey had none, and another quarter had only makeshift provision contrived within an ordinary classroom, often inconveniently placed in relation to other work going on in surrounding rooms. Of all the "practical" subjects, it had the least satisfactory provision.

419. Equipment is often similarly inadequate. Whereas with the other "practical" subjects the equipment is installed before any teaching can begin, with music the reverse practice is commonly followed: the teacher has to begin with virtually nothing and build up very slowly through the years, with his equipment supplied by small grudging instalments, often of poor quality. Yet sheet music, books, musical instruments, records, a tape recorder, as well as access to radio and television, are all essential teaching tools, and particularly valuable for work with the less able pupils. Brass band work, for example, has often proved most successful with pupils of quite limited general ability, and a practical approach through instrumental playing can be much more effective than "appreciation" classes. But a set of instruments is out of the reach of most schools if they have to provide it out of their ordinary annual capitation allowances: new schools need a foundation grant for equipment in music as for any other major branch of the curriculum.

420. It seems to us that some schools are being asked the near impossible, and although they sometimes contrive to do it, that music will not make anything like its full contribution to the education of many boys and girls unless much better provision is made. In areas where this provision is good, there is abundant evidence to show that pupils of all kinds of ability can respond to opportunity. Music can clearly be a potent force in the lives of many young people. It is a natural source of recreation, and one form of activity which can be carried on from school through adult life; its contribution to both the school community and the larger community can be notable. It deserves generous encouragement.

[1] See paragraph 671.

6

CHAPTER 18

Science and Mathematics

A. SCIENCE

421. A boy is usually excited by the prospect of a science course. What is it that appeals to him? He experiences a sense of wonder and a sense of power. The growth of wheat, the birth of a lamb, the movement of clouds put him in awe of nature; the locomotive and telephone he sees as man's response; the switch and the throttle are his magic wands. If he cannot produce a sunset he can change the colour in his test tube. He comes readily to his teacher hoping most to learn how to control events, though from time to time, as he grows older, he stops to ask why things behave as they do. In some way we have to show him how scientific knowledge is acquired, by what hard means advances are made. If he finds this dull, his teachers must accept part of the blame. The girl may come to the science lesson with a less eager curiosity than the boy, but she too will need to feel at home with machinery and will be subject to the prestige which science has in the world. In the future she may earn her living in as scientific an occupation as the boy. Whether science to her is friend or enemy she will be better equipped by having some inkling of its nature.

422. What are the essentials of the scientific method? To see, to wonder why, to attempt explanations, to test these by taking a closer look, is a common enough sequence of experience. The scientist repeats this process deliberately and in a controlled situation, learning to look closely, record accurately and say clearly what inferences have been made. It is not necessary to do anything esoteric to get the feel of being a scientist in this sense. But, for most of the pupils we are discussing, this is best obtained by trying out the process in practical work.

423. It is the next steps that are more difficult, and much more adult. They involve a personal willingness to give way to fact rather than to maintain prejudice. The mature scientist has a sense of the tentativeness of even the best scientific theories, he knows that somewhere along the line it becomes a matter of judgement whether a scientific law is worth retaining or not. How much of this can be presented to and absorbed by how many of our pupils is simply not known. But the teaching should not actively encourage naive attitudes of acceptance of revealed truth in the science lesson. The more naive the pupils, the more important this negative principle is. Too much of the tradition of science teaching is of the nature of confirming foregone conclusions. It is a kind of anti-science, damaging to the lively mind, maybe, but deadly to the not so clever. For them, in science as in mathematics, the spirit of genuine enquiry is essential.

424. The common practice of exploring a wide field in the first years of the science course, perhaps under the heading of general science, provides all the opportunities that we need. All the topics found in the typical science course, and many others, can be used. They will rarely be elementary in the sense of belonging to the elements of the formal development of the subject.

425. A girl may know that when she pedals, her bicycle generator can light the lamps. She may not wish to take a generator to pieces, but by enquiry she can find out that the school or home lighting is probably produced by another generator, driven by a steam turbine, at the nearest power station. Using a pressure cooker with the weight removed, and a paper windmill, but taking care to avoid a scalding, she can simulate a turbine. How does the steam get such power? Let her watch water boiling in a beaker, let her use a thermometer, let her find how long the water takes to come to the boil, how much longer for one quarter to boil away. How much further the topic can be pursued depends upon her willingness to speculate and to follow up her ideas. It may be appropriate to discuss the heat from a gas fire, or a coal fire, and to remember the coal at the power station. Quite probably it is too early to discuss how the sun's heat got into the coal, or into her muscles so that she could pedal. It is almost certainly unwise at this stage even to appear to exhaust the subject, which can be left open for further examination and experiment later. A train of thought has been followed; experience has been used as a basis for ideas; as a by-product, and, for a moment, something about the nature of scientific enquiry may be appreciated. Like so many by-products, in relation to the less able, this one will run to waste if it is not deliberately garnered. The technique is no hard selling one, it demands the well placed question here and there, the odd five minutes of insight at the end of an hour and a half in the laboratory. We would hope that by the time they are fourteen many of our boys and girls will have a tolerably clear idea of what it means, in the school science course, to take a scientific attitude to a question. Transference to other situations may have to wait on the maturity of the pupils themselves.

426. The field of science is so wide that what is done in schools can jump from one facet of the subject to another without much sense of cohesion developing. This appears quite suitable to the roving curiosity of the pupils when they enter the secondary school. By about the third year it would be appropriate to concentrate on a few relatively extended pieces of work rather than a large number of excursions into this or that aspect of the subject. At this stage a certain ruthlessness in selecting what will be attempted and what will not is essential. Even when a topic for enquiry has been selected, the ramifications to which it can lead need to be kept under control, if a sense of definite accomplishment is to result. On a farm for example there are many more things than milk yields, cropping, manuring and the like. There are heavy awkward things to move about, gates whose hinges must take a strain, tractors which at the price of dramatic changes in the liquid with which they are fed put energy at the farmer's service. This wealth of possibilities is an opportunity rather than an embarrassment. It could allow teacher and pupil jointly to discuss and settle what they will pursue; to take the pupils into partnership is to bring an adult element into the situation from the point of view of personal relationships as well as subject matter.

427. Conversely, seemingly limited topics can be made, with a little ingenuity, to yield something particular the teacher may have in mind. Measuring the temperature of a greenhouse at various points at a given level could give a near at hand example of isotherms, moving a kitchen table involves leverage, friction, centre of gravity and force (if it is moved by slightly raising one end before pushing it, rather than by just pushing). To find material for science

for our pupils it is only necessary to look around. This immediacy is just what they need. It should give them a certain kind of alertness to their surroundings and some commonsense in coping with them. School and life will not remain in separate compartments. The one will reinforce the other.

428. Perhaps this is sufficient to make the point that a great deal of real science can be extracted from relatively few enquiries. To be of its fullest value it needs a good deal of unhurried discussion and writing up what the pupil has done and discovered from the whole exercise. It is all the more appropriate for our pupils for that. Science is a practical subject ready-made for doing more for the "basic skills" than most—not forgetting reading, for sometimes it will be possible to use written instructions in the form of worksheets or general guidance cards. Moreover, science is well placed to encourage the use of books both for reference and for general interest. There is a particularly good supply of such books and their variety stretches from those which simply supply information to books fully worthy of the title "literature". They should be readily available and fully used. As science receives more time, with the improvement in the supply of science teachers, great care needs to be taken not to fill the extra time with too much additional subject matter. No amount of increase in quantity could compensate for lack of quality. This applies as much to the keeping of good records by the pupil as to any part of the work. Good records will help to give shape to what can become a rather untidy process of learning, and will help to give the confidence that comes from a sense of accomplishment. They are more important as a means of showing the pupil what he has done, than as a check by the teacher.

429. The need for practical work, often done in conjunction with the teacher, is probably much greater for our pupils than for the abler ones. An abler pupil can generalize (not without danger) from a few examples and apply his general conclusions to other situations, but our pupils need a greater variety of experience before generalizations can begin to form in their minds. They need to come at their work frequently enough too. Just to "do science" for a double period each week may be merely to provide them with long enough intervals in which to forget. For this reason alone the contribution that other subjects (mathematics and geography in particular) can make towards their scientific education is doubly valuable in the present condition of scarce resources. Once again we underline the fact that the need of our pupils for team work among the staff as a whole is greater than that of abler pupils.

430. With very slow pupils, who have limited powers of consciously transferring experience in one situation to a different situation, it may rarely be possible to generalize effectively. What has science to offer them? It can provide an absorbing activity in the solving of a very simple problem: "How can I get water from the tap to turn the wheel round?" "How can I get these seeds to germinate quickly?" In the solving they will be thinking of possibilities (hypotheses) and the means of trying them out (experiments) without consciously knowing that this is scientific method. Their disappointments can be educative and their successes triumphant. They will then have something to talk about, perhaps draw, or even write about. Many experienced teachers of the very slow have found in very simple science a means of re-energizing the disheartened.

431. Most of what we have said about the earlier part of the course is applicable to the spirit in which science will be taught in the later years too. But, as far as the content of the work is concerned, there could be dramatic changes for many pupils in their fourth and fifth years in the secondary school. The principle of choice applies easily to science, but perhaps some rethinking needs to be done about the range of choice that could be offered. As things are, the choices which are available usually correspond to the formal divisions of the subject—physics, chemistry, biology. It is doubtful whether these divisions have a natural relationship with the requirements of our pupils. We should prefer to see choices much more organically linked to what pupils want to be, or to a particular interest, or to some part of their curriculum.

432. For some, a natural choice would be the science which is particularly relevant to an occupation or to a further education course which they hope to follow. For some girls, a course might be based on investigating the nature and qualities of apparatus and materials used in the home as we suggested in the last chapter; it might require a different laboratory from what is now the standard kind. Some schools already run successful courses organized around rural crafts and occupations; they are good not only for their direct scientific purpose but also because looking after living things is good for people, and acquaintance with the countryside as the home of a basic industry can help to develop responsible attitudes in our pupils. Could this be matched for the town by using some other industry; building might be a case in point? It would be worth while to discover whether effective courses of study can be built around, say, electrical apparatus and circuits (or the internal combustion engine) which are a combination of handicraft and science. Here the word handicraft is to be interpreted very widely and the time for both handicraft and science would be brigaded. We have in mind something more wide ranging than a course in, say, motor vehicle maintenance, for, unless some of the larger scientific ideas are distilled, it will remain a course about engines alone —useful but of limited illumination. These are only examples, merely an indication of the kind of direction in which it may be fruitful to go.

433. If we are to begin where our boys and girls are, it will not be at the beginning of a logically organized course but somewhere in the middle. Perhaps with "How does an electric motor work?" "What are the factors which determine the heating power of an immersion heater?" Such questions could be tackled from actual investigation of simple enough models by finding out what the important factors in the situation are and investigating them further. But it would need a large supply of apparatus which is rather different from what is customary at present, apparatus in the form of easily assembled and dismantled kits which make up into something which works and can be seen working. There is opportunity, too, for making models in the handicraft room—rough and ready models which work and which are suitable for pupils who find working to accurate limits difficult, as well as the more sophisticated models which give great pleasure because they look so good and work so well when they are well finished. The whole question of courses and materials for teaching science to the ordinary boy or girl needs bold and thorough experiment. It may be that some courses offered by the school could be short courses of a term or two.

434. It may be said that some of these suggestions would lead the school into regions suitable only for industry or for further education. There are two

kinds of reply. The first is simply to ask what is wrong with a school course which overlaps with industry or further education. It is often said that the schools should give as general a grasp of scientific principles as possible and leave the applications to industry or to further education. Doubtless there is much truth in this, but it can be inhibiting. A general grasp comes out of particular instances. There is some danger of saying to the schools "You are out of touch, but you mustn't touch". The fewer the boundaries between school, industry and further education the better for all. What is quite certain is that the schools would need to have good liaison with industry and with further education if they are to put the most appropriate items into their syllabuses and to treat them appropriately too. Secondly, we would reiterate that we are thinking of courses which use interest in a technology to give starting points for important pieces of work in science, not as confining the science to a kind of technological training.

435. The pupils are living and will live in a world which is permeated with scientific reference. It is not a mere side issue that science at school should help them to deal with this situation. Once again the science teacher is in a strong position. His material is ready to hand, sometimes it will actually be sent through the post to his home and to those of his pupils. The laboratory notice board could act not only as a platform for good scientific matter, but as a pillory for bad. The pupils will not be slow to bring material and not slow to see that "Contains the new phenolthiocene" is meaningless, or that statements beginning "It has been scientifically proved . . ." need taking with some caution. A teacher, willing to be led up the garden a little, will do a great deal to help pupils to read in an adult manner, not just to read.

436. It is not only pseudo-science but real science that will come within the ambit of class discussion. Much scientific knowledge, even of science teachers, is hearsay; some one trustworthy is being believed. The pupils, interested in what is sometimes called "magazine science" are in much the same case. They talk about atoms, molecules, electrons and they may read about a large number of other so called particles. Could they not discuss the credibility of what they read? It is so easy to slip over into the land of uncritical wonder. They might be stirred by the thought that all our theories represent temporary resting places in an unending quest. Emotion and science are not utter strangers. Might not Newton's famous words about being on the sea-shore with the whole ocean of truth undiscovered before him make an appeal to ordinary boys and girls as much as to the sixth-former?

437. Even their own generalizations might receive a more careful look towards the end of the course. To "explain" pressure in terms of the random motion of gaseous molecules which are like very small billiard balls is to replace what has been seen by what is imagined. To look closely at Boyle's Law with the mind's eye is to see that, if it were universally true, air would need to be infinitely compressible—and where do molecules go then? Even a slow class which has enjoyed its science course may be willing to entertain such questions. We do not yet know how far it is possible to go if we are willing to draw on all the faculties of quite ordinary people, and it is important to remember that a time will come when the leaving age will be sixteen, with all this means for greater maturity.

438. Science leads, not only to its own problems, but straight to moral problems too. It does so in the outer world, and it follows automatically that it should do so in school. This is not just a matter of atomic bombs. The advance of medical knowledge brings its problems, and it has helped to present this and the next generation with the problem of the pressure of population on food supply. Such a matter might come up under health education, or under rural studies with its reference to crops, fertilizers, the struggle to improve wheat strains and the like. Again, a substantial course on the science relative to the internal combustion engine could connect up with what this invention has done to our lives as individuals, as sociable as well as social beings, and it is directly relevant to the world's energy resources. To have "done" such problems once in current affairs or modern history is not quite enough. Awareness is re-inforced by discovering awareness in many other people; even at the lowest, to find that "Old Stinks" (or his modern equivalent) is human is something. He may even, with propriety, discuss whether it is right to assume that what is not amenable to scientific investigation is somehow unreal. It is not unthinkable that the notice board in the science laboratory should sometimes display a poem; poets as well as scientists are observers.

439. The difference between knowing the facts and in some measure committing oneself to a personal attitude about their bearing on one's own actions stands out most clearly in that part of the science curriculum which deals with sexual reproduction. It is becoming clearer every day that, in the society in which we now live, the schools cannot contract out of the whole question of sexual conduct. The facts, as part of the make-up of the natural world, will be dealt with by science teachers; some, but not necessarily all, will also be the teachers who deal specifically with the problems they pose for personal conduct. The fact that in other directions, too, science leads to questions of moral principle, will help to put the specifically sexual questions in a more general framework. One of the main questions at issue, in the personal side of sexual behaviour, is how free we really are in our own actions when another personality (whether the child or the partner) is involved. Whatever doubts and hesitations teachers in our schools may have about positive moral teaching, surely they will not doubt that one of the cornerstones of civilized existence is the principle that nobody, merely for his own ends, has rights in the life of another. This is what resistance to the great political heresies of our times is about. It lies behind the long struggle for freedom from slavery, and behind much of our hard won legislation on conditions of labour. Should it not be put to our pupils that they too are subject to the same principle? If they are slower at seeing connections and arriving at generalizations than others, is it not all the more necessary that they should be shown that the connections exist? This is a matter for the policy of the school as a whole; the teachers of science will need to know clearly what this policy is. Nowadays, the challenge to express an opinion may crop up without notice in a most uninhibited manner from the pupils themselves. At least the major answers should be ready.

440. Finally, a point about the science course itself. It would be comparatively easy to go through an interesting and useful course without dwelling on the great unifying concepts—the energy chain, evolution, the balance of nature, the simpler quantitative laws (perhaps understood pictorially) and the like. They may be beyond some pupils, but those who have any chance of

grasping them, even though apparently fleetingly, should have the opportunity.

441. Mathematics has much to offer to boys and girls of ordinary ability at the secondary stage. It has a self-evident usefulness which can be a great advantage in arousing the interest of pupils who become bored by classroom tasks that may appear to them to be unrelated to their everyday experience.

442. Mathematics is a difficult subject, but not as difficult as it is often made out to be. Most people have a greater capacity for mathematical understanding than they are aware of, and a large reservoir of undeveloped mathematical competence certainly exists among youngsters of ordinary ability which good teaching and an enlightened approach could reveal. Few, if any, of our pupils are ever likely to become mathematicians, but some may well come to find satisfaction in mathematical work if its purpose has first been clearly seen and confidence established through the successful use of mathematics as a tool.

443. Recently and dramatically both the flavour and range of the mathematics which children are experiencing in an increasing number of primary schools are changing almost out of recognition. The secondary schools of the future can expect to base their mathematics teaching on foundations of interest and understanding to an extent that has never been possible before. These developments present a challenge and opportunity at the secondary stage.

444. The basis of all practical mathematics is a sound knowledge of the "facts" of elementary arithmetic—addition and multiplication tables, tables of quantities in common use. Many of our children will not have acquired facility in the four processes of addition, subtraction, multiplication and division in the primary schools, at least not with any permanence or security, and when, at the secondary stage, the four processes are found to have been inadequately learned, mere repetition of elementary exercises will fail to put matters right. Calculation must be re-introduced as an adjunct to more adult practical tasks that the pupils are anxious to do well but which cannot be tackled without the use of some mathematics.

445. Multiplication tables left unused are easily forgotten and other calculation skills can be as quickly lost. To keep these arithmetical tools in good condition is as important for all boys and girls, whatever their vocational interests, as for carpenters to keep their chisels sharp. Regular and fairly frequent practice in computation is therefore essential. The teacher of mathematics who has pupils of less than average ability needs a close knowledge of what they are doing outside the periods given to mathematics and must comb all the other subjects in which they show interest for material with which to build good lessons in mathematics itself. The teacher is presented with a serious difficulty in that to draw all examples from actual situations may leave uncovered or insufficiently practised important mathematical concepts which pupils could profitably master, given the opportunity and a reasonable amount of time. Just to do calculations about imagined real situations will not necessarily make an exercise "practical". Nor will this prevent boredom. The areas of carpets can be found too often.

446. The teacher seeking graded exercises may well feel the necessity of turning to textbooks. Unfortunately, textbook problems can rarely illustrate spontaneously the immediate interest or activities of the pupils. They tend inevitably to be artificial, too plainly, in the pupils' eyes, contrived in order to make work and take up classroom time. Even today, many textbook problems are unrealistic—halfpennies in money sums of over £100—merely in order to complicate a computation; or are drawn from situations which our pupils never meet. Examples from country life may have no relevance for the city dweller; problems about high blocks of flats may be meaningless for the pupil living in a rural area. There is no release for the teacher from the need for forethought, invention and a great deal of time week by week spent in the preparation of fresh material for purposeful classroom work. The essence of good teaching of mathematics for our pupils lies in variety and continuous adaptation, each new opportunity being seized as it arises.

447. Several recent publications give good examples of the kind of mathematical work derived from real situations which we have in mind and material of this nature is being used with marked success in many schools. Almost unlimited opportunity for valuable and stimulating lessons can arise from school activities; from the study of local activities or farm life, for example, from local history and geography, social science, biology. Pitching a tent, buying and bottling fruit, calculating crop yields can all lead to constructive mathematical work. Map-reading, surveying, the study of contours, meteorology, navigation, dressmaking—all these can provide the right kind of incentive. Even the "new mathematics" may have something to offer for some of our pupils where there is a well-qualified and well-versed enthusiast on the staff.

448. Though the schools need more mathematical expertise at their disposal than they have at present or are likely to have in the near future, almost all members of staff can and should help. The teacher with direct responsibility for mathematics must guide other members of staff in exploiting every situation which can lead to interesting mathematical work. The specialist will need to advise non-specialists on how to introduce mathematical ideas in logical sequence through their own particular subjects or interests. Careful guidance will be necessary if fragmentation is to be avoided and in order to ensure a common precision in the use and language of mathematics. If the best advantage is to be taken of the many opportunities for stimulating interest that arise in the general work of the school, the staff must work as a team. There will need to be a clear school policy and regular meetings to secure the proper planning and co-ordination of the mathematical work.

449. The less able the pupils, the simpler the work will need to be, the less rigorous the approach and the more closely related to practical needs. But an approach in which at least some of our pupils wake to the need for mathematics and see the purpose in terms of a vocation or leisure pursuit can revolutionize attitudes and reveal unexpected mathematical aptitude. The basic mathematical equipment for successful everyday living must be acquired before leaving school. Personal budgeting and "social arithmetic"—gas and electricity accounts, what rates and taxes are about, how local and welfare services are paid for, and even their cost—should find a place in the curriculum of every pupil, not necessarily in the mathematics periods. The

decimalization of British money, and, eventually we hope of weights and measures, will remove a serious stumbling block in the teaching of mathematics. Considerable emphasis can profitably be given to the use of decimals and to the decimal system generally.

450. In calculation, as in reading, there is inevitably for many pupils a good deal left to be done at the secondary stage. Facility in calculation comes only with time, with practice and with increasing maturity and understanding of mathematical ideas. The emphasis in calculation should always be on accuracy rather than on speed, for speed is of little consequence—it grows of itself from a habit of accuracy. Success and confidence is all-important whether at the primary or secondary stage and computation should be done in short and easy stages. Facility cannot be acquired once and for all by a concentrated drive, but grows through constantly applying previously learnt mathematical techniques in new contexts. A drive for accuracy of a "brush up your calculations" type when pupils are in sight of leaving school and there is a strong vocational motive can, however, prove most rewarding.

451. There is particular value in taking advantage of the pupils' increasing vocational interests during the last years of school and in relating a wider range of mathematical work to employment and to the work of colleges of further education.

452. To teach the use of tables, ready reckoners, charts and diagrams, and to give ample practice in the use of rulers, tape-measures, the compass, protractor, set-squares, vernier callipers and measuring instruments of all kinds is important. Engineering drawing has special interest for boys; and girls, too, can show talent for technical drawing if they are given the right encouragement. There can usefully be some undisguisedly vocational studies, for example in running savings schemes, designing and executing controlled experiments in rural studies, costing, and catering.

453. A desk calculating machine can widen the scope of the enquiries which can be tackled by a class and makes possible all manner of social and physical statistical investigations which are well within the understanding of pupils of ordinary ability in the secondary schools. Some mathematical models and working apparatus which are nowadays produced commercially are both well constructed and beautiful to look at; a carefully selected collection can be a great asset to mathematics teaching. Pupils should be encouraged also to construct apparatus and illustrative material for themselves.

454. For this, a well-equipped mathematics room is needed to which pupils can go for practical project work in mathematics as well as for formal lessons. Flexibility in the timetabling of mathematics work and in the use of the mathematics room is desirable to allow for both single and double periods. It is not suggested that all mathematics teaching should take place in a special room.

455. Rapid developments are being made in the use of teaching machines and the techniques of programmed learning; these may prove to be valuable aids to teachers both with new work and for revision. Much research remains to be done before the contribution that they are likely to make to the teaching of our pupils can be assessed. Any real success with teaching machines will depend on teachers having adequate induction courses and on well-designed programmes becoming readily available which teach the kind of mathematics

that makes sense for our pupils. Mechanical aids can be of great help in remedial work.

456. Much has been said in this chapter about computation and practical arithmetic. A broader outlook to the mathematical syllabus as a whole is, of course, required. We are encouraged by the extent of the new thinking that is taking place all over the country about the teaching of mathematics and by the enthusiasm shown by teachers in attending courses on mathematics. There is no lack of ideas, but judgement is required in their application and this can come only with experience in the actual teaching situation.

457. Have we developed far enough new approaches to mathematics for the slow arithmetician comparable to the successful new approaches to reading for the backward reader? Pupils who are backward in mathematics need not necessarily be excluded from assisting classmates in some of the practical mathematics work undertaken—they can gain something by noticing how others set about a job and even by holding the end of a measuring tape if this contributes to an understood purpose.

458. Some classes are seriously hampered by having to include pupils who, though not necessarily backward in other subjects, need remedial treatment in mathematics. If remedial work is required, it needs to be given in separate small groups: the presence of the teacher and individual help is essential. There can be no prescribed rules: every case in unique.

459. Most adults who have experienced success either in academic work or practical or physical activity can look back and pick out some particular moment of time when the subject "went critical". The learner suddenly catches the knack of riding a bicycle, of playing piano arpeggios, of feeling the rhythm of a poem. Professional mathematicians have these moments of enlightenment throughout their successful working lives, for in mathematics as in the other sciences, and, indeed, in most subjects and activities, understanding may come suddenly and unexpectedly, only after long periods of groping endeavour. So it is for children. Many adults, perhaps most, "get by" with minimum rule-of-thumb techniques in mathematics which bear no relationship to the real language of mathematics and which cannot lead to understanding. Our aim in the teaching of mathematics to all pupils, to those of average and below average ability no less than to those with marked academic talent, should be to bring them to an interest in the content of mathematics itself at however modest a level. For success, the teachers with special responsibility must themselves have a real enthusiasm for mathematics and for mathematical ideas and language, and this must be based on good personal mathematical attainments and experience. Teachers must also have a sympathetic understanding of the interests, needs and difficulties of their pupils, and a thirst for experiment in finding and exploiting mathematical situations which arise in the pupils' daily experience.

460. Mathematics and science, closely interlocked, are the basis of the most revolutionary of recent developments in society and in the everyday lives of all young people. Even the slowest pupils are interested in progress and success, and in demonstrating that mathematics can contribute towards success. We may best hope to give all pupils before leaving school some realization of its intrinsic value.

CHAPTER 19

The Humanities

A. ENGLISH

461. The use of language in thought and in communication must enter into every part of the curriculum. English, as a subject primarily concerned with care for words, clearly has a distinctive contribution to make, yet it is doubtful if that contribution is at present as effective as it might be. Of the general sincerity and frequent skill of the teaching there can be no question; real illiteracy in the formal sense is comparatively rare. But there seems a very general feeling that the ordinary boy and girl should leave school with a better command of English than they in fact appear to possess. Have aim and method in English teaching kept pace with what we know about young people and how they learn? And does English teaching take sufficient account of the relation between school and the world beyond? For the pupils are a product of both and so is the command of language which they need for maturity.

462. The teachers of English tend to think of their subject from three different but related points of view: as a medium of communication, as a means of creative expression, and as a literature embodying the vision of greatness. They are trying to offer all pupils the freedom of all three, and rightly do not think of the weaker boys and girls as living in a kind of nature reserve, debarred by lack of ability from the great things of our civilization. That way lies apartheid. But in practice many of the weaker pupils never seem to reach the point at which real English begins. Some teachers, including many who have never been trained for teaching English, give them a watered down version of what they remember from their own grammar school experiences. Much use is made of text books providing endless exercises in comprehension, composition and the like. There are rough books and best books, the former filling up more quickly than the latter with laborious writing. Commas are inserted, spelling corrected. Occasionally free composition produces a shapeless mess in which the memory of many televised Westerns often seems to be still riding the range of the pupil's mind. Poetry is "done": drama may occur on Friday afternoon and towards Christmas . . .

463. When handled with competence and conviction, the traditional teaching pattern can enlist interest and encourage progress. But it is too seldom about anything of much potential importance to the pupil; where there is little to talk about, conversation or discussions cannot flourish. What is learned today tends to be forgotten tomorrow; it is not applied to other subjects. Nor, though plenty of work seems to be going on, do teacher or pupil seem to expect much real progress. There is little pleasure or respect for skill.

464. The weaker pupils in the third or fourth year do not seem to mind too much, even where, as is not uncommon, the text books seem a tired survival from the junior school. But good humoured tolerance often passes into a somewhat cynical attitude which may in turn become definite rejection, when reading means little to these pupils, and writing less. What they already have

of either seems enough for their needs later on. And when it comes to speech, there is often a deep-seated corporate resistance to the very notion of "talking posh".

465. But the pupils are not merely a product of school. Their standards in speech, as in much else, reflect those of their families. They have heard much about the outside world from older relatives already in jobs, as well as from newspapers, magazines, the cinema and television. The last appears particularly potent, if only because so many particularly of the less able pupils have imbibed so much of it. Like the other mass media it tends to mirror and over-emphasize certain aspects of our society which are at variance with the values of school—not for nothing is the screen schoolmaster usually a buffoon. No wonder if school is regarded as something to be tolerated.

466. Yet we must not forget all the ordinary pupils who happily make good progress. Nor are boys and girls as grown-up as they would like us to think; many a young man has left coffee-bar, fruit machine and girl friend to play, with or without a younger brother, with the toys of childhood. And under their veneer of sophistication these young people know they are not yet properly equipped to face the outside world. But their misgivings are inarticulate. They need help and will accept it if this can be done without loss of face.

467. The overriding aim of English teaching must be the personal development and social competence of the pupil. And of all the different aspects of English, speech has by far the most significant contribution to make towards that development. Inability to speak fluently is a worse handicap than inability to read or write. Though boys and girls learn to speak long before they go to their first school, every school carries a major responsibility for its pupils' speech. This is not essentially a matter of accent or pronunciation, although in a mobile society it is realistic to recognize that the pupils who have no alternative to a strictly local vernacular may be at a disadvantage in later life. But far more important is the need to ensure that they can speak easily, clearly and with interest, and have something to talk about. Personal and social adequacy depend on being articulate, that is, on having the words and language structures with which to think, to communicate what is thought, and to understand what is heard or read. The pupils need in school experiences which will not only help them to find the words but also give them confidence to express them. Any definition of literacy for them must include an improved command of spoken English, particularly in understanding argument and in trying to put a point of view. Side by side with speech comes its partner listening; conversation presupposes both, but too few pupils ever learn to listen carefully, to the teacher or to each other. Here the teacher's example is all-important; when he teaches, is it all monologue or a reasonably balanced dialogue in which the pupils get a fair chance; is he interested in what they have to say?

468. Real communication begins when the words are about experience, ideas, and interests which are worth putting into language. The teacher can initiate and encourage; he cannot do the work for the pupils, but he can suggest work that is clearly worth doing and help them to do it. Only he can find out what interests his pupils, and he must begin, though not end, with that. The initial experience will be that of home, school and the immediate background,

though young people's curiosity will soon take them beyond that. There is so much to discuss, not only local and domestic questions, but also such themes as fashion, death, the rate for the job, marriage, football, abstract art, the prospect of human survival, or bringing up children. Hobbies such as fishing, vintage cars, and aircraft all offer possibilities which point beyond their own first beginnings—for discussion will not satisfy for long.

469. Books, magazines and the library are, or should be, there to help. The library ought to be the power-house of words and ideas: it is the more regrettable that large numbers of secondary schools—three-fifths of the modern schools in our survey—are still seriously deficient in library accommodation.[1] Even where facilities are good, it requires resource and persistence to contrive that the less able pupils really benefit from them. It seems likely that there is often a notable drop in the quality of books available to many pupils when they move from the primary to the secondary school, partly because there is a tendency for schools to cater most fully for their ablest pupils, and partly because it is not easy to provide, at least for the older pupil of really limited reading ability, books which are sufficiently simple and yet appropriately adult in content and vocabulary. The latter problem becomes even more acute when the pupils leave school. Even with the large numbers of boys and girls to whom the mechanics of reading present no serious difficulties, there is a need to enlist interest and to establish reading habits which will persist beyond school. Valuable co-operation exists in some areas between schools and public libraries, and deserves wider extension. Certainly it is not enough merely to persuade pupils to acquire a public library ticket, nor simply to insert "library" periods into the school time-table.

470. The library, fully equipped and used, has much to offer. There are paper backs, books of reference, and periodicals about anything from railways to homemaking. Assignments on topics appropriately related to the pupils' interests and experience, yield, as well as information, the pleasure of working seriously on one's own. The results may not be wonderful at first, but the excitement of making discoveries and advancing is catching; the pupils will not be unaffected by the gradual enlarging of their powers which will follow. But much will always depend on the individual pupil; every pupil is an unknown country which the teacher approaches like a water diviner, and only when he touches the springs of interest will language begin to flow.

471. Seeking information is one aspect of the use of books. Techniques of reading remain important, not least when the pupil has nominally learned to read. Practice in slow, careful reading, practice in rapid reading, work (much of it going deeper than traditional "comprehension" questions) to link reading with speaking and writing can all help; good reading aloud by a teacher may be much appreciated by the class. In the long run quality of reading usually depends upon will and interest. Many adults manage quite happily with little reading and less writing; the pupils know it, even though they also will accept that one cannot really go very far in contemporary life without either. In a world where the spoken word is so much more important than it was, we cannot assume that all our pupils will take reading or writing seriously unless

[1] Details are given in paragraphs 677–681.

we show them (rather than preach) the value of both. This means taking account once again of the pupils' background and interests—and also of their personal history; some, particularly of the weaker ones, associate reading and writing with six or seven years of continuous failure, and these salvage cases are the most difficult of all. Yet even at fourteen it is not too late to make a fresh start, provided that the start really is fresh; it is useless to go on boring the pupils of this age with books from the primary school, and one remembers the story of the young man of nearly fourteen given up by his teachers as a hopeless illiterate, who ran a successful betting book under cover of his children's primers; when challenged, he is alleged to have replied: "You don't think I can be bothered with all that muck".

472. Given a basic literacy, the work in the later part of the school life may be increasingly concerned with the use of literacy: having learned, in some degree, how to handle words, the pupils have to be helped to learn now not to be handled by them. They need not merely to read, but to read with increasing sensitivity. This may require more attention to what pupils read at their own level, to help them formulate their own responses in words, and so be in a better position to criticise for themselves. Work of this kind, in relation to popular magazines and newspapers and advertising, is to be found in the schools but needs to be done more widely and systematically.

473. Nor should this more perceptive approach to reading be confined to popular journalism or what the pupils may voluntarily seek for themselves. All pupils, including those of very limited attainments, need the civilising experience of contact with great literature, and can respond to its universality, although they will depend heavily on the skill of the teacher as an interpreter. Sympathetically presented, literature can stretch the minds and imaginations of the pupils, and help to illumine for them, in wider human terms, their own problems of living. In so difficult a task the teacher will need a greatly extended range of books from which to choose, and all the help which professional readers and actors on records and radio and television can give. Indeed, in in all its work in speech and reading and writing, the English department will have special need of these aids and of others such as tape recorder and film, as both sources of material and methods of teaching.

474. Here we should wish to add a strong claim for the study of film and television in their own right, as powerful forces in our culture and significant sources of language and ideas. Although the study of these media has for some time been accepted in a small number of schools as an important part of the curriculum, in the majority of schools they are used only as visual aids for the presentation of material connected with other subjects. Again, making a film is frequently seen as an interesting and unusual practical activity especially for the less academically gifted child; film and television clubs may be organized after school hours for the showing of feature films or informal discussion of evening programmes: all these ways of using film and television are valuable and constructive, and their extension is commended elsewhere in this report. The most important and most general use of these media, however, as major means for the mass communication of cultural experiences, is not generally dealt with in schools any more than it is in colleges or universities. Little attention is paid to the degree to which film and television enter into and influence the lives of our pupils and to these media as legitimate means for the

communication of personal experience alongside literature, music and painting.

475. The culture provided by all the mass media, but particularly by film and television represents the most significant environmental factor that teachers have to take into account. The important changes that take place at the secondary stage are much influenced by the world offered by the leisure industry which skilfully markets products designed for young people's tastes. The media help to define aspirations and they offer roles and models. They not only supply needs (and create them) but may influence attitudes and values. Little as yet has been effectively undertaken in schools in the way of offering some counter balancing assistance. We need to train children to look critically and discriminate between what is good and bad in what they see. They must learn to realize that many makers of films and of television programmes present false or distorted views of people, relationships, and experience in general, besides producing much trivial and worthless stuff made according to stock patterns.

476. By presenting examples of films selected for the integrity of their treatment of human values, and the craftsmanship with which they were made, alongside others of mixed or poor quality, we can not only build up a way of evaluating but also lead the pupils to an understanding of film as a unique and potentially valuable art form in its own right as capable of communicating depth of experience as any other art form. Just as we have traditionally thought it important to broaden children's response to and experience of literature and music, so we must now offer a comparative education in the important and powerful visual media, both because these media at their best have much that is valuable to offer and simply because communication in the twentieth century is becoming increasingly visual. The making of films when allied to studies of this kind becomes a much more potent educational instrument. One of the difficulties in extending this work is the shortage of teachers equipped to tackle it. While there is a supply, even if inadequate, of specialist and other teachers with some training in literature, music, art and drama, there are very few teachers equipped to deal with the art forms that most closely touch the boys and girls of this report. We are glad to note that some training colleges have begun to respond to this challenge by offering courses in film both as major and minor elements in a course.

477. English comes within the sphere of the liberal arts for the pupils covered by this enquiry. It is not always easy to remember this; and yet, where there is real progress, such things as colour, feeling, tone, rhythm and the pleasure of language are surprisingly often playing a part. Heart is involved as well as head. It is of course within poetry and drama that the use of language goes deepest. Nobody should have to teach poetry against his will, but without it English will never be complete; poetry is not a minor amenity but a major channel of experience. The best starting point is likely to be the present, and there is a great deal of contemporary verse to draw on, including ballads, songs and even limericks. How far the great poetry of earlier ages can be introduced with advantage only the teacher can say. Good reading by the teacher and the use (too rare in many schools) of records of spoken poetry will help the pupil to broaden his range; from listening to reading (in a group as well as individually) is a second step; from reading to writing is a third. In a number of schools very ordinary boys and girls are writing verse with

pleasure, and the result, however simple, can be a moving and sometimes beautiful comment upon experience.

478. Though drama comes, by school tradition, into the English field, it is a creative art embracing much more than English. Perhaps its central element is, or should be, improvisation. It involves movement as well as words—that is one main reason why an outsize classroom or a small hall is really essential for English teaching. Drama can include miming and acting everyday situations or familiar stories, playwriting and play reading: all are relevant for the pupils covered by this enquiry, so long as we respect the limits of their understanding. It is useless, for example, to take them out of their depth in dramatic literature. If they read plays, they must be helped to realize that a play is not just the words in the book but much more besides.

479. Drama can offer something more significant than the day-dream. It helps boys and girls to identify themselves with well known men and women of whom they have heard or read. By playing out psychologically significant situations, they can work out their own personal problems. Here is one way in which they can be helped to reconcile the reality of the world outside with their own private worlds. Once this begins, education has something on which to build. In short, drama, along with poetry and the other arts, is not a "frill" which the less able can safely omit or relegate to a minor position on some Friday afternoons. Art is not an expensive substitute for reality. It is through creative arts, including the arts of language, that young people can be helped to come to terms with themselves more surely than by any other route.

480. It is a matter of some concern that the educative experience of drama in all its forms is too often, despite notable exceptions, restricted or denied to pupils. In school, the reason is often lack of suitable teachers, or of accommodation; outside, in many areas, there are too few opportunities for seeing high quality productions in the theatre. The stimulation of interest in the professional theatre, and encouragement to feel that it is part of their own, not an alien, culture, is particularly important for the older boys and girls, if they are not to miss this source of enrichment of their adult lives.

481. The best way to study writing is to practise it. Children only learn writing by writing, and they are best prepared to write about their own experiences. These free out-pourings have much of the character of free verse: they are shapeless often, and lack control over words, grammar, spelling and punctuation. Gradually, improved writing develops. With some of our pupils it may never become completely mature or adult, but it can be encouraged by understanding teachers. Teachers whose sole standard is correctness can dry up the flow of language and shackle creative and imaginative writing before it is under way. Precision and logical arrangement of ideas may well be sought but will not readily be found. Of the quotations (both extracts from longer pieces) which follow a headmaster writes:

"These would never have been written had correctness been our care. This boy of fifteen must only have bottled up his feeling for his pigeons. The quantity of output would have suffered and the quality of natural expression have been lost. The tenderness of the first passage, and the professional appraisal of the racing birds in the second, spring from real experience, creative enjoyment, and a pupil teacher relationship that develops confidence."

(a) (Part of a story, A Pigeon to be Remembered):

"Every day David looked at his egges to see if they were hatching, taking great care not to alarm the birds or touch the egges. He soon got downhearted and thought his egges would never hatch, and then one day to his great joy he saw his first baby pigeon, it sat there with it large eyes shut and all its golden doun beutifieing its otherwise ugly stature. He smiles as he shut the door of his small coop, and then suddenly he thought such a terrible thought that he ran almost in tears to his mother, and spluttered the words out, mother only one egge has hatched. A great smile came over his mothers face and she said they don't hatch at ones. A great smile came over his face, and he told her of his little baby pigeon and asked her if she wanted to see it, no she said let his sleep now he will be tired"

(b) (from a description of preparing entries for racing):

"It was about half past five, as I went down to the loft, the weather was fine, the wind was in the East. I loocked out accross the sky and said to my self I hope it stays as fine as this. After fidling around in my pocket I finally found my key and opened the lock. The usualy rumpus happened, My big black Cock Bird called Sulky Sam jumped on my shoulder, and started to pick my ears in his usual way, this earned him the name of Sulky Sam. I picked him up of my shoulder and loocked at him carefully, he was one of six candates, two of which would race. I loocked into his eyes, and grunted contentidly, it was good and bright, and the core was beutifully white. I ran my hand gently down his side and felt his beutifully hard body and silky feathers. I then opened his wing and saw every flight and secondry in beutiful condition. I brushed my fingers down his wing and it squeked and a lot of bloom came off it.

The next bird I came across was a hen and soon as I laid hands on I thought she seemed lively. She was in lovely condition, and had the things about her I was looking for. Her wattle was lovely and white and she handled beutifully. She was also sitting correctly. The Black and this hen were my candidates."

482. Writing is most likely to flourish in an atmosphere of ideas, discussion and reading, but it remains a difficult art and must be recognized as such. As far as the technicalities of English are concerned, balance is needed: spelling and punctuation must be taken seriously, but not with such ferocity that (as often happens) the pupil gives up trying. Spelling games do no harm if they are brief; a close link between writing and recent reading also helps. But while English spelling remains what it is, some even of our ablest pupils will always have trouble with it, and a few have spelling problems which call for treatment beyond the resources of the ordinary class teacher. Punctuation is best learned where there are ideas to express and points to make; full stops and commas should be friends, not enemies, if one has something to communicate. Correction involves a good many technical points beyond the compass of this report; not all mistakes need be scored through, the real problem is to touch the pupils' pride in giving the best that is in them. In reading and

writing alike, we might learn from the primary school practice of carefully checking the progress of individual pupils from stage to stage.

483. A wide and generous course of English should do much to prepare these pupils for life in an adult society; it is vocational in the best possible way. Such a course should provide a good foundation of workmanlike English, in that it will enable boys and girls in later life to read instructions or pass on messages, or write a letter, or jot down a record. The course will almost certainly have included practice in writing real letters, both personal letters, for example, to a member of the class in hospital, and more formal letters, such as those to firms asking for a leaflet or arranging a visit. Some special help, but not much, will be needed, if it is necessary to write letters of applications for employment; but those devastating make-believe applications in laborious, unreal letters should not often be needed, In any case too much must not be expected: the employer who wants his employees to be proficient in the written word will probably have to provide specialized linguistic practice as part of the training given to new entrants, however well the school does its work. But these are not the only, or even the most important vocational aspects of English. In whatever job, and at whatever level of skill, the pupils may subsequently be working, they will all need to enter into effective relations with other people, if they are to work efficiently and happily. What they take with them from school in improved powers of speech, and in sympathetic insight into human relationships gained through literature, will be of great value to them here. To achieve success in their work, even in the narrowest sense, the boys and girls will require an experience of English that is far from narrow. To those objectors who say in effect "Cut out the frills. You haven't the time, and the pupil hasn't the capacity, for more than the three Rs; this is the only way to deal with illiteracy", we repeat, as we have argued earlier, that such a restricted programme defeats its own ends.

484. English is distinctive in the curriculum in that it is both all-pervasive and yet has relatively little subject matter of its own. In the greater part of the pupils' work concerned with communication, with the acquisition of information and with the recording and evaluation of experience, English performs a service function to other subjects: it is the other subjects which supply the content, and the occasions for strengthening the pupils' resources in language. English must not be a subject narrowly ensphered within its own specialist boundaries; neither must it disappear altogether. It has distinctive experiences to offer: there will, for example, always need to be timetable periods in which the main emphasis falls on imaginative literature, and it is not easy to see how other subjects could take these over. The English lesson, too, is most likely to offer those opportunities which allow adolescents to write out of themselves what they are not always prepared or able to talk about: in the writing, deeply personal thoughts and feelings may be disguised or transmuted. Some of the least able pupils most need these opportunities.

485. But there are schools in which much, perhaps even most, of the speaking, reading and writing are taught through the medium of other subjects, or through projects of various kinds. Project work offers the incentive of a unified and challenging task, and also a means of bringing together diverse subjects, although projects cannot always cover all the important points; as the pupils get older, the various fields of knowledge are likely to be wider and

more sharply defined than for younger pupils, regardless of ability. Whatever the pattern of organization, the content of other subjects provides the pupils in any event with a great part of their verbal education. Not only are they continuously using ordinary English which is common to all occasions; but they are acquiring a series of important special vocabularies which enlarge the field in which their minds are active. There is a particular literacy required in all subjects which should be carefully fostered by those who teach them. They are, perhaps, more likely to do this if sufficient time is allowed for the purpose (as it often is not at present) and if the objective is thought of as a necessary part of what they are thelmseves teaching rather than as a contribution to "English" which is somebody else's business.

486. We feel considerable disquiet at the possible impact of examinations on English teaching. The proposed examination for the Certificate of Secondary Education is designed for boys and girls whose capacity varies from just below G.C.E. standard to a little below the middle of the ability range. Since the new examination will concern only those who stay on until sixteen, it is not likely at first to be taken by very many of the less able pupils. But when all have a five year course there may be a real danger of distorted teaching as a result of too many candidates in the third and even fourth quarter of ability being put through unsuitable tests. We should not wish to see the main emphasis in Form 5C (and probably in 4C and 3C as well) being devoted to answering examination questions, instead of learning English. And, if we may judge by G.C.E. experience, preoccupation with examinations would tend to perpetuate a teaching pattern in which the whole form is treated as a single unit, at the expense of individual and group study.

487. To many good judges our suggestions will probably seem not so much unreasonable as Utopian. There are all the physical difficulties so often mentioned in this report. Even more serious is the shortage of trained teachers. Not many teachers without knowledge or training can teach the subject in the way that we have tried to suggest, however great their devotion and natural skill. And the supply of real specialists capable of making good heads of department or deputy heads, who would give a lead in the right direction, is drying up. Many schools have made great strides in English as in other subjects during the past decade, but today some of the best are full of misgiving. The quality of English teaching threatens to become worse; if it does, the weakest pupils will suffer most because the dominant pattern of teaching is always likely to be, for the non-specialist working without help, that which is set by the ablest groups and which is inappropriate for those with which we are concerned. We face, then, a crisis which is even now not sufficiently recognized, because it is a crisis of quality as much as of quantity. The challenge in teacher training is formidable. This is partly a matter of supply and organization, but it is more than that alone. It involves a wider recognition of what these pupils need. They deserve the best.

B. A FOREIGN LANGUAGE

488. In our survey, just under a third of the modern schools provided some foreign language teaching, mainly in French, and largely confined to the

ablest pupils.[1] In the country as a whole at the present time, a foreign language is probably taught to about a third of the pupils in perhaps half of the modern schools. It is clear that very large numbers of boys and girls, including most of our "average" as well as the "below average" pupils, as yet have had no opportunity of learning a foreign language. The reasons for this are partly historical, partly related to the shortage of really skilled and fluent language teachers. There are nevertheless signs that this situation is beginning to change, and we think it wholly desirable that it should.

489. There are several reasons why boys and girls of all levels of ability should have the opportunity of learning a foreign language. One has an important connection with their urgent need, already discussed in relation to English, of improved powers of communication. Learning to speak in a foreign tongue offers one more experience of the significance of words as tools, as means of indicating particular objects or actions or ideas; and as a result of this, though very simply in the case of the more limited pupils, they may begin to think about the use of words in their own language. While we should not suggest that very backward boys and girls still struggling to attain the barest literacy in their own language should be burdened with another, there is every likelihood that other pupils, whose poor attainments stem from disturbed early schooling or adverse environment rather than lack of native wit, might be helped, by the stimulus of a foreign language well taught, to apply fresh energy to the learning of their own.

490. Indeed, some of us would consider this the most important reason of all, that the learning of a new language may give confidence to those pupils who need it most—the less than average, those who have often had difficulty with English. The feeling that they too can express themselves, however simply, in a foreign tongue can increase their self-respect and improve their general attitude to learning. We have long accepted that children of relatively limited general ability in Switzerland, the Netherlands, and the Scandinavian countries acquire a simple, spoken knowledge of other languages: we should not deny the opportunity to our own children. In spite of frequent assertions to the contrary, there is no solid evidence that, comparing like with like, our people have less aptitude for languages than those of other nations.

491. In the past, the people of this country have had their closest links with the English speaking world and have generally lacked the incentive which some other European countries have had to learn a foreign language. But circumstances are changing, and are already beginning to create a climate of opinion which may be very favourable to language teaching on a much wider scale. Not only in our national economic life, for which it is highly important that as many people as possible should be able to cross the language barrier, but in private life, the links with the rest of Europe are growing stronger every day. The notable increase in recent years of facilities for foreign travel, both by school parties and by families and young people on holiday, has provided a strong motive for acquiring at least a "tourist" knowledge of another language—as witness the interest and persistence with which many thousands of adults have followed broadcast language series.

492. When young people and adults travel abroad, as increasing numbers certainly will, it is important that they should go wanting to make contact

[1] See paragraphs 633–635.

with the people of the country, and ready to appreciate their distinctive way of life. This attitude is more likely to develop through the learning of the language, than by merely reading about the French or Germans or Italians— although obviously there will still be a need for considerable reading in English about the country in question, to supplement a modest acquaintance with the language. For many of our pupils, both the language and the supplementary reading stimulated by the possibility of a visit may valuably enlarge their general stock of ideas and of knowledge. Here is one more window on the world, a chance to extend their experience through contact with a different people and culture.

493. The question arises as to which foreign language should be taught. French is the usual one because there are more people available to teach it. It is not, however, the easiest in its early stages, and Spanish and Italian have been more successfully taught to the less able pupils in some schools. The difficulty is to ensure a succession of good teachers, whatever language is chosen. Continuity of teaching, always important in the learning of a language, is essential in the weakest groups. The teachers must be fluent and have an easy command of the language. The approach must be an oral one; the argument for teaching a language is valid only if the pupils can speak what they know. We accept the fact that some will never speak more than a few simple sentences but many will do more that that and will be able to write simply as well. It will be, with rare exceptions, only the most able who will speak fluently and write accurately. Nevertheless we would not deny even to the least able the privilege and the fun of being able to say a few simple things in a language other than their own.

494. Opinion varies as to how long average and below average pupils can go on learning a language. The experience over seven years of one comprehensive school is that a language can be taught to girls of all levels of ability for at least three years, and that in spite of the great demands it makes on the patience and ingenuity of the staff, it is well worth doing for the sake of the pupils. If there can be continuity of teaching, it would seem that a language can profitably be studied to the end of the fifth year by average girls though probably not by the least able. But the truth is that although we know this is happening in one school, and probably in others, there is too little experience nationally of trying to teach a foreign language over the whole, or most, of the ability range for anyone to gauge the limits and possibilities. Quite certainly there is evidence that many more boys and girls could respond to an opportunity.

495. Current trends are all in favour of letting them try. A large-scale experiment supported by the Ministry and the local education authorities is even now introducing a foreign language into primary schools. Before long, many boys and girls will in any case be arriving at their secondary schools with an awakened interest in the speech and customs of another country, and will be disappointed if they cannot continue with the language they have begun to learn.

496. Happily, just at the time when the demand for teachers of foreign languages may rise sharply, there have been striking advances in teaching techniques based on the use of audio-visual aids, which offer ways of considerably supplementing the teacher's own resources. These methods, which

put an emphasis on lively communication through speech, as opposed to an analytical, text-book approach, could have special significance for our pupils. But as yet too few schools in this country have had experience in using these methods, or possess the necessary equipment, for the full possibilities to be assessed. Many more schools need to be equipped to take full advantage of materials and techniques involving the use of film-strips and tape recorders, listening booths, and radio and television programmes designed especially for this purpose.

497. We welcome the present interest in language teaching, at both the primary and the secondary stage, and believe that extended experiments are highly desirable, in methods of teaching and learning over the whole range of ability, and in the choice of the language taught. Given good conditions, a foreign language, taught in a well-conceived oral course and enlivened wherever possible by direct contacts with a foreign country, might well be one of the most stimulating subjects in the curriculum for some of the pupils of this report.

498. Finally, there is a significant world trend towards more language learning. Europe as a whole is ahead of this country in including a foreign language. and often two, in the general education of a much larger proportion of its citizens. Humanly and economically speaking, insularity is behind the times.

C. THE PROPER STUDY OF MANKIND

499. The importance of history and geography, or the social studies in which they are sometimes merged, seems obvious. A man who is ignorant of the society in which he lives, who knows nothing of its place in the world and who has not thought about his place in it, is not a free man even though he has a vote. He is easy game for "the hidden persuaders". A society in which he and his like predominate is at their mercy. We may turn Abraham Lincoln's saying to our situation: 'this nation cannot survive half slave and half free'. Too often, however, the boys and girls with whom we are concerned do not see this. Geography and perhaps even more frequently history lessons are expendable as far as boys, and to a less extent girls are concerned. They cannot buy anything with this kind of kowledge as they can with physics and shorthand; they are not always willing to pay for it with hard work as they will for the skills of handicraft or dressmaking. Henry Ford's "history is bunk", did they but know it, expresses exactly what they feel; but, of course, Henry Ford is as dead to them as Queen Anne—or history.

500. This is a grimly pessimistic view. In so far as it is true it represents a grave danger. But, while it holds good of many pupils in many schools, we see no reason why this should go on. If other schools can tell a different story, and they can, we are not confronted with a psychological barrier which prevents people of below average intelligence, that is to say about half the nation, forming a responsible and reasoned opinion about public affairs. Optimism is possible. The important thing is to discover and apply the means by which it can be justified.

501. They will be found in classrooms. A 16 mm film about an Indian village has just been shown. Here are to be seen temple and mosque, dung cakes and wooden plough, the monsoon bank of earth and nearby the building of a large concrete dam soon to result in a permanent water supply and the gift of

electricity. Here in a Birmingham classroom in 1963 is present at one time a recapitulation of many thousands of years of human history. Maps, statistics, first-hand descriptions may lead on to questions of climate, food, birth-rate, clothing, caste, nationalism, religion, and governmental planning.

502. The film has raised questions. The answers call for contributions of many kinds from many groups of pupils. Discussion alone is not enough. Its purpose is to decide on a programme of work and to evaluate work done. In between comes the work. This requires the provision of much source material. Standard reference books will be needed; good maps; an indexed collection of pictures and diagrams. Some will be to hand in the geography room; some in the school library; the public library system will be involved. Eventually, when some final worrying area of ignorance remains to be explored— but, if the teacher is wise, only then—reference may be made to the Commonwealth Institute or to the Indian or Pakistan High Commission. The pupils will have been investigating real problems, using adult sources of information and becoming involved in a world situation in which they may have a part to play.

503. In another school boys and girls of the same age are engaged in what one might call a series of confrontations. Here, magnified, is a rubbing of a George VI half-crown with its superscription "Ind. Imp." and the date. Next to it on the display board, is a similar rubbing of a Victorian half-crown—how by the way was this obtained? The dates are compared and the heyday of the British raj is fixed. The class are debating what shall be put opposite the half-crowns. The Indian flag? Mahatma Ghandi's spinning wheel? Is the latter already as dated as the George VI half-crown? Why? We are back to the population problem. Then, pictures. "Forty years on", a line of melody from the school song, a silhouette of Harrow Hill and the pictures of Jawaharlal Nehru and Winston Churchill. Questions again: What brought Nehru to Harrow? Will other Indian boys in the future do the same sort of thing? Would they understand the language if they did? We are back before we know it to Lord Macaulay and on to this year's debates in the Indian parliament on English as an official language. Another confrontation: Mr. Ghandi again, but this time gathering salt, not spinning kadar. Side by side with this picture there is a recent photograph of English demonstrators sitting down in Trafalgar Square. What is the connection? And, incidentally, had Mr. Ghandi any connection with South Africa? Why did he choose salt? What has this to tell us about poverty; and, if the class is up to it, about elastic and inelastic demand?

504. Once again a full programme of work is mapped out; once again adult sources will be used; once again the boys and girls will become involved in a situation which calls, first, for understanding and then for commitment. Who was right and who wrong? This is the first question they ask. What was right and what wrong in each side's action and why? That is the second question. The second question leads on to the third, which is very like the first but with a subtle difference. Who was right on balance?

505. These two lessons, or series of lessons, on India may stand as tokens to represent a whole programme of work designed to set ordinary minds working on world problems. Some parts of the programme, however, would be set much nearer home—almost on the doorstep or no further away than a school

journey's distance. The identification of land forms, the influence of geology on landscape, the principles involved in national parks and nature reserves, the rights of different kinds of country users—young and old, walkers, motorists, naturalists and farmers, this is a totally different sequence from the Indian ones. It starts with the immediate experience of the perceptive eye and the field-sketching hand, but it too may lead on to the making of social judgements. Another home-based sequence, using immediate experience but this time of human relations, might study the ebb and flow of East and West as seen in the pupils' family history—uncles and aunts settled or working overseas, new neighbours from abroad; the epitome of world history in one of its main transformations as crystallized in grandfather's war and father's war—here the school in the slums is at no disadvantage and possibly somewhat better off than others. There is plenty of material which a good teacher can use to secure an intellectual and emotional break-through from the classroom with its text book and its lessons to the real world of human problems. To secure this break-through is more important than to explain the mechanics of the ballot—more difficult, no doubt, but more likely to hold the pupils' attention.

506. But the teacher needs space and time if he is to succeed.[1] He needs space because his room will have to serve as a base, a workshop and a store. He needs good facilities for mechanical aids—projector, record player, tape-recorder, radio and T.V. receiver. He needs these to give the actuality of quasi-immediate experience to studies which time or space put at a distance. He needs a working surface where models can be made, a tracing table, perhaps a photo-copier (certainly ready access to one), map chests, filing cabinets, book-shelves. He needs time. The total time allowed by the school for English subjects is often adequate, sometimes generous. But when it is dispersed between three and four teachers with three or four different "subjects"—social studies, current affairs, history, civics, geography—none has enough elbow room to undertake a programme of work such as we have suggested. The time needs concentrating, and the values specially associated with the various subject names secured by ringing the changes among them.

507. Something in depth for a short time rather than a little of everything all the time is probably the right approach anyhow for the boys and girls with whom we are concerned. A relatively short spell of work at a given theme— a term at the most—culminating in some definite evidence of achievement is a good formula. The evidence of achievement may take the form of an exhibition, the production of a class book, the making of a film strip, perhaps with a commentary recorded on tape—there are many possibilities. Different themes lend themselves to different methods; the important thing is that all pupils should be able to take part. Such a wide range of expression is possible that this general participation can usually be secured—but it does not happen without careful planning in advance. It is indeed often possible to get senior boys and girls so interested in what they are doing that homework does not so much have to be set as suggest itself. Some of it may even take the agreeable form of an evening's viewing—but with a constructive and critical purpose.

508. A programme of this kind will have failed if it does not lead to knowing what evidence is and what it will prove. At one time a class will be interpreting

---

[1] Present conditions are described in paragraphs 641 and 682.

for themselves physical evidence: they will be learning, for instance, how to read landscape and how to interpret a map. A short time at a Field Studies Centre will make both map and science come alive for them. At another time they will be setting social facts against social facts. They will come to see that in any economic problem some facts will tell in one direction and some in another; that some groups of people will naturally pay more attention to one set than the other; and that this personal bias is something that they must guard against in themselves. The personal and social advantages of different forms of space heating is an obvious example. They may, and should, go on to problems where only some of the facts are known, but a decision has to be made. There is much argument, for instance, about streaming in schools. It will take a long time to find out what its true consequences are, but meanwhile schools have to be carried on. This is the sort of situation that could profitably be examined. It is possible to move from co-operative situations like this, where everybody is trying to find out the truth or the best course to take, to situations in which there is no longer this common purpose. In war, for instance, the enemy's position has to be inferred in face of appearances designed to mislead. Boys and girls of quite poor academic ability are often well aware that a good deal of propaganda falls into this last category. They feel that they are being got at, that they are not being told the truth, or at least only carefully doctored truth. They develop a protective cynicism which leads them to disbelieve everything; a more hopeful defence would be provided by an elementary training in evidence and how to handle it.

509. Even more important, perhaps, than this scientific approach to factual evidence is an ability to enter imaginatively into other men's minds. What is to be cultivated here is psychological sensitivity and intuitive awareness rather than rational fact-finding. It is important to keep good company and great company. People count. They count not only in their private lives but publicly. People make history. It is an enlarging of the spirit for our boys and girls to meet great men and to respond to them as men did and still do. The racy but rich speech of Abraham Lincoln can still hold fifteen year-olds in twentieth century England and show them as it showed men a hundred years ago what things are worth more than living. It is important, too, to know bad company and to avoid it. Evil men also have power. Were those who followed Hitler necessarily worse men than those who rallied to Churchill? Why did they do it? Might we not have done the same? How did some of his own people stand out against him? These are sobering questions which ordinary young people ought to face.

510. Need a teacher select his programme with an eye to more than its momentary acceptability to his pupils and its effectiveness in getting his pupils to pause long enough to think? If he remembers that there is nothing quite so dead as last year's sensation, he will probably conclude that he ought to have some better principle of selection than topicality.

511. Probably in history he will decide that in the last years at school he must choose contemporary themes which will help his pupils to understand the world in which they live, not only the world into which their fathers were born. History in schools now often, but by no means always, reaches 1939 and edges towards 1945. But in 1945 the Indian peninsula was still politically united and part of a British Empire; China was not yet Communist; and Africa was still a network of colonies and mandated territories with only a

distant prospect of becoming anything else. The first atomic bomb had only just been exploded; Everest and not the moon was still the summit to be reached. History which does not take account of these and similar revolutionary changes will not seem to the limited minds of our boys and girls to be the history of their world. This does not mean that the cavemen and the open fields of their earlier years were just childish stories. They will find them still existing: no longer in our past but in other peoples' present. English boys and girls need to get some idea of this compression of millenia of human development into one African generation and of the economic and psychological problems that go with it. They need, too, to understand the problems of India and China which are economically similar to Africa's but psychologically different because Asia is a continent of old and proud cultures. Some of our very modern history will take us back to very ancient times.

512. What is living and important in the world in 1963 cannot be explained only by what has happened since 1945. This is certainly true even when the topic is the U.S.A. and the U.S.S.R. in the world today. In British history perhaps the most important thing to do with the pupils before they finally leave school will be an assessment of Britain's true position in the world of to-day, an assessment which must be based on knowledge of the past as well as the present. Here is material for a life study, not for a year's work however generous the time allowance. The teacher will have to choose between the barest outline of events and the selection of limited topics which can be studied in sufficient detail to bring them to life. If he chooses the latter course, and this seems more likely to give his pupils understanding, he will want to select his topics carefully to give as representative coverage as he can to four or five themes of history today.

513. The same principles apply in geography. The list of possible topics is far too long for any school to exhaust. Once again the choice must lie between large tracts of barren outline and a few typical problems studied in depth. Once again the latter is the promising solution. A clear break in the syllabus is useful at the end of the third year, involving a change from a systematic course to selected case studies. It should not mean losing intellectual coherence. A wise teacher will probably distribute his fields of study as widely as possible so that examples are given of differences of climate and relief, different stages of economic development and differences in race and culture. The progressive nature of the work will not be determined by the sequence of examples, but by the depth at which they are tackled. Thus a detailed study of an Indian village if taken in the third year might stop short at vivid description. If taken in the fifth year it might initiate a discussion on the precise meaning of "a low standard of living" illustrated by comparative figures for Malaya, Britain and the U.S.A., leading on to a consideration of how the standard could be raised.

514. Most of the illustrations in this chapter have been drawn from history or geography. Often very much the same ground was being covered, though in one case the approach was that of a historian, in another that of a geographer. No attempt has been made to set out all that history or geography can do for the education of the average and below-average boys and girls during their schooldays. We have concentrated on certain things and certain lessons which they need especially to learn during their last year or two at school and which we think history and geography can usefully teach them. We do not really

mind which does it. There are more than a sufficient number of teachers of both to meet the needs of the schools. It is only fair, however, to add that many of them would feel themselves singularly ill-equipped to undertake the kind of work which is suggested in this chapter. There is need for a review of what history and, to a rather less extent, of what geography is taught in higher education. There is quite certainly need for a large programme of in-service training.

515. Can historians and geographers do all that boys and girls need in this sphere? It seems to us that the answer must be "no". Most of the illustrations we used lead on into the field of moral judgements. No review of the world situation can fail to show boys and girls how strong and how various are the faiths by which men live. They are bound to encounter and admire the conviction and self-sacrifice which many Communists display. They will discover how Protestant pastor, Roman Catholic priest and Communist cell-leader alike were tried in the ordeal of Buchenwald and not found wanting. They will find, too, how men of all faiths can be cruel and evil, often with the highest possible motives. Both discoveries need thinking about. Turning back to one of our original illustrations, they will grossly misunderstand Mr. Ghandi, if they fail to realize something of the subtlety of his relation to Christianity.

516. This involves among other things knowing what Christianity is. There is a straightforward teaching job to be done here. Just what do Christians believe about God and man, life and death? Many fourteen year-old boys and girls will not know unless they are taught—but it is often assumed that they know this already. An information service is important, and they ask for it. In their last years at school there is need also to help them to see the difference that being a Christian makes, or should make, to the answers that have to be given to problems of living. Some of these problems are personal and immediate; some are collective and social—relations with parents and with friends of the opposite sex; problems of conflicting loyalties to friends and to moral standards; nuclear weapons and the colour bar; the care of the old and thalidomide babies. Problems such as these, and others mentioned in Chapter 7, come up clearly in any discussion about human beings which is more than skin deep. They lend themselves to treatment in the same kind of way as many of the themes already discussed in this chapter. Good teaching may often involve contact with those working outside the school. These contacts should be welcomed; they are part of the process of relating the school to the world. But this kind of contact is not the whole of the answer. Christianity is not to be defined as the religion of Englishmen. It is sometimes difficult for boys and girls to realize this and what it implies. They can be helped to do this if, for instance, they are brought into contact with the problems of Christians who lapsed under Mau Mau persecution and have since wished to come back to their faith. What line should the Church take? This was a burning question in the first Christian centuries; it still is. It cannot be solved without probing deeply into the heart of man and the heart of the Christian religion; to observe Africans answering it is sometimes to shame ourselves.

517. In some schools it may be possible to bring the school's religious instruction into close association with the social studies with which this chapter has been mainly concerned. It should gain. But there is always need to remember the double conscience clause—the right of the pupil to be excused,

the right of the teacher not to suffer professionally because he does not choose to give religious instruction. There is also a right of pupils to be taught. Until there is a much better supply of skilled and knowledgeable teachers the right to religious education at a true secondary level is bound in some schools to be little more than nominal.

CHAPTER 20

The Organization of the School and the Deployment of Staff

A. ORGANIZATION

518. Some forms of school organization make it easier than others for pupils to recognize the vocational interest which can mean so much to them in their later years at school. Some have a built-in factor of choice which helps to associate pupils with the work they are doing. A head who agrees with the general line of argument we have put forward will naturally test his plans to see if they make it easy for his pupils to feel that the education they are getting is practical and realistic, has vocational interest and relevance, allows some measures of choice and helps them to make wise decisions for themselves.

519. Most heads inherit an established organization; they adjust it to meet changing needs and their own wishes but they never have quite the free hand that comes to those who build up a new school from the start. This chapter will serve its purpose better if it presents itself with the coveted opportunity of a clean slate. It assumes a four-form entry secondary modern school of something over 500 pupils. How will the head set about his task? There are, of course, certain things he will have to take for granted. The size of his school, for instance, and whether it is to be co-educational will have been decided before he is appointed. So, too, will the range of ability it is to serve— whether it is to be a modern or a comprehensive school. But, within this given frame-work, he is free to make his own plans to realize his general aims.

520. Our terms of reference relate to pupils of average and below-average ability; but the head has to consider the organization of the whole school including that minority, perhaps a quarter of the total, who are above the median in intelligence. The wide range of ability which all modern schools contain presents real teaching problems. This must find some reflection in the way the school is organized. The commonest form is a simple division by ability, even though it may be half-concealed by various tricks of nomenclature The head will certainly be aware that "streaming", which starts well down in the primary schools, is a matter of acute educational controversy. He may decide, as we have done for our part, that this not something on which he can at present make up his mind for two reasons. First, an informed review of the consequences of this form of organization can only take place when much detailed investigation has been done. Work on this is only now beginning on a substantial scale, and much will depend on what the National Foundation for Educational Research finds out in its new enquiry. Secondly, judgement must start where the practice starts—in the primary school and not in the secondary school with which he, and we, are concerned. Both of us have to deal with an inherited situation.

521. But, while the head may be in a situation of suspended intellectual judgement, he has to make operational decisions.[1] He cannot leave the

---

[1] The present practice in schools in our sample is described in paragraphs 643 and 644.

organization of his school until the experts have pronounced. And what he decides involves provisional judgements. He may possibly have taught as an assistant in a large school in which there were eight forms to a year, all graded by ability. We doubt, however, if he will regret that his four form-entry will prevent such an apparently fine degree of discrimination. He is likely, we think, to feel that on balance this type of organization would increase the feeling of educational inferiority and rejection in the lower forms without corresponding teaching advantages.

522. Many European countries reject the idea of streaming (except that variety which is involved in the difference between selective and non-selective secondary schools). Instead they keep down, as we used to do, pupils whose work is not good enough to justify promotion. Anybody planning a new school organization will be interested in their experience, as we have been; and will wish to make further enquiries about it; but it seems very unlikely that he will adopt it. If the head has taught in a small primary school or in one of the very few one form-entry schools, he will have had experience of doing without streaming and relying instead on different teaching groups for different subjects within the same form, and on some system of individual assignments. He may well wish to encourage his heads of departments to write something of this kind into their subject schemes of work and indeed to enquire about programmed learning, but this does not mean scrapping any idea of arranging his forms by ability.

523. In a new school the first problem of organization is to arrange for the initial intake of eleven year-olds. It seems most probable that the head will decide on some division by ability to cover the work of the first two or three years. He may hesitate between a straight four-fold grading and a system of "topping and tailing" with two middle forms of roughly comparable ability, but few will chose any other system. Even in a large modern school it is doubtful whether a finer grading is necessary.

524. Should this system be carried further up the school? Should it go right to the top? It does in most modern schools; and it is probable, therefore, that the head will have this possibility well in the fore-front of his mind. But the situation is changing so rapidly that there are several new factors to think about. Two are especially important. They are linked together. How long does he expect his pupils to stay at school? How much value does he put on giving them some freedom of choice? Most heads started teaching when boys and girls usually left school as soon as they were fourteen; until a few years ago nearly all left at fifteen. The older senior elementary school course was one of two years and a bit; the compulsory secondary modern school course is now only four years,[1] and in some districts this is still its normal length, but in large parts of the country a five year course is becoming common for many pupils. This, subject to the necessary Order in Council, is already its statutory length. The presumption that one form of organization is right for the whole secondary school is not as strong as it was. Almost certainly the head of a new school will want to start his planning on the assumption of a five year course for all—or, at present, for as many as can be persuaded to take it.

---

[1] A substantial proportion of pupils, however, are still legally able to leave school before they complete their fourth year.

525. What are the right tactics to adopt in order to see that as many boys and girls as possible get secondary education to sixteen? The first point is a negative one. It is important to avoid a form of organization which forces on parents and pupils the necessity of "signing on" for an "extended course" if they want to stay at school to sixteen. This can happen where those pupils who are proposing to take an external examination at the end of five years are grouped together in one form from the beginning of the third or fourth year. This usually involves a certain amount of re-shuffling between the A and B forms. It carries with it the implication that those who do not elect to enter, or perhaps in some cases are not put into, the examination stream will be leaving when they become fifteen, which is thought of as the normal thing to do. If the head decides on this pattern of organization he may build up a strong examination form and give valuable opportunities to his abler pupils; but it will be at the expense of the rest. In his school the raising of the minimum school-leaving age to sixteen will still amount to a revolution instead of the gentle rounding off of an evolutionary process.

526. The head's problem is to find an organization which will give his most ordinary pupils the same encouragement as the ablest to get their second wind so that they may finish their school course as strongly and optimistically as they began it. He may remember the change of heart which he himself experienced when in his schooldays his bent for languages or for science was first allowed to influence his time-table. Ten years ago a similar kind of personal stock-taking and readjustment of curriculum for the less able grammar school pupils helped to check the spate of "premature leaving". An appetite for a longer secondary education is often created in girls of barely average ability by the provision of special courses which meet their desire for something going beyond school work as they have hitherto known it. If the tonic is to work, it must be an individual prescription. To give short-hand and typewriting to a girl who wants something to do with child care is to invite her to leave at the earliest opportunity. Variety of provision, then, is necessary to fit individual need, capacity and interest. On the whole, the balance of advantage lies with some form of organization which in the last two years of the five-year course takes more account than in the lower forms of the pupils' wishes. An organization which relies in the senior years on streaming by attainments—by definition the weak point of our boys and girls—is not likely to encourage them voluntarily to complete a five-year course.

527. When should this change in organization be introduced? Those schools which carry out such a reorganization do so normally either at the beginning of the third or fourth year. It is a difficult decision to make until the fifth year is established on a firm and wide basis. As long as most boys and girls leave as soon as they can, it is rational to feel that they will be more likely to stay if they have "signed on", so to speak, by the third year. Our advice, however, would be strongly in favour of choosing the fourth year. There are two reasons for this. First, many of the new interests to be catered for are vocational. We think thirteen too young an age at which to give a vocational slant to a pupil's education or to expect him to expect him to make a vocational choice. Secondly, as soon as some have "signed on" the remainder (who to-day are the majority) will in their own minds have "signed off."

528. One way in which organization can take account of interests is through the provision of carefully defined courses with an occupational bias. They

give a centre of unity to the later stages of school life. This need not, however, stand in the way of experience in each of the three main curriculum fields which we have distinguished. Probably some of the work done in each of the three fields will be related to this central theme; some will be the more invigorating for standing apart from it. What the head has to consider from the time-table angle may be illustrated by an actual example. This course is called "Technical Building". The fourth year time-table analysis gives the following results.

A. Humanities: 410 minutes per week

B. Mathematics and Science: 530 minutes per week

C. "Practical Subjects": 560 minutes per week

D. Total school hours per week: 1500 minutes

E. Time spent on Building (225 minutes) and Directly Related Subjects (e.g. Mechanics, Maths, Architectural History) 680 minutes per week. Total: 905 minutes.

529. Would such a course, and others like it, do what he has in mind? This is probably something which he will find hard to decide. Organization on a course basis has great merits. It gives its members a feeling of belonging together in an activity that is both purposeful and educational. They have status; and are not isolated units in a nondescript form clearly below the best in the school. There is a rough recognition of differences in ability without loss of face. The academic courses have a different objective, but not a more important one than building is to builders. They are doing something that they have chosen with care, which belongs to the "real world" and, it may be, to their own future real world.

530. At this point a number of questions arise. First, this course and many like it, is a "package deal". The pupil chooses his course. After that he may not do much more choosing. In this school, for instance, he cannot be a builder and a musician, though he could be an engineer and a musician. Secondly, while a boy in the building course will have had a good secondary education which will stand him in good stead whatever he decides to do, there may be a concealed risk that other boys from other courses will be at a disadvantage if they later want to become employed as builders. This is something a head will want to guard against before starting a course with an occupational bias. No career ought to be closed to a boy or girl who did not enter an appropriate occupational course at fourteen. Thirdly, while it is easy to discover good courses with an occupational bias for pupils of average ability, it is not easy to carry the process much further down the line. The number of times that "General", "Practical", "Modern" appear in the list of courses in schools organized in this way tells its own depressing story. The head may well remember how in the war the undoubtedly high morale of those who belonged to a "private army" was sometimes gained at the expense of those who were left behind in their original units.

531. Another way by which variety, choice and individual prescription can be provided for all pupils is by the system of options and sets which has long existed in grammar schools. This recognizes that there must be almost as many reasons why boys and girls choose a particular subject as there are pupils in the set. Some will be there for vocational reasons, others because they like the

subject or the teacher, or because they are good at it. The unity which a course engenders is not easy to secure—there is no "private army" to belong to—but it is easier to arrange to meet individual preferences for unusual combinations of subjects. It allows too, for the study of the same subjects at various depths by different pupils—for handicraft for example, both as a major subject and for recreational use with a smaller time allocation. These possibilities may be especially important to below-average boys and girls. Fortunately for them, they do not need a certificate witnessing to a particular combination of subjects: there is, therefore no pattern externally imposed upon their education beyond the basic demands of literacy and numeracy. It is possible, and necessary, to plan their course to take advantage of whatever talents and interests they have. These are not always the obvious ones. A boy may want to cook, a girl to build a canoe. If the school organization can bend to make this possible, it may be their educational salvation.

532. If the head decides on a very flexible organization, he will do so realizing the extra work entailed. An organization of this kind only works successfully if the time-table making is expertly done. The greater the variety offered, the more complicated the task. Once it is agreed that some element of specialist teaching is essential difficulties begin. They accumulate when attention is paid to the need for different subjects for periods of varying lengths—the contrast, for instance, between short, daily practice in French and a continuous spell of craftwork to which we have already referred. Time-tabling is a difficult art and one that proves more difficult year by year as schools grow bigger and options become more numerous.

533. But, if the organization stops at the time-table, there will be unnecessary disaster ahead for a good many boys and girls. The curriculum has become a long à la carte menu with all the possibilities of indigestion that this implies. A sound education is only to be secured in this way if each pupil's selection is carefully scrutinized to see that it makes sense. not only term by term, but longitudinally in sequence over the years. This involves a clear knowledge by those who advise boys and girls not only of possible subject permutations and combinations but also of what is taught set by set under various subject names. There has to be, so to speak, a book of the school and a book of each pupil. One way of matching them is by a tutorial organization which provides each pupil with some member of staff to take interest in all of his work year after year—an admirable system where there is sufficient staff stability to make it practicable. Another way, which does not depend quite so much on staff stability, is by a form-master system. The important thing is the devolution of responsibility.

534. The complexities of running a school are great. A good head needs skill as well as wisdom and character. Teachers have many opportunities as assistants of learning from one another; when they become heads they have no immediate colleagues to whom they can turn for quick advice. They need help to acquire the new and different skills which are demanded of those who run a school. There are a considerable number of opportunities nowadays for heads to meet together in short courses and conferences to discuss these matters; the demand for them grows. There is need for more.

535. These, then are some of the thoughts which must run through the mind of any head asked to build up a new secondary school, whatever its size. The

decisions he finally makes must depend on the resources to his hand. There is no one finally right solution. He, like his pupils, must exploit his strengths, and not try to provide everything that an ideal school would do. There is no ideal school. His resources lie, first in his own school and to some extent are controlled by its size. Formerly small schools offered only restricted opportunities. This was not in the main because they were small, but because they were built and equipped as schools for boys and girls who went to work as soon as they were fourteen. Now that they have older pupils, many small schools have discovered means of fostering individual work and some are providing sufficient variety of experience to meet the educational needs of most of the pupils with whom we are concerned.

536. Of course, a big school can offer a range of vocationally directed courses which is beyond a small school's internal resources. The advantage is important, but not, necessarily decisive. The head of a small school has resources outside his staff and his buildings on which he can draw. He may have pupils—perhaps one or two in a hundred—who have a strong bent which he cannot adequately satisfy though a neighbouring school could. In such instances transfer is right. More frequently he will find that by careful planning with a local technical college he can provide the vocational aspect of a course which a larger school would find from its own resources. If this means sending his boys and girls out into a more adult world for part of their time at school, it may be no bad thing. The head may also be able to draw into the school the part-time help of those in the local community who have special skills not found among his colleagues. The less his school, or any school, is an island to itself the better. If it is to serve this generation it needs to be joined to the mainland of life by a causeway well-trodden in both directions.

B. STAFF

537. A head's real struggle comes when he turns from the blue-print of organization to the deployment of staff. We have said in Chapter 12 something about the qualities needed by those who are going to teach the pupils with whom we are specially concerned and about the education and training which is most likely to make them good teachers. Here we are concerned with the actual problem as, for instance, it faces the head of a four form-entry co-educational school of about 500 pupils when he sits down to make his time-table.

538. It is probable on the basis of the knowledge we have gained from our survey that his time-table analysis will show for fourth-year pupils the equivalent each week of two days for the humanities, one day for mathematics and science and two for the "practical subjects" in the extended sense we have given this term.[1] These are, of course, only rough approximations and the range is considerable. A school, however, which drastically curtails the time spent in one of these fields is not providing a suitable secondary education. Reference to Part Three of this report shows that a few schools are not. It does not matter which is the area of the curriculum that is impoverished; in this trinity none is before or after other since all are necessary.

539. Occasionally what we consider a serious maldistribution of time may be the deliberate result of a different outlook or education from ours and an

[1] See paragraphs 626–630.

alternative assessment of the needs of growing boys and girls. This is probably not common. More often it is the result of deficiencies in buildings and of difficulties in staffing. All of us know schools where there is no gymnasium and where, almost as a direct consequence, there is no properly qualified teacher of physical education. All of us know schools where one of the craft rooms is closed for lack of a teacher, or where science is taught in an ordinary classroom by somebody whose knowledge is clearly inadequate. The head of a school in such a position is bound to tailor his time-table to the measure of his staff and his equipment and not, as he would wish, to the growing stature of his pupils. In extreme cases this amounts to a curriculum so grossly disturbed as to justify the sweeping condemnation expressed in the previous paragraph. More often it amounts to a distortion of what the school would like in the balance of individual subjects, although compensating adjustments may keep the three fields reasonably well proportioned. Sometimes pupils have to be given what the staff can teach them, even though the school may feel that this is not the fare best suited to their needs but only the next best.

540. A co-educational secondary modern school of 500 pupils will probably have a staff of thirteen or fourteen assistant masters and nine or ten assistant mistresses.[1] This is enough to fill the vacant places on the time-table, but after what fashion? What kind of background have the teachers? The head's first problem is that there will almost certainly be a fair number of newcomers about whom he knows little or nothing beyond their paper qualifications. A third of the men and half the women are likely to have been with him less than three years, and a good many others will have come and gone during that period. Two or three of his staff will only be teaching part-time; they are probably married women. Nearly half his full-time women assistants are likely to be married. If they have young children, he will learn to dread the winter with its risk of infectious diseases and other illnesses.

541. Some of the teachers will have been students in teachers' training colleges before the last war. They are the professional general practitioners: they provide the most stable and the most flexible part of the staff, but promotion has carried many of them on to more specialized duties. They will have been accustomed to take their own form for both English and arithmetic; but their training and most of their experience in their formative years was with younger boys and girls than those with whom we are mainly concerned. Another group will have come from the general teachers' training colleges since the war. They will have made a deeper study of one, or sometimes two, subjects than their pre-war colleagues did, but this often means that they feel unfitted, certainly in their earlier years of teaching, to teach other subjects. A third group are the men and women who come from the specialized colleges for the "practical subjects". Just over a quarter of the staff ought to have this background, but these have been the hardest vacancies to fill so that there may be fewer. There remain the graduate teachers—perhaps four or five all told. We must expect a great increase in their number in the near future as a result of the expansion of the universities and the diversion of students from general training colleges to teach in primary schools. We are warned that many of the new graduates will be untrained.

542. It is with the help of these men and women that the head must make his time-table. One of his main anxieties may well be the staffing of the

---

[1] The staffing of the schools in our sample is described in chapter 24.

humanities—an odd situation at a time when every newspaper and every other White Paper proclaims a national shortage of scientists and technologists. The problem in the humanities is one of quality rather than of quantity. By quality we are not of course referring to personal inadequacies of character but to professional deficiencies in knowledge of the subjects and of insight into the problems of teaching. These come from the kind of specialized higher education which many incoming teachers have received, and from the lack of any professional training from which many of them suffer. The gravity of the present situation is known to every head; but, because its effects are to be detected only by a clinical judgement, it is largely concealed from administrators and statisticians. No safety rules prohibit the use of an English classroom because there is nobody qualified to teach English; but, if there is no science teacher, the laboratory will be shut, and the woodwork room will be out of use if there is no handicraft teacher. It is possible, therefore, to see and count the deficiencies in these subjects, and others like them; but in the humanities, the truism that "every teacher is a teacher of English" is in practice so perverted that it might often as well read "anybody can teach English".

543. Out of his staff of twenty-two or twenty-three teachers the head has to find the equivalent of nine full-time teachers to cover this group of subjects. Where can he find them? At first sight this ought not to be difficult. Four-fifths of the graduates teaching in modern schools have arts degrees. The trouble is, however, that the way in which they are divided among the arts subjects is very unlike the way in which the schools divide their time between the humanities. Two-thirds of the modern schools give more than half their total time allocation for the humanities to English itself. Only a quarter of their graduate teachers with arts degrees have their qualification in English. There are almost as many history graduates as English graduates teaching in modern schools, although more than three times as many periods, and quite often four times, are given to English as to history. The balance of specialization among training college students is probably not very different, and under present policy they will no longer provide a direct supply of teachers for senior forms in secondary schools.

544. It is clear that the head of a typical school of 500 pupils will have much less difficulty in finding the equivalent of nine teachers for the humanities or English subjects in general than in finding four who are really competent to tackle the intellectually and imaginatively exacting job of teaching English, or one to lead in the equally demanding work of religious instruction. With a head of department post to offer he will probably succeed in getting one specialist English teacher. With luck he may find two. After that he is very likely to have to share out the work between teachers who would rather be doing something else which they are better qualified to undertake. He may very reluctantly be driven to dividing the English of one form between several teachers, perhaps giving "poetry" to one and "composition" to another. This sort of expedient happens far too often, and will continue to occur as long as the supply and training position is unchanged. The boys and girls of our report are the victims of this kind of situation more often than they should be. If there is only one teacher specially qualified to teach English, he cannot be everywhere in a subject which has so many periods to fill. If he is not employed with the examination forms, there may almost be a breach of

faith to those who have stayed on voluntarily to work for G.C.E. If he concentrates on them, then the boys and girls who are our special concern may be left to indifferent teachers of English because their work is not going to be brought to any external measurement. Both courses are unjust. Often one of them has to be chosen. As long as the supply is as inadequate as it is at present, some unfortunate boys and girls will suffer. All that we dare demand of the head of a school is that it should not be the same boys and girls all the time.

545. A precise matching of supply and demand subject by subject would probably be impossible and, even if it could be achieved, would have serious disadvantages. These would be most obvious in the teaching of those subjects to which a relatively short time allocation is given. Religious instruction, history and geography are all subjects to which two periods a week are commonly given. On this basis one specialist teacher could as far as the time-table goes cover all the work. It would however entail teaching some 500 boys and girls each week. This is too heavy a price to pay for expertise, and too unfair on the expert. Some boys and girls, and we would include nearly all those with whom we are especially concerned, are only able to learn anything from a teacher whom they know and who knows them.

546. On the other hand a return to a general practitioner basis in the "classroom subjects" as a whole seems equally undesirable and indeed impracticable if the kind of work sketched out in the last few chapters is to be attempted. This cannot be done on the basis of general knowledge and being a few lessons ahead of the class. Above all, few teachers are really competent to teach both English and mathematics in a secondary school, especially to the older pupils with whom we are concerned. A reasonable higher education for anybody proposing to teach the boys and girls of this report should in any event make him able to teach more than one subject. It would probably give him a wide degree of competence in one of the broad fields of the humanities, mathematics and science or the "practical subjects"; and would, we think, quite often fit a teacher who had a major qualification in one of the first two fields to take a share in the third, or a teacher whose major qualification was in one of the "practical subjects" to take some part in one of the first two fields, provided that he was not asked to teach something for which he has had no professional training.

547. Some interchange of disciplines of this kind would often be an advantage to the pupils with whom we are most concerned. They are perhaps more likely to pay attention to what a teacher tells them about their speech or writing if they have seen him making something in the workshop or in the kitchen. Certainly a teacher who sees his pupils working in a number of quite different situations will have a much truer idea of their individual needs than if he only teaches them one subject. He can then arrange their work so that one subject supports another and so that both are more likely to meet the individual pupil's individual need. An interchange would also have the advantage of giving those teachers, who at present always teach whole classes, the opportunity of working more closely with individuals in the half classes which are normal in many practical subjects. The individual conversation which is impossible with thirty boys and girls in a forty minute period is both practicable and essential with fifteen during a double period of craft work. English teachers, who are also competent craftsmen, could both learn and contribute much in this way. Married women, who have brought up a family, have much

that they could contribute to housecraft, given some little additional training, as well as to their own subject whatever it may be.

548. We have concentrated on the problem of finding teachers for the humanities, and for English and religious instruction in particular, because it is here that many people see no problem at all. This does not mean that we ignore the problems of staffing in the other two major fields. They are indeed acute. But the urgent needs in these fields have been generally and officially recognized and action taken so that a head who is familiar with the general pattern of teacher training and the provision of specialist wings to meet the known shortages may reasonably feel that in a few years' time the supply in these fields will be better, though there is no guarantee that the wastage through marriage of women teachers of practical subjects will not offset the improved supply.

549. Few school time-tables can today be made with the confidence that the right staff will be there to do the job that ought to be done. It is indeed remarkable how well the schools have "made do". But it is important to remember that "making do" will not do. Our schools will not be what they should until we give them the teachers they need.

Part Three

What the Survey Shows

CHAPTER 21

The 1961 Survey

A. THE NATURE OF THE INFORMATION

550. Repeated references have been made in earlier chapters of this report to the survey carried out for the Council in 1961 in modern and comprehensive schools. The purpose of this part of the report is to set out in non-technical language the nature of the enquiries and the main conclusions. It is followed by a Statistical Appendix containing a fuller description of the methods used, of some of the results and a justification of the judgements made.

551. Surveys were arranged in a representative sample of modern and comprehensive schools with the co-operation of the local education authorities and by the willing help of the headmasters and headmistresses. The amount of work falling on the schools was heavy, and the Council is greatly indebted to them for all the trouble they took. The few remaining all-age schools (which educated only 2·7 per cent of the age group in 1962) were excluded as were the grammar and technical schools in which are to be found a small proportion of the abler boys and girls within our terms of reference.

552. Our terms of reference are to advise on the education of pupils aged 13 to 16 and the survey was arranged to throw light on conditions affecting them. We were not concerned with the younger pupils in secondary schools. The enquiries fell into three main parts. In the first, the heads were asked to write freely about their problems, the background of their pupils, their schools and their staff; about their methods, their difficulties and their successes. We have quoted freely from what they wrote in earlier parts of the report, especially in chapters 2, 3 and 8, and wish we could have quoted more. The second section of the survey took the form of four exacting questionnaires. The first was concerned with an analysis of the time-table of pupils in their fourth year. This is summarized in chapter 23. Another questionnaire dealt with particulars of staffing and provided the material for chapter 24. We asked for particulars of the school premises; the answers form the basis of chapter 25. The last of these four questionnaires enquired about examination and non-examination candidates. This information, together with the data about individual boys and girls, described in paragraph 554, is used in the next chapter.

553. Our terms of reference rightly separate pupils of average from those of below-average ability. Most members of both groups—most in fact of the secondary school population—are in modern schools. National educational statistics and some educational writing treat the modern schools as if each was homogeneous and as if all were roughly uniform. Nothing could be further from the truth. It was, then, implicit in our task that we should dispel this illusory unity. The means we used was the administration of a standardized test which enabled us to compare pupil with pupil and school with school. If we had only been concerned with comparing the pupils inside their own schools, we could have relied on the head's estimates of their relative attainments; but a comparison of these estimates with the results of the standardized tests

shows that any generalized statements about pupils in modern schools made on this basis would have been most misleading because schools differ so much in the quality of their intake. The test used was the one which has been employed for the Ministry's reading ability surveys of 1948, 1952 and 1956. In addition to the simple ability to read words a fairly extensive vocabulary is required to do well in this test, and we have felt justified in using it as a general measure of where boys and girls stand in their school work in regard to one another. It has helped us to identify the pupils with whom we are particularly concerned, and to see how they differ among themselves as well as by contrast with others. This test was taken by all fourth-year pupils in the samples of modern and comprehensive schools. The latter of course included a due proportion of abler boys and girls who in other areas would have formed the grammar school population.

554. The last source of information available for our survey was a questionnaire about individual pupils which was completed for every third boy and girl in the fourth year in the survey schools. This gave us some strictly objective information about the pupils—their attendance record, their height, and whether or not they received free school dinners, for instance; some indirect objective reporting—the forms were completed by teachers, not pupils—about such matters as belonging to youth clubs and delivering newspapers; and some subjective judgements of attitudes such as amenability to school discipline.

555. In addition to this new material we have drawn also on some of the information gathered for the Council's previous report, Fifteen to Eighteen. The material used was that collected in the National Service Survey of 1957–58 which is fully described in Part II of Volume II of Fifteen to Eighteen. This National Service Survey took place immediately before the end of conscription. It could not be repeated now. A representative sample of nearly 7,000 recruits were interviewed after they had taken the normal Army intelligence and attainment tests. They proved to be very nearly a true cross-section of the whole population of young men. From this survey we have drawn information about the occupational and family background of former modern school pupils of three levels of ability. No questions were asked in 1961 about home background.

B. RISING AVERAGES

556. The detailed results of the survey are the subject of the following four chapters, but two general conclusions are given here and in the following section. The first is that, although this report is about the academically less successful, it is a success story that we have to tell. In interpreting our terms of reference perhaps the most important thing to bear in mind is that what an average boy or girl knows is not a fixed quantum for all generations, but something liable to change. There are indications of marked improvement over the last fifteen years. There is opportunity for more improvement to come and reason to expect it. The four reading test surveys and the National Service Survey tell the same story of rising averages. The army's measure of ability is a battery of intelligence and attainment tests. The tests were standardized in 1947 and recorded in a form in which the top and bottom group each represented ten per cent of the population and the intervening four

groups twenty per cent each. But ten years later, when these tests were used for our National Service Survey, 58 per cent of the intake instead of 50 per cent fell into the top three groups, and the bottom two groups comprised only 21 per cent of the intake instead of the original 30. It is true that men who were 18 in 1947 had spent their later years of elementary education (secondary education for all was yet unborn) in the disorder of the war years so that something would clearly have been wrong if there had not been a sensible improvement in attainment test results between 1947 and 1958. The same argument would apply to the improvement in the reading test results between 1948 and 1952. We were making up obviously lost ground. But the later tests of 1956 and 1961 show that we are now going forward into new territory. The position of pupils aged 14 years 8 months in modern schools at the four dates is shown in the following table, and diagrams 7A and 7B at the end of this chapter illustrate the same point.

Table 1. The Reading Tests 1948–1961

Year	Average Score	Gain in Months (7 months = 1 point)
1948	18·0	—
1952	18·4	3
1956	18·9	6
1961	21·3	23

557. Today's average boys and girls are better at their books than their predecessors half a generation ago. There are reasons to expect that their successors will be better still. One is the working out of the social handicaps which are so marked in their influence on present educational achievements. A fifth of the boys with whom we are concerned have fathers who are un-skilled manual workers;[1] only eleven per cent come from the homes of non-manual workers. In this very disparity there is hope. It is difficult to believe that a good many children in middle-class homes, where educational sights are set on a reasonably high standard of attainment, would not have done much worse at school if they had been born in homes where there was no tradition of homework and where the social and marketable value of educa-tion was not fully realized. Pretty certainly, too, more unskilled workers' children would do better at school if they had the persistent encouragement of parents who believe that their children can and must reach a reasonably high educational standard. The National Service Survey strongly suggests this. One would expect a man in the top ten per cent in ability to obtain at least four passes in G.C.E. at ordinary level. Most of the recruits in this category did so, but the proportion who did not grows steadily from left to right of this profile:

Table 2. Proportion of men in the top 10 per cent in ability who had not achieved 4 Ordinary Level passes in G.C.E. (National Service Survey)

Father's Occupation			
Professional or Managerial	Clerical etc.	Skilled Manual	Semi-skilled or Unskilled Manual
5%	14%	23%	34%

[1] Two-thirds of the children of unskilled manual workers fall into the test groups clearly within our terms of reference.

Similarly men whose test results place them in the middle of the ability range must be unusually persistent and diligent if they are to pass four subjects in G.C.E. Recruits who achieved this are found in significant numbers on the left of this profile but dwindle to a handful on the right.

Table 3. Proportion of men in the middle of the ability range who achieved at least 4 Ordinary Level passes in G.C.E. (National Service Survey)

	Father's Occupation		
Professional or Managerial	Clerical etc.	Skilled Manual	Semi-skilled or Unskilled Manual
20%	8%	6%	3%

558. The gap between the ends in each of these two profiles is wide, but it is narrowing. Unfortunately there is no statistical evidence from modern schools, but we can illustrate the process from the grammar schools. What can be proved to be happening there is reported by the heads we consulted to be true also of modern schools. One of the outstanding factors in the maintained grammar school situation as it existed in 1953, when our Early Leaving survey was made, was the way in which the children of manual workers, and especially of unskilled and semi-skilled workers, lost ground during the course compared with the children of non-manual workers.[1] Between 1953 and 1961 there has been a general improvement in standards in which all occupational groups have shared. There is, also, and it is this which is particularly important, a tendency for the lower occupational groups to show a somewhat greater improvement than the higher ones. The evidence is given in the Statistical Appendix on page 293. This is a first instalment of what can be expected as manual workers become increasingly familiar with what secondary education offers their children.

C. CONTRASTING ATTAINMENTS

559. The second general conclusion from the survey evidence is the contrasts which exist between school and school. It is obviously important to pin-point these differences as far as possible and for this purpose two methods of classification were used. The first was an analysis in terms of the neighbourhoods served by schools. From the evidence provided by their heads, schools were divided into groups according to the type of neighbourhood they predominantly served:

Table 4. Distribution of Pupils by Neighbourhoods

	Percentage of fourth year pupils
Rural	12%
Mining	7%
Council Estate or New Town	33%
Problem Area, i.e. an area of bad housing with a high concentration of social problems	18%
Mixed, i.e. a combination of several of the above or with a high proportion of owner-occupied houses	30%

[1] "Early Leaving" p. 18.

a range of schools based on social class, distinction.

To make certain that we had a sufficient number of schools in the most difficult possible neighbourhoods a special group of twenty schools in slums was added. This group stands outside the representative sample and is never included with it in tabulations.

560. The second classification was into geographical regions. When information from individual pupils' questionnaires was being analysed the geographical classification was by Ministry of Education Divisions—a Northern group comprising the Northern, East and West Ridings and North-Western Divisions; a Midland group comprising the Midland, North Midland and South-Western Divisions (more of the people in this division live in the Bristol, Somerset and Gloucester area than in Devon and Cornwall); and a Home Counties group comprising the four Divisions which include and touch London—Eastern, Metropolitan, South-Eastern and Southern. Where the schools' as opposed to the pupils' questionnaires were being analyzed the schools were divided into three zones—those within 80 miles of London; those between 80 and 160 miles from London and those beyond this distance. This method of classification could not be used for the pupils' questionnaires because it had not been punched on the Hollerith cards used for analysis. Neither basis is free from inconsistencies, but the method of zones seemed to be less awkward than the divisional one. The outer zone includes all the North Country on both sides of the Pennines down to Sheffield and Manchester, while very few of the schools in the sample are in the extreme south-west. The middle zone includes the Black Country, the Potteries, the Leicestershire, Nottinghamshire and Warwickshire industrial areas, the Bristol and Gloucestershire industrial belt and many rural districts. The inner zone includes all the home counties and extends to Ipswich, Oxford and Southampton. Its schools have a distinctly better record in the test than the schools in the middle and outer zones. The range between zones is 1·6 points.

561. Other methods of classification were used and are described in succeeding chapters such as the condition of the buildings and the staffing position in the schools. Of all these groupings the classification by neighbourhood was the one which proved most enlightening. The range in the mean test score between the five groups was 1·8 points, equivalent to a range of 12 months in reading age. The special group of schools in slums had a mean score which was a further 1·28 points below that in the problem areas, the lowest scoring neighbourhood in the sample. Diagrams 8A and 8B at the end of this chapter illustrate this.

562. Far more significant, however, was the range in the means between individual schools. Nine points, equivalent to five and a quarter years, separated the schools with the highest and the lowest reading test scores. Within each neighbourhood group, the range was considerable. This can be illustrated by comparing the distribution among schools in the problem areas, where the group average is lowest, with that in the mixed neighbourhoods where the group average is highest.

Table 5. Comparative Test Scores in Problem Areas and Mixed Neighbourhoods

Neighbourhood	Test Scores										No. of Schools
	25	24	23	22	21	20	19	18	17	16	
Problem Areas	—	—	3	7	3	6	4	2	4	1	30
Mixed Neighbourhoods	3	4	7	11	9	5	2	—	1	—	42

563. It is important to remember that the reading test represents attainments after nine years of education, not only three years in a secondary school. It is a cumulative achievement that is being measured. Setting test scores against factors such as staff ratio (which may change overnight) or even staff turnover (of which we had only three years' knowledge) was not likely to prove highly significant, and did not do so, though differences there were in the case of turnover. The neighbourhood in which a boy or girl lives, however, is usually a constant throughout his life and could be expected to be more meaningful, as it was. The most striking thing, however, is the way in which individual schools differ. There is no need to be a fatalist.

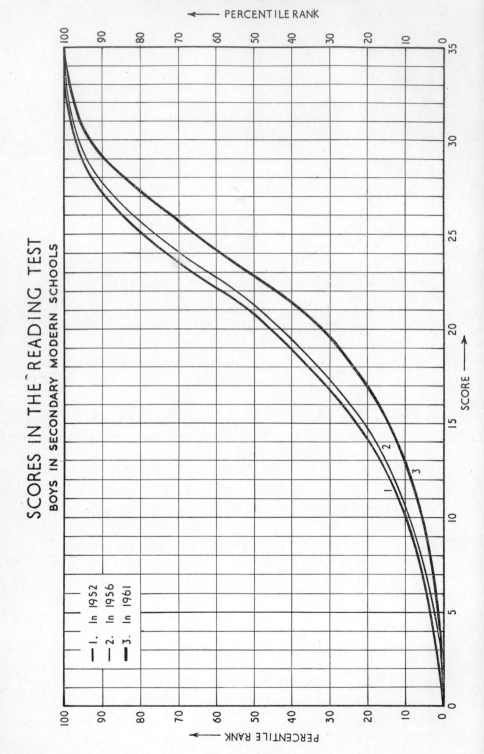

Diagram 7a

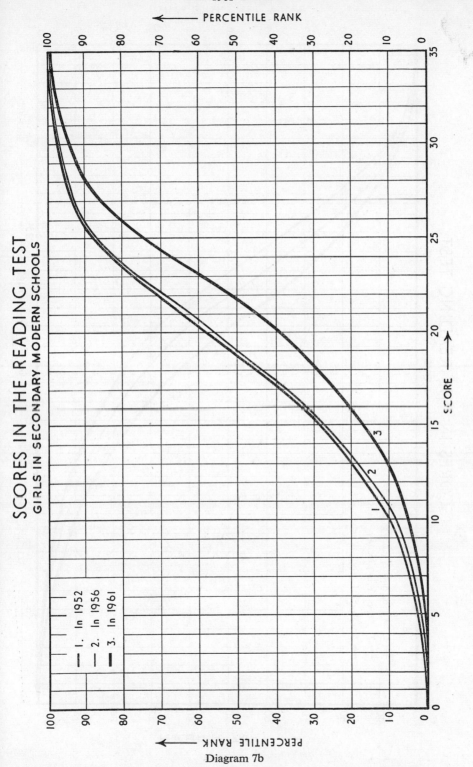

SCORES IN THE READING TEST

GIRLS IN SECONDARY MODERN SCHOOLS

← PERCENTILE RANK

PERCENTILE RANK ←

SCORE →

1. In 1952
2. In 1956
3. In 1961

Diagram 7b

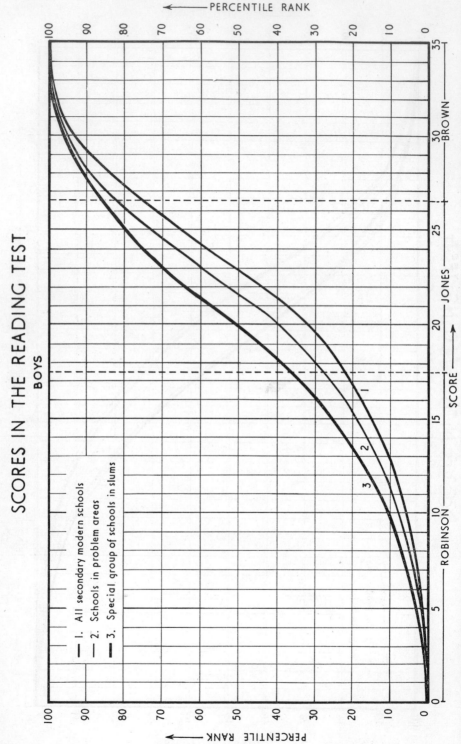

Diagram 8a

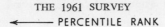

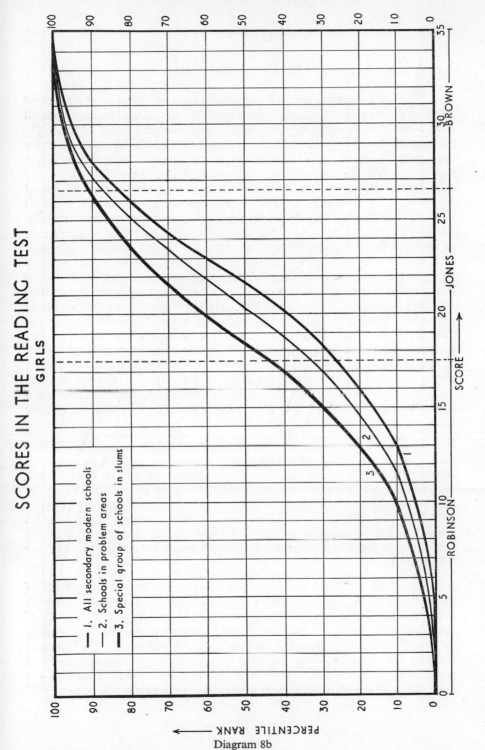

Diagram 8b

CHAPTER 22

The Boys and Girls

564. Who are the average and below-average pupils of our terms of reference? Are they distinguishable except by their record of success and failure in school work? Are their backgrounds and their needs much the same or markedly different? The 1961 survey, and the National Service survey carried out for the Council's report on Fifteen to Eighteen, provide information which has been helpful in clearing our minds on these and similar questions. We have used these surveys as a source from which we have drawn the material for portraits or profiles of imaginary boys and girls who may be taken to represent the upper, middle and lower reaches of the modern school population at the age of fourteen. All are between 14 and 15 years of age—the average age is 14 years, 8 months. We have unoriginally named them Brown, Jones and Robinson. More precisely, Brown stands for all those in modern schools who score 27 or more on the reading test; whose average score is very close to the score on the ninetieth percentile and who form roughly the top quarter in ability of modern school pupils. Similarly Jones stands for all those whose scores are between 18 and 26; whose average score is close to that on the fiftieth percentile, and who form the two middle quarters of the age-group. Robinson stands for those who scored 17 or less; whose average score is close to that on the tenth percentile and who provide the bottom quarter in ability. These definitions are shown graphically in diagrams 8A and 8B. Brown, Jones and Robinson are, then, primarily shorthand terms to avoid the repetition of lengthy definitions. They also underline the fact that, although we are using percentages, we are still dealing with human beings.

565. The information we have about the boys and girls in the sample is limited to certain questions of fact. We know a little about their physique, their family background, where they live, their school work and their social life. We know nothing about the imponderables which are ultimately much more important—the personal characteristics which make them happy or discontented, loved or disliked, useful members of the community or a drag on society. In the following paragraphs boys and girls are dealt with separately and in that order. These generalized descriptions are to be found in the three "B" sections.

566. Each "B" section is preceded by accounts supplied by their schools of three individual boys or girls who were included in the sample. Names have been changed. These boys and girls have been chosen to give some idea of how great may be the difference between human beings who are rightly included for teaching purposes in the same classification. The contrast between the individual case histories in the three "A" sections and the generalized profiles which follow them in the "B" sections illustrates the risks involved in generalizing from limited personal experience.

I. "BROWN" OR THE TOP QUARTER IN ABILITY

A. THREE REAL PEOPLE

567. *Jim's* father is a mechanic and has one other child, a girl. Apart from physical education, Jim's work was good. He was a prefect, a member of the cricket club, Young Farmers' Club and a good actor in the dramatic society. He earned extra pocket money as an errand boy. He is now at a technical college doing a one-year full-time course and is hoping to get an engineering apprenticeship in the merchant navy. He is a bright, pleasant, intelligent boy, rather short and light for his age. His attendance was almost perfect—he only missed school on five half-days in his third year. He left school as soon as he was entitled to.

* * *

568. *Tom's* father, a works manager, thought of sending his son to a private school, but found that boys were entering his firm having passed G.C.E. examinations in secondary modern schools. As a result he rented accommodation so that his boy could come to us. We found that the boy had an immense fund of general knowledge, but was below standard in most basic attainments. At the end of the second year he still had difficulty with mental arithmetic and basic English skills. We began to wonder whether we were expecting too much from him, but the educational psychologist assessed him as "Above Average Intelligence". Individual coaching in English and arithmetic was arranged. In the meantime Tom was featuring in school plays and played in the junior rugger side. In the fourth year, following great perseverence, a marked advance was made. In the autumn of 1962 he obtained Group One passes in G.C.E. in chemistry and history—and lower level passes in language and literature. At this moment he is taking five more subjects—including physics and maths.

He has been recommended for a Sixth Form Scholarship at an independent school open to outstanding boys from secondary modern schools. He is a prominent member of the school sailing club and has his own boat. He is Deputy Head Boy.

* * *

569. *Susan's* father is a farm foreman. She is a tall girl, one of four children, and now works in an accountant's office. She was a prefect for two years and interested in all her school work and in many school activities—the dancing club, the swimming club, the choir, the record group and the stamp club. She was in the hockey eleven and keen on athletics. She stayed for a fifth year and has taken G.C.E. in English.

* * *

B. TWO IMAGINARY CHARACTERS

DESCRIPTION OF JOHN BROWN

570. *His Physique*

John Brown is probaly rather above average height for his age of 14 years 8 months, 5 ft. 5 ins. or a fraction more, well-built and weighing about 8st. 7 lbs., which is again a few pounds more than the average. He is likely to be a week or so older than most of the other boys who entered the school at the same time.

571. *His Family*

There is well above an even chance that John Brown's father is a skilled manual worker; in the general population as a whole there is a slightly less than even chance that a man will be in this category. About one in five of all the Browns have fathers who are white collar workers; one in four are the sons of semi-skilled or unskilled workers. The non-manual workers are a little under-represented; the unskilled and semi-skilled are in about the usual proportion. Rather less than a third of the Browns have three or more brothers or sisters; the same proportion have just one brother or sister, while one in six is an only child. Really large families are rare. There are very few Browns on the free dinner list.

572. *Where he lives*

There are Browns of course, in every part of England; but there is a marked tendency for them to congregate in London and the Home Counties. Similarly, the kind of school in which to start looking for John Brown would be one serving a neighbourhood where a fair proportion of owner-occupied homes send their children to the modern school. But there is no neighbourhood, however depressing, in which there are no Browns. They account for 12 per cent of the pupils in the special group of schools in slums, though of course they are disproportionately few there and in the "problem areas" generally. In the school with the most Browns they account for half the fourth-year boys; in the school with fewest, they form only six per cent.

TABLE 6. PROFILE OF THE BROWN BOYS

Age

Average Age 14 years 8 months

Height

Under 5' 0"	5%	5' 4"–5' 7"	49%
5' 0"–5' 3"	23%	5' 8" or more	23%

Weight

90 lbs. or less	6%	131 lbs.–150 lbs.	21%
91 lbs.–110 lbs.	26%	151 lbs. or more	8%
111 lbs.–130 lbs.	39%		

Father's Occupation

Non-Manual Worker:		Manual Worker:	
Professional or Managerial	7%	Skilled	59%
Clerical, etc.	11%	Semi-skilled	14%
		Unskilled	9%

Size of Family

Only Child 17%

Number of Brothers or Sisters:		Three	13%
One	30%	Four	7%
Two	23%	Five or more	10%

Free Meals

Receive free school dinners 3·5%   Do *not* receive free school dinners 96·5%

Where They Live

REGION

Ministry Divisions	Browns	Jones and Robinsons
Metropolitan; E.; S.E.; S.	46%	38%
N.; E. & W. R.; N.W.; N.M.; M.; S.W.	54%	62%

NEIGHBOURHOOD

	Browns	Jones and Robinsons
"Problem Areas"	13%	18%
Rural	11%	12%
Council Housing	30%	29%
Mining	6%	11%
Mixed Areas	40%	30%

573. *His School Work Generally*

It would be surprising if John Brown's work was not well above average since the only qualification for being Brown is to do well on a test which demands native wit sharpened by school work. Clearly a good many Browns have improved on their position in the "eleven plus". Indeed, at fourteen John Brown has done better than a fifth of the boys in grammar schools. It is worth noting that a quarter of the Browns managed to get their attainments up to this level, which is a national one, although they were in schools which set them no regular homework.

574. *What examinations will he take? When will he leave school?*

If Brown attends a school where external examinations are taken at the end of the fourth year, he is more than likely to be a candidate—over four-fifths are. But only just over half the Browns have this opportunity.

Nearly half the Browns are likely to stay on for a fifth year. But, since about a third of them are pupils in schools which have no fifth year courses, it is safe to say that, when Brown is offered the chance, he is almost certain to take it. At the end of that year he will in all probability become a candidate for an external examination, probably the G.C.E. at Ordinary level, very likely in four subjects.

575. *His Attitude to School*

One cannot quite rule out the possibility that John Brown will be "agin the government", but it is exceedingly unlikely—only two per cent of the Browns are noted as being especially difficult in their attitude to discipline, while three-quarters are particularly co-operative. Truancy, or unjustified absence, is hardly a problem: only three per cent are reported as troublesome in this respect, while the total amount of school work that is missed each year by absence for any reason is likely to be less than a fortnight's.

Brown is very unlikely to neglect his homework, but he is less likely to be co-operative over school uniform. In schools where fourth-year boys are expected to wear uniform, a quarter of the Browns refuse. On the other hand, in schools where uniform is voluntary a quarter still regularly wear it.

576. *His Activities outside the classroom*

Although John Brown is twice as likely as most modern school boys to have homework to do, he is just as likely to find time to take on some kind of out-of-school paid job—a paper round is the most probable choice. The majority of Browns don't, but two out of five have some employment of this kind. Brown has a better chance than Jones or Robinson of playing regularly in a school team, but this is still a distinction which only one Brown in three is likely to earn. Similarly, he has a considerably better chance than most of becoming a school prefect; but, even so, only one in five had achieved this by the time our census was taken. Rather over a third belong to school clubs or societies while a clear majority are members of outside youth clubs. Five per cent of Browns might better have been called Crichton since they are both prefects and games colours, as well as belonging to school societies and outside youth clubs. The average score on social participation of all the Browns is 1·4 out of a possible 4. A quarter of the Browns have no social activities of which we have knowledge.

Homework

In Forms *without* Regular Homework   23%
In Forms *with* Regular Homework   77%
(Properly done 95%; Fail to do it 5%)

Probable Length of School Life

Likely to leave as soon as possible   46%
Likely to complete Fourth year but not start Fifth   12%
Likely to stay on for Fifth year   42%

External Examinations

FOURTH YEAR EXAMS
Proportion of Browns who are candidates
In Schools which take these Exams 85%   In All Schools 38%
FIFTH YEAR EXAMS
Proportion of candidates who are Browns 49%

Attitudes

DISCIPLINE
Thoroughly Co-operative   72%   Especially Difficult   2%
ATTENDANCE
Some Truancy   3%   Absence from all causes in
                                       3rd year   1–2 weeks
UNIFORM
Refuse to wear it although expected 25%   Wear it although voluntary   26%

Activities Outside the Classroom

SOCIAL
Prefect or similar post   22%   Belong to school societies   35%
Member of school team   30%
(Connected with School)
Belong to Youth Club 56% (Unconnected with School)
EMPLOYMENT
Have Paid Job 42% (Unconnected with School)

577. *Her Physique*

Mary Brown is probably one and three-quarter inches shorter than John but only about one pound lighter. Her height of 5 ft. 3¼ ins. and weight of 8 st. 6 lbs. puts her rather above the average for girls of her age (14 years 8 months).

578. *Her Family*

We have no family details for girls—the National Service Survey from which these details are drawn was necessarily confined to men—but there is no reason to suppose that Mary Brown's circumstances are markedly different from John's. The only known difference is that a slightly higher proportion are on the free dinner list—4·5 per cent.

579. *Where she lives*

Mary Brown is even more likely than John to live in the Home Counties. Over half the Brown girls live there compared with two-fifths of all other girls. There is a less than proportionate chance that Mary Brown will live in a problem area and a better chance than numbers alone would suggest that she will come from a mixed neighbourhood, but the differences are not so great as with the Brown boys. In the special group of schools in the worst slum areas one in ten of the girls in the fourth year are Browns. In the school with the most Browns they provide two-fifths of the fourth year girls; in the school with the lowest proportion they form only 4 per cent of the total.

580. *Her School Work*

Naturally enough Mary Brown is a hard worker like John. She is likely to have done better by the age of fourteen than nearly a quarter of the girls in grammar schools. Nearly a quarter of the Brown girls, like the Brown boys, have got where they are although they went to schools which set them no regular homework.

TABLE 7. PROFILE OF THE BROWN GIRLS

Age

Average Age 14 years 8 months

Height

Under 5′ 0″	6%	5′ 4″–5′ 7″	42%
5′ 0″–5′ 3″	48%	5′ 8″ or more	4%

Weight

90 lbs. or less	6%	131 lbs.-150 lbs.	15%
91 lbs.–110 lbs.	31%	151 lbs. or more	6%
111 lbs.–130 lbs.	42%		

Free Meals

Receive free school dinners 4·5%   Do *not* receive free school dinners 95·5%

Where They Live

REGION		
Ministry Divisions	Browns	Jones and Robinsons
Metropolitan; E.; S.E.; S.;	54%	41%
N.; E. & W.R.; N.W.; N.M.; M.; S.W.	46%	59%

NEIGHBOURHOOD		
	Browns	Jones and Robinsons
"Problem Areas"	17%	22%
Rural	11%	11%
Council Housing	38%	36%
Mining	2%	5%
Mixed Areas	32%	26%

Homework

In Forms *without* Regular Homework	23%
In Forms *with* Regular Homework	77%

(Properly done 95%; Fail to do it 5%)

581. *What Examinations will she take? When will she leave school?*

Mary Brown is less likely than John to sit for an external examination in the fourth year of her secondary course though, if she attends a school that takes these examinations, there is a two to one chance that she will be a candidate. She is just as likely as John to stay on for a fifth year. This means that, if her school provides the opportunity, she can almost be counted upon to take it. There is every likelihood that if she takes a fifth year, she will be an external examination candidate.

582. *Her attitude to School*

Mary's attitude to school rules is closely similar to John Brown's with one major and one minor exception. She is a good deal less likely to refuse to wear school uniform if her school expects it, but she is rather more likely to be absent from school without a reasonable excuse. In other respects she is, like John Brown, a thoroughly satisfactory member of the school community.

583. *Her Activities outside the Classroom.*

The main differences in the social life of Mary and John Brown, as far as we know them, are two. Mary is unlikely to have a part-time paid job. This is pretty certainly in part a reflection of a difference in home duties. She is also a good deal less likely than John to play for a school team. This is not because Mary Jones and Mary Robinson are more likely to be picked; but because games play a less important part for girls than for boys, and because the size of teams for many girls' games is smaller than for boys'. There are in fact in the sample roughly twice as many boys as girls who play regularly for a school team. This accounts for the slightly lower average score on social participation of the Brown girls compared with the boys— 1·3 activities out of 4 instead of 1·4. For the same reason there are fewer Admirable Crichtons—3·5 per cent instead of 5·4 per cent take part in all four kinds of social activity. A quarter take no part in any of the activities of which we have knowledge.

PROFILE OF THE BROWN GIRLS (*contd.*)

Probable Length of School Life

Likely to leave as soon as possible	48%
Likely to complete Fourth year but not start Fifth	9%
Likely to stay on for Fifth year	43%

External Examinations

FOURTH YEAR EXAMS
Proportion of Browns who are candidates
In Schools which take these exams 63%   In All Schools 50%

FIFTH YEAR EXAMS
Proportion of candidates who are Browns
Candidates 52%

Attitudes

DISCIPLINE
Thoroughly Co-operative   75%   Especially Difficult   2%
ATTENDANCE
Some Truancy   5%   Absence from all causes in
3rd year   1–2 weeks
UNIFORM
Refuse to wear it although expected   10%   Wear it although voluntary   28%

Activities Outside the Classroom

SOCIAL
Prefect or similar post   26%   Belong to school societies   37%
Member of school team   19%
(Connected with School)

Belong to Youth Club 51% (Unconnected with School)

EMPLOYMENT
Have Paid Job 16% (Unconnected with School)

II. "JONES" OR THE TWO MIDDLE QUARTERS IN ABILITY

A. THREE REAL PEOPLE

584. *Robert* came from a poor home. He lived with his mother, three brothers and two sisters. His father was often away from home, serving with the forces. The general health of the family was well below standard and his mother gave the impression of being harrassed, probably due to family worries and difficult economic circumstances. Robert was often absent in order to help his mother. When at school, he was well-behaved, helpful and rather quiet. He gave considerable help in a school athletics project, digging out high jump and pole vault pits and approach run-ups. He worked hard for his pocket money by putting in coal for local residents. Robert was good at practical subjects but weak in the basic subjects. He had intelligence, but his progress had been seriously retarded by frequent changes of school and by frequent absences. Eventually, the family left the area by doing a "moonlight flit". (*Exact* details about this boy are somewhat scanty.)

* * *

585. *Jane's* father is self-employed—a business man. Jane is well above average height and weight. She was in the B stream at school, went on to take a commercial course in a technical college and is now working in an office. Her work in housecraft at school was as good as that of girls in the A stream. Her form was not given regular homework to do, but Jane asked for some and did it. She belonged to a youth club, but held no school offices. She did not take a fifth year course, but stayed on one extra term to take a fourth-year examination.

* * *

586. *Sheila* is the eldest of five children. Her father, a capstan lathe operator, lives on a housing estate where many of the families come from slum clearance areas. All his children attend school badly, and Sheila missed the equivalent of twenty weeks' work in her third year. Her father did not always know of these absences, but even after warnings from the school attendance officer did not try to enforce his authority. In her last year at school Sheila worked in a café on Saturdays, and on one occasion at least she was working there when she was supposed to be absent from school because of illness. She went to work in the printing industry and is still with the same firm one and a half years later.

Sheila did not do very well in any kind of school work. Her teachers felt she did not work to capacity and her frequent absences made it difficult to interest her and gain her co-operation. She never joined any school societies and did not distinguish herself in games or physical education.

She was inclined to be silly in class, and inattentive; but I do not remember any occasion when she was guilty of more serious faults such as stealing. During her last two years at school she was very interested in boy friends and talked about them frequently to the visitor who takes the girls for sex education and mothercraft.

* * *

8

B. TWO IMAGINARY CHARACTERS

DESCRIPTION OF JOHN JONES

587. *His Physique*

John Jones is 14 years old. He is probably about 5 ft. 4½ ins. in height though he is quite likely to be any height between 5 ft. 3 ins. and 5 ft. 7 ins. and, of course, may be even taller or shorter. He is most likely to weight a little under eight and a half stone, though any weight between seven stone and nine stone would not be uncommon and the total range is, of course, considerably wider even than that. It would not be easy to pick John Jones out of a crowd simply on his physique.

588. *His Family*

More likely than not John Jones is the son of a skilled manual worker, but a third of the Jones boys are the children of semi-skilled or unskilled workers. Only one in eight comes from a white collar worker's home. Half as many again of the Jones boys come from unskilled and semi-skilled workers' families as there would be on a strictly proportionate division of the population; similarly there are among them a quarter more sons of skilled workers than might arithmetically be expected. A quarter of the boys like John Jones have one brother or sister, a fifth have two, over two-fifths have three or more. There is only a one in eight chance of John Jones being an only child. There are few like him on the free dinner list.

598. *Where He Lives*

There is no special part of England or particular type of neighbourhood in which one would set out to look for Jones. He is to be found everywhere and in all modern schools, whose backbone he forms. There are rather fewer boys like him than might arithmetically be expected in the Home Counties and in schools serving mixed neighbourhoods where there is a good deal of owner-occupied housing, but the differences are not great.

TABLE 8. PROFILE OF THE JONES BOYS

Age

Average Age 14 years 8 months

Height

Under 5' 0"	6%	5' 4"–5' 7"	44%
5' 0"–5' 3"	32%	5' 8" or more	18%

Weight

90 lbs. or less	8%	131 lbs.-150 lbs.	19%
91 lbs.–110 lbs.	32%	151 lbs. or more	6%
111 lbs.–130 lbs.	35%		

Father's Occupation

Non-Manual Worker :		Manual Worker:	
Professional or Managerial	4%	Skilled	55%
Clerical or other Non-Manual	9%	Semi-skilled	16%
		Unskilled	16%

Size of Family

Only Child 13%

Number of Brothers or Sisters:		Three	16%
One	24%	Four	11%
Two	20%	Five or more	16%

Free Meals

Receive free school dinners 4·5%   Do *not* receive free school dinners 95·5%

Where They Live

REGION

Ministry Divisions	Jones	Browns and Robinsons
Metropolitan; E.; S.E.; S.	36%	41%
N.; E. & W.R.; N.W.; N.M.; M.; S.W.	63%	59%

NEIGHBOURHOOD

	Jones	Browns and Robinsons
"Problem" areas	17%	18%
Rural	12%	12%
Council Housing	29%	29%
Mining	11%	8%
Mixed Areas	31·%	33%

590. *What Examinations Will He Take? When Will He Leave School?*

In the fourth year, which is likely to be his last, there is an even chance that John Jones will be in a form which is given regular homework. Given the chance, two-fifths of the Jones boys will sit for an external examination of some kind in the fourth year.

Allowing for the number of schools which have no fifth forms, it is probably true to say that, where there is an opportunity to stay on, about a quarter of the boys like John Jones will take it. If John has a fifth year at school, it will almost certainly be with the intention of taking an external examination. At present about half the total number of fifth form external examination candidates are boys like John Jones. Many, if not most, of them are candidates for examinations conducted by the various regional examining unions, though quite a few take one or two subjects in G.C.E. They are likely to sit for the new Certificate of Secondary Education.

591. *His Attitude to School*

There is little adverse to be said about John Jones and boys like him; indeed, two-thirds of them are thoroughly co-operative in school. There is a little trouble over school attendance, but not much; and a little more over homework, which ten per cent neglect. The one losing battle which schools fight with them is over uniform. Nearly two-fifths of those who are supposed to wear it do not in fact do so.

592. *His Activities Outside the Classroom*

Two-fifths of the boys like John Jones have some regular part-time paid work usually of the paper round description. John Jones has a one in seven chance of becoming a school prefect or holding some similarly important post, and twice as good a chance of playing regularly for some school team. Half the boys like him belong to outside youth clubs and similar societies, and over a quarter to school societies. But nearly a third (31 per cent) of them do none of these four things, although some three per cent do everything—they are prefects, play for school teams, belong to school societies and outside youth clubs. Out of the four social activities on which we have information the average score of boys like John Jones is 1·2.

PROFILE OF THE JONES BOYS (*contd.*)

Homework

In Forms *without* Regular Homework   48%
In Forms *with* Regular Homework   52%
(Properly done 90%; Fail to do it 10%)

Probable Length of School Life

Likely to leave as soon as possible   74%
Likely to complete Fourth year but not start Fifth   10%
Likely to stay on for Fifth year   16%

External Examinations

FOURTH YEAR EXAMS
Proportion of Jones boys who are candidates
In Schools which take these Exams 41%   In All Schools 19%

FIFTH YEAR EXAMS
Proportion of candidates who are Jones boys 51%

Attitudes

DISCIPLINE
Thoroughly Co-operative   64%   Especially Difficult   2%
ATTENDANCE
Some Truancy   6%   Absence from all causes in
3rd year   1–2 weeks
UNIFORM
Refuse to wear it although expected   38%   Wear it although voluntary   8%

Activities Outside the Classroom

SOCIAL
Prefect or similar post   14%   Belong to school societies   28%
Member of school team   28%
(Connected with School)

Belong to Youth Club 50% (Unconnected with School)

EMPLOYMENT
Have Paid Job 42% (Unconnected with School)

DESCRIPTION OF MARY JONES

593. *Her Physique*

Mary Jones is probably about one and three-quarter inches shorter than John Jones and about two pounds lighter. Her height of 5 ft. 2¾ ins. and her weight of 8 st. 3 lbs. are about average for girls of her age (14 years 8 months).

594. *Her Family*

In the absence of information about Mary Jones' family background we must assume that it is similar to John's. The proportion of girls like her who get free school dinners is fractionally higher at five per cent than for Jones boys.

595. *Where She Lives*

Mary Jones, like John, forms the backbone of all modern schools in all parts of the country and all types of neighbourhood. There are rather more girls like her in schools serving council housing estates and rather fewer in the schools in problem areas than mere arithmetic might suggest; but even in the worst slum areas she and her kind provide nearly half the total number of girls in the schools.

TABLE 9. PROFILE OF THE JONES GIRLS

Age

Average Age 14 years 8 months

Height

Under 5′ 0″	7%	5′ 4″–5′ 7″	37%
5′ 0″–5′ 3″	53%	5′ 8″ or more	3%

Weight

90 lbs. or less	6%	131 lbs.–150 lbs.	11%
91 lbs.–110 lbs.	39%	151 lbs. or more	5%
111 lbs.–130 lbs.	39%		

Free Meals

Receive free school dinners 5%   Do *not* receive free school dinners 95%

Where They Live

REGION

Ministry Divisions	Jones	Browns and Robinsons
Metropolitan; E.; S.E.; S.	43%	44%
N.; E. & W.R.; N.W.; N.M.; M.; S.W.	57%	56%

NEIGHBOURHOOD

	Jones	Browns and Robinsons
"Problem" areas	20%	23%
Rural	11%	12%
Council Housing	38%	34%
Mining	4%	4%
Mixed Areas	27%	27%

Homework

In Forms *without* Regular Homework   40%
In Forms *with* Regular Homework   60%
(Properly done 94%; Fail to do it 6%)

596. *What Examinations Will She Take? When Will She Leave School?*

Mary Jones, like John, is expecting to leave school as soon as she is legally old enough. Only one in five of the girls like her will stay on for a fifth year, but that is partly because many of them are in schools which do not provide fifth-form courses. Mary Jones is rather more likely than John to be in a form which gets regular homework, but even so two-fifths of the girls like her are not. There is virtually nothing to choose between John and Mary Jones in the matter of external examinations. Boys and girls like them provide about half the fifth year examination candidates—usually not for G.C.E. If her school takes an external examination in the fourth year there is one chance in three that she will sit for it.

597. *Her Attitude to School.*

The odds are strongly in favour of Mary Jones getting into no serious disciplinary trouble. If she does it will probably be because she will not wear the uniform the school expects—a fifth of the girls like her are difficult over uniform, though this is not nearly so high as the corresponding figure for boys. There is on the other hand among the girls rather more of a tendency to stay away from school without adequate excuse, though once again the number affected is small—only about one in thirteen of the girls like Mary Jones plays truant. Mary Jones is likely to have missed altogether about a fortnight's school in the previous year, just a little more than John. When homework is set, it nearly always gets conscientiously done—in the kind of form in which Mary Jones is likely to be, it would be surprising if more than one or two girls gave trouble in this respect.

598. *Her Activities Outside the Classroom*

There are probably two main differences between Mary Jones and John. Mary is very much less likely to have any kind of part-time paid job—only one in six of the girls like her have regular paid jobs compared with two out of five boys like John. Then she has a better than one in five chance of becoming a prefect or holding some similar post (something more important than a form office), compared with his one in seven chance. She is less likely to play games for a school team, but the difference is small considering the smaller number of players in many girls' games. Nearly a third (30 per cent) of the girls like her take no part in any of the social activities of which we know; but four per cent are prefects, members of school teams and belong both to school societies and youth clubs. The average score of girls like Mary Jones is 1·2 out of the four social activities which we know about.

PROFILE OF THE JONES GIRLS (*contd.*)

Probable Length of School Life

Likely to leave as soon as possible   72%
Likely to complete Fourth year but not start Fifth   9%
Likely to stay on for Fifth year   19%

External Examinations

FOURTH YEAR EXAMS
Proportion of Jones girls who are candidates
In Schools which take these Exams 38%   In All Schools 22%

FIFTH YEAR EXAMS
Proportion of candidates who are Jones girls 48%

Attitudes

	DISCIPLINE	
Thoroughly Co-operative	67%	Especially Difficult 3·5%
	ATTENDANCE	
Some Truancy	7·5%	Absence from all causes in 3rd year 2 weeks
	UNIFORM	
Refuse to wear it although expected	21%	Wear it although voluntary 11%

Activities Outside the Classroom

SOCIAL
Prefect or similar post   22%   Belong to school societies   26%
Member of school team   20%
(Connected with School)

Belong to Youth Club 52% (Unconnected with School)

EMPLOYMENT
Have Paid Job 16% (Unconnected with School)

III. "ROBINSONS" OR THE BOTTOM QUARTER IN ABILITY

A. THREE REAL PEOPLE

599. *Bill* is an only child, who lives with his parents in a semi-detached house. His father is a miner. His attendance at school was satisfactory, and there were usually acceptable reasons for his occasional absences. His general health was always good but he was a nervous boy and had the habit of biting his nails. Occasionally he was impatient and irritated and lost his temper. His conduct was usually good with occasional lapses.

At the age of 12 he appeared before a Juvenile Court for larceny of axes and hammers but was given a conditional discharge. He was easily led. The educational psychologist found him to be educationally retarded and recommended him for a special class. He continued, however, in the secondary school, where he was always in the "C" stream. He was very backward in the basic subjects. He also lacked athletic ability and did not participate in the sporting life of the school, but he was a likeable boy. Art was his best subject, in which he was very interested. He was quite good, in his class, at woodwork and metalwork. He worked in the house doing odd jobs and liked helping his mother. He earned a fairly regular supply of pocket money after school and in the holidays.

* * *

600. *Joan* lives on a housing estate in a good district. Her father is a salesman and Joan is an only girl, well below average height and weight.

Her attendance was not good, partly due to family difficulties and partly due to poor physical health. Her father and mother quarrelled frequently and the mother was often ill with nervous trouble. They both wished to do their best for Joan but they quarrelled about her future career. After she left school she came back several times to talk to members of the staff about her troubles. She appeared to have no relatives who could help or advise her. For a time the father left home and Joan, who wished to stay on for a fifth year, had to leave and find work. She passionately wanted to be a nurse but her work was much too poor. Her first employment was at a hairdresser's but she soon lost this post and another similar one because she was not very good at the work. She then went to a shop as a window-dresser but again could not do the work successfully and she is now working in the shop as a sales assistant. She was very well behaved and was friendly and courteous but too nervous to take any active part in school life. She was a member of the junior branch of St. John's Ambulance Brigade but even here she was unable to pass the various tests and so could not make any progress.

* * *

601. *Bert* was only 5 ft. 1½ inches tall and weighed just 7 st. 7 lbs. His attainments were very poor when he came to the secondary school, and he left with a reading age of eight years and four months. His I.Q. at the time of the eleven plus examination was 73. He has one elder brother who went to the same school where he had been a thorough nuisance. Bert himself was a pleasant, cheerful lad on the surface, but inclined to be a trouble-maker or so his teachers thought. Neighbours, too, complained to the school of his bad influence over their children and particularly of his filthy language if they took him to task. He lived in a poor housing area, and he and his brother were left to their own devices in the evening while his parents went out. Neighbours reported that quarrels were a regular and noisy domestic feature. Bert was given to occasional, quite unexplained absences from school. He missed over three weeks' work in his third year. He spent about an hour and a half a day on a paper round, but took no part in any voluntary school activities nor did he belong to a youth club.

B. TWO IMAGINARY CHARACTERS

1. DESCRIPTION OF JOHN ROBINSON

602. *His Physique*

John Robinson is rather short for his age of 14 years 8 months—about 5 ft. 3¾ ins. and rather light at just 8 stone. But there are plenty of boys like him who are tall or heavy, and it would not be possible to identify Robinsons by their build alone. They tend to be just a little younger than other boys who entered the secondary school at the same time.

603. *His Family*

Nine out of ten boys like John Robinson come from the homes of manual workers. The proportion whose fathers are semi-skilled or unskilled is getting on for twice that in the whole population (38 per cent instead of 22). A quarter come from really large families—those with six or more children; only one in fourteen are only children and one in six from families with two children. One in twelve are so poor that they have free school dinners.

604. *Where He Lives*

In the "problem areas" there are half as many Robinsons again as there are boys like Brown and Jones. In the schools in the worst slum areas over a third of the boys (36 per cent) are of John Robinson's kind. There are proportionately rather more Robinsons in the North and Midlands than in the rest of England, and this is still true even when allowance has been made for the fact that there are more problem areas in these regions than in the south. In the school with most Robinsons they form over a third of the whole fourth year age-group; the smallest proportion of Robinsons in any school is 3 per cent. These variations are important in assessing what chance John Robinson has of achieving any distinction in school activities.

TABLE 10. PROFILE OF THE ROBINSON BOYS

Age

Average Age 14 years 8 months

Height

Under 5' 0"	14%	5' 4"–5' 7"	37%
5' 0"–5' 3"	35%	5' 8" or more	14%

Weight

90 lbs or less	16%	131 lbs.–150 lbs.	14%
91 lbs.–110 lbs.	32%	151 lbs. or more	4%
111 lbs.–130 lbs.	34%		

Father's Occupation

Non-Manual Worker:		Manual Worker:	
Professional or Managerial	2%	Skilled	53%
Clerical or other Non-Manual	7%	Semi-Skilled	18%
		Unskilled	20%

Size of Family

Only Child 7%

Number of Brothers or Sisters:		Three	17%
One	17%	Four	14%
Two	20%	Five or more	25%

Free Meals

Receive free school dinners 8·2%   Do *not* receive free school dinners 91·8%

Where They Live

REGION

Ministry Divisions	Robinsons	Jones and Browns
Metropolitan; E.; S.E.; S.	42%	46%
N.; E. & W.R.; N.W.; N.M.; M.; S.W.	58%	54%

NEIGHBOURHOOD

	Robinsons	Jones and Browns
"Problem" areas	24%	16%
Rural	10%	12%
Council Housing	31%	29%
Mining	12%	9%
Mixed Areas	23%	34%

1. DESCRIPTION OF JOHN ROBINSON (*contd.*)

605. *What Examinations Will He Take? When Will He Leave School?*

It is almost certain that John Robinson will leave school as soon as he can; even when allowance is made for modern schools without provision for a fifth year, it is unlikely that one in seventeen of those Robinsons who have the opportunity will take it. Only a quarter of the Robinsons get regular homework to do. Where boys like Robinson attend schools which take an external examination in the fourth year about one in ten become candidates.

606. *His Attitude to School*

There is a good chance that John Robinson will be reckoned to be thoroughly co-operative in all matters of school discipline, though one in ten of the boys like him are considered especially difficult. Where the school expects fourth year boys to wear uniform, it has a stiff struggle to enforce it on the Robinsons—half of them refuse. Nearly a fifth of the Robinsons who are given homework to do fail to do it regularly. Attendance too is fairly often a problem—one in six or seven sometimes plays truant, and their absences, justified and unjustified, during the third year of the secondary course added up to between two and three weeks on an average.

607. *His Activities Outside the Classroom*

It would be too much to expect many boys like John Robinson to take a prominent part in school activities, but one in fourteen do become prefects or hold some similarly important position—purely form offices were not counted—and one in five plays regularly for a school team. They are much more likely to take part in activities unconnected with the school—three times as many belong to youth clubs and the like as to school societies, and the same proportion (two out of five) have a part-time paid job. Nearly half (45 per cent) do not figure in any of the four social activities; a very few (just over 2 per cent) score four out of four, but the average score for all Robinsons is only 0·8.

1. PROFILE OF THE ROBINSON BOYS (*contd.*)

Homework

In Forms *without* Regular Homework 76%
In Forms *with* Regular Homework 24%
(Properly done 82%; Fail to do it 18%)

Probable Length of School Life

Likely to leave as soon as possible 93%
Likely to complete Fourth year but not start Fifth 4%
Likely to stay on for Fifth year 3%

External Examinations

FOURTH YEAR EXAMS
Proportion of Robinson boys who are candidates
In Schools which take these Exams 10%   In All Schools 4%

FIFTH YEAR EXAMS
Proportion of candidates who are Robinson boys NIL

Attitudes

DISCIPLINE
Thoroughly Co-operative 55%   Especially Difficult 10%
ATTENDANCE
Some Truancy 15%   Absence from all causes in 3rd year 2–3 weeks
UNIFORM
Refuses to wear it although expected 51%   Wears it although voluntary 6%

Activities Outside the Classroom

SOCIAL
Prefect or similar post 7%   Belong to school societies 13%
Member of school team 20%
(Connected with School)

Belong to Youth Club 40% (Unconnected with School)

EMPLOYMENT
Have Paid Job 41% (Unconnected with School)

608. *Her Physique*

Mary Robinson at a probable 5 ft. 2¼ ins. is an inch and a half shorter than John, but like him probably weighs just eight stone. Both are well below the average for their age of 14 years 8 months. Both, too, are a little younger than others who entered the school at the same time.

609. *Her Family*

There is no reason to suppose, though we lack evidence, that Mary Robinson's family differs from John's. Her father is almost certainly a manual worker—more likely than not a skilled worker, but with a considerably greater chance of his being a semi-skilled or unskilled worker than their numbers in the whole population suggest. About one in sixteen are poor enough to receive free school dinners.

610. *Where She Lives*

Well over half the girls like Mary Robinson live in the Midlands or the North compared with just half all other girls. There are fewer girls like her in the schools serving housing estates, new towns or socially mixed neighbourhoods and more in problem areas than strict arithmetic would suggest. In the schools in the worst slum districts nearly half the girls (45 per cent) are of the same kind as Mary Robinson. In the school with the highest proportion of Robinsons they account for four-fifths of the fourth-year girls; in the school at the opposite extreme they form 4 per cent of the age-group. These variations need to be remembered when considering Mary Robinson's chance of distinction in school activities.

TABLE 11. PROFILE OF THE ROBINSON GIRLS

Age

Average Age 14 years 8 months

Height

Under 5′ 0″	13%	5′ 4″–5′ 7″	28%
5′ 0″–5′ 3″	58%	5′ 8″ or more	1%

Weight

90 lbs. or less	10%	131 lbs.–150 lbs.	11%
91 lbs.–110 lbs.	42%	151 lbs. or more	3%
111 lbs.–130 lbs.	34%		

Free Meals

Receive free school dinners 6·6%   Do *not* receive free school dinners 93·4%

Where They Live

REGION

Ministry Divisions	Robinsons	Browns and Jones
Metropolitan; E.; S.E.; S.	44%	50%
N.; E. & W.R.; N.W.; N.M.; M.; S.W.	56%	50%

NEIGHBOURHOOD

	Robinsons	Browns and Jones
"Problem" areas	26%	19%
Rural	12%	11%
Council Housing	32%	38%
Mining	6%	4%
Mixed Areas	24%	28%

Homework

In Forms *without* Regular Homework   64%
In Forms *with* Regular Homework   36%
(Properly done 78%; Fail to do it 22%)

611. *What Examinations Will She Take? When Will She Leave School?*

It is virtually certain that Mary Robinson, like John, will leave school as soon as she can. Even where she has the opportunity of a fifth year there is not much more than a one in fourteen chance that she will take it—but this is just a little better than the picture for boys. Mary Robinson is more likely than John to take an external examination if she gets the chance—and if this does not involve staying for a fifth year. About one in eight become candidates for minor examinations in schools where fourth year examinations are held. Only one in three of the Robinson girls gets homework to do—few enough, but distinctly more than with the boys.

612. *Her Attitude to School*

This is very like John Robinson's. Over half the Robinson girls are thoroughly co-operative and rather fewer girls than boys are reported as exceptionally difficult (7 per cent). But truancy is more of a problem, and quite a serious one since one in five or six have unjustifiable absences and the average time lost in the third year from all causes was the equivalent of three weeks. Although fewer girls than boys refuse to wear uniform if it is demanded, the proportion of those like Mary Robinson who give trouble in this way is high—36 per cent. Over a fifth of the minority who are set homework neglect to do it.

613. *Her Social Activities*

There is little real difference between the record of the Robinson girls and boys. Neither can be expected to shine in school affairs, but Mary has a one in ten chance of becoming a prefect or holding some similar post and a one in seven chance of playing for a school team. Fewer Robinson girls than boys belong to youth clubs and far fewer (only one in seven) have a part-time job. About half (49 per cent) do not figure at all on the list of social activities, only one per cent score four out of four, and the average score for girls like Mary Robinson is 0·75.

PROFILE OF THE ROBINSON GIRLS (*contd.*)

Probable Length of School Life

Likely to leave as soon as possible	94%
Likely to complete Fourth year but not start Fifth	2%
Likely to stay on for Fifth year	4%

External Examinations

FOURTH YEAR EXAMS
Proportion of Robinson girls who are candidates
In Schools which take these Exams 13%   In All Schools 8%

FIFTH YEAR EXAMS
Proportion of candidates who are Robinson girls Nil

Attitudes

DISCIPLINE

Thoroughly Co-operative   55%   Especially Difficult   7%

ATTENDANCE

Some Truancy   18%   Absence from all causes in
                                     3rd year   3 weeks

UNIFORM

Refuse to wear it although expected   36%   Wear it although voluntary   8%

Activities Outside the Classroom

SOCIAL

Prefect or similar post   10%   Belong to school societies   15%
Member of school team   14%
(Connected with School)

Belong to Youth Club 35% (Unconnected with School)

EMPLOYMENT
Have Paid Job 14% (Unconnected with School)

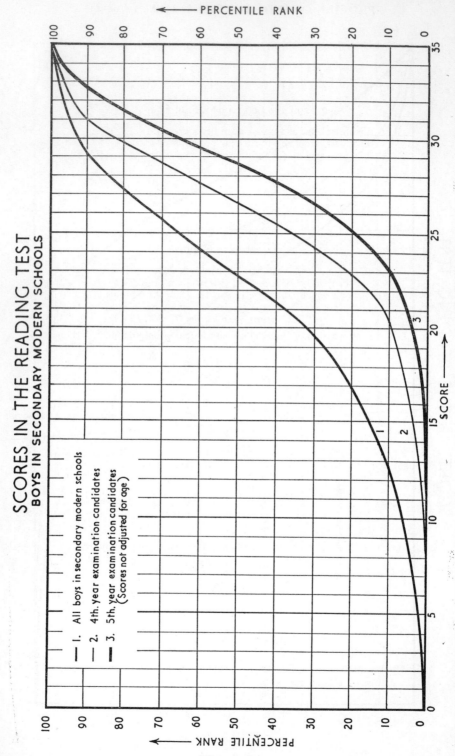

Diagram 9a

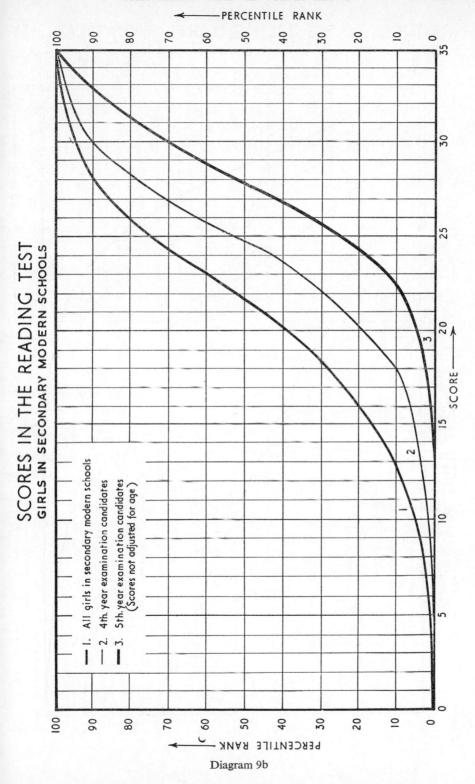

Diagram 9b

ATTITUDES TO DISCIPLINE IN RELATION TO ABILITY

BOYS

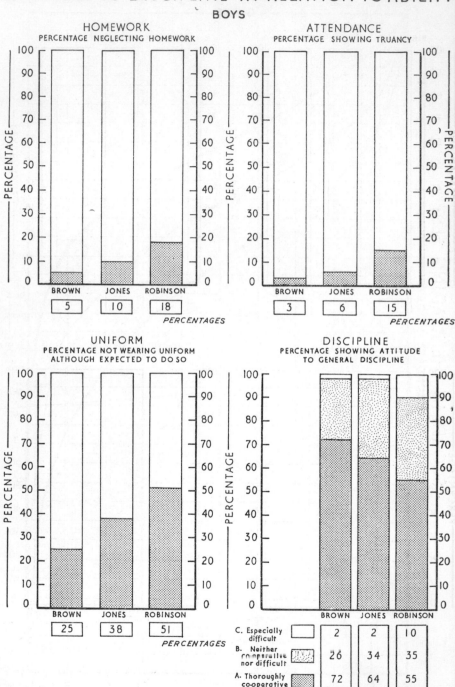

Diagram 10a

ATTITUDES TO DISCIPLINE IN RELATION TO ABILITY

GIRLS

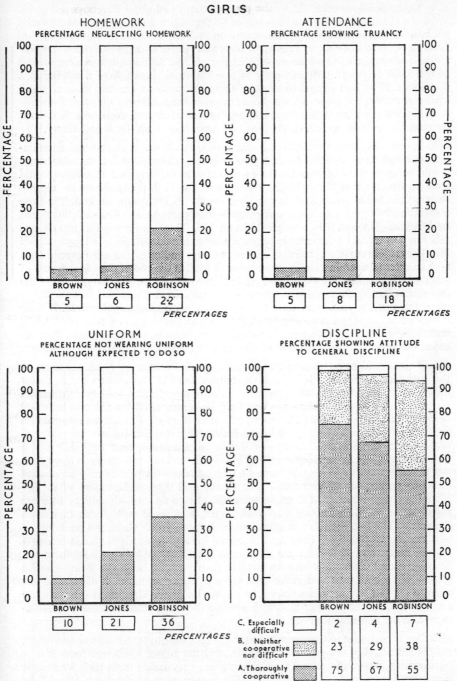

Diagram 10b

IV. BROWN, JONES AND ROBINSON

614. In the previous three sections over 6,000 boys and girls[1] were reduced to six symbolic characters. Only one item out of all the information we possessed formed the basis of characterization—performance on a scholastic test. This was appropriate because our terms of enquiry refer us to boys and girls of average and below-average ability and require us to advise on their education. We deliberately therefore looked at the 6,000 boys and girls as nearly as possible from the angle of a teacher in a classroom. If we had wished to think of them primarily as a games master, youth leader or newsagent might do, we should have selected different pieces of information to form the basis of characterization. Instead of Brown, Jones and Robinson we might have built up Athos, Porthos and Aramis or Tom, Dick and Harry.

615. It was likely from the beginning that Brown would sit for an external examination and stay on at school for a fifth year. The only doubtful point was whether he would be given the opportunity. It was also always unlikely that Robinson would want to do either of these things. The reasons for both probabilities are clear— Brown was chosen because of his good test results, Robinson for his bad. The close association between test results and entering for external examinations is illustrated by Diagrams 9A and 9B on pages 224 and 225. They also bring out clearly one other important fact—the value in terms of academic achievement of a longer school life. The middle curve represents the scores of boys and girls who were expecting to take an external examination in the summer of 1962 at the end of their fourth year of secondary education; the right hand curve the scores of fifth year candidates in the same schools. The boys and girls whose scores are recorded on the right hand curve were, therefore, a year older than those represented by the middle curve. If their scores are adjusted by the appropriate age allowance the two curves become virtually indistinguishable. The fifth year candidates score more points not because they are more intelligent but because they are older, and have had an extra year's education.

616. There could be no obvious certainty about what the survey would show about the activities of Brown, Jones and Robinson outside the classroom. A factor analysis was, therefore, made of which details are given in the Statistical Appendix on page 294. The conclusions reached may be summarised for the non-technical reader in this way. The extra-classroom activities of which we received information are five– school posts of responsibility and authority, membership of a school team, of a school society, of a youth club or similar organization, and the holding of a part-time paid job. Brown, Jones and Robinson all tend either to figure in more than one of these ways or to abstain from all. The activities themselves may be divided into two groups—those associated with school and those independent of it. The school based activities tend to go together and also to tie up with ability—they are associated more with Brown than with Jones, and more with Jones than with Robinson. The two activities independent of school—youth clubs and paid jobs— also tend to go together. They are not closely related to academic achievement— Brown, Jones and Robinson are all equally likely or unlikely to take them up. Another useful distinction between the five activities can be made. Being given a responsible school post and being chosen for a team are marks of distinction not open to all, but anybody can belong to a school society. The first two are closely associated with one another and with ability; the third stands half-way between them and the non-school group.

617. Pupils' attitudes to their school and the school's attitude to pupils are no doubt closely linked. They are not unchangeable, and the power to change them is to a considerable extent the school's. In this respect they differ from such important factors as homes and neighbourhoods. The survey gives information about four

[1] The third of the modern school sample for whom individual questionnaires were completed.

attitudes—to homework, to attendance, to the wearing of uniform and to discipline generally. Diagrams 10A and 10B show that the connection with ability is close. Robinson is much more likely than Brown to stay away from school, to neglect his homework (or not to get any), to refuse to wear school uniform and to be especially difficult to control.

618. Granted that a Robinson is more often an unsatisfactory pupil in these various ways than a Brown is, the question still remains open whether it is these propensities which help to make him Robinson, a boy bad at work, or whether he falls into these bad habits because he is only and inescapably Robinson. As the Jacobite toast had it

"But which Pretender is and which is King,
God bless us all, that's quite another thing."

It may be that if points of friction could be removed, whenever no serious principle is involved, and if more interesting and suitable work could be provided, the differences in attitude to school which at present tend to distinguish Brown, Jones and Robinson might disappear.

V. OUR BOYS AND GIRLS IN COMPREHENSIVE SCHOOLS

619. Brown, Jones and Robinson, are all, by definition, pupils in modern schools. But there are pupils in comprehensive schools who are like all three, and pupils in grammar schools who are like Brown and Jones. The proportion of pupils in comprehensive schools who are in fact like them is brought out in Diagrams 11A and 11B on pages 230 and 231. Brown at 14 is as good as many grammar school pupils, and needs treating accordingly so that he may feel their equal and achieve as good results.

620. There is a contrast in principle between Brown, Jones and Robinson in their modern schools and their twins, so to speak (pupils with the same test scores), in comprehensive schools.[1] Part of it is clearly to be seen in the diagrams on pages 230 and 231 and part can be inferred from them. The part that is visible is that the twins of Jones and Robinson form a much smaller part of the whole comprehensive school than Jones and Robinson do of the modern school. This is an exaggerated case of the differences that arise between modern schools themselves where the range extends from a school with one per cent only of Browns at one extreme, to a school with only one per cent of Robinsons at the other end. The other part of the contrast, the part that has to be inferred, is that the twins of all three—Brown, Jones and Robinson—are necessarily junior members of a comprehensive school whereas they would have been seniors in a modern school. This is because, again by definition, Brown, Jones and Robinson are fourteen years of age and comprehensive schools have many pupils of seventeen and eighteen.

621. Are there any significant differences in activities outside the classroom and in attitudes to school between Brown, Jones and Robinson and their twins in comprehensive schools? Unfortunately one can only give an answer for Brown and Jones. For one reason or another the number of individual questionnaires received from comprehensive schools for pupils in the Robinson range of scores was only half the proportion that the total test results showed them to form in the comprehensive schools as a whole. The actual number of Robinson questionnaires received was too small to make it possible to estimate with any confidence activities or attitudes within this group. The point is further discussed in the Statistical Appendix on page 281.

[1] No genetic reference is intended by the metaphor.

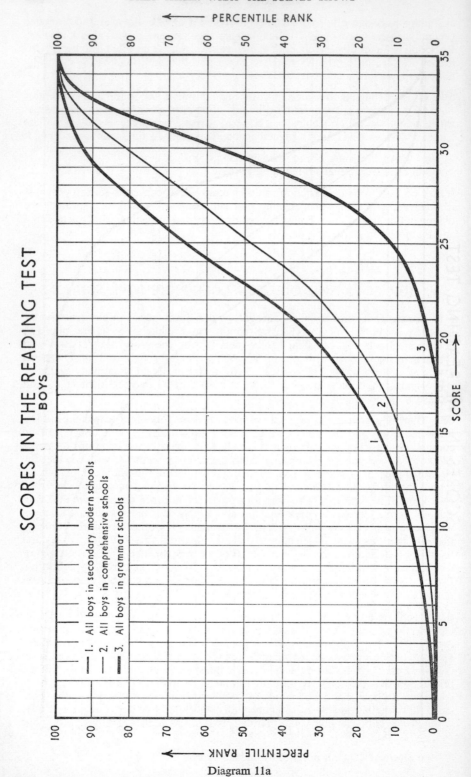

Diagram 11a

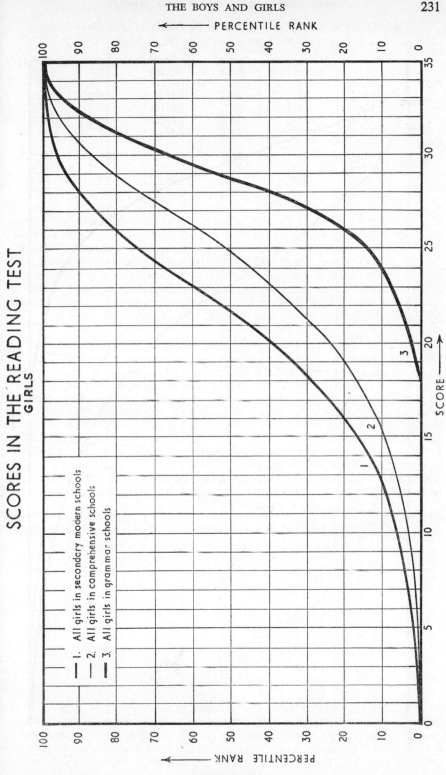

SCORES IN THE READING TEST
GIRLS

PERCENTILE RANK

1. All girls in secondary modern schools
2. All girls in comprehensive schools
3. All girls in grammar schools

SCORE

PERCENTILE RANK

Diagram 11b

Table 12. *Extra-Classroom Activities in the Fourth Year in Modern and Comprehensive Schools*

		Responsible School Post	School Team	School Society	Youth Club	Paid Job
Boys						
Brown	Mod.	**22%**	*30%*	**35%**	*56%*	*42%*
	Comp.	**6%**	*28%*	**51%**	*49%*	*37%*
Jones	Mod.	**14%**	**28%**	*28%*	*50%*	*42%*
	Comp.	**8%**	**19%**	*32%*	*45%*	*48%*
Girls						
Brown	Mod.	**26%**	**19%**	**37%**	**51%**	*16%*
	Comp.	**5%**	**10%**	**15%**	**22%**	*15%*
Jones	Mod.	**22%**	*20%*	*26%*	**52%**	*16%*
	Comp.	**6%**	*15%*	*23%*	**39%**	*20%*

622. In Table 12 which deals with activities outside the classroom, differences which are statistically significant are shown in Bold type and those which are not free from sampling fluctuations in italic. The same device is used in Table 13. School societies play a bigger part and outside youth clubs and organizations a smaller part in the life of comprehensive than of modern school pupils. Brown and Jones would have had a smaller chance of reaching a position of authority or playing for a school team if they had gone to a comprehensive school—no doubt because they would still be only middle school pupils.

623. Table 13 shows that there are no significant differences over attendance or neglect of homework (though the comprehensive schools set it to virtually all the pupils of this ability range and the modern schools only to three-quarters of the Browns and half the Jones). The comprehensive schools expect all their pupils to wear uniform and secure it with very few exceptions. A considerable number of modern schools do not expect fourth year pupils to wear uniform and those which do have considerable difficulty in enforcing it. There is no significant difference about the proportion of pupils said to be especially difficult over discipline; but, as Diagram 12 shows, the comprehensive schools have a markedly smaller proportion who are said to be thoroughly co-operative. This, like other differences, may well be due to the fact that Brown and Jones are among the oldest pupils in modern schools while their twins are only halfway up the comprehensive schools.

Table 13. *Attitudes to School in the Fourth Year in Modern and Comprehensive Schools*

		Neglecting Homework	with some truancy	refusing to wear uniform
Boys				
Brown	Mod.	*5%*	*3%*	**25%**
	Comp.	*7%*	*2%*	**2%**
Jones	Mod.	**10%**	*6%*	**38%**
	Comp.	**7%**	*3%*	**6%**
Girls				
Brown	Mod.	*5%*	*5%*	**13%**
	Comp.	*1%*	*2%*	*Nil*
Jones	Mod.	*6%*	*8%*	**20%**
	Comp.	*7%*	*6%*	**1%**

624. Another analysis shows that there is virtually no difference in the proportion of Browns who will complete a five-year course in those modern schools which provide the opportunity and the proportion of their twins doing so in comprehensive schools. There is, however, rather less likelihood of Jones staying on in his modern school, if given the chance, than there is of his comprehensive school twin doing so.

ATTITUDES TO DISCIPLINE
IN SECONDARY MODERN & COMPREHENSIVE SCHOOLS

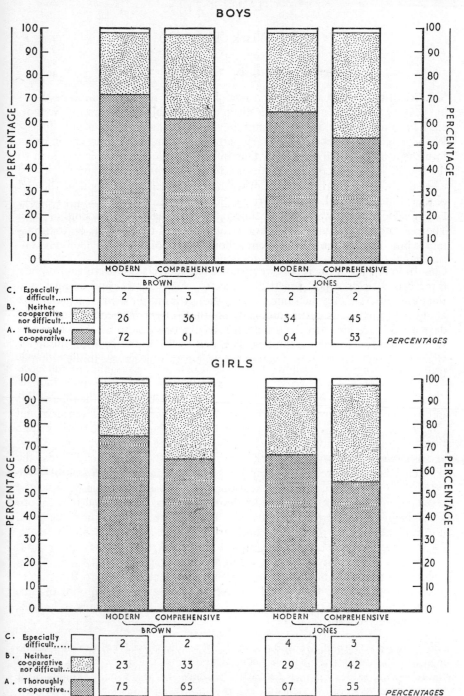

Diagram 12

CHAPTER 23

The Work They Do

625. Most countries can provide a straightforward time-table analysis showing year by year how much time is given to each subject. We cannot. Schools are free to make their own plans and they take great advantage of this liberty. We have had to impose an arbitrary pattern on conflicting practices in order to present an intelligible picture. Our information, moreover, is confined to the fourth year in secondary modern schools. We have a horizontal view of what the boys and girls with whom we are concerned are doing near the end of their time at school, but the vertical element is altogether lacking: we have no evidence about how long their time-tables have had the same kind of look. There is another limitation. We know the names of the subjects on the time-table; but their content varies from school to school.

626. In Part Two of the report we grouped the subjects of the curriculum into three broad fields—the "practical subjects", mathematics and science, and the humanities. Using the same classification, the simplest way to generalize about the fourth-year curriculum is to say that roughly the equivalent of two days a week are given to the practical subjects, one day to mathematics and science, and two to the humanities. This is a useful approximation though it slightly exaggerates the time given to the practical subjects and to the humanities.

627. The next step to a clearer picture is to distinguish between the time-tables of boys and girls. There are roughly three boys and three girls in co-educational modern schools to every two boys and two girls in single sex schools. The time-table analysis shows that in both types of school there are some differences between boys and girls in the time given to the three broad fields: the difference is rather greater between boys and girls in single sex schools than between boys and girls in co-educational schools. In part this may be the result of differences in outlook, but some at least of it is caused by the convenience in co-educational schools of making allocations of time correspond in those subjects for which boys and girls separate—for physical education, for instance, or the crafts. The simplest way of expressing the difference is to say that boys in boys' schools spend on an average the equivalent of half a morning a week more in the maths and science field than do the girls in girls' schools, who in turn spend a correspondingly greater amount of time on the practical subjects. In co-educational schools the difference still exists, but is roughly halved.

628. Far greater than the differences in time allocations between boys and girls are the differences between school and school. This is brought out in the following table, which is arranged in steps of five per cent. This is done because five per cent of a school week is a quarter of a day's work; and, thus, ten per cent is a half-day and twenty per cent the equivalent of one day a week.

Table 14. Average time spent by boys and girls in their Fourth Year in Modern Schools in the Three Curriculum Fields.

| | BOYS | | | GIRLS | | |
| Percentage of Working Week | Practical Subjects | Maths and Science | Humanities | Practical Subjects | Maths and Science | Humanities |
	No. of schools	No. of schools	No. of schools	No. of schools	No. of schools	No. of schools
60–56	—	—	2	—	—	1
55–51	—	—	—	1	—	2
50–46	4	—	8	14	—	8
45–41	25	—	27	30	1	25
40–36	36	—	55	40	—	53
35–31	37	7	23	26	3	24
30–26	12	32	2	3	12	2
25–21	1	63	—	1	46	—
20–16	1	14	—	—	49	—
15–11	1	1	—	—	4	—
10 or less	—	—	—	—	—	—
No. of schools	117	117	117	115	115	115

629. To some extent, as with the differences between boys and girls, these variations are caused by a differing diagnosis of the needs of pupils; but this is not the whole, and is probably not the major cause of variety. A comparison of this chapter with chapter 25 makes it clear why at any rate some of these variations occur. Where provision for a subject is inadequate somebody must go short. But, because we have only an analysis of fourth year time-tables, it is impossible to relate the time given to a subject or field of education to the adequacy of the physical provision for it since some schools prefer to pinch, if pinch they must, at one stage of the course and some at another. The same conditions apply as a result of staffing difficulties of the kind discussed in chapter 24. The results could not be better expressed than by the head who wrote to us "time-table analysis is chancy: I seldom finish the term with the time-table I started with". It is not surprising that in their general comments many heads made it clear to us that their curriculum is not what they think right; but only the best that they can do in the circumstances.

630. The time allocations given in Table 14 are the average of the separate fourth year form allocations. These averages often conceal a wide and important variation from form to form; but on the other hand many schools make little or no distinction in the time they give to their abler and their less able pupils, at least as far as the three broad fields of the curriculum are concerned. Both aspects are brought out in Table 15 overleaf where, as in the previous table, the device of five per cent steps is used. In schools with less than a five per cent variation the reason for varying totals may well be a difference in the length of morning and afternoon periods rather than a difference in policy. A major reason for the different treatment of different forms is the belief that a common time allocation makes little sense in a modern school—it is useless to treat the Browns and Robinsons of the last chapter as though they need the same kind of time-table because they go to the same school. In some schools, therefore, the time given to mathematics drops steadily as one moves from the forms where there are most Browns to those where there are most Robinsons. Other schools hold the same belief in the need for separate

Table 15. *Variations in Time Allocations to the Three Curriculum Fields within Individual Schools*

| Range between Forms | BOYS | | | GIRLS | | |
| | Practical Subjects | Maths and Science | Humanities | Practical Subjects | Maths and Science | Humanities |
Percentage of Working Week	No. of schools	No. of schools	No. of schools	No. of schools	No. of schools	No. of schools
No variation	15	17	16	13	18	12
1–4	29	43	40	28	39	36
5–9	30	28	32	35	31	35
10–14	27	20	14	16	17	19
15–19	5	5	6	8	9	3
20–24	9	4	7	7	—	7
25–29	2	—	1	5	—	2
30–34	—	—	1	3	1	1
No. of schools	117	117	117	115	115	115

treatment, but draw a different conclusion—in these schools the process is reversed and the time given to mathematics rises as one moves from the Browns to the Robinsons. Examples of both principles occur among the schools with wide variations in Table 15.

631. We have written first about three broad fields of the curriculum both here and in Part Two rather than of the individual subjects for two reasons— because it is easier to hold three variables in mind than ten, and because we have wished to be positive about the need for all pupils to gain adequate experience in all three fields without being restrictive about the choice of the individual subjects through which this experience is given. This permissiveness, which is part of the English educational tradition, might be expected to lead to a very wide range of subjects being studied with marked differences in the curriculum from school to school and between pupils in the same school. A variety of historical reasons, however, have in fact kept schools to a considerable measure of uniformity, and the work of analysis soon showed that it was possible to identify a typical modern school programme which would be common to most pupils in most schools. Diagram 12 illustrates the position. There was little difficulty about the list of subjects to be included— Religious Instruction, English, history, geography and current affairs or civics form the humanities group. Mathematics and science stand together. Technical drawing, handicraft or the domestic crafts, art, music and physical education make up the normal practical subjects. The problem was not to choose the subjects, but to decide how much time each would get in a typical school. The same wide differences between schools and between forms within the same school, which we found in the three fields of the curriculum, necessarily recur in individual subjects.

632. The circular form of the diagram brings out other relations between subjects than those symbolised by our three curriculum fields. Technical drawing, for instance, is placed among the practical subjects because of its relation to craft work, but it is neighbour also to mathematics and might well have been included in that field. If this had been done, the proportion of the curriculum which boys devote to the field of mathematics and science would have been increased from 24 per cent to 30 per cent, and the gap between boys and girls in that field and in the field of the practical subjects

FOURTH YEAR CURRICULUM IN A TYPICAL SECONDARY MODERN SCHOOL

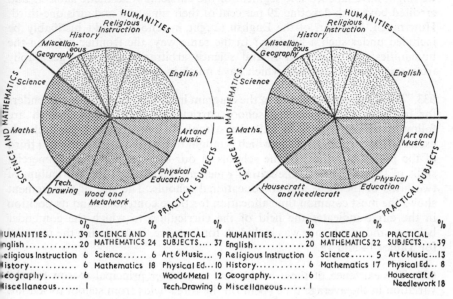

BOYS

HUMANITIES........39	**SCIENCE AND**	**PRACTICAL**
English..............20	**MATHEMATICS** 24	**SUBJECTS**....37
Religious Instruction 6	Science......6	Art & Music...9
History............6	Mathematics 18	Physical Ed...10
Geography.........6		Wood & Metal 12
Miscellaneous......1		Tech.Drawing 6

GIRLS

HUMANITIES........39	**SCIENCE AND**	**PRACTICAL**
English..............20	**MATHEMATICS** 22	**SUBJECTS**....39
Religious Instruction 6	Science......5	Art & Music...13
History............6	Mathematics 17	Physical Ed...8
Geography.........6		Housecraft &
Miscellaneous......1		Needlework 18

COMMON ADDITIONAL SUBJECTS

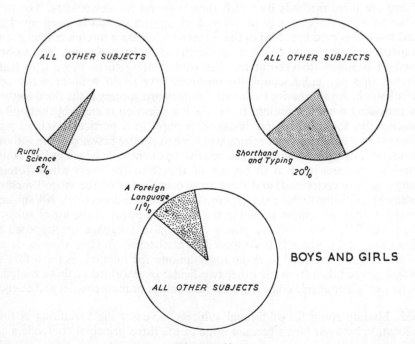

BOYS
ALL OTHER SUBJECTS

Rural Science 5%

GIRLS
ALL OTHER SUBJECTS

Shorthand and Typing 20%

A Foreign Language 11%

ALL OTHER SUBJECTS

BOYS AND GIRLS

would have been widened accordingly. Similarly, the subjects which lie on either side of the frontier between the humanities and the practical subjects suggest by their proximity another basis of classification which we might have employed. Art, music and literature clearly have much in common, and we might have labelled one segment of the curriculum aesthetic subjects and credited boys with devoting 29 per cent of their time to it and girls one-third. How much, however, of the English taught in schools could justifiably be included under such a heading? In the same way, the frontier between the humanities and mathematics and science arbitrarily separates geography from science—two subjects which have much in common.

633. The three smaller circles in the diagram indicate three serious contenders for inclusion in the modern school curriculum—rural studies which are followed by some boys in half the schools in our sample (girls' schools excluded); a foreign language which is taught to between a quarter and a third of the pupils in a third of the schools in our sample; and the commercial skills of shorthand and typewriting which are included in the curriculum of two-fifths of the girls' and co-educational schools. The size of the segment shows the most common time allocation for these contenders and its position in the circle indicates the field of the curriculum to which the contender belongs, and in which it was included, for instance, in preparing the material for Tables 14 and 15.

634. The existence of these contenders is another principal reason for the variation in the average time spent on the three fields from school to school, and on the range of time from form to form in the same school. The average time is affected because the price that has to be paid for the inclusion of one of these subjects is not always found from other subjects in the same field. There are three methods by which time is found for newcomers. The time given to other subjects may be reduced though no subject is given up. This first method is used in a third of the forms which learn a foreign language and a quarter of the forms which take shorthand and typewriting. The second method is simply to cut out another subject altogether—those who learn French in a particular school, for instance, have to do without music and needlework. An alternative to this straightforward surgery is the third method of providing a pool of options from which a selection is made by the pupil or teacher. By this method, for instance, a pupil in a particular school who chooses shorthand and typewriting will have to choose between doing without housecraft or without science. The relative frequency of the second and third methods is three to two in favour of the third (options) where foreign languages are concerned, and three to two in favour of the second method (straight exclusion) where the commercial skills are concerned. All subjects in the typical curriculum shown in the diagram appear in the list of subjects dropped. The only half exceptions are English language (as opposed to literature) and arithmetic (as opposed to mathematics). Over three-quarters of the subjects excluded to make room among the humanities for a foreign language are taken from the other two fields; over a third of those excluded in favour of commerce come from the humanities or mathematics and science.

635. Finding room for additional subjects increases the variations in time allocation between forms because none of the three principal contenders are

usually taught to the whole age-group. Rural studies is much more frequently taught to Robinson than to Jones and to Jones than to Brown; a foreign language in the fourth year (whatever may have been the case in junior forms) is normally reserved for the abler pupils. The commercial skills, too, are on the whole the preserve of the abler girls (though only rarely of those able girls who learn a foreign language).

636. A third main reason for the larger variations in time for various subjects from school to school and from form to form is the introduction of external examinations. This is perhaps most clearly seen in the provision for science. Table 16 compares the time allocation in the best fourth year form in a school ("A") with that in the poorest fourth year form ("C"), excluding small remedial groups. The time given to science in the fourth year generally is in most schools either identical with that in the "C" column or considerably nearer to it than to the "A". Where there is a substantial difference between forms, it is the "A" form which stands apart.

Table 16. *Time Given to Science by Boys and Girls in "A" and "C" Forms in the Fourth Year in Modern Schools*

Schools with Time Allocation	"A" Forms		"C" Forms	
of Minutes per Week	Boys	Girls	Boys	Girls
Over 315	3	2	—	—
275–315	2	2	—	—
230–270	7	3	—	—
185–225	9	9	2	4
140–180	36	21	16	6
95–135	29	20	36	24
50–90	28	41	54	63
Up to 45	2	2	3	5
Nil	1	15	6	13
No. of schools	117	115	117	115

The forms in the top half of the "A" columns are getting a normal grammar school allowance of time and the pupils in them, like grammar school pupils, are preparing for external examinations, usually for the General Certificate of Education at ordinary level. The extra time they get has to be taken from other subjects, almost certainly in the case of science from subjects in other curriculum fields. The effect of preparing for an external examination is, therefore, first, to increase the differences between forms in the amount of time given to the examined subject; and, secondly, to introduce similar differences in time allowances for the other subjects indirectly affected. In 1961 over three-quarters (77 per cent) of the modern schools prepared candidates for either fourth year or fifth year external examinations. Over half the schools (55 per cent) and a fifth of the fourteen year-old pupils in them (21 per cent) were preparing for fifth year examinations. In these schools there is a marked distinction between the time analysis of the examination candidates and of other pupils.

B. MATHEMATICS AND SCIENCE

637. A few notes may be given about the individual subjects of the curriculum field by field. It is convenient first to finish the field of science and

mathematics. The extent to which the various branches of science are taught to fourth year forms containing boys and girls is as follows:

Table 17. Description of Science Taught in Fourth Year Forms

	Boys	Girls
General Science	84%	65%
Biology	10%	30%
Physics	12%	2%
Chemistry	3%	1%
No science taught	3%	12%

NOTE:—The percentages add up to more than 100 because some forms study more than one branch.

638. There is as wide a range in the time given to mathematics as there is to science; but here there is no clear distinction between "A" and "C" time allowances, partly no doubt because of the opposing views held by schools as to whether the stronger or the weaker pupils need more time. Mathematics is, however, the subject in which boys' and girls' schools most clearly diverge as Table 18 shows.

Table 18. Time Given to Mathematics by Boys and Girls in Forms in Single Sex and Co-educational schools

Minutes per week	Boys' Schools	Co-educational Schools	Girls' Schools	All Schools
	%	%	%	%
320–360	4	2	—	2
275–315	3	4	1	3
230–270	51	25	10	27
185–225	39	53	33	47
140–180	3	16	45	19
95–135	—	Trace	11	2
50–90	—	—	—	—
Up to 45	—	—	—	—
Number of Forms (=100%)	119	345	116	580
Average number of minutes per form	260	215	180	205
Percentage of Forms doing only arithmetic	10%	12%	31%	15%
Average number of minutes per week in these forms	225	200	130	175

Naturally, it is for the most part the weaker pupils who only do arithmetic, but less than half (44 per cent) of the forms concerned are in fact the bottom forms in the fourth year in their schools, while in six schools no fourth year girl does any mathematics as opposed to arithmetic.

C. THE PRACTICAL SUBJECTS

639. The range of time given to each of the various subjects in the practical group is wide with the exception of physical education. The great majority of schools spend between 8 and 11 per cent of the week (110 to 155 minutes) on this subject. This figure covers two-thirds of the boys and half the girls in "A" forms and three-quarters of the boys and two-thirds of the girls in "C" forms. The extreme range of time is from 20 per cent for boys and 17 per cent for girls to nothing for both boys and girls but these extremes occur in only

one school. The position in the other subjects in this field is set out in Table 19 which brings out the fact that the distinctions between boys and girls (who spend more time in this field) are greater than between "A" Forms and "C", except that far more "C" forms than "A" are without technical drawing.

Table 19. Time Given to the Practical Subjects by Boys and Girls in "A" and "C" Forms in the Fourth Year in Modern Schools

Minutes per week	Technical Drawing (Boys)		Craft[1]				Art and Music			
	"A" Forms	"C" Forms	"A" Forms		"C" Forms		"A" Forms		"C" Forms	
			Boys	Girls	Boys	Girls	Boys	Girls	Boys	Girls
	%	%	%	%	%	%	%	%	%	%
Over 315	—	—	2	16	2	11	—	—	—	1
275–315	—	—	5	16	5	25	—	—	1	3
230–270	—	—	3	18	6	26	2	3	5	7
185–225	1	—	9	25	6	24	6	11	13	17
140–180	13	2	43	10	42	7	27	40	32	41
95–135	17	6	27	6	31	4	26	26	25	20
50–90	48	50	7	3	6	3	24	13	18	8
Up to 45	8	8	—	—	—	—	4	4	1	2
Nil	13	34	4	6	2	—	11	3	5	1
No. of Schools (=100%)	117	117	117	114	117	115	117	115	117	115

1 Craft for boys means woodwork and/or metalwork plus in three schools engineering, motor engineering and building construction respectively. For girls it means housecraft and needlework. The two "additional subjects" referred to in paragraph 633 (rural science and the commercial skills) are not included in this table.

640. The position of music is far less satisfactory than that of art and the studio crafts, and in both these aesthetic subjects more boys than girls go without—especially able ones. Half the boys and two-thirds of the girls in "A" forms have both art and music in the fourth year; in the "C" forms these proportions rise to two-thirds of the boys and virtually all the girls. But over a third of the boys' schools and seven per cent of the co-educational schools have no music at all in the fourth year, and nearly a third (31 per cent) of all fourth year forms containing boys provide no music for them, though in twenty-four of these forms in co-educational schools there is music for the girls.

D. THE HUMANITIES

641. The central position in the field of the humanities is naturally taken by English, which has the lion's share of the time though the proportion that this bears to the whole varies widely among the schools in the sample. Since there is little difference between the practice of boys', girls' and co-educational schools, these are not distinguished in the following tables.

It will be seen that, except where examination sets are involved, the time given to each individual subject except English itself in the field of the humanities is small although their combined allowance is often considerable. This has a bearing on the extent to which they can be used as a vehicle of English teaching.

Table 20(A). Time Given to the Humanities and the Proportion of this Time given to English as a Separate Subject.

Humanities Minutes per week	No. of Schools giving the following proportions of this time to English						Total No. of Schools
	35–39%	40–44%	45–49%	50–54%	55–59%	60% or more	
600 or more	—	3	2	4	10	2	21
550–599	1	7	6	15	4	4	37
500–549	6	2	7	11	11	5	42
450–499	1	2	7	13	11	—	34
400–449	—	2	3	2	2	—	9
Under 400	—	—	—	—	2	—	2
No. of schools	8	16	25	45	40	11	145

NOTE: Foreign languages are excluded from Column 1 for the purposes of this table.

Table 20(B). Time Given to other Subjects in the Humanities

Percentage of Forms receiving the following number of minutes per week

	270–230	225–185	180–140	135–95	90–50	Under 50	Nil
Religious Instruction	—	—	—	—	80	18	2
History	—	—	4	23	61	1	11
Geography	—	—	6	24	58	1	11
Social Studies	1	1	4	4	3	4	83

NOTES:(a) The figures for Religious Instruction refer only to the county schools in the sample: in the voluntary schools the time was much longer. Optional sets preparing for external examinations were also excluded.

(b) In 5 per cent of the forms history is an alternative to some other subject, usually geography.

(c) In 4 per cent of the forms geography is an alternative to some other subject, usually history.

(d) Where social studies occur it is usually, though not always, as a substitute for history and geography.

642. There is, then, a great variety of provision within the individual schools, though this variety is concerned more with the distribution of time between subjects than with the number of subjects taught.

E. THE POWER TO CHOOSE

643. How far does the individual pupil have any say in his own particular assignment? The schools in the sample were organized in different ways and this has a bearing on the answer. The three main varieties are an organization based on ability and attainments (over which the individual pupil has only a long term indirect influence through his industry or lack of it); an organization based on the term at which pupils are expected to leave school (this is fixed largely by their date of birth); and an organization based on a special bias in the type of course, usually in preparation for a particular examination or in association with a particular career. It is this type of organization which probably comes closest to meeting the pupils' wishes. The extent to which the three types were found in the sample is shown in Table 21.

Table 21. Basis of Form Organisation in the Fourth Year

Schools whose Fourth Year Forms are wholly or partly based on	All Schools	Size of School			Type of School		
		Small	Medium	Large	Boys	Girls	Co-educational
	%	%	%	%	%	%	%
Ability and Attainments	76	81	77	64	93	54	78
Term of leaving	17	13	14	28	3	36	14
Type of Course	21	12	21	43	7	39	20
No. of schools (=100%)	144	68	48	28	30	28	86

NOTES: (1) Percentages add up to more than 100 because some schools use different methods in making up different forms.
(2) Size of School is defined in the Statistical Appendix on page 279.

There are two important contrasts to be seen in this table. Girls' schools are much more inclined to use the "type of course" organization than boys' schools, and large schools than small ones. The former contrast is partly caused by an easy division of girls into those who want a commercial course, those who want an academic course and those who would like one in which the domestic subjects and the arts play a large part. Boys' vocational needs are more nearly satisfied by the ordinary subjects of the curriculum in their customary combination. The latter contrast is to be explained by the difficulties which small schools would find in staffing and equipping an organization based on several differently biased courses each serving a few pupils.

644. There are other ways by which a pupil can exercise some element of choice over the work he does than by electing to follow one course rather than another. Without changing one's form, it is possible, if the school so arranges its work, to choose one subject rather than another. A scrutiny of the time-table analysis makes it possible to give a rough estimate of the extent to which in fact individual pupils have some power to select at least a portion of the work they do. This estimate is set out in Table 22.

Table 22. Options Between Subjects in the Fourth Year in Modern Schools

Is there any element of choice of subject?	All Schools	Size of School			Type of School		
		Small	Medium	Large	Boys'	Girls'	Co-educational
	%	%	%	%	%	%	%
Yes	48	31	52	82	57	57	42
No.	52	69	48	18	43	43	58
No. of Schools (=100%)	144	68	48	28	30	28	86

NOTE: Size of School is defined in the Statistical Appendix on page 279.

The element of choice is often *larger* than indicated in the table because this could take no account, for instance, of the range of choice open in the art room. The element of choice is often *smaller* than would appear from the table because the opportunity is often confined to the abler candidates, who are invited to select their strongest subjects with a view to an external examination; and because in other instances the range is often restricted to a choice between woodwork and metalwork.

645. Two ways of describing the time given to subjects and fields of the curriculum have been used in this chapter. Sometimes the actual number of

minutes per week has been given; sometimes the percentage of the working week. Readers may wonder why the more familiar unit of "periods" was not employed. There are two reasons. First, periods vary in length from thirty to forty-five minutes so that comparisons on this basis would have been unreliable. Secondly, a number of schools arrange their time-table on cycles lasting more than the five days of a school week. The teaching periods given to subjects in these schools will be different in successive weeks and neither figure will correspond to the allocation in a school on a normal five day cycle. We have used minutes instead of periods to make it easier to express all the allocations in terms of a notional five day cycle. But there is a difficulty in comparisons between schools expressed in minutes. By far the commonest length of actual teaching week (i.e., excluding assembly, registration and "breaks") is 1,400 or 1,425 minutes but the range is very considerable. A comparison of minutes may also be misleading because some schools allow a short interval between periods to allow for movement of staff or pupils while others regard one period as starting the moment the previous one stops. It was impossible to overcome these difficulties of interpretation, and the comparisons between schools expressed in percentages of the working week are calculated from the basis of each school's own stated total working time.

CHAPTER 24

The Men and Women who Teach Them

646. "Are you going to stay with us, Sir?" was the question which greeted the hero of a recent novel about a modern school as he got to know the boys in his form. They had had a long experience of transient teachers and had not enjoyed it. Were they particularly unfortunate, or is this what must be expected? The schools in our sample were asked to report their staff changes since September, 1958, so that we might know how many comings and goings of teachers the Browns, Jones and Robinsons of our report had known in their secondary modern schools.

647. There must, of course, always be changes in school staffs. Experienced teachers reach retiring age, promising men and women get promotion and young men and women are appointed to fill their places. This is a natural and a healthy process. In addition the years covered by our enquiry have been years of increasing numbers of pupils in secondary schools and extra teachers have been appointed to meet the bulge. There were 14 per cent more men and 11 per cent more women teachers in the schools in our sample in 1961 than in 1958.

648. There is no precise way of deciding from the information in our possession what a normal and healthy turnover would be, but it is necessary to have some kind of yardstick by which to judge the present position. Probably few heads of schools would wish to appoint a man or woman to the staff who would not stay at least three years with them. Heads of training colleges and university departments of education would probably advise their students to stay three years in their first post. Allowance must be made for young teachers who run into difficulties in their first school and are well advised to move to another school where they can avoid the mistakes they have made. Older men and women may find promotion unexpectedly come their way within three years of joining a school staff. It seems reasonable to suppose that somewhere between 10 per cent and 15 per cent of new appointments may rightly move on within three years for one or other of these reasons. The period under review in our survey was one of three years. We know for each school how many men and women were appointed to the staff after September, 1958, up to and including September, 1961. If the argument of this paragraph is sound, we should hope that the schools would still have on their staffs somewhere between 85 and 90 per cent of those appointed during this period. A school with a holding power of this order is in a healthy condition.

649. An index of "holding power" was calculated for all schools. Holding power was defined as the proportion of teachers appointed to the staff after September, 1958, who were still in post in September, 1961. On this basis the overall holding power of schools where men teachers are concerned was 65 per cent and for women teachers 58 per cent. Even if our estimate of a healthy situation in the last paragraph proves somewhat too exacting, the contrast between it and these figures indicates an unhealthy state of affairs in modern schools generally.

650. To some extent this is clearly a national problem—one consequence of the general shortage and wastage of teachers and the greater opportunity of promotion to graded posts since 1956. The difference between the holding power index for men and women teachers is no doubt associated with the early wastage of married women teachers. In the conditions which prevailed in the 1930's, both generally and among teachers, the holding power of the schools was almost certainly greater.

651. But excessive turnover is not only a national problem. The differences in holding power between schools are more than can be explained by sampling fluctuations. Some variation is in any event to be expected just as it is when twenty coins are each tossed ten times. But undue variation—and what is undue in this context can be evaluated mathematically—would be evidence of something odd in the coins themselves. So here the variation is more than would arise accidentally, and is evidence of real differences in holding power not only between categories of schools, but between schools in the same category.

652. The distinction between various kinds of neighbourhood has often been useful in interpreting the data from our survey. The school staffing situation is no exception. Thus, while the average holding power index for men in modern schools is 65 per cent, in socially mixed neighbourhoods it is 70 per cent and in rural schools 76 per cent. In the special group of slum schools it is only 34 per cent. The full picture by neighbourhoods is given below.

Table 23. Index of Staff Holding Power by Neighbourhoods

	Rural	Mixed	Council	Mining	Problem Areas
Men	76%	70%	67%	58%	55%
Women	69%	57%	58%	60%	56%

653. These differences are not unexpected and they are certainly important, but perhaps even more important is the fact that these groups are far from homogeneous. The differences between schools in the same type of neighbourhood are often greater than can be explained by chance in the sense in which we have used it. Only the group of rural schools is free from these significant variations and its record, at least for men teachers, approximates to that which we set up as a model in paragraph 648. It is reasonable from our data to infer that the quality of the school as a community can on occasion increase or lower its holding power, proving stronger than the effects of the neighbourhood in which its work is done. Some schools at least can help themselves.

654. The distribution of the schools in the sample between the three regional zones shows only small differences between them in holding power, though of course great differences within each zone. The position is shown in the following table.

Table 24. Index of Staff Holding Power by Regions

	Men	Women
Inner Zone	64%	55%
Middle Zone	69%	64%
Outer Zone	62%	59%

When allowance is made for the fact that a high proportion of the rural schools in the sample are in the middle zone differences between zones cease to be statistically significant.

655. Another illustration both of the importance of group factors and also of the even greater importance of individual factors is given by an analysis of holding power in relation to the quality of the school premises. A comparison was made between the staffing position in those schools which are really well-found both in buildings and playing fields with those which are very seriously deficient on both counts. One would expect the former to attract and retain staff and the latter to lose teachers at a more than average rate. And so they both do. The holding power of the well-found schools as a group is 74 per cent for men compared with the overall figure of 65 per cent. For the really poor schools the index is 61 per cent. Clearly having good buildings is an important advantage in keeping a stable staff, especially while most schools are indifferently housed. The disadvantage of a bad building is rather less but may be expected to be aggravated as schools of this kind dwindle in number. But these advantages and disadvantages are not finally decisive. There is sufficient variation between the individual schools in each group to make it clear that a school in a bad building can get and keep a stable staff, and that the best architects cannot guarantee one.

656. Up to this point we have been concerned with a school's holding power over new appointments to the staff. To complete the picture it is necessary to consider also the numbers of staff who have been in post since before September, 1958. The over-all staffing position of the schools in the sample in September, 1961, was made up in the way Table 25 indicates.

Table 25. Staffing of Modern Schools in the Sample in September, 1961

Men Appointed		Women Appointed	
In or before Sept. 1958	After Sept. 1958	In or before Sept. 1958	After Sept. 1958
56%	44%	45%	55%

Those in the first column of each panel had been in the school at least as long as the boys and girls who took part in our survey—some of them, of course, very much longer. Over the country as a whole there is, then, a reasonable core of at any rate short term stability. The second column of each panel, however, presents altogether too flattering an impression.

657. The true picture is, perhaps, best given in the form of the flow diagrams on the following page. The first shows roughly what might be expected in a hypothetical school with twenty men on the staff. In three years the head would have had dealings with thirty-five instead of twenty masters. The second diagram brings out how much heavier the turnover is where women teachers are concerned. In a hypothetical school with twenty women assistant mistresses the head would have had dealings with forty-one, more than twice the original complement, during the three-year period.

658. The two diagrams illustrate the kind of experience which the boys or girls in our sample might expect to meet in single sex schools. But most of them in fact are pupils in co-educational schools, and there at least the girls would probably escape the worst disturbances caused by turnover in girls'

MEN TEACHERS IN A HYPOTHETICAL SECONDARY MODERN SCHOOL, 1958—1961

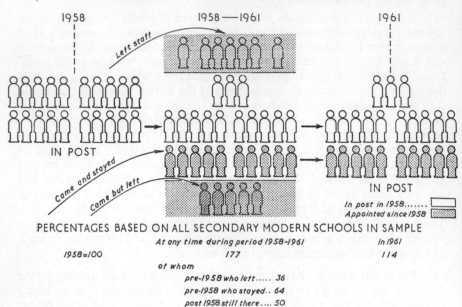

PERCENTAGES BASED ON ALL SECONDARY MODERN SCHOOLS IN SAMPLE

	At any time during period 1958-1961	In 1961
1958=100	177	114

of whom

pre-1958 who left..... 36
pre-1958 who stayed.. 64
post 1958 still there.... 50
post 1958 who came
and went.... 27

WOMEN TEACHERS IN A HYPOTHETICAL SECONDARY MODERN SCHOOL, 1958—1961

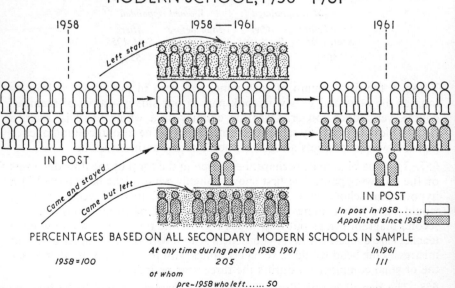

PERCENTAGES BASED ON ALL SECONDARY MODERN SCHOOLS IN SAMPLE

	At any time during period 1958 1961	In 1961
1958 = 100	205	111

of whom

pre-1958 who left...... 50
pre-1958 who stayed... 50
post 1958 still there... 61
post 1958 who came
and went.....44

Diagram 14

schools. The following analysis of the staffing of all modern schools in the sample was made to illustrate the part played by women teachers in general and by married women in particular in 1961.

Table 26. *Number of Single and Married Women Assistants on the Staff of Modern Schools*

Type of School	Full-Time Assistants			Part-Time Assts.		Total	
	All Assts.	Single Women	Married Women	All Assts.	Married Women	All Assts.	Married Women Assts.
Boys	555	13	12	13	6	568	18 (3%)
Girls	484	231	243	79	59	563	302 (55%)
Coeducational	1,699	379	352	158	104	1,857	456 (24%)
All	2,738	623	607	250	169	2,988	776 (26%)

CHAPTER 25

The Schools They Go To

A. INTRODUCTION

659. The pictures between pages 108 & 109 show how varied are the secondary schools attended by the boys and girls with whom we are concerned. This chapter is concerned with these differences.[1] Some schools, to use a current idiom, clearly have everything; some virtually nothing. How many of each are there? And how many in between? Where does the balance lie? In Part Two of this report we were concerned to illustrate from our own observation and from the evidence given to us the kind of teaching which is most likely to be effective with ordinary adolescents. In this chapter we try to see how often at present it is practicable to expect this kind of education. The question is looked at first subject by subject. The order of treatment follows the order of chapters 17, 18 and 19—the "practical subjects" are treated first, and in the same order as there; they are followed by science and mathematics, and then by the humanities. Finally, an attempt is made to classify the schools as a whole in terms of their structural suitability for the job they have to do.

660. The area required for playing fields is laid down by regulation. For the rest the yardstick we have used wherever we could are the suggestions made in the Ministry's current Building Bulletins. These are in no sense mandatory, but they do represent a realistic view of the physical standards which ought to be attained by a reasonably good secondary school built in the second half of the 1950's. They must not be taken as representing our own views of what is desirable either room by room or for a school as a whole, but they provide an intelligible standard of comparison based on enlightened but conservative practice.

661. Starting from this basis we have made a fourfold classification of the data provided by the schools. The four main grades are:

A. Satisfactory specialist accommodation.

C. Makeshift accommodation.

B. Some specialist accommodation, but inadequate in quantity.

D. No provision.

Minor divergencies from these classifications are indicated as they occur. The analysis refers solely to space; we have no indication of the suitability of equipment. Category B refers to a temporary phenomenon, a discrepancy between the number of pupils and the amount of specialist accommodation. It can be put right either by a reduction of the total school roll or by the provision of additional specialist accommodation. There is no need to scrap the existing provision. Category C, on the other hand, will not do, and with few exceptions ought to go. It refers to accommodation of the kind pictured in plates 7 and 8b. As far as the education of the pupils at present in school is

But not with the particular schools illustrated. None of them was included in the sample for our survey.

concerned Category C offers far less satisfaction than Category B but is better than the nothing of Category D.

B. THE PRACTICAL SUBJECTS (see Chapter 17)

662. We start our tour of the schools with the art room. Half the schools have a room or rooms which come up to the expected standard. In the middle zone the proportion is two-thirds—68 per cent. A further third have some specialist provision, which is however inadequate either because the room is too small or because there are not enough rooms for the size of the school. One school in eight has no art room.

663. Some three-fifths of the co-educational and boys' schools have adequate provision for handicraft. None has no provision, though occasionally it is at a "centre" away from the school. The usual provision is for both woodwork and metalwork. A third of the schools could only provide woodwork, including a number whose provision is adequate in quantity. The small co-educational schools are plainly at a disadvantage in providing a variety of crafts for boys. Nearly two-thirds of them (62 per cent) are only equipped for woodwork. Nine-tenths (93 per cent) of the boys' schools of the same size can offer both woodwork and metalwork. Only three schools, all among the large co-educational schools, have any provision for engineering, and no other "heavy crafts" such as building were reported in our sample. These are the only modern schools in a position to offer the range of workshop crafts for boys which our report implies for the future.

664. About one in eight of the boys' and co-educational schools report some provision for rural science or, more frequently, for gardening. Not quite half of them have set aside a classroom as well as ground for this work. These rooms vary in size from 420 to 670 square feet. Other schools have small huts (some only 210 square feet in size), or potting sheds or greenhouses. Two which teach rural science have no special accommodation—one reported that, when it rained, it had "gardening in the library and kitchen". Two girls' schools out of twenty-eight have some provision. Neither has a classroom; one has a hut, the other a potting shed and greenhouse. Schools in all five of our neighbourhood groups—rural, mining, problem area, council estate and mixed areas—were among those which had special rural science classrooms.

665. Over half the girls' and co-educational schools have adequate housecraft rooms, including nearly two-thirds (64 per cent) of those in the middle zone. None is without provision, though occasionally it involves going to another school or to a separate housecraft "centre". The provision for needlework is worse. Ten per cent of the schools have no special room, and in two-fifths the provision is clearly inadequate, normally taking the form of a makeshift adaptation of a small classroom furnished and used for general class teaching as well as for needlework. It is no doubt easier to improvise some kind of a needlework room than a metalwork shop so that the girls in small co-educational schools are less at a disadvantage for variety in craftwork than the boys. Only one-fifth of these schools had no needlework room; two-thirds had no metalwork shop.

666. The survey distinguished three forms of provision for physical education —gymnasium; playing fields; and swimming baths. Playing fields were graded

into three categories: "A" where the provision was fully up to the regulations; "B" where the provision was sub-standard but amounted to at least half the prescribed acreage; and "C", where it was below this. No school was without any provision for field games. Schools with access to detached playing fields provided or rented by the L.E.A. have been placed in category "B" apart from a few where the provision was clearly either "A" or "C".

667. Thirty per cent of the schools have playing fields up to the prescribed standard—this proportion holds roughly good in all three zones. Among the neighbourhoods it is exceeded in schools serving rural areas (45 per cent) and council estates or new towns (40 per cent), but falls seriously short in the problem areas where only 13 per cent of the schools have good outdoor facilities, and over three-quarters (77 per cent) have less than half the prescribed acreage.

668. Two-fifths of the schools have a gymnasium of suitable size and a further tenth have a small one. Even so, half have none at all. This does not, of course, mean that there can be no indoor physical education. Most schools have an assembly hall, though 4 per cent have none, and 8 per cent share their hall with another school. About a fifth of the schools have a single hall which has to serve for assembly, as a dining room and for physical education in all its indoor forms including dancing as well as gymnastics, and, very often, for drama and music as well. Often the classrooms open off this central hall. Schools of this type are found in all zones and in all neighbourhoods. One is illustrated in plate 7. This leaves about a third of the schools which have to use the assembly hall for indoor physical education, but in which the position is not complicated by its use for dining. Some small schools have been built with a large hall especially designed for use as a gymnasium—perhaps ten per cent of the schools fall into this category. A higher proportion of schools in the outer zone than in the other two have no separate gymnasium (60 per cent compared with 50 per cent). More in the outer zone also have either a small gymnasium of less than 2,000 sq. ft. or have to share a gymnasium with another school—11 per cent in the outer zone compared with 8 per cent in the other two. Schools which serve council estates or new towns tend to be of relatively recent date and consequently nearly two-thirds (63 per cent) have an adequate gymnasium. On the other hand three-quarters of schools serving problem areas or mining villages have none.

669. Good indoor provision compensates for restricted playing fields and playgrounds only in relatively few instances. The more general rule is that schools which are fortunate in one respect are fortunate in both. Thus, nearly two-thirds of the schools (62 per cent) which have adequate playing fields have also sufficient gymnasium provision at least as far as area is concerned, and only just over a quarter (27 per cent) have none. On the other hand, less than a fifth (18 per cent) of the schools whose outdoor facilities are thoroughly unsatisfactory have an adequate gymnasium, and three-quarters have none.

670. Only one school in seven has no opportunity of teaching its pupils to swim. Four-fifths (79 per cent) use public baths and 6 per cent have their own swimming pool. Most of these are small learners' pools, usually financed partly at least by the individual schools with the aid of parents and often with some of the constructional work done by self-help. One school uses the sea. It proved impossible to assess how much use the schools could make

ACCOMMODATION FOR THE PRACTICAL SUBJECTS

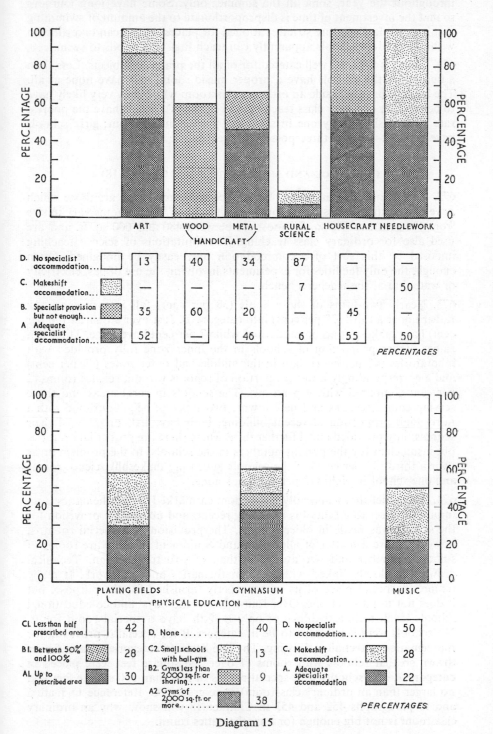

Diagram 15

of the public baths because circumstances varied so greatly. Some use them throughout the year, some in the summer only. Some have long journeys so that the investment of time is disproportionate to the amount of swimming that is possible. Some are strictly rationed for places, others can take all who wish to go. Most schools apparently can teach first year pupils to swim.

671. Music is the least well catered for of all the practical subjects. Less than a quarter of the schools have a proper music room, half have none at all. The balance have set aside an ordinary classroom which may very likely have to be used for ordinary class teaching as well. Boys' schools have the poorest rate of provision—only one in six has a proper music room; girls' schools have the best—one in three possesses a real music room.

C. SCIENCE AND MATHEMATICS (see Chapter 18)

672. The schools in Category C for science accommodation are those which have only adapted classrooms for science teaching. These rooms vary in size from 430 sq. ft. to 700 sq. ft.; most are between 480 and 600 sq. ft. and are used also for ordinary class teaching. The limitations of science teaching imposed by this sort of accommodation may easily be imagined. Often enough, the only facilities for experiments involving the use of gas, electricity or water are at the teacher's bench.

673. Nearly two-fifths of the schools (38 per cent) fall into category A; rather under a third (29 per cent) into category B. Just over a quarter (26 per cent) have makeshift accommodation, while 7 per cent have none. There is a rather higher proportion of schools in the inner zone fully provided with laboratories (42 per cent) than in the middle and outer zones (37 per cent) and a correspondingly lower proportion of schools without science rooms (2 per cent compared with 9 per cent). The schools in rural areas and those serving council estates and new towns, two types of neighbourhood with a fairly high proportion of recent building, both have half or more of their schools fully provided and a further third where there are proper laboratories but insufficient for the present numbers in the schools. In the problem areas over a third (37 per cent) of the schools have only makeshift science rooms and one school in eight (13 per cent) has none.

674. The belief that a specially large room earmarked for mathematics is an important asset to a school is relatively recent, and no specific provision for the subject was made in older schools. The provision of a special room is, however, more a matter of allocation and equipment (if there are rooms of sufficient number and size available) than of structural design. Technical drawing is closely linked with both mathematics and craftwork. It really requires a special place of its own properly furnished for the purpose, but it does not usually get one. Over four-fifths of the boys' and co-educational schools teach technical drawing; only a sixth have a special room for it. No schools were considered to be in category B for specialist provision for mathematics or technical drawing. The line between categories A and C was drawn so that schools with rooms of over 500 square feet were placed in category A and schools with special rooms of less than 500 square feet (i.e. no larger than an ordinary classroom) were graded C. Reference to plate 5 and to paragraphs 452 and 453 in Chapter 18 will show why an ordinary classroom is not big enough for a mathematics room.

675. One school in eight has a special room for mathematics—9 per cent are in category A and 4 per cent in category C as columns 2 and 3 in Diagram 8 show. Most of these schools are either co-educational or boys' schools, but one in seven of the girls' schools has a special mathematics room. Eighty-seven per cent of the schools are in Category D. For technical drawing the proportions in the various categories are: Category A—11 per cent; C—2 per cent; D—87 per cent. These are the proportions given in Columns 2 and 4 of the diagram, but it might be fairer to reckon the percentages on boys' and co-educational schools only on the ground that none of the girls' schools provided separate accommodation and that technical drawing is at present almost, if not entirely, a boys' subject. On this assumption 14 per cent of the schools concerned are in category A, 3 per cent in category C and 83 per cent in category D. Five per cent of the boys' and co-educational schools have special rooms for both mathematics and technical drawing.

676. There is less provision of special rooms for mathematics and technical drawing in the outer zone than in the other two—18 per cent compared with 24 per cent. Schools which serve mixed neighbourhoods account for 55 per cent of all special rooms for mathematics and technical drawing, but only 38 per cent of the total number of schools.

D. THE HUMANITIES (see Chapter 19)

677. It is now a commonplace that the school library is as essential for work in the humanities (though not only in them) as the laboratory is in science. Like the laboratory, however, it was not included in the schedules of the old elementary schools. One must therefore expect to find a good deal of improvisation and a good deal of going without; and so one does.

678. The information provided by the survey was analysed into six categories:

A —schools with a proper library reserved for library use;

B —schools with a proper library which has also to be used for ordinary class teaching;

C_1—schools with a classroom reserved for exclusive library use;

C_2—schools with a classroom allocated for a library but used also for ordinary class teaching;

C_3—schools with a small stock room, prefects' room or the equivalent in area converted into a library;

D —schools without any library room.

The proportions in each category are:

A —26 per cent	C_2—19 per cent
B —13 per cent	C_3— 6 per cent
C_1—15 per cent	D —21 per cent

679. The categories can usefully be grouped together in two ways. The first method distinguishes schools with libraries built for the purpose (categories A and B); schools with improvised libraries (categories C_1 to C_3); and schools without libraries (category D). Roughly two-fifths have libraries built for the purpose; two-fifths have improvised libraries and one-fifth no library at all. The second method distinguishes schools where a room of whatever kind is exclusively reserved for library work (categories A, C_1 and C_3); schools where

ACCOMMODATION FOR SCIENCE AND MATHEMATICS

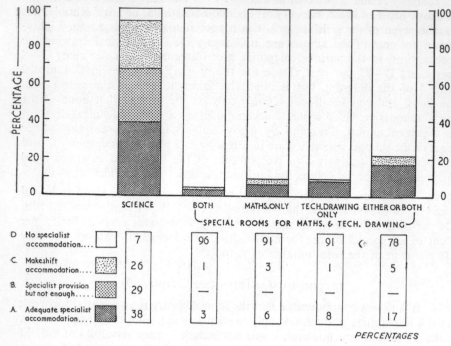

	SCIENCE	BOTH	MATHS. ONLY	TECH. DRAWING ONLY	EITHER OR BOTH
D. No specialist accommodation....	7	96	91	91	78
C. Makeshift accommodation....	26	1	3	1	5
B. Specialist provision but not enough.....	29	—	—	—	—
A. Adequate specialist accommodation....	38	3	6	8	17

SPECIAL ROOMS FOR MATHS. & TECH. DRAWING

PERCENTAGES

ACCOMMODATION FOR THE HUMANITIES

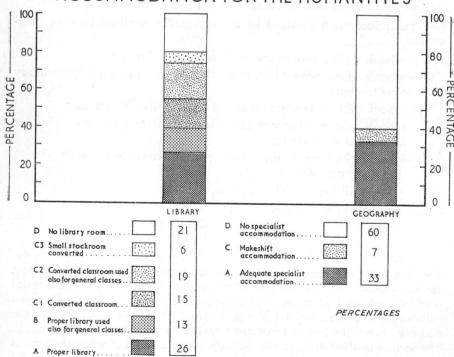

LIBRARY   GEOGRAPHY

	LIBRARY
D No library room......	21
C3 Small stockroom converted........	6
C2 Converted classroom used also for general classes..	19
C1 Converted classroom...	15
B Proper library used also for general classes..	13
A Proper library......	26

	GEOGRAPHY
D. No specialist accommodation......	60
C. Makeshift accommodation......	7
A. Adequate specialist accommodation......	33

PERCENTAGES

Diagram 16

the books are kept in rooms which are used for ordinary class teaching (categories B and C_2); and schools without library rooms (category D). On this basis nearly half (47 per cent) of the schools have rooms used exclusively for library purposes, a third (32 per cent) have library rooms which are also classrooms and a fifth (21 per cent) have no library rooms at all.

680. The schools with libraries built for the purpose are, of course, found in all parts of the country and in all kinds of neighbourhoods, but they are most common relatively among schools serving rural districts, where reorganization is often of recent date, and in schools serving council estates or new towns. Two-thirds of the rural schools (65 per cent) and over half (55 per cent) of the schools serving council estates or new towns have proper library rooms. This compares with only a quarter of the schools serving the three other kinds of neighbourhoods studied—problem areas, mining districts and areas of mixed housing.

681. It seemed probable that there might be a positive relation between the possession of a library room and achievement on the reading test which, as explained elsewhere, calls for a fairly extensive vocabulary as well as the ability to decipher print. The library categories were, therefore, analysed by the mean score on the test of the schools in each category which gave the following results.

Table 27. Reading Test Scores and Library Provision

Schools with Library Rooms used exclusively for that purpose	Schools with Library Rooms in use also as classrooms	Schools without Library Rooms
Category	Category	Category
A —21·2	B —21·8	D—21·3
C_1—20·5	C_2—21·4	
C_3—20·4		

There is a wide range of scores within each category. All three regions and all five neighbourhoods are represented among the schools in each of the columns above, and each is represented by schools with an extensive variation of scores. There is room for various interpretations of a result which is itself surprising.

682. Two-fifths of the schools have rooms set apart specially for geography. Most of them are bigger than an ordinary classroom—a third of all schools have geography rooms of more than 500 square feet. No other arts subject has anything like comparable provision, though three of the geography rooms are used also for history. The outer zone and the schools serving problem areas and mining villages are again educationally below par in this respect— only 14 per cent of them have large geography rooms; rather more (17 per cent) have been able to allocate an ordinary classroom for the subject; but this leaves over two-thirds without any special provision.

E. THE SCHOOLS AS A WHOLE

683. Thus far we have been concerned with accommodation for individual subjects of the curriculum. It was possible, though not probable, that the deficiencies might be so divided that, while no school was perfect, few schools

were very bad. A scoring system was therefore adopted for each of the items shown in the diagrams—suitable accommodation was given 3 points; accommodation otherwise suitable but inadequate in quantity or used also for other purposes was given 2 points; makeshift accommodation of all kinds, 1 point, and to schools where no special provision was made no points were awarded. On this basis the schools were divided into three groups.
Schools scoring:

Less than one-third possible points	Between one-third and two-thirds	Over two-thirds
16%	56%	28%

Four schools scored full marks; five scored less than one-sixth of the possible points. The average score for all schools was 54 per cent of the possible maximum.

684. A further analysis was made to see whether the situation was more serious in some parts of the country or in some types of neighbourhood than others. It was probable, for instance, that deficiencies would be fewer where there either had been an influx of new inhabitants sufficient in number to call for a new school, or where the replacement of all-age schools by separate primary and secondary schools had recently taken place. This expectation is borne out by the following analysis:

Table 28. Adequacy of School Premises analysed by Neighbourhoods

	Rural Areas	Council Estates or New Towns	Problem Areas	Mining Areas	Mixed Neighbourhoods
Average Score per school	57%	64%	46%	44%	52%
Proportion scoring less than one-third	1 in 7	1 in 10	1 in 6	1 in 6	1 in 4
Proportion scoring more than two-thirds	1 in 3	1 in 3	1 in 8	Nil	1 in 3

685. These scores measure the presence or absence of specialist accommodation; they do not take into account the general suitability of the buildings.

THE SCHOOL BUILDINGS AS A WHOLE

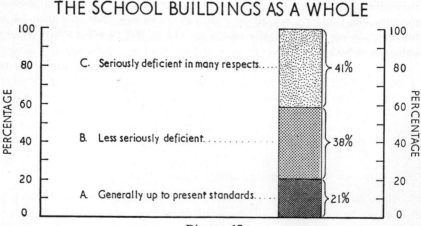

C. Seriously deficient in many respects..... 41%

B. Less seriously deficient............ 38%

A. Generally up to present standards..... 21%

Diagram 17

Once again, reference to the pictures between pages 108 and 109 will immediately make clear the qualitative differences between old schools and new. How many schools fall into each category? An N.U.T. survey,[1] made within a few weeks of our own but using different methods, asked for the date of the earliest part of the buildings of each school. In the following table our results, which refer to the main structure of the school, are compared with the results of the N.U.T. survey. The correspondence is remarkably close.

Table 29. Age of Modern School Buildings

Dates	C.A.C. Sample %	N.U.T. Survey %	Dates
1875–1902	20	20	Before 1900
1903–1918	21 ⎫	⎧ 20	1900–1914
	⎬ 44	45 ⎨ 5	1920–1929
1919–1944	23 ⎭	⎩ 20	1930–1944
1945 or later	36	35	1945 or later

686. There is clearly great leeway to be made up. The main buildings of at least half of the schools were intended for much younger children than those by whom they are now used and for a much more restricted curriculum. But this does not give the whole extent of the problem. It is by no means safe to assume that the third of the pupils who are in post-war schools are suitably accommodated. Nearly half of these schools (46 per cent) are so grossly overcrowded that we have had to place them in category B or even in three instances into category C in the final diagram of this chapter. Categories A, B and C in this diagram apply to the school buildings as a whole the same standards of judgement which in earlier tables were applied to the individual specialist parts. The main difference is that, whereas for the earlier diagrams schools were only placed in category C if their specialist accommodation was improvised, for this diagram a number of schools whose buildings were good or at least satisfactory in themselves were downgraded to category C because of such consequences of overcrowding as the use of the hall by two classes for ordinary class teaching, the use of stockrooms as "form bases" and similar misappropriations of space. The overall picture is that one-fifth of the modern schools are generally up to standard, but two-fifths are seriously deficient in many respects.

[1] "The State of Our Schools", page 11, Table 1.

Acknowledgements

We are glad to acknowledge our debt to all those who have contributed to the making of this report. A list of individuals and organizations who presented oral or written evidence, and in many cases both, is given in Appendix I; for their time and trouble and interest we are indeed grateful.

The text bears frequent witness to the extent to which we have drawn freely on the experience of teachers and others in daily contact with the business of education. We are notably indebted to the heads and staff of the schools involved in our surveys, both for their personal statements which have helped so vividly to illumine the background to their work, and for the factual detail they supplied. We realise how much time and care must have gone into their well-documented replies, and appreciate their patience in dealing with supplementary queries. To them, and to the local education authorities whose co-operation made the surveys possible we repeat our thanks.

Similar ready co-operation made it possible for us to visit 46 schools, colleges of further education and day continuation schools in 20 different local education authority areas throughout England, as well as four schools in Wales and six in Scotland. We also visited works education centres, a naval training establishment, and two Approved schools: to all our hosts on these occasions we are most grateful for enabling us to see so much in the time available.

We greatly valued the opportunities we enjoyed also of paying informal visits for discussion with staff and students at training colleges and departments of education.

Our enquiries took us abroad, and we were fortunate in being able to visit schools of many different types in France, Holland and Switzerland, and we record our thanks to the staffs of all the institutions concerned and the representatives of the various Ministries and Government services in those countries for much information and hospitality, and invaluable assistance in arranging the programmes of the visits. We also had the benefit in the Council of the recent experience of several of its members who paid independent visits to Australia, Germany, Holland, Sweden and U.S.A.

Among the staff of the Ministry of Education in this country, we particularly wish to express our thanks to members of the Development Group of the Architects and Building Branch, for the diagrams and commentary on school design included in Part I, Chapter 11. We have also drawn heavily on the experience of Her Majesty's Inspectors, both through discussions with individuals and through written evidence contributed by the Panels of the Inspectorate.

In a period of just over two years, we have met on some 70 days, including five weekend conferences. It is difficult to avoid the trite when expressing gratitude to those who have carried the major responsibility for our report. "Setting up a Committee" is easy enough but it is quite another matter to make if function. Our enquiry has involved a mass of paper work which, described in weight, volume or content would be incredible to the uninitiate.

Evidence, survey, statistics, recording and writing have involved a formidable skill on the part of those who have served us. It is difficult adequately to express our gratitude to Mr. R. J. W. Stubbings, H.M.I., Mr. J. W. Withrington, H.M.I., and Miss K. A. Kennedy for all they have done for us as Assessors. Particularly we want to thank Mr. D. G. O. Ayerst, H.M.I. whose experience as an Assessor with the Central Advisory Council spreads over no less than three of its assignments and whose cumulative widsom has been of peculiar value. The sampling design of our survey of schools, as well as the interpretation of its results, has been the work of Mr. G. F. Peaker, C.B.E., H.M.I. This is the third occasion on which the Council expresses its gratitude to him for expert assistance of this nature and we would like to wish him well in the responsibilities of a similar kind which he is undertaking for U.N.E.S.C.O. We are also grateful to Miss M. L. Smith, our Clerk, for her indefatigable labours mainly behind the scene.

But, above all, we owe a debt to our Secretary, Miss M. J. Marshall, H.M.I. who has guided us with unerring and charitable competence towards our proper objectives. To her and to the Assessors we are grateful for the patience shown to us sometimes, we must admit, when they might have been provoked to act otherwise. We have all learnt much in the past two and a half years both from those who have given evidence to us, from our visits and from our protracted discussions among ourselves but, probably, our most effective mentors have been our colleagues on the staff of the Ministry of Education and our gratitude to them is abounding.

(*Signed*)

John Newsom (*Chairman*)	B. Paston Brown
R. II. Adams	Elizabeth M. Pepperell
Catherine Avent	A. H. Quilley
D. B. Bartlett	J. Scupham
S. W. Buglass	E. L. Sewell
S. M. Caffyn	A. M. Simcock
A. B. Clegg	W. J. Slater
Basil Fletcher	J. E. Smith
F. D. Flower	C. A. Thompson
A. J. N. Fuller	N. G. Treloar
H. Frazer	D. Winnard
M. G. Green	*Assessors*
H. W. Hinds	K. A. Kennedy
Audrey Hirst	D. G. O. Ayerst, H.M.I.
R. M. T. Kneebone	R. J. W. Stubbings, H.M.I.
Kathleen Ollerenshaw	J. W. Withrington, H.M.I.
	M. J. Marshall, H.M.I.
	(*Secretary*)

The Council is indebted to the following publishers for permission to quote short extracts from their publications:

William Heineman Ltd., *Saturn over the Water* by J. B. Priestley.

W. H. Allen and Company, *Saturday Night and Sunday Morning* by Alan Sillitoe.

MacGibbon and Kee Ltd., *Absolute Beginners* by Colin MacInnes.

Pergamon Press, *Home, School and Work* by M. P. Carter.

Councils and Education Press Ltd., *Education* Issue of 15th June 1962.

Thanks are also due to the Architect and Building News for permission to use Plate 1 (a).

APPENDIX I

A. List of Witnesses who gave Oral (and in most cases Written) Evidence (in addition to those from Government Departments)

(i) ASSOCIATIONS OF LOCAL AUTHORITIES AND OF EDUCATION COMMITTEES

Association of Education Committees

Mr. R. G. Robinson, Chairman of the Advisory Committee of the Association.
Sir William Alexander, Secretary of the Association.
Mr. B. S. Braithwaite, Chief Education Officer, East Sussex.
Alderman A. Moss, Vice-President of the Association.
Dr. F. Lincoln Ralphs, Chief Education Officer, Norfolk.
Mr. W. G. Stone, Director of Education, Brighton.
Alderman J. Wood, President of the Association.

Association of Municipal Corporations

Alderman Mrs. E. V. Smith, Chairman of the Education Committee of the Association.
Alderman L. E. Haines.
Mr. S. R. Hutton, Chief Education Officer, Southport.
Mr. G. W. Cutts, Borough Education Officer, Widnes.
Mr. K. P. Poole, Assistant Secretary of the Association.

County Councils Association

Sir Alan Lubbock, Chairman of Hampshire County Council, Chairman of the Education Committee of the Association.
Sir Offley Wakeman, Bt., C.B.E., Chairman of Shropshire County Council, former Chairman of the Education Committee of the Association.
Commander D. S. E. Thompson, R.N., County Councillor and Chairman of the Kent Education Committee.
Mr. J. H. P. Oxspring, M.B.E., Chief Education Officer, Staffordshire.
Dr. F. Lincoln Ralphs, Chief Education Officer, Norfolk.
Mr. L. W. K. Brown, Deputy Secretary of the Association.

London County Council

Mrs. M. McIntosh, Chairman of the Education Committee.
Mrs. Helen C. Bentwich, Chairman of the Primary and Secondary Schools Sub-Committee of the Education Committee.
Mr. W. F. Houghton, Education Officer.
Dr. E. W. H. Briault, Deputy Education Officer.

(ii) ASSOCIATION OF CHIEF EDUCATION OFFICERS

Mr. G. H. Sylvester, President of the Association, Chief Education Officer, Bristol.

Dr. B. E. Lawrence, C.B.E., Treasurer of the Association, Chief Education Officer, Essex.

Mr. H. Martin Wilson, C.B.E., Secretary for Education, Shropshire.

Mr. H. Oldman, Secretary to the Association, Chief Education Officer, York.

(iii) ORGANIZATIONS REPRESENTING TEACHERS

Association of Head Mistresses (Incorporated)

Miss E. M. Huxstep, Chairman of Sub-Committee.
Miss R. N. Pearse, O.B.E., President of the Association 1962–64.
Miss A. F. Bull, Past President.
Miss P. M. Adams.
Mrs. R. Shaw.

Association of Teachers in Colleges and Departments of Education

Mr. E. G. Peirson, Principal, City of Worcester Training College.
Dr. William Taylor, Principal Lecturer in Education, College of the Venerable Bede, Durham.
Professor J. W. Tibble, Director of the Institute of Education, The University, Leicester.
Mrs. E. Tidy, Principal Lecturer in Education, City of Coventry Training College.

Association of Teachers in Technical Institutions

Mr. T. Driver, Technical College, Doncaster, President of the Association.
Mr. E. E. Robinson, Brunel College of Technology, Vice-President of the Association.
Mr. C. J. Tirrell, M.B.E., Principal of the Technical College, Crewe, Treasurer of the Association.
Mr. W. Ing, Member of the Executive.
Mr. Edward Britton, General Secretary of the Association.

National Association of Head Teachers

Mr. J. W. Watts, President of the Association.
Mr. J. H. Chantler, J.P.
Miss D. M. Parncutt.

National Association of Schoolmasters

Mr. T. Casey, President of the Association.
Mr. R. Hall, Vice-President of the Association.
Mr. L. G. Harris.
Mr. M. A. Langdell.
Mr. B. F. Wakefield.
Mr. A. C. E. Weston.
Mr. A. S. Massingham, Assistant Secretary of the Association.

National Union of Teachers

Miss M. A. Stewart, Junior Vice-President of the Union.

Mr. D. G. Gilbert, Chairman of the Education Committee of the Union.

Mr. J. W. Hand, Vice-Chairman of the Education Committee of the Union.

Mr. M. J. C. Clarke, Chairman of Panel A of the Union's Education Committee and Chairman of the Union's Advisory Committee for Special Education.

Mr. S. W. Exworthy, Chairman of Secondary Modern Schools Advisory Committee.

Miss M. O. M. Morris, Assistant Secretary to the Union's Advisory Committee.

Mr. F. M. Newrick, Assistant Official to the Education Department of the Union.

(iv) OTHER INSTITUTIONS AND ORGANIZATIONS

British Employers' Confederation

Mr. W. M. Larke, General Manager, Stewarts and Lloyds Ltd., Bilston and Vice-Chairman of the Educational Sub-Committee of the Confederation.

Mr. J. Brosgall, Educational Adviser to Unilever Ltd. and Member of the Industrial Education and Training Committee of the Association.

Mr. D. D. Sim, Secretary to the Industrial and Training Department of the Confederation.

Central Council for Health Education

Dr. A. J. Dalzell-Ward, Medical Director, Central Council.

Dr. W. S. Parker, Medical Officer of Health, Brighton.

Institute of Youth Employment Officers

Mr. C. P. Walton, Secretary of the Institute.

Mr. V. B. Bray, County Youth Employment Officer, Cheshire.

Standing Conference of National Voluntary Youth Organisations

Miss M. Robinson, Members Council Adviser, National Association of Youth Clubs.

Mr. H. Higgins, National Association of Boys' Clubs.

Mrs. H. Burgess, J.P., Girl Guides Association.

Miss J. Lines, Girl Guides Association.

Miss A. Bailey, Young Women's Christian Association.

Miss S. Matthews, Young Women's Christian Association.

Brigadier D. Meynell, Hon. Secretary of the Standing Conference.

Trades Union Congress

Mr. J. O'Hagan, O.B.E., Member of the General Council and the Education Committee.

Mrs. E. McCullough, Member of the General Council and the Education Committee.

Mr. G. F. Smith, Member of the General Council and the Education Committee.

Mr. R. A. Jackson, Assistant, Education Department.

(v) INDIVIDUAL WITNESSES

Mr. B. Bernstein, Institute of Education, University of London.
Mrs. J. Floud, Official Fellow of Nuffield College, University of Oxford.
Dr. M. E. M. Herford, D.S.O., Appointed Factory Doctor, Windsor and
    Slough District.
Mr. B. Jackson, Director, Advisory Centre for Education, Cambridge.
Mr. L. Paul, Research Fellow, Industrial Welfare Society.
Mr. D. A. Pidgeon, Senior Research Officer, National Foundation for
    Educational Research.

The Council also wishes to record its gratitude to the Bishop of London,
the Bishop of Salford, the Rev. H. A. Hamilton, and Dr. Kathleen Bliss
for accepting the Council's invitation to meet them and for the help they
rendered the Council on that occasion.

B. List of Other Organizations and Persons Who Submitted Written Evidence, Memoranda or other Data

Association of Physical Education of Great Britain and Northern Ireland.
Association of Teachers of Domestic Science.
Association of Women Science Teachers.
Boys' Brigade.
Boy Scouts Association.
British Council of Churches.
British Film Institute.
British Red Cross Society.
British Transport Commission.
Catholic Education Council.
Central Council for Physical Recreation.
Church of England Board of Education, Schools Council.
City and Guilds of London Institute.
Communist Party, Education Advisory Committee.
Congregational Youth and Children's Department.
Consumer Advisory Council.
Electricity Council.
English Association.
Gas Council.
Geographical Association.
Girl Guides Association.
Historical Association.
Institute of Christian Education at Home and Overseas.
Institute of Handicraft Teachers.
Institute of Personnel Management.
London Association for the Teaching of English.
Mathematical Association.
Modern Language Association.
National Association of Inspectors of Schools and Education Organisers.
National Association of Youth Service Officers.
National Coal Board.

National Council for School Sports.
National Rural Studies Association.
National Savings Development Committee.
National School Sailings Association.
National Society for Art Education.
Physical Education Association of Great Britain and Northern Ireland.
Society of British Esperantist Teachers.
Society for Education Through Art.
South East Regional Association of Education Officers.
Special Schools Association.
Union of Shop, Distributive and Allied Workers.
United Kingdom Atomic Energy Authority.
Workers' Educational Association.
Young Christian Workers.

Mr. C. Adams, Culverhouse Boys' County Secondary School, Essex.
Mr. M. Ableway.
Mr. J. R. Armstrong, Chief Education Officer, Joseph Lucas Ltd.
Mr. G. H. Bantock, Reader in Education, University of Leicester, (advance copy of a chapter from a forthcoming book, "Education in an Industrial Society").
Mr. M. P. Carter, Department of Sociological Studies, University of Sheffield (advance copy of "Home, School and Work").
Mr. W. B. Everett, Headmaster, Huntingdon County Secondary School.
Dame Anne Godwin, General Secretary, Clerical & Administrative Workers Union.
Mr. R. F. Goodings ⎰ Institute of Education, University of London. (Joint
Mr. S. Pratt ⎱ memorandum included as Appendix of this report).
Mr. E. H. Heelas, Inspector of Schools, Birmingham.
Mr. L. J. Hewitt, Director of Guidance, Board of Education, Hamilton, Ontario.
Mr. J. Heywood, Nuffield Fellow, College of Advanced Technology, Birmingham.
Mr. D. Holbrook, Fellow of King's College, Cambridge (advance copies of two books, "English For The Rejected" and "The Secret Places").
Mr. G. Jahoda ⎧ Senior Lecturer in Social Psychology, University of
Mr. A. D. Chalmers ⎨ Glasgow (copy of report, "The Youth Employ-
⎩ ment Service, A Consumer Perspective").
Mr. T. Lewis, Department of Education, University of Bristol. (Copy of Diploma Thesis).
Mrs. M. Leopold, Manager, Comptrollers Staff Office, J. H. Lyons Ltd.
Mr. R. C. McGregor, Training College Lecturer.
Mr. R. Morley, Headmaster, Broadlands County Secondary School, Somerset.
Mr. R. W. Palmer, Windsor Grammar School for Boys.
Mr. R. T. Rivington, Institute of Education, University of Sheffield.
Mr. F. R. Rogers.
Mr. C. A. Slack, Headmaster, Abbey Grange Church of England School, Leeds.
Mr. N. J. Spearing.
Mr. J. Webb.

APPENDIX II

Sex Education

(An account of how one school tackles the task, written by the Headmaster)

1. My report on sex teaching is based on seventeen years' experience in a mixed school. Its central theme is that the vast majority of boys and girls, as they grow up and before they reach the leaving age, have a normal curiosity about sex. Once they know they are at liberty to speak freely to their teachers, they will discuss general and personal problems with a wholesome frankness new in this generation. The testing time comes when they leave school and go to work. Promiscuity then there may well be but our evidence is of intense loyalty and generosity in boy and girl friendships while they are still at school.

2. We have problems with some of our boys and girls but we would woefully misrepresent what goes wrong if we spoke of them in sensational terms. Current standards of morality in the adult world have not affected their behaviour at school so completely as to make our interpretation of goodness out of date. They have more than an inkling that, as they grow older, they will have problems to face and decisions to make which are of vital concern to them. We prepare them to meet these by initial protection, by personal help rather than through arid schemes of work which avoid the main issues, by religious teaching humanly interpreted and by moral guidance firmly but sympathetically offered.

3. Given the friendly interest of the staff, how does the school plan its aid for pupils going through adolescent development? The biological approach is the obvious one. Our younger children, especially the girls, quickly come to terms with the facts of the reproductive processes. Some visual aid material is available but there is not enough to enthuse about. Careful selection of the best slides is made. Whenever we have had a lively pets club or some school livestock the beginnings of sex discussion in mixed groups have been completely uninhibited. From there we find no difficulty in taking the next step to the human situation.

4. In Health Education and Housecraft the mistress comes close to the needs of the senior girls. Her emphasis is held steady on sex as a healthy and natural interest. She notes and approves it openly, allaying fears concerning the onset and development of menstruation, discussing marriage and the birth and care of children and planning the homes they hope to have in the future. From these subjects arise many group and personal outpourings that need the wise teacher and sympathetic listener. A married woman with children of her own is invaluable here.

5. The girls' interest in their dress and appearance forms an essential part of sex teaching. Girls are helped to make the most of themselves. They are advised about over-emphasising their physical characteristics. Why shouldn't they? The answer is given directly and with no attempt to avoid issues. It is related immediately at this stage to the difference between healthy attractiveness for boys and the flaunting of sexual differences to enflame.

6. To our deputy-head go the girls with the more intense personal problems. Gossip, misunderstanding, first encounters with sexual incidents are explained and a line of conduct indicated. She advocates many and diverse interests to keep the body active and the mind alert so that sex takes no inordinate place.

7. My school's teaching on sex is positive rather than negative. We put the value of moral behaviour before the possible unpleasant consequences of sexual experiment. We aim to make "love", "honour" and "respect" words of significance in our school life, and as familiar as "practical" and "vocational" are in other departments of our work. In terms of human happiness they will almost certainly mean more.

8. In Religious Knowledge lessons and in talks with their form teachers the children are invited at the senior stage to ask their questions. Nearly all are completely and sincerely serious. They want to know. The teacher may be discussing the Marriage Service. "With my body I thee worship". His teaching is clear and precise. Our pupils know that many people in our district and in the wider world do not live by these standards. The teacher holds to his belief that, when we fall from grace, forgiveness and a new start are always possible to all who honestly admit their wrong and seek ways of putting it right. He does not take a holier-than-thou position, but represents himself as being fallible as they are. He shares their need to love and respect their neighbour.

9. My Housecraft teacher finds that work done in Biology and Religious Education lessons provides a natural introduction to her talks with the senior girls. This is not fortuitous. There is continuous reference being made privately and in our regular staff meetings to problem cases and to the progress of our teaching. My teachers are experienced in assessing when talks about sex and marriage to the fourth year pupils are opportune. They follow no hard and fast scheme of work. The idea runs counter to their feelings about the subject.

10. The work of one fourth year form teacher illustrates this. He has treated these subjects very fully this year. They are based on current topics or on those arising our of religious teaching on marriage.

1. Teenage courtship
2. Pre-marital sexual experience
3. Unmarried Mothers, based on an excellent series in a Sunday Newspaper
4. Newspapers and Sex
5. Divorce, arising out of Leo Abse's Bill
6. Vice and the current scandal
7. Abortion and the problem of Thalidomide babies
8. Venereal Disease, illustrated in a recent I.T.V. Programme, and watched by some of the form.

This is a formidable and daunting list. Our method ensures that no subject will be treated cold on a particular day.

11. There is a danger in all of our group, or form, discussions. We want to give no superficial introduction. We prefer the personal approach by pupil to teacher. These quotations underline the problem:

(a) "I find the difficulties lie in the wide difference in maturity in any age group. If only one could segregate the absolute innocents from the obviously well-informed". Housecraft Teacher.

(b) "Sex. I have not finished my course as a teenager. And this subject as not really hit me in the eye yet. But it is the subject I shall have to think about". Boy—15 years.

(c) "The question of sex is always cropping up in front of teenagers, and it is wrong. Was sex thrown at our fathers when they were our age? No. Then why throw it at us. You get fed up of the word, and I think the more you discuss it over a certain level the more harm it does. When somebody tells you that you get a tremendous thrill out of intercourse you are likely to try it at the first chance you get". Boy—15 years.

12. Yet unexpectedly we have seen a large group meeting succeed. Two hundred girls in the 14–15 age group were gathered in our school for a day's conference. The opening talk was so sensibly and clearly given as to create an atmosphere in which any topic could be broached. Small groups met for discussion and produced written questions that were fairly answered. A husband and wife spoke of their first romantic feelings for each other, then of their physical attraction and so on to their marriage and lasting companionship. The day made its mark. Its weakness lay in the impossibility of any follow-up.

13. B.B.C. Television programmes such as "Going to Work" have afforded an excellent introduction to mixed viewing and discussion. Taped recordings of a series of lessons called "The Other Sex" from "The Bible and Life" Sound Broadcasts for Schools have enabled the whole of the fourth year to follow significant material in small groups. The result has generally been that after collective discussion children have stayed behind to ask questions privately. This is the outcome of our work that gives the greatest satisfaction.

14. Few men staff feel comfortable about giving boys sex instruction. The girl stands to suffer more. The unmarried mother who elects to keep her child has a tremendous struggle ahead. So we speak more often to the girls. But we are wrong if we shirk a vital issue. Boys need help no less. Their body changes offer private means of satisfying newly experienced desire. They feel guilty or unclean. They are reassured medically and morally. Their experiments, their sense of the girls' challenge to their growing manhood, are met by honest, forthright explanation from those older members of staff who feel they can approach the subject without embarrassment.

15. The duty of the older boy to honour the girl he loves is readily appreciated and supported. Our boys and girls are often far more censorious about sexual morality than adults. The plight of the girl deserted by her false lover provides no amusement to the toughest group of boys. They, too, have sisters and know what these desertions mean. They can well understand "love with honour". The phrase may help them in the future. The point is further made by a member of staff:

"I do not pride myself into thinking that what I say will necessarily have any effect upon their future behaviour, but at least the facts have been presented to them together with what I hope are reasonable arguments, and

when they reach the stage of being involved in personal relationships they are
able to face them having some knowledge. This knowledge could result in
experiment, as some people argue, but at the same time ignorance of these
matters more often can result in painful consequences".

16. We realise that our pupils are faced with temptations greater than we
experienced owing to the widely understood practice of birth control and the
increasing simplicity of the methods adopted. We do not avoid mentioning
contraception and fornication in our lessons. How much should be told is
our problem. We stop short at positive teaching. A few of our pupils become
knowledgeable, daring and amoral. The majority do not. We know that the
information we withhold will most probably be passed on in the usual way
before marriage by persons least suited to give it, that the goodness and virtue
that we champion will be sorely tried, and that fear, strain and unhappiness
will result. Yet my teachers feel that they cannot accept a responsibility that
rightly belongs to parents.

17. Accordingly, books and illustrated papers dealing with sex, whilst
existing in up to date form in the classroom for the use of teachers, are not
lent indiscriminately to boys and girls unless their parents indicate that we
should continue giving advice beyond the place where they feel competent
to pursue the subject. Parent Teacher meetings and personal interviews with
parents occur and are felt to be the wisest in the face of difficulties. Doctors
and nurses can be called upon for help in a joint undertaking between school
and home but the moral charge remains with the parents.

18. In a world swinging between the sentimentality and slush of many of the
pop songs, the visual debauchery of our lurid paper backs and the uncovering
of vice rings in our daily newspapers we are at a disadvantage. Our young
people are growing up, starry-eyed or cynical, needing what is best and meriting
it. We ought to have as support their parents' example and our own, but we
must admit that both can be very insecure and shaky. It is a challenge all
schools must meet. Here we are trying to face it without preaching, without
heavy moralising, but with sympathetic understanding. We care intensely for
these boys and girls.

11

APPENDIX III

This evidence has been submitted by Mr. R. F. Goodings and Mr. S. Pratt, of London University Institute of Education.

They wish to stress that this is a personal submission, not a document from the Institute as such.

THE DEPLOYMENT OF TEACHERS AND THE EDUCATION
OF THE AVERAGE CHILD

(1) We start from two truths which we hold to be, though not self-evident, at least incontrovertible. First, the strength of an educational system depends upon the quality of its teachers. However enlightened the aims, however up-to-date and generous the equipment, however efficient the administration, the value to the children is determined by the teachers. Secondly, there is in this country a desperate shortage of teachers.

(2) From these propositions it follows that the education of practically all children must in some measure suffer. We are concerned to suggest that it is the education of the children of average and less than average ability which will suffer most. The effect for them will be so serious that unless some solution is found to this problem, all other beneficial proposals for their education must be rendered almost wholly nugatory.

(3) The quota system secures that no area shall exceed a certain nationally defined maximum staffing establishment. It does not and cannot necessarily ensure that the less fortunate areas shall not fall below a certain minimum. It places a limit on the affluence of the rich but only partially alleviates the poverty of the poor. And differences of this kind tend to increase not decrease. An area becomes short of teachers because it is, for various reasons, unattractive. It becomes increasingly unattractive once it is generally known to be seriously short of teachers. These forces serve to deprive certain areas of the quantity of teachers they need if they are to fulfil their statutory obligations to their children.

(4) It is less generally recognized that the same kind of forces operate as between types of school. The selective schools which cater for both ends of the ability range i.e. the Grammar and the E.S.N. schools, can both offer attractions to teachers which are not available to the schools which cater for the average. In the Grammar school the Sixth Form gives more than prestige and academic standing—both powerful inducements in themselves. It rapidly raises the Burnham group of the school and consequently breeds graded posts from which even staff who do not themselves teach the Sixth can benefit. A similar salary advantage is added to that of small classes in the E.S.N. school. There is also a vocational satisfaction in helping the sub-normal which is less easily felt in teaching the average. The effect is that the teaching resources of an area reach the Secondary Modern Schools last. In a scarcity situation the average child has the poorest access to the essential educational resource—teachers. And again a disparity of this kind tends always to

increase. The more teachers a school has, the more it is likely to get. Conversely, heads of under-staffed schools are often reluctant to advertise all their vacancies since they will know that their chances of recruiting anybody at all diminish proportionately with the length of the list.

(5) We have so far considered the quantitative effects of the teacher shortage on the secondary education of the average. But shortage of numbers is almost invariably accompanied by a qualitative shortage which greatly exacerbates the problem. An advertised vacancy in a favoured area will generally present the authorities with a choice of applicants. And, since it is reasonable to assume that most appointing authorities, whether heads or administrators, are professionally competent, the best teacher secures the post. A shortage area will therefore be able to recruit only from among others' rejects who similarly are likely to be, in one way or another, less satisfactory teachers. This remains true even when the quantitative staffing position is apparently satisfactory. So again as between types of schools; the average child gets substantially less then his share of the outstanding teachers.

(6) Clearly, and mercifully, there are exceptions; an excellent teacher may wish to teach in a generally unfavoured area because his home or his fiancée is there, or in a secondary modern because he feels he particularly wants to work in such a school. But these exceptions do not significantly disturb the general pattern. An outstanding teacher drawn to a shortage area for non-professional reasons will usually seek appointment in a selective school. And since he is good and the area is short he will get the post. A vocational impulse which leads a first-rate teacher to seek work with non-gifted children very often inclines him to the least able of all—the E.S.N. The exceptions to the picture we have outlined seldom, therefore, benefit the average child.

(7) The pedagogical implications of this situation scarcely need to be stressed. No one would suppose that the average child needs less or less competent teachers than any other, though it might be argued that he needs more and better. Certainly the C and D streams in a secondary modern school might well benefit disproportionately from small classes and the best of teaching. Simply as a matter of social justice their claim to a bigger share of such resources is undeniable, but these are precisely the children for whom the provision of both sorts is the least satisfactory. Further, solutions to a serious staffing shortage seldom benefit the average or can be sought in terms of their needs. Thus, for example, the creation of an extended course may attract teachers but will often only impoverish further the provision within the school for the less able. Advertisements offering "opportunities for work with backward classes" are rare indeed.

(8) We conclude therefore that, if proposals to improve educational provision for the group under consideration are to have any reasonable chance of application on anything more than a token scale, such proposals must be linked with carefully constructed plans to ensure that the country's secondary school teaching strength is deployed in a manner appropriate to the task.

Several measures have been attempted in the effort to obtain a distribution of teachers more nearly concomitant with the aims expressed in the Education Act of 1944. None could fairly be described as positive in nature; all have been either palliatives or pipe-dreams.

(9) Reliance on an all-round improvement in the supply of teachers is clearly pointless in the face of a shortage not expected to fall significantly below 50,000 (assuming current policies only) for the next twelve years (N.A.C.T.S.T. Seventh Report). Even if the shortage were to be arbitrarily eliminated by raising the "maximum" size of classes for an interim period to correspond with the supply of teachers actually available, the consequent improvement in the numbers of teachers for children of average ability would not be paralleled by a corresponding increase in the quality, especially in the shortage areas. Only the overproduction of teachers (and the consequent unemployment of some of them) giving the schools at the back of the queue for teachers a worthwhile choice of candidates, would make a significant difference.

(10) A more rational policy of siting training colleges in difficult areas may help to bring forward teachers with local ties in these areas but such a policy is increasingly irrelevant when one of the attractions of the teaching profession is the relative freedom of the teacher to seek a post anywhere in the country.

(11) Inducements in kind—housing, removal expenses paid, generous provision of study leave, of courses for teachers, and of books and materials for classroom use are important examples—each have their advantages and disadvantages, but there is an overriding disadvantage which they have in common. The existence of the quota scheme implies that some well-placed authorities would, but for its existence, willingly pay to employ more teachers. Since such authorities are as free as any other authority to use inducements in kind, it follows that they would spend money in doing so if their use by shortage authorities (or shortage types of school) became a significant threat to their own staffing position. Inducements in kind are therefore either ineffective or, if effective, self-defeating unless their use is restricted to particular areas, categories of school, or both.

(12) The quota scheme has been used as a method of limiting the quantitative maldistribution of teachers between Local Education Authorities. Recent reports suggest that in this it has succeeded admirably, especially in coping with problems arising from the introduction of the standard three-year training course. Its major limitation is however a serious one; no account is taken of the distribution of the best teachers who, being generally in the strongest position in competition for the most popular posts, tend to drift away both from shortage areas and from posts in which the principal concern is with the age and ability groups under review. An advantage of the scheme is that it sets a limit to the number of vacancies which can be advertised at any one time and therefore has some inhibiting effect upon the high rate of mobility of teachers from post to post. At the price, perhaps, of some otherwise unnecessary unemployment of geographically immobile teachers, the quota scheme is effective in improving the distribution of teachers; but its influence on the distribution of teaching ability is haphazard.

(13) The only effective method now generally employed by Local Authorities in mitigating the effects of teaching shortages is that of accelerated promotion. Teachers needed for particular posts are offered promotion at a relatively early stage in their careers. The approach has the disadvantage that it is only applicable when a considerable proportion of the available posts carry special responsibility allowances—not a characteristic of posts concerned mainly with children of average and less than average ability. Also, when the

technique can be used, considerable ingenuity is required if undesirably high rates of staff turnover are to be avoided.

(14) We submit that each of these measures, or indeed any likely combination of them, is inadequate if the purpose is to ensure that the teaching of children within the Council's terms of reference is not to be unduly handicapped by the concentration of the effects of the continuing teaching shortage in this field, especially where schools in shortage areas are concerned. What is needed is a *positive deployment policy* for secondary school teachers (and indeed for primary school teachers also). By this is meant a policy under which relevant distinctions between various categories of need and between various categories of teachers are made and steps taken, if necessary by adjusting the salary structure for teachers, to match needs with teacher supply so far as the overall supply of teachers permits.

(15) As examples of elements contributing to such a policy, the following may be useful. The first suggestion has similarities, at the national level, to the County Unattached system now operating in many areas. It involves the introduction of an element of direction into the terms of employment of some, but not all, teachers with adequate compensation provided for less favourable terms of service. The second suggestion emphasises the possibility of spending money not only to improve the overall supply of teachers, but also to further accepted aims of deployment policy while relying on the inducement principle to select the teachers concerned.

(16) e.g. (i) The introduction of a considerable salary differential in favour of teachers who, under contract, would accept direction to any school in the country for which the L.E.A. concerned could satisfy Her Majesty's Inspectors that no suitable applicant was available, would give high quality, geographically mobile teachers the opportunity to work where they were most needed and would give them sufficient reward to compensate for the loss of amenities in an equivalent post elsewhere. Admission to the panel of these contract teachers would be competitive if the differential were adequate, but it is reasonable to assume that L.E.A.s would be most unlikely to make unreasonable requests for the services of "panel" teachers owing to the possibility of withdrawal of such teachers by Her Majesty's Inspectors.

(17) e.g. (ii) It would seem reasonable to draw a distinction between two objectives of salary policy for teachers, which might be pursued through different forms of negotiation.

The distribution of a global sum of money allocated to teachers on grounds of social justice, overall teacher supply position or any other criterion concerned with the relationship of the teaching profession to the world at large is properly, as at present, a matter for agreement between teachers and their employers, the L.E.A.s.

The use of *additional* money by the Ministry of Education and the L.E.A.s in order to reach a more satisfactory deployment of the teaching resources available to them should surely be a matter for *decision* by these bodies alone (although they might well *consult* the teachers nevertheless). The teachers' response would be made through the lists of applications.

(18) We have found it impossible to suggest changes of any promise whatever which do not involve salary changes, although it is conceivable that there may be some such solution. We have also satisfied ourselves that fruitful consideration cannot be given to the Council's terms of reference without giving detailed attention to the problem of the deployment of teachers. We would therefore submit that not only is a positive deployment policy required but also that the broad principles upon which the determination of teachers' salaries are based require close examination if realistic proposals are to be made to meet this requirement.

RICHARD F. GOODINGS.

SIMON PRATT.

25th February 1963

APPENDIX IV

COPY OF LETTER SENT TO THE MINISTER ON THE TRAINING OF TEACHERS

7th February 1963

My Dear Minister,

As you are aware, the Central Advisory Council are shortly to report to you on the education between the ages of 13 and 16 of children of average and below-average ability. At the last meeting of the Council we discussed in particular the form of training most suitable for the teachers of such children. We were aware that this matter, which is of such importance to us, must also concern the Committee now sitting under Lord Robbins, and as we were so emphatic and united in our views, I as Chairman felt it to be a matter of urgency that I should inform you of them in the hope that if you think fit you will pass them on to Lord Robbins and his Committee.

We were unanimous in our opinion that an intending teacher whose personal and professional training are carried on together over a span of at least three years is much more likely to become a successful teacher of less able children than one who completes a degree course in a special subject and follows it with a year of training.

Briefly, we believe experience to show that "concurrent training" and "consecutive training" tend to produce different kinds of teachers. The former, because it entails a prolonged study of child development over a three-year period coupled with a study of a range of subjects, is more likely to produce teachers who succeed with the less able child. The latter tends to produce teachers who, having studied an academic subject in depth, are anxious to impart it to children sufficiently able to master it and derive satisfaction from it.

We do not deny that there is a considerable overlap between these categories, but, whereas the teacher trained to deal with the less able child will have little difficulty with the more able in his early years, the teacher who is trained in the expectation of presenting his subject to the more academically minded children is likely to be ill-equipped, discontented, and consequently less competent in teaching his subject (or, as is so often the case, some other subject) to slower children.

We are, of course, aware that within the resources at present being applied to teacher training the country's need for primary school teachers has led to a limitation for the time being of the number of secondary school teachers trained by the three-year colleges. We are deeply concerned lest what we hope will be a temporary expedient should be assumed to have educational merit on which long-term proposals for training might be based.

In informing you of these matters I am, of course, well aware that the National Advisory Council on the Training and Supply of Teachers is the proper body to advise on teacher supply. Since, however, the kind of training most likely to produce the best teachers for a large proportion of secondary school pupils is an issue of fundamental importance to our present concerns as a Council, I hope you will find it possible to submit our views, on which we are unanimous, to Lord Robbins and his Committee at this stage in their deliberations.

There is perhaps just one final point which I ought to make. We are concerned less with existing institutions than with types of training. It may well be that new patterns of training will emerge in the newer Universities or in existing Colleges. What we do believe, however, is that the longer study of teaching problems coupled with the study of a wider range of subjects generally speaking produces better teachers of the less able children than a more specialised course followed by a markedly shorter period of training.

Yours sincerely,

The Rt. Hon. Sir Edward Boyle, Bt., M.P.,   JOHN NEWSOM.

Minister of Education,

Ministry of Education,
Curzon Street House,
W.1.

APPENDIX V

Statistical Detail of the Survey

This appendix, which is contributed by Mr. G. F. Peaker, C.B.E., H.M.I., gives a brief account of the sampling design of the survey, and a few examples of the more detailed tables from which the short tables in the main text have been condensed.

1. THE SAMPLING DESIGN

1.1 The Modern School Sample

The main object of sampling design is to get reliable information at low cost. Previous experience of some of the variables suggested that with a stratified sample of about 150 modern schools the standard errors would turn out to be small enough for the purpose in hand. At the present time a sample of this size includes about 18,000 pupils in the fourth year, and since the most onerous task undertaken by the selected schools was to provide detailed information about fourth year pupils it was decided to reduce the 18,000 to 6,000 by sub-sampling within the selected schools.

The sampling fraction was 1/24. Before the sample was drawn the schools were stratified by size, sex and region. For size the schools were divided into large, middling and small, the middling group covering the range from 400 to 600 pupils. With this definition there are about the same number of pupils in each stratum, while the schools are divided in the ratio 3:5:7. There are fewer single sex than co-educational modern schools, the proportion being 1:1:3 for boys', girls' and mixed. To produce the regional stratification the draw was made systematically with random starts, beginning from the northern end of the Scottish border and working through to Land's End. To provide a quick means of estimating standard errors in complicated cases the draw was made twice, producing two independent and interpenetrating samples of 75 modern schools, each as follows:

	Boy's	Girl's	Co-educational	Total
Large	3	3	9	15
Middling	5	5	15	25
Small	7	7	21	35
Total	15	15	45	75

No attempt was made to stratify by neighbourhood, chiefly because it seemed better to ask the schools to classify their own neighbourhoods rather than to impose on them an external and possibly outdated or otherwise erroneous description. Consequently neighbourhood was included in the questionnaire and not in the prior stratification.

1.2 Schools in the Slums

Chapter 3 of the report is about a special group of schools that did not form part of the sample, but was selected by a supplementary procedure for this reason. It was clear from prior knowledge that the probability sample would include about 30 schools in areas of the kind described as "problem neighbourhoods" in paragraph 559. But if the neighbourhoods of all the 3,606 modern schools in the country at the time of the survey could be ranked in ascending order, beginning with the deepest slums, it is an arithmetical fact that half the possible samples of 150 schools would not include any of the most extreme 16 neighbourhoods. All samples being equally likely the risk of omitting all the most extreme tenth of the neighbourhoods is only one in 10,000,000, which is not the sort of risk that needs attention. On the other hand the risk of not including any of the most extreme 3% of these neighbourhoods is one in a hundred. This is a risk that deserves respect, and therefore some supplementary procedure seemed advisable, to make sure of including a few of these 109 neighbourhoods in the survey, even in the somewhat unlikely event of their being omitted from the probability sample.

For this purpose Her Majesty's Inspectors working in the L.C.C. area and the five largest and two other county boroughs were each asked to nominate three schools (six in the case of the L.C.C.) as being those for which the neighbourhoods were the most difficult. From these lists a final selection of 20 schools was made. Since these areas together include about a sixth part of the population of the whole country, and since the proportion of difficult neighbourhoods in them must at least be greater, and perhaps considerably greater, than that in the rest of the country, it is reasonable to suppose that the neighbourhoods of these 20 schools are among the most difficult in the whole country. The evidence subsequently collected in the survey confirmed that their circumstances were far more difficult than those of most schools, and the method of selecting them gives ground for thinking that some of them at least are very close to the foot of the scale.

The inverse problem, of estimating how many schools in the country are represented by this special group, is attended by more uncertainty, but upper and lower limits can be reached by the following arguments. If 3% of the modern schools in the whole country had neighbourhoods as bad as those in the special group there would be 108 such neighbourhoods altogether, of which rather more than 20 would fall in the sixth of the country from which the schools of the special group were chosen. If 10% of neighbourhoods in the whole country were as bad there would be 360 such neighbourhoods altogether, of which rather more than 60 would fall within the sixth of the country from which the special group was chosen. In the former case the judgment shown in selecting the 20 neighbourhoods for the special group would have been remarkably accurate; in the latter it would have been rather poor. Consequently 3% and 10% may be regarded as the upper and lower limits, and splitting the difference between them gives 7% as a rather loose estimate of the proportion of schools in neighbourhoods as bad as those of the schools in the special group. This estimate is compatible with the estimate from the probability sample that 20% of the neighbourhoods fall into the "problem" class, since this class should include, but be considerably larger than, the "slum" class as here defined.

1.3 Comprehensive Schools

The comprehensive schools form a much smaller class than the modern schools, so that a larger sampling fraction is needed for them. On the other hand they are much more homogeneous. These opposing considerations taken together suggested that a sample of 12 schools—two boys', two girls', and eight co-educational—would be enough to give estimates with reasonably small standard errors, and such a sample was in fact taken.

1.4 Sub-sampling of Pupils Within Selected Schools

The schools were asked to give detailed information about one in three of their fourth year pupils, and to select these pupils from their registers systematically with a random start. For this purpose each school was given one of the first three digits. A very accurate check against bias in the sub-sampling was available in the shape of the scores in the Reading Test. If the rule of selection is strictly followed the sub-samples will be single stage samples of the pupils in the selected schools, with pupils as the primary sampling units. Consequently the standard errors for means and class proportions can easily be calculated, by the rules for simple random sampling. Such a calculation ignores the gains from systematic selection compared with purely random selection, but this merely means that the estimates of error are slightly too large.

For the modern schools the agreement was excellent. The differences between the sample and the sub-sample estimates were well within their standard errors. But in the case of the comprehensive schools something went wrong. The sub-samples gave mean reading scores for girls and for boys that were excessive by four and five times their standard errors respectively. Comparing the numbers in the score groups 0 to 11, 12 to 17, 18 to 23, 24 to 29, and 30 to 35, for boys and girls together, gave a chi-squared of 37, on 4 degrees of freedom, which is preposterous. Owing to the pressure of other work it was a long time before the comprehensive school sub-samples reached the head of the queue for coding, so that by the time this heavy bias was discovered many of the boys and girls had left school, and nothing could be done to correct it. To expedite the coding, the sub-sampling fraction for comprehensive schools had been reduced from one in three to one in six—that is to say, only half the returns were coded—but a post mortem showed that the bias had occurred before this point.

Since the comprehensive school sub-samples contained too few Robinsons and too many Browns all the estimates based on them are subject to a doubt, and this applies particularly to the Robinsons, for whom the absolute, as well as the relative, numbers are very small. (See paragraph 621).

2. THE READING TEST

2.1 The Choice of Test

The test chosen was the one that had been used for the National Reading Surveys described in "Standards of Reading 1948/1956".[1] Paragraph 5 of this pamphlet describes the test and paragraphs 72–74 explain and justify the use to which it was put. This choice had the advantage of giving a useful by-product. The 1961 results formed another link in the chain of surveys extending from 1948, and provided evidence that the progress observed in 1952 and 1956 was still continuing.

It will be noted that in the surveys of 1948, 1952 and 1956 the test was used as a measure of progress. In 1961 it has again been used as a measure of progress. But it has also been used as a measure of ability for the classification of individual pupils. At first sight this seems to involve a contradiction. How can the same test be used both as a measure of improvement in the achievement of the schools, and as a measure of ability in the pupil? If the test is a measure of ability, how can the schools claim credit for an improvement in the test scores? If, on the other hand, it is a measure of achievement, how can it be used as a measure of ability? There is in fact nothing either illogical or unusual in such a dual use. The same questions might be asked of the records of athletic performances. Do these measure the native ability of the athletes concerned, or do they measure the effects of training? They do both. No amount of training would have enabled William Bunter to defeat Roger Bannister on the track. None the less a trained Bunter could have knocked one or two minutes off the time of an untrained Bunter for the mile. A trained Bunter would still have been lapped by an untrained Bannister, but this does not show that training is useless. Athletic excellence depends mainly on natural endowment, but can be improved by training. Intellectual excellence depends mainly on native wit, but can be improved by education. Where native capacity is equal, or nearly so, training or education dominates. Where training or education are not very different native capacity dominates. This holds not only for individuals, but also for groups. It is likely that the distribution of native ability among the crews of two of Her Majesty's ships is much the same; the fact that one ship has better seamanship or gunnery than the other is the effect of training. The crews of Beatty's ships could read; most of Nelson's men could not. This again is not a difference of native ability but a difference of education. The performance itself is a function both of native ability and of the effects of education. Which predominates depends upon the kind of comparison that is being made. If the comparison is between individuals whose education has been much the same, ability is dominant; if it is between groups each covering much the same in range of ability, then ability tends to cancel out and the effects of education predominate.

Englishmen in general do not know Chinese because they have had neither occasion nor opportunity to do so. For the same reason Chinese do not know English. To conclude that the ignorance of English common among Chinese was a mark of lack of wit would be a monstrous absurdity into which no one

[1] Standards of Reading 1948/1956 (Ministry of Education Pamphlet No. 32).

is likely to fall. But in less extreme cases very similar conclusions have been reached and maintained. The general principle, which is of great importance in judging the future possibilities of education, is therefore worth re-stating, though it has for long lacked the charm of novelty. Macaulay, for instance, wrote in 1854, in his report on the appointment of Indian civil servants by open competition:—

"The marks ought, we conceive, to be distributed among the subjects of examination, in such a manner that no part of the Kingdom, and no class of schools, shall exclusively furnish servants to the East India Company. It would be grossly unjust, for example, to the great academical institutions of England, not to allow skill in Greek and Latin versification to have a considerable share in determining the issue of the competition. Skill in Greek and Latin versification has indeed no direct tendency to form a judge, a financier, or a diplomatist. But the youth who does best what all the ablest and most ambitious youths about him are trying to do well, will generally prove a superior man; nor can we doubt that an accomplishment by which Fox and Canning, Grenville and Wellesley, Mansfield and Tenterden first distinguished themselves above their fellows, indicates powers of mind, which, properly trained and directed, may do great service to the State. On the other hand, we must remember that in the North of this island the art of metrical composition in the ancient languages is very little cultivated, and that men so eminent as Dugald Stewart, Horner, Jeffrey and Mackintosh would probably have been quite unable to write a good copy of Latin alcaics, or to translate 10 lines of Shakespeare into Greek iambics. We wish to see such a system of examination established as shall not exclude from the service of the East India Company either a Mackintosh or a Tenterden, either a Canning or a Horner."

So much for the general principle. Here we are concerned to apply it to comparisons in which the reading test plays a part, and we have to decide in each case whether the comparison is one in which it is reasonable to suppose that native ability averages out, or nearly so, in which case estimates of general progress or retrogression are appropriate, or whether it is one in which occasion and opportunity average out, or nearly so, in which case judgments of ability can reasonably be made.

The first comparison with which we are concerned is that between the whole modern school population in 1956 and the corresponding population in 1961. In 1961 the average score, over the whole sample, was very considerably in advance of the average score in the 1956 sample. It would be grossly unreasonable to suppose that, in so short a period, there could have been any marked change in the total native ability of the whole of the youth of England. The proportion of that youth that attends other kinds of school is very much the same in 1961 as in 1956, from which it follows that the total ability of modern school pupils must still be much the same. The advance must therefore be an effect of education in the widest sense, of which education in school is at least a major part. It is reasonable, therefore, to regard the advance as in part an achievement of the schools, for which they are entitled to credit.

Another comparison is between the schools in the 1961 sample and those in the special group of schools in the slums. It was to be expected that the adverse environment of the latter would have a depressing effect on the test scores, and that these would therefore be lower on the average than those in the sample, unless either the natural ability of the pupils or better staffing in the schools of the special group compensated for the effects of environment. There is no reason to suppose that the natural abilities of the pupils in these schools are, on the whole, either much superior or much inferior to those of pupils in modern schools at large, and the fact that on the average their scores were very substantially lower may therefore be regarded as an effect of environment, somewhat mitigated by the more favourable staffing ratios enjoyed by these schools. On the average there were two pupils fewer per teacher in the special group schools than in the sample schools. It cannot be doubted that this is an advantage, but it is not enough to close the gap. It can only reduce it.

In comparisons between large groups it is mainly differences of education and environment that emerge. On the other hand in comparisons of individuals within groups where environment and education are much the same it is mainly differences of ability and native wit.

2.2 Bias in the Test

The test has a well marked bias of about a point in favour of boys. This has been steadily evident in the three previous surveys, and it appears again in 1961. Most tests have such a bias, sometimes strong and sometimes weak, sometimes in favour of girls and sometimes in favour of boys. The reason for regarding it as a bias, rather than as a mark of superiority in the boys (or the girls) is simply that the sign varies from test to test.

To locate the bias in this case a rather lengthy piece of analysis was done with the co-operation of members of one of the Ministry's short courses. The scripts from twelve large mixed schools in the sample were used for this purpose. From the scripts from each school four sub-samples—two for boys and two for girls—were drawn systematically, giving 48 sub-samples and 960 scripts for analysis. Between sub-samples within schools and sexes there were no significant variations. Pooling the sub-samples for boys and for girls within each school and subtracting gave, for each of the 35 questions in the test, twelve independent estimates of the bias, one being derived from each of the twelve schools. From these twelve estimates a mean estimate, and its standard error, was calculated for each question. The 35 standard errors thus obtained did not differ significantly from the corresponding binomial estimates. In other words there was no evidence that the bias had a school component.

Altogether the 480 boys produced 10,637 right answers, and the 480 girls 10,110, the average scores being 22·16 and 21·06, and the bias 1·10. On 25 of the questions the boys had a higher score, with a total excess of 592; on 10 questions the girls did better, with a total excess of 65. Question 28 by itself accounted for more than a fifth of the total bias, with 273 successes for boys (57%), and 149 for girls (31%). There were three other questions where the boys' successes exceeded the girls' by more than 10%, and five more where the excess was over 5%. These nine questions together account for 452 out of the net 527 by which the boys' score exceeded the girls'.

Although the data from these twelve schools locate the bias they do not provide the most accurate estimate of it. In the complete sample there were 90 mixed schools, of which 88 replied, and their data supply an estimate of 0·90, with a standard error of 0·12. The 59 single sex schools that replied yield a much less accurate estimate of 0·83 with a standard error of 0·41. If these are pooled they give 0·87, with a standard error of 0·18 for all schools. But, since the estimate for single sex schools is blunted by the difference between schools within each kind, it is better to take the accurate mixed school estimate by itself. This shows that the bias is very steady. In fact the scatter in the relevant table is no more than would occur if the scripts, instead of being divided into boys' and girls', were divided alphabetically without regard to sex, though in this case the mean would be approximately zero instead of 0·9. This means that for the sex difference there is no component of variation between schools. The difference between the sexes for boys' and girls' schools vanishes when it is adjusted by the difference found in mixed schools.

It would have been possible to take account of the bias in defining Brown, Jones and Robinson and their sisters in the main text, and to have adjusted all the tables in which this nomenclature is employed accordingly. But it would have been extremely laborious to do so, and on the whole it seemed enough to draw attention to the bias and leave the tables as they stood.

2.3 The Reliability of the Reading Test

The tables prepared to locate the bias in the test served also to estimate the reliability. By dividing the twelve schools into two groups of six, and comparing the scores on the questions with odd and with even numbers four independent estimates of reliability were obtained, namely 0·92 and 0·91 for boys and 0·90 and 0·88 for girls. Pooling these gives 0·90 with a standard error of 0·009. The latter does not differ significantly from the 0·006 obtained by the simple random sampling formula, so that once again there is no evidence of difference between schools.

A reliability co-efficient of 0·90 is high for a ten minute test containing only 35 questions. It corresponds to 0·95 for a test of double the length.

3. GENERAL NOTES ON TABLES

1.1 TO 3.3

These notes are supplementary to those attached to the tables themselves.

Table 1.1 shows the mean scores for modern schools in the reading test. It is noteworthy that there is a range of nine points, from 25 to 16. There is, as would be expected, an even larger range in the quartiles. For example, the lower quartiles range from 24 to 11.

Table 1.2 gives a number of pupils in score ranges each covering six points. These sample frequencies are graduated in table 1.3 to give the scores corresponding to every tenth percentile rank. It is from these data, and the corresponding data in later tables, that diagrams 7, 8, 9 and 11 have been drawn.

It will be seen that the nine point range between school means shown in table 1.1 corresponds to about 50 percentile ranks, and the eleven point range in the lower quartiles to more than 60.

Table 1.4 shows the improvement from 1956 to 1961, and its standard error. The improvement can be stated as 2·4 points, or as 17 months, or as 17 percentile ranks in the middle of the scale.

In table 2.1 the school mean scores are arrayed by zone and by neighbourhood. The middle zone extends from 80 to 160 miles from London. The outer zone covers the six northern counties and Cornwall completely, with most of Cheshire and Devon, and a fringe from other counties. Ipswich, Kettering, Chipping Norton and Southampton are just inside the inner zone.

The summary at the foot of table 2.1 gives the mean scores for neighbourhoods within zones, and the weighted and the unweighted means of these means. The weighted means of means for the three zones take account of the varying proportions of kinds of neighbourhood within zones; the unweighted means of means eliminate this. There is a similar relation for the weighted and unweighted means of means for neighbourhoods. The scores for the outer zone are somewhat higher than those for the middle zone, but decidedly lower than those for the inner zone. Since the variance per school is 2·96 these means all have a standard error of about 0·25, so that the differences are not negligible. They are however smaller than the differences between neighbourhoods shown at the foot of the summary. The fact that there is a preponderance of small schools in problem neighbourhoods is mainly responsible for the lower scores of small schools shown in table 1.1.

Table 2.2 compares the mean scores for all modern schools, schools in problem areas, and the special group of schools in the slums. It will be seen that, although two of the special group have lower scores than any schools in the other groups, yet there are five schools in the special group with scores at or above the general average. This is a notable achievement.

In Table 2.3 the corresponding deciles for pupils are given. Diagrams 8A and 8B have been drawn from these data.

Tables 3.1 and 3.2 give the mean scores and deciles for all fourth year pupils, fourth year examination candidates, and fifth year examination candidates. Diagrams 9A and 9B have been drawn from these data.

Table 3.3 gives the deciles for all pupils, for fourth year examination candidates and for fifth year examination candidates in comprehensive schools, with the deciles for grammar schools in 1956 added for comparison. One of the twelve comprehensive schools in the sample failed to supply this information; among the eleven schools who did reply the range of school means was from 26 to 22, and the variance per school was 0·90. The mean score for the group was 24·4, with a standard error of 0·29.

Table 1.1 Mean Scores for Modern Schools in the Reading Test

There were 150 schools in the Modern School Samples, grouped by size and sex as shown below. Middling Schools had between 400 and 600 pupils on roll.

School Mean Score	Boys' Schools Large	Middling	Small	Girls' Schools Large	Middling	Small	Mixed Schools Large	Middling	Small	All Schools
25		1						1		2
24	2		2				2		1	7
23	2	2	5		4		4	3	2	22
22		3	1	3	2	4	4	9	12	38
21	2	1	2	2	2	2	3	4	10	28
20			3		1	4	3	7	9	27
19		2	1		1	1	2	3	4	14
18		1						2		3
17						3			2	5
16									1	1
Schools Replying	6	10	14	5	10	14	18	29	41	147
Schools not Replying				1				1	1	3
Total	6	10	14	6	10	14	18	30	42	150
Mean Score	23·00	21·40	21·86	21·60	21·70	20·00	21·61	21·00	20·73	21·15
Variance of school means										2·96

	Mean Score
All Boys' Schools	22·09 ± 0·31
All Girls' Schools	21·10 ± 0·32
All Mixed Schools	21·11 ± 0·18
All Schools	21·30 ± 0·14

The definition of the middling size group (400–600) was chosen so that the numbers in the populations were roughly equal. Within size groups the means for schools and for pupils approximate closely, between size groups equal weights are appropriate, and between sex groups weights of 1, 1, 3 for Boys, Girls and Mixed. This leads to the estimate $21·30 \pm 0·14$ for all pupils, which agrees very closely with the estimate 21·34 obtained directly from pupils' score groups in the next table. It is rather larger than the unweighted mean for all schools at the foot of the right hand column above, because size is neglected in reckoning the latter, and large schools score rather higher than small. This difference is significant, at the 5% level, but ceases to be so when the scores are adjusted for environment.

The difference between the scores of girls and boys is a feature of the test, and can be traced to half a dozen of the 35 questions (see 2.2).

Table 1.2 Modern Schools

Grouped Scores for Pupils in the Reading Test.

The differences between boys in boys' schools and in mixed schools are not significant, nor are those for girls. Pooling gives:—

Reading Score	All Boys No.	Frequency %	Cumulative Frequency %	All Girls No.	Frequency %	Cumulative Frequency %
0— 5	128	1·3	1·3	53	0·6	0·6
6—11	622	6·6	7·9	623	7·2	7·8
12—17	1352	14·2	22·1	1643	19·0	26·8
18—23	3110	32·7	54·8	3126	36·2	63·0
24—29	3593	37·8	92·6	2780	32·1	95·1
30—35	705	7·4	100·0	421	4·9	100·0
Total	9510	100·0		8646	100·0	
Mean Score	21·78			20·90		
Mean Score for all pupils			21·34			

This table gives 6·21 and 5·89 as the standard deviations of the scores for boys and girls respectively, and pooling gives 36·6 as the variance per pupil. The harmonic mean of the number of pupils per school is close to 100, so that

if S and P are the components per school and per pupil (within schools) S + P
= 36·6 and S + P/100 = 2·96, from the previous table. This gives S = 2·6
and P = 34·0. For the later estimates based on subsamples of pupils S +
P/100 must be replaced by S + 3P/100 and 2·96 by 3·84.

Table 1.3

The data in the preceding table give the following distribution when graduated. The 1956 results, adjusted to the same age, are inserted for comparison.

Rank	Boys		Girls	
%	1961	1956	1961	1956
90	29·1	26·6	28·0	25·8
80	27·4	26·9	26·0	23·5
70	25·8	23·3	24·4	21·6
60	24·1	21·8	23·1	20·3
50	22·8	20·2	21·7	18·9
40	21·4	18·8	20·2	17·3
30	19·6	17·1	18·3	15·6
20	16·9	14·4	16·0	13·5
10	12·8	10·3	12·9	10·7
Mean Score	21·8	19·5	20·9	18·5

Table 1.4

This table shows the improvement in reading standards in modern schools
since 1956. The 1961 sample on the average was four months younger than
the 1956, and on the average scored 1·8 more points in the test. The age
allowance is seven months to the point, so that the improvement can be
expressed either in points or months, as follows:—

			Improvement from 1956 to 1961	
	1956	1961	Points	Months
Mean Score	19·5	21·3	1·8	13
Standard error	0·42	0·14	0·44	3
Age	15y 0m	14y 8m	0·6	4
Total Improvement			2·4	17

It may be noted that the standard error in the estimate of the improvement
arises almost entirely from the standard error for 1956, which is three times
that for 1961. This was because the case studies that played an important part
in 1956 made it necessary to have three-stage sampling, with the selection
of 23 L.E.A. areas as the first stage. This extra stage enlarged the standard
error, since the variation between L.E.As. is not inconsiderable.

The major source of uncertainty, however, is not the sampling of pupils,
but the sampling of tests. It is well known that different tests give somewhat
different results, but this knowledge is vague, whereas knowledge about the
sampling of pupils is precise, for the reasons given in the text. None the less,
taking both hazards together, it seems reasonably safe to say that the improvement is not less than one year and not more than two.

Table 2.1 Reading Test Scores (School means) by distance from London (zone) and neighbourhood

Key

1. Rural
2. Mining
3. Problem
4. Council House and New Town
5. Miscellaneous

	Outer Zone (more than 160 miles from London)						Middle Zone (Between 80 and 160 miles from London)						Inner Zone (Within 79 miles from London)						Grand Total
	1	2	3	4	5	Total	1	2	3	4	5	Total	1	2	3	4	5	Total	
25																	2	2	2
24					1	1					2	2				3	1	4	7
23		3		1	2	6				1	3	4	1		2	6	3	12	22
22	1	1	4	7	6	19	2	1		1	2	6	2		3	5	3	13	38
21		1	3	3	1	8	4		1	3	4	12	2			3	3	8	28
20	2	1	5	3	1	12	4		2	2	3	11	1		1	1	1	4	27
19		4		2	2	8	1	1	1		2	5					1	1	14
18			1			1					1	1			1			1	3
17			2			2			2			2			1			1	5
16									1			1							1
Number of Schools	3	10	15	16	13	57	11	2	7	7	17	44	6	0	8	18	14	46	147
Mean Score	20·67	20·30	20·33	21·19	21·77	20·91	20·64	20·00	18·57	21·14	21·29	20·61	21·50	—	20·88	22·17	22·50	21·96	21·15

Means of Means

Neighbourhood

	1	2	3	4	5
Zone Outer	20·67	20·30	20·33	21·19	21·77
Middle	20·64	20·00	18·57	21·14	21·29
Inner	21·50	—	20·88	22·17	22·50
Means of Means { Weighted	20·90	20·25	20·07	21·61	21·82
Unweighted	20·94	20·15	19·93	21·50	21·85

Means of Means

	Weighted	Unweighted
Zone Outer	20·91	20·85
Middle	20·61	20·33
Inner	21·96	21·44
Means of Means	21·15	20·87

Variance per school 2·96

Table 2.2

Mean scores per school for (1) All modern schools and (2) the schools in problem areas, in the sample, and (3) the special group of schools in the slums.

School Mean Score	All Modern Schools	Sample Schools in problem areas	Special Group Schools in the Slums
25	2		
24	7		
23	22	3	1
22	38	7	1
21	28	3	3
20	27	6	1
19	14	4	5
18	3	2	4
17	5	4	2
16	1	1	
15			1
14			
13			1
Total	147	30	19
Mean Score per school	21·15	20·07	18·79
Standard deviation per school	1·72	2·05	2·37

Table 2.3

The deciles corresponding to the preceding table are:—

Rank %	Boys All Modern Schools	Boys Schools in Problem areas	Boys Schools in the slums	Girls All Modern Schools	Girls Schools in Problem areas	Girls Schools in the slums
90	29·1	28·2	27·9	28·0	27·2	26·2
80	27·4	26·2	25·1	26·0	25·2	23·5
70	25·8	24·5	23·1	24·4	23·6	21·7
60	24·1	23·0	21·4	23·1	22·0	19·9
50	22·8	21·5	19·9	21·7	20·4	18·4
40	21·4	20·0	18·1	20·2	18·8	16·9
30	19·6	18·0	16·1	18·3	16·9	15·1
20	16·9	15·4	13·5	16·0	14·5	13·0
10	12·8	11·4	9·9	12·9	11·4	9·9
Mean Score	21·8	20·6	19·3	20·9	19·8	18·2

Table 3.1

Mean Scores in the Reading Test of candidates for external examination in Modern and Comprehensive Schools.

	Modern Schools B.	Modern Schools G.	Comprehensive Schools B.	Comprehensive Schools G.
All 4th Year Pupils	21·8	20·9	24·2	23·9
4th Year Examination Candidates	25·7	24·0	28·3	28·0
5th Year Examination Candidates	27·6	27·2	28·4	27·8

Table 3.2

The deciles for candidates in modern schools are:—

Modern Schools

	Boys			Girls		
Rank %	All 4th Year Pupils	4th Year Candidates	5th Year Candidates	All 4th Year Pupils	4th Year Candidates	5th Year Candidates
90	29·1	31·0	32·6	28·0	29·9	32·9
80	27·4	29·8	31·5	26·0	28·4	31·4
70	25·8	28·7	30·4	24·4	27·0	30·0
60	24·1	27·6	29·5	23·1	25·7	28·9
50	22·8	26·6	28·6	21·7	24·8	27·9
40	21·4	25·5	27·6	20·2	23·7	26·8
30	19·6	24·2	26·5	18·3	22·1	25·7
20	16·9	22·8	25·2	16·0	20·3	24·4
10	12·8	20·3	23·2	12·9	18·1	22·5
Mean Score	21·8	25·7	27·6	20·9	24·0	27·1

Table 3.3

The deciles for external examination candidates in comprehensive schools in 1961, and those for grammar school pupils in 1956, are:—

	Boys				Girls			
	Comprehensive Schools (1961)			Grammar School (1956)	Comprehensive Schools (1961)			Grammar Schools (1956)
Rank %	All 4th Year Boys	4th Year Candidates	5th Year Candidates	All boys aged 15·0	All 4th Year Girls	4th Year Candidates	5th Year Candidates	All girls aged 15·0
90	31·4	32·1	32·6	32·6	30·7	31·8	33·5	32·2
80	29·9	31·1	31·5	31·7	28·9	31·0	32·1	31·2
70	28·4	30·3	30·7	31·0	27·5	30·2	30·7	30·4
60	26·8	29·5	30·0	30·3	26·2	29·4	29·5	29·6
50	25·2	28·7	29·4	29·6	24·9	28·6	28·3	28·7
40	23·8	28·0	28·7	28·7	23·2	27·7	27·3	28·1
30	22·0	27·1	27·5	27·7	21·3	26·7	25·9	27·2
20	19·5	26·0	26·3	26·5	19·1	25·4	24·3	26·0
10	15·7	24·3	24·2	24·6	15·5	23·3	22·1	24·0
Mean Score	24·2	28·3	28·5	28·8	23·9	28·0	27·8	28·2

4. THE RELATION BETWEEN THE READING SCORE AND HEIGHT, WEIGHT AND AGE

The average height of the boys and girls was 64·5 and 62·8 inches respectively. The average weights were 116·9 and 114·7 lbs. The standard errors are a tenth of an inch and two thirds of a lb.

The London County Council Survey ("Report on the heights and weights of school pupils in the county of London in 1959") gives 64·6 and 62·9 inches and 119 and 116 lbs. for boys and girls of the same age, namely the year group centred on 14 years 8 months. The London figures have been obtained by interpolation in the table on page 30 of the L.C.C. report. The number of schools in the London sample is not given. It seems likely to have been smaller than the number in our national sample, but on the other hand it was possible to make more use of stratification in London, so that the standard errors are likely to be much the same. The agreement between the London and the national estimates is remarkably close. The difference of 2 lbs. in the average weight for boys is about twice its standard error, but the other three differences are well within the range of sampling fluctuation. The national sample showed no differences clear of sampling fluctuation between zones or neighbourhoods; to find such differences it was necessary to go to the special group of schools in the slums. This perhaps reffects the social and economic changes of the last quarter of a century, which have, in London itself, been narrowing the gap between the physique of children in different districts. The nine educational divisions of the county of London now show a range of only 1·5% in stature for boys and 1·8% for girls. For weight the ranges are 1·6% for boys and 2·6% for girls. These ranges are less than they used to be, and it may well be that the same tendency for the backward districts to catch up holds throughout the country as a whole.

Even the differences shown by the special group are quite slight. In this group the average height was 63·2 and 62·0 inches for boys and girls respectively, the weights being 112·5 and 115·6. Since this group was purposively selected the standard errors are, strictly speaking, unknown. If the selection is treated as random they turn out to be 0·27 inches and 1·8 lbs. The boys in the special group fall short of the national average by 1·3 inches and 4·4 lbs., and the girls by 0·8 inches. These are all clear of sampling fluctuation, taking the standard errors as above. The average weight of the girls in the special group is 1·1 lbs. greater than the general average, the standard error of this excess being 1·9 lbs.

For the comprehensive schools no reliable estimates of height and weight could be made, owing to the bias in the sub-sampling in these schools that has been mentioned in 2.2 above. That they would be slightly greater than in the modern schools may be inferred from the correlation with the reading scores given below.

The statistics calculated from the modern school sample to explore the relations between height, weight, age and reading score are given in Table 4.

Table 4

This table gives the statistics calculated from the modern school sample for the relations between height, weight, age and reading score. They are as follows:—

	Boys			Girls		
	Mean	s.d.	C.V.	Mean	s.d.	C.V.
1. Reading Score	21·8	6·2	28%	20·9	5·8	28%
2. Height (Inches)	64·5	3·4	5·3%	62·8	2·6	4·2%
3. Weight (Pounds)	116·9	20·2	17·3%	114·7	18·5	16·1%
4. Age	14y 8m	3·3m	2·0%	14y 8m	3·3m	2·0%
5. Shape (Weight/Height^3)		12%			15%	

6. Correlations:

	Boys			Girls		
	Height	Weight	Age	Height	Weight	Age
Reading	·1563	·1572	·0853	·1622	·1169	·0577
Height		·7240	·1399		·4814	·0759
Weight			·1188			·0839

With age held constant

Reading Score	·1464	·1487		·1585	·1127	

7. Regressions on age:

	Boys	Girls	
Reading	1·9	1·2 points per year	
Height	1·7	0·7 inches per year	
Weight	8·7	5·6 pounds per year	

With age held constant—*continued*

8. Regression coefficients for reading score on height, weight, and age:

	Boys			Girls		
	Height	Weight	Age	Height	Weight	Age
Reading Score	0·0823	0·0902	0·0632	0·1359	0·0478	0·0433
Standard Errors*	±0·0251	±0·0250	±0·0174	±0·0207	±0·0208	±0·0182

* A safety factor of about 1·5 is needed to cover the additional variation from the fact that the sampling is two-stage.

9. The multiple correlations of reading score with height, weight and age are 0·180 (boys) and 0·174 (girls), and the variances and co-variances of the regression coefficients are:

	Boys					Girls			
	Height	Weight	Age			Height	Weight	Age	
Height	629	−451	−34	X10⁻⁶	Height	430	−206	−15	X10⁻⁶
Weight	−451	625	−11		Weight	−206	431	−21	
Age	−34	−11	304		Age	−15	−21	333	

The standard errors are the square roots of the diagonal elements and have already been inserted in (8) above.

5. CLOSING THE GAP

Paragraph 558 refers to "a tendency for the lower occupational groups to show a somewhat greater improvement than the higher ones." Part of the evidence for this emerges from a comparison of Table 12 in "Early Leaving" with Table 12 in the Supplement to Part 2 of "Statistics of Education 1961". The data in "Early Leaving" relate to the age group that entered grant aided grammar schools in 1946, and those in the Supplement to leavers from grant aided grammar schools in 1961. Those members of the former cohort who left school with four O level passes or fewer would for the most part leave in 1951, so that, both for this category and its complement, the proportions are on much the same footing, at a ten year interval. Taking the complementary proportions—those who achieved at least five O level passes, including those with various combinations of A level passes, we have:—

	Boys 1961 %	Boys 1951 %	Boys 1961/1951 %	Girls 1961 %	Girls 1951 %	Girls 1961/1951 %
Professional and Managerial	77	69	112	70	69	101
Clerical	62	53	117	63	55	115
Skilled	56	48	117	51	43	119
Semi-Skilled and Unskilled	41	31	132	34	28	121

It will be seen that on the whole there has been an improvement of about 17% over the ten years, but that within this total improvement there has been a levelling up, which is most marked towards the foot of the table.

Parental occupation was not recorded for the boys and girls in the modern school sample of the 1961 Survey, but since most of the parents fall into the two groups at the foot of the table above it is reasonable to conclude that the improvement shown in the successive reading surveys is another aspect of this process of closing the gap.

6. VOLUNTARY ACTIVITIES

The data collected for each boy and girl in the sub-samples include information about five voluntary activities. The five activities and the numbers and percentages of boys and girls in the modern schools engaging in them, were as follows :—

	Boys		Girls	
	N	%	N	%
Holders of responsible School Posts	469	14·4	570	19·4
Sports Representatives (School Team)	868	26·7	535	18·2
Members of School Club	868	26·7	734	24·9
Members of other Clubs	1592	48·9	1400	47·5
Part-time Paid Employment	1349	41·4	453	15·4
Total	5146	158·0	3692	125·4

(i.e. the 3257 boys shared 5146 activities, an average of 1·58; and the 2945 girls shared 3692 activities, an average of 1·25).

If membership of a school club made membership of an outside club neither more nor less likely the expected number of boys belonging to both would be 26·7% of 48·9% of 3,257, that is to say, 424. The actual figure is 557—an excess of 133—which means that members of School Clubs are more likely than non-members to belong to outside Clubs, and vice versa.

When the same principle is applied to the 32 combinations of the five activities it produces tables with 32 rows and 26 degrees of freedom, for which chi-squared is 885 for boys and 828 for girls. These tables condense to:

Table 6

Number of Activities	Boys O	E	O—E +	−	Girls O	E	O—E +	−
0	684	448	236		889	647	242	
1	1005	1148		143	1007	1219		212
2	869	1088		219	617	801		184
3	448	472		24	298	242	56	
4	196	94	102		113	34	79	
5	55	7	48		21	2	19	
	3257	3257	386—386		2945	2945	396—396	

There are far more boys and girls with no activities, or with the maximum possible, than would be the case if the propensity to join one activity was independent of the propensities to join others. The evidence is conclusive in favour of a common factor, or general propensity. This propensity is positively correlated with height and weight, and also with the reading score. If R, P, T, C, K, E stand for reading, school post, school team, school club, other club and part-time employment respectively the extraction of two factors and a rotation give the patterns:

	Boys I	II	h²		Girls I	II	h²
P	·76	·00	·58	P	·66	·00	·44
R	·36	·07	·13	T	·67	·07	·45
T	·57	·15	·33	C	·58	·16	·36
C	·54	·30	·38	R	·43	·19	·22
K	·33	·54	·40	K	·31	·41	·26
E	·01	·36	·13	E	·08	·40	·17
Total			1·95	Total			1·90

which account for 32% of the variance in each case. The angles between the successive vectors, in the order in which they occur above, are 11, 4, 14, 30 and 29 degrees (boys), and 6, 10, 9, 28 and 27 degrees (girls), with angles of 88 and 80 degrees between the extremes P and E.

The lengths of the vectors are squared in the third column, and the angles and lengths together give patterns that accord with expectation. P is, so to speak, the extreme "school" factor, and E the extreme factor for outside activity. In both patterns these form the wings, with K closer to E, and R, T and C closer to P, though the order of these three differs from boys to girls. The relative shortness of the vectors for R and E indicates that they have less in common with the other four than the latter have among themselves.

For the boys a third factor with a heavy negative loading on T and light positive loading on R and E accounts for another 12% of the variance, but the third factor for girls is less clear cut.

7. NOTE ON HOLDING POWER (Chapter 24)

Since every teacher was either an original member or a newcomer, and either stayed to the end of the period or left, there are four exclusive and exhaustive classes, u, v, x, y, giving (1) $u/(u + v)$ and (2) $x/(x + y)$ for any school as the proportions of (1) the original and (2) the newcomers staying to the end of the period. The second of these is the school's "holding power" for newcomers as defined in chapter 24.

For a category represented in the sample by n schools the holding power is therefore estimated by the ratio

$$p = S(x)/S(x+y)$$

with a standard error $\sqrt{\dfrac{nQ}{n-1}} \Big/ S(x+y)$

where $Q = p^2 S(y^2) - 2pqS(xy) + q^2 S(x^2)$.

The standard error thus obtained can be compared with the binomial estimate. If it is significantly greater there is evidence that the schools in the category differ in holding power; if not, not. Similarly for original members. There was more frequent evidence of differences between schools in the same category for newcomers than for original members. Some of the latter no doubt had moved to more congenial schools before the period began. Others, perhaps, had come to appreciate the wisdom of Mrs. Gamp's advice to young Bailey.[1]

[1] "He was born into a wale", said Mrs. Gamp with philosophical coolness, "and he lived in a wale; and he must take the consequences of sech a sitiwation."

(*Dickens: Martin Chuzzlewit chapter 49.*)

Index

Printed in England for Her Majesty's Stationery Office by Henry Blacklock & Co. Ltd., Manchester, 8.
Wt. 3167—C57.   K280.   10/63.   H. B. & Co. Ltd.   GP3321.